Understanding Biblical Gender Equality

Hope Abigail Freeman

Understanding Biblical Gender Equality

Hope Abigail Freeman

Copyright © 2011 Hope Abigail Freeman

All rights reserved.

Pictures, images, and quotes are copyright their respective owners.
www.WalkInTruth.net

Thanks to Jesus Christ, for helping me to write this, and for setting me free. This book is dedicated in His service, and also dedicated to my daughters and my son.

Table of Contents

Introduction	7
Titus 2, Genesis 3, Ephesians 5 and Submission	9
1 Corinthians 14:34-35 Silence in the Churches	15
Genesis 3 Desire	29
1 Corinthians 11:1-16 Heads and Coverings	47
Eph 5 Marriage – Part 1 – Submit Yourself	75
Eph 5 Marriage – Part 2 – Love Your Wife	87
Eph 5 Marriage – Part 3 – Love and Submit	107
Genesis – The First Marriage	121
Genesis – The First Marriage Problems	141
Genesis – The First Marriage Problems Continued	161
Genesis – Setting a Pattern of Marriage Problems	133
Lessons from the First Marriage	209
1 Timothy 2 – Female Teachers, etc.	231
A Pause for a Romans 13 Study	253
Humanity's History	265
Jesus, Women, and the Law	293
1 Peter 3 – Actions Louder Than Words	309
1 Timothy 3 – Female Deacons, etc.	341
The Truth of the Church's History	359
Many Who Are Last Will Be First	379
In Conclusion	409
Resources	432

Introduction

This work is a new look at what the Bible has to say about women and men, in all their many roles and ways of relating to God, to the world, and to each other.

Walking in Truth

"My people are destroyed for lack of knowledge..." Hosea 4:6

In the Bible, the first type of knowledge mentioned is the knowledge of Good, and the knowledge of Evil, from the fruit of the tree of the knowledge of Good and Evil. And in eating from the tree, men and women have come to know both Good and Evil.

But the hard part in life, and a central focus in living a righteous life, is to come to be able to distinguish the difference between what is Good and what is Evil. How many people have been destroyed or had their life ruined because they could not tell the difference between Good and Evil, or between what is True, and what is False?

The most important Truth that anyone needs to know is that Jesus Christ is the Son of God and the only way to right standing with God and eternal life. If you don't know this most important Truth, the Bible teaches it will lead to your eternal destruction.

At the same time, not knowing the truth in this life about a topic can also lead to destruction in this mortal life.

In you walking out your life, if you think what is false to be true, and what is evil to be good, this is the most essential knowledge that you lack, which will lead to destruction in your life. But if you walk out your life knowing Good to be Good, and Evil to be Evil, if you know the Truth to be True, and the False to be False... then this is the essential knowledge you can have that will prevent destruction and lead you towards prosperity in your life, that God wants you to have.

"Woe unto them that call evil good, and good evil; that put darkness for light, and light for darkness; that put bitter for sweet, and sweet for bitter! …Therefore as the fire devoureth the stubble, and the flame consumeth the chaff, [so] their root shall be as rottenness, and their blossom shall go up as dust: because they have cast away the law of the LORD of hosts, and despised the word of the Holy One of Israel." Isa 5:20,24

This is how important it is to walk in truth, and why our loving God, who wants to prosper us, says, "I have no greater joy to hear that my children walk in truth" 3 Jn 1:4

"For I know the thoughts that I think toward you, says the LORD, thoughts of peace and not of evil, to give you a future and a hope. Then you will call upon Me and go and pray to Me, and I will listen to you. And you will seek Me and find Me, when you search for Me with all your heart. I will be found by you, says the LORD, and I will bring you back from your captivity…" Jer 29:11-14a

Chapter One
Titus 2, Genesis 3, Ephesians 5 and Submission

We're going to start with Titus 2, with a focus on the part relating to "submission".

Titus 2:1-5 (YLT) "And thou — be speaking what doth become the sound teaching; aged men to be temperate, grave, sober, sound in the faith, in the love, in the endurance; aged women, in like manner, in deportment as doth become sacred persons, not false accusers, to much wine not enslaved, of good things teachers, that they may make the young women sober-minded, to be lovers of [their] husbands, lovers of [their] children, sober, pure, keepers of [their own] houses, good, subject to their own husbands, that the word of God may not be evil spoken of."

The word for "subject" here is "hupotassomenas", which is the same root word of hupotasso used in Eph 5 referring to wives being "submissive" to husbands. This word hupotasso would be better translated as "submit themselves" to their own husbands. Here the instruction is for older women to teach the younger to submit themselves to their husbands. In all places in which the Bible directs instructions directly to wives, telling them to submit such as Eph 5, the word hupotasso is reflexive, which means that this is something wives are told to do to themselves, like wash themself, or dress themself. Hupotasso is always directed towards wives to "submit themselves".

Here, the stated reason why is so "that the word of God may not be evil spoken of." The phrase "evil spoken of" is an ok translation, as the word in Greek is "blasphemetai", which according to Strong's mean "abusive, speaking evil" and Thayer's says "to speak reproachfully of, rail at, revile, calumniate". (I prefer the Thayer's to the Strong's as it is generally more reliable in my opinion.)

The "word of God" here seems like it must refer to the Bible, specifically the Old Testament as of this point in time. This is an assertion, but if Paul was referencing only to his own letters and the Gospels as scriptures would not seem likely. It is far more in keeping with Paul's writings to see the "word of God" here to mean the Old Testament. So basically Titus 2 says that it is sound teaching that women should be submissive to their own husbands so that people will not rail at or speak reproachfully about the Word of God, which was the Old Testament at this time.

This reason makes sense if a lack of submission of wives to their husbands would create a stumbling block or tempt people to think (incorrectly) that the Old Testament has some flaw in it, that people would use as opportunity to speak evil of the Old Testament. And it only makes sense if the Old Testament does, in fact, speak on wives being submissive to their husbands.

Therefore somewhere in the Old Testament there is something that verifies that women should, as Christians, be submissive to their own husbands. Yet, nowhere in Titus 2:1-5 do the verses specifically say that the Old Testament actually says "wives submit to your husbands". Titus 2 does not say that it is written in the Old Testament "wives submit to your own husbands". But something must be written in the Old Testament that would result in that wives should be submissive to their own husbands, else the Old Testament would be falsely criticized and reviled at.

So, I read the whole Bible and could not find a place in the Old Testament where it says "wives submit to your husbands" or "women submit to men". I looked. I sought. I did not find.

What I did find was Genesis 3:16, which says that "he will rule over you" or "he will govern over you" and that is how I read it, not "he shall rule over you" but that "he will rule over you". This is an important difference, because "he shall rule" implies that God is giving permission, which He is not because he is describing something evil and unwanted, because all the things here are the negative consequences of the fall that God is listing:

Gen 3:14-19 The LORD God said to the serpent, "Because you have done this, Cursed are you more than all cattle, And more than every beast of the field; On your belly you will go, And dust you will eat All the days of your life; And I will put enmity Between you and the woman, And between your seed and her seed;
He shall bruise you on the head, And you shall bruise him on the heel."

To the woman He said,
Multiply, I will multiply your pains, and your conception in pain you shall bring forth children;
Your desire will be for your husband, and he will rule over you."

Then to Adam He said, "Because you have listened to the voice of your wife, and have eaten from the tree about which I commanded you, saying, 'You shall not eat from it';
Cursed is the ground because of you;
In toil you will eat of it All the days of your life.
"Both thorns and thistles it shall grow for you;
And you will eat the plants of the field By the sweat of your face
You will eat bread, Till you return to the ground,
Because from it you were taken;
For you are dust, And to dust you shall return."

Now, as much as pain in childbirth, a cursed ground, and eating dust, are negative repercussions of the fall so also is "he will rule over you" also a negative repercussion of the fall. God is not giving the man permission to rule over the woman here, but rather God is speaking to the woman and is letting the woman know of the worst consequences of the fall into sin. Some of those consequences include God placing a curse on the snake, and on the ground, putting enmity between the woman and the snake, and causing multiplying of the woman's pain of childbearing. But no where here does God say that He will cause the man to rule over her, or give permission for him to do so, but rather this is stated as a negative consequence of the fall that naturally follows and extends from her and the man's new, sinful, nature.

So I do not read this as "he shall rule" but instead "he will rule". As "he will rule" implies that it is going to happen, like "it will rain" which simply put means, it's going to happen. The question here is whether God is talking about negative consequences of sin, and He is. As such, "he will rule over you" is a negative consequence of the fall into sin.

So how does "he will rule over you" relate to Titus 2? Because God is giving a prophecy in Gen 3:16. God is stating the facts in Genesis 3:16. It is a fact "He will rule over you". It's going to happen. And that's what I see, looking over the history of humanity. Husbands have ruled over wives. Men have ruled over women. It has happened. And as a trend in the world, it makes sense that a sinful man is going to beat a sinful women every time, if for no other reason than his superior physical strength. He is stronger and she is weaker.

So what is being said in Titus? That there is another way for the Old Testament statement "he will rule over you" to be true. That what God says will happen, will happen, that "he will rule over you", that husbands will rule over their wives.

But there is more than one way that this can be true: The old way, seen throughout history and in the Bible itself, is that the husband rules over his wife through a forceful sinful domination. The new way is the way described in Eph 5 and other places in the New Testament, a way of the wife voluntarily submitting herself and showing respect, and the husband loving and honoring the wife. This new way replaces the old way, for Christians.

Eph 5:21-33
And be subject to one another in the fear of Christ.
Wives, submit yourselves to your own husbands, as to the Lord. For the husband is the head of the wife, as Christ also is the head of the church, He Himself being the Savior of the body. But as the church submits to Christ, so also the wives ought to be to their husbands in everything.
Husbands, love your wives, just as Christ also loved the church and gave Himself up for her, so that He might sanctify her, having

cleansed her by the washing of water with the word, that He might present to Himself the church in all her glory, having no spot or wrinkle or any such thing; but that she would be holy and blameless. So husbands ought also to love their own wives as their own bodies. He who loves his own wife loves himself; for no one ever hated his own flesh, but nourishes and cherishes it, just as Christ also does the church, because we are members of His body. FOR THIS REASON A MAN SHALL LEAVE HIS FATHER AND MOTHER AND SHALL BE JOINED TO HIS WIFE, AND THE TWO SHALL BECOME ONE FLESH.
This mystery is great; but I am speaking with reference to Christ and the church. Nevertheless, each individual among you also is to love his own wife even as himself, and the wife in order that she respects her husband.

And this means that women should be submissive because that is another way, a new way, a Christian way, that replaces the old way of a husband trying to dominate. There are good rulers and bad rulers, and a good way to govern and a bad way to govern. Both the old bad domination and the new good accepted leadership of a willing follower can both be true under the statement "he will rule over you". But they are worlds apart, like night and day! And it is the honor of the wife to carry out God's word by being submissive to her own husband, protecting the Bible from people speaking evil against it, and in doing so strengthening her witness.

Still what is submission? More on just what submission Is in another article. Still, nothing so far has defined submission any more than describing it as part of a replacement for the man dominating his wife. And Nothing so far has said women are to be submissive to men, but rather only that wives are to be submissive to their own husbands.

Chapter Two
1 Corinthians 14:34-35 Silence in the Churches

To be extremely to the point, I believe the historical evidence of 1 Cor 14:34:35 shows it to be a gloss.

By that, I mean it was not in the original letter of Paul to the Corinthians, and years later someone added these verses into the text falsely. In short, God did not write 1 Cor 14:34-35 nor intend for these verses to be in the Bible, nor counted for establishment of doctrine.

For scholarly historical evidence of this fact, you can check out this page here:
https://www.linguistsoftware.com/payneessays.htm
This is research you probably have never heard of, because it is new, dated 95, 98, and as late as 2004. Change comes slow to the church.

You can read major papers on this there:
"The Text-Critical Function of the Umlauts in Vaticanus, with Special Attention to 1 Corinthians 14.34-35: A Response to J. Edward Miller"

"Ms. 88 as Evidence for a Text Without 1 Cor 14.34-5"

"Fuldensis, Sigla for Variants in Vaticanus, and 1 Cor 14.34-5"

"There is, however, substantial evidence for the existence of a text that omitted1 Cor 14.34–5. It has been widely argued on internal grounds and on transcriptional probability that 14.34–5 was not in the original text of 1Corinthians. In AD 546 or 547 Bishop Victor of Capua had the end of 1Corinthians 14 rewritten in the bottom margin of codex Fuldensis omitting vv.34–5. Clement of Alexandria († pre AD 215) cites 1 Cor 14.6, 9, 10, 11, 13, 20 yet calls both men and women without distinction to silence in church, indicating that 1 Cor 14.34–5 was not in his text of 1 Corinthians. Further evidence of a text of 1 Corinthians 14 without vv. 34–5 is that none of the Apostolic Fathers or the next generation of church fathers gives any indication of awareness of 1 Cor14.34–5. The most logical explanation of the features of ms. 88 is that it was copied from a Greek manuscript without 1 Cor 14.34–5. All of the other

explanations require an implausible assumption such as inadvertent displacement, intentional displacement later reversed, or derivation from a Western manuscript. The one other possibility, derivation from a non-Western manuscript with vv. 34–5 after v.40, requires the existence of a reading which no known non-Western Greek manuscript through the twelfth century supports. The explanation that 88 was copied from a manuscript without vv. 34–5 does not depend on the scribe of 88 having access either to a Western manuscript or a non-Western manuscript with a reading totally out of keeping with its textual tradition. On this explanation, the source from which the scribe of ms. 88 copied vv. 34–5 presents no difficulty, since it could have come from any Greek text containing 1 Cor 14.34–5. The evidence that ms. 88 was copied from a text of 1 Corinthians 14 without vv. 34–5 provides additional external support for the thesis that vv. 34–5 were not in the original text of 1Corinthians 14."

-Philip B. Payne PhD, <u>Ms. 88 as Evidence for a Text Without 1 Cor 14.34-5</u>

For anyone who cannot believe that the Bible could contain an uninspired addition, please look at what Jesus said at the end of the Bible,

"For I testify unto every man that heareth the words of the prophecy of this book, If any man shall add unto these things, God shall add unto him the plagues that are written in this book: And if any man shall take away from the words of the book of this prophecy, God shall take away his part out of the book of life, and out of the holy city, and [from] the things which are written in this book." Rev 22:18-19

Apparently Jesus acknowledged that words could be added or taken away; that such was possible. But at the same time, Jesus also said, "For truly I say to you, until heaven and earth pass away, not the smallest letter or stroke shall pass from the Law until all is accomplished." Matt 5:18 and "the scripture cannot be broken" John 10:35.

Which is why I believe the original has been preserved, and can be known, though perhaps not at face value in any 1 perfect manuscript, but rather over the whole of all the manuscripts. And this includes the historical manuscripts analyzed above, which show that 1 Cor 14:34-35 was not in the original and earliest manuscripts.

And truly, in some modern translations passages are included which were not in the original, and there is evidence for this, like the passage of the adulterous woman in John 8. And some of the same evidence for it being a gloss overlaps with the evidence that 1 Cor 14:34-35 is a gloss. Often that passage in John 8 is italicized or bracketed off with a footnote, which says these verses are not found in the earliest manuscripts. At the very least, the evidence in the case of 1 Cor 14:34-35 is weighty enough to warrant the same measure in modern translations that John 8 receives, of being noted with italicization or bracketing that there is evidence that these verses were not in the earliest manuscripts. Although, there is more evidence besides the historical for why I think a note is warranted.

Besides this scholarly evidence, there is also the test of internal witness in the Bible, which shows that these verses contradict the rest of the Bible, which I will attempt to show below.

The Lack of Internal Biblical Consistency

I've included the verses surrounding 1 Cor 14:34-35 for context. This passage is talking about people speaking in tongues in church, and how it all must be done in an orderly manner. Earlier in this letter, 1 Cor teaches about praying and prophesying and other gifts of the spirit. No restriction is placed upon women using their spiritual gifts. In other places in the NT, women use their gifts, such as tongues during gatherings of believers, which was their church service. Yet here it is commanded that women be silent in church.

1 Cor 14:30-40 "But if a revelation is made to another who is seated, the first one must keep silent. For you can all prophesy one by one, so that all may learn and all may be exhorted; and the spirits of prophets are subject to prophets; for God is not a God of confusion but of peace, as in all the churches of the saints. *The women are to keep silent in the churches; for they are not permitted to speak, but are to submit themselves, just as the Law also says. If they desire to learn anything, let them ask their own husbands at home; for it is improper for a woman to speak in church.* Was it from you that the word of God first went forth? Or has it come to you only? If anyone thinks he is a prophet or spiritual, let him recognize that the things which I write to you are the Lord's commandment. But if anyone does not recognize this, he is not recognized. Therefore, my brethren, desire earnestly to prophesy, and do not forbid to speak in tongues. But all things must be done properly and in an orderly manner."

Let's take a closer look at verses 34 and 35. These verses make several assertions that need to be analyzed one by one.

1. Women are to be submissive to men, because no woman is to speak whether she is married or not.
2. Silence shows submission.
3. All women must learn from their husbands at home.
4. Therefore, All women must have husbands in order to learn.
5. "The Law" says that women are to subject themselves.

Let's start with,

"The Law" says women must subject themselves

The Law refers to the first 5 books of Moses. The Law does not say that women are to subject themselves. Go ahead and read the Bible. It's not there. The closest thing to this might be "he will rule over you" in Genesis 3:16, which does not mean "submit yourself to him". Submission is not the same thing as domination. Gen 3:16 cannot apply as an example of "subject themselves just as the Law also says" because "he will rule over you" does not describe the woman "submitting herself" but rather domination by the husband. God did not tell Eve she would subject herself, or that she even should subject herself, in Genesis, or to women in the Old Testament at all. It's not there. So verse 35 says something that is a lie. The Law, the first 5 books of Moses, does not say anywhere that women are to submit themselves. This is a lie. And the Word of God does not contradict itself. In the Law, it also does not say that women have to submit to men, period, which also is implied here. More on that in a minute.

All women must learn from their husbands at home

This is directly contradicted by 1 Tim 2:11-12:
"Let a woman in quietness receive instruction with entire submissiveness. But I do not allow a woman to teach or exercise authority over a man, but to be in quietness."

The Greek here for "quietness" is "hesychia" which means to be quiet, but not silent. It also means to not meddle in the affairs of others, but to keep to ones own business, and this may be the actual usage of the word in these verses.

The word in Greek for "silence" is "sigao". This is the word used in 1 Cor 14 (which also says "not permitted to speak" as an additional defining of silence as silence). We have 2 different words here, one saying women need to be quiet or not meddlesome, the other word saying they may not verbally speak at all. 1 Tim 2 contains Paul's instructions to Timothy as a leader in the church in Ephesus, saying Timothy should let a woman learn. In context, this means a woman learning under the church, in the church.

Additionally, the particular word translated as "submissiveness" in 1 Tim 2 implies a classroom setting. The sense here is that the women may learn in church quietly and in an orderly manner, like a classroom. The word for submissiveness here in 1 Tim 2 is not hupotasso, as is the word for submit in marriage verses, but the word "hupotage" which is also translated as submit, but is a word more commonly used to describe being set in an organized fashion, and is more reflective of the kind of submission of a student in a classroom rather than the special submission between

a husband and wife, or a king and his kingdom, which is in the special word case hupotasso in Greek.
In contrast, 1 Cor 14 says "if they desire to learn anything let them ask their own husbands at home". So these are two very different verses, one claiming women may be taught in church in an implied classroom setting, the other claiming women must learn at home from their husbands. Thus 1 Cor 14 directly conflicts with 1 Tim 2. And the Word of God does not contradict itself. *(*We will cover some of the verses on this page later in more detail as to other aspects*)*

Also, the idea that women should only learn from their husbands is directly contradicted by the relationship that each believer has to the Holy Spirit, John 14:26 and 16:13

"But the Comforter, [which is] the Holy Ghost, whom the Father will send in my name, <u>he shall teach you all things</u>, and bring all things to your remembrance, whatsoever I have said unto you." "But when He, the Spirit of truth, comes, <u>He will guide you into all the truth</u>; for He will not speak on His own initiative, but whatever He hears, He will speak; and He will disclose to you what is to come."

and also speaking of the Holy Spirit,
"As for you, the anointing which you received from Him abides in you, and you have no need for anyone to teach you; but as His anointing teaches you about all things, and is true and is not a lie, and just as it has taught you, you abide in Him." 1 John 2:27
Jesus said the Holy Spirit would teach all things to believers, in whom He indwells.
"For I know that this will turn out for my deliverance through your prayer and the supply of the Spirit of Jesus Christ" Phil 1:19

The Holy Spirit is also called the "Spirit of Jesus", so when the Holy Spirit teaches us, Jesus teaches us. This directly contradicts that women should only learn from their husbands at home, and shows that men and women with the indwelling Holy Spirit of Jesus are equally meant to be able to learn from Him directly. 1 Cor 14:34-35 completely seems to ignore and contradict this reality of the Holy Spirit guiding all believers into all truth directly, in the Spirit of Jesus' personally teaching each Christian.

Another point to be made: Women seemed free to learn and talk while with Jesus, and I see no mention of our Lord ever putting these kinds of restrictions on women. In fact the Bible records that Jesus spoke to women, and taught women himself, both alone and in mixed groups, and generally encouraged their learning.

Luke 8:1-3 "And it came to pass afterward, that he went throughout every city and village, preaching and shewing the glad tidings of the kingdom of God: and the twelve [were] with him, And certain women, which had been healed of evil spirits and infirmities, Mary called Magdalene, out of whom went seven devils, And Joanna the wife of Chuza Herod's steward, and Susanna, and many others, which ministered unto him of their substance."

John 4:5-10, 22-27 "Then cometh he to a city of Samaria, which is called Sychar, near to the parcel of ground that Jacob gave to his son Joseph. Now Jacob's well was there. Jesus therefore, being wearied with his journey, sat thus on the well: and it was about the sixth hour. There cometh a woman of Samaria to draw water: Jesus saith unto her, Give me to drink. (For his disciples were gone away unto the city to buy meat.) Then saith the woman of Samaria unto him, How is it that thou, being a Jew, askest drink of me, which am a woman of Samaria? for the Jews have no dealings with the Samaritans. Jesus answered and said unto her, If thou knewest the gift of God, and who it is that saith to thee, Give me to drink; thou wouldest have asked of him, and he would have given thee living water."…"Ye worship ye know not what: we know what we worship: for salvation is of the Jews. But the hour cometh, and now is, when the true worshippers shall worship the Father in spirit and in truth: for the Father seeketh such to worship him. God is a Spirit: and they that worship him must worship him in spirit and in truth. The woman saith unto him, I know that Messias cometh, which is called Christ: when he is come, he will tell us all things. Jesus saith unto her, I that speak unto thee am he. And upon this came his disciples, and marvelled that he talked with the woman: yet no man said, What seekest thou? or, Why talkest thou with her?"

Luke 10:38-42 "Now it came to pass, as they went, that he entered into a certain village: and a certain woman named Martha received him into her house. And she had a sister called Mary, which also sat at Jesus' feet, and heard his word. But Martha was cumbered about much serving, and came to him, and said, Lord, dost thou not care that my sister hath left me to serve alone? bid her therefore that she help me. And Jesus answered and said unto her, Martha, Martha, thou art careful and troubled about many things: But one thing is needful: and Mary hath chosen that good part, which shall not be taken away from her."

Everywhere else in the New Testament it can easily be accepted that women were using their spiritual gifts right beside the men in their church setting. In Acts, many believers of both genders were in Jerusalem, on the day of Pentecost, when the believers spoke in tongues, including the women who had been followers of Jesus.

Acts 1:13-14, 2:1-4 "And when they were come in, they went up into an upper room, where abode both Peter, and James, and John, and Andrew, Philip, and Thomas, Bartholomew, and Matthew, James [the son] of Alphaeus, and Simon Zelotes, and Judas [the brother] of James. These all continued with one accord in prayer and supplication, with the women, and Mary the mother of Jesus, and with his brethren."..."And when the day of Pentecost was fully come, they were all with one accord in one place. And suddenly there came a sound from heaven as of a rushing mighty wind, and it filled all the house where they were sitting. And there appeared unto them cloven tongues like as of fire, and it sat upon each of them. And they were all filled with the Holy Ghost, and began to speak with other tongues, as the Spirit gave them utterance."

Lydia held church meetings, fellowship of believers, in her house, Acts 16:14-15, 40:
"And a certain woman named Lydia, a seller of purple, of the city of Thyatira, which worshipped God, heard [us]: whose heart the Lord opened, that she attended unto the things which were spoken of Paul. And when she was baptized, and her household, she besought [us], saying, If ye have judged me to be faithful to the

Lord, come into my house, and abide [there]. And she prevailed upon us."... "After Paul and Silas came out of the prison, they went to Lydia's house, where they met with the brothers and encouraged them. Then they left."

It seems unlikely that we are to assume so very much that Paul made her keep silence in her own house. The whole idea is very wrong.

Lydia is not the only instance of church being held in a woman's house,
Col 4:15 "Greet the brethren who are in Laodicea and also <u>Nympha and the church that is in her house</u>."
Acts 12:12 "And when he had considered the thing, he came to <u>the house of Mary the mother of John</u>, whose surname was Mark; <u>where many were gathered together praying</u>."

Do you think that John Mark told his mother Mary to keep silence during a gathering of believers in her own house? Let me put it this way: Do you think your mother would feel like you are honoring her (as per the 10 Commandments) if you told her she needed to not speak during a church service she was holding in her own house, on account of her being a woman?

I would think not.

<u>Therefore, all women must have husbands in order to learn</u>

On to the next point, how ridiculous it is to suppose that all women must marry! This directly contradicts Paul's advice in 1 Cor 7:8, 25-40. This is the same letter! It makes no sense whatsoever that Paul would directly contradict himself in the same letter, nor that God would contradict Himself in the same letter.

"But I say to the unmarried and to widows that it is good for them if they remain even as I. Now concerning virgins I have no command of the Lord, but I give an opinion as one who by the mercy of the Lord is trustworthy. I think then that this is good in view of the present distress, that it is good for a man to remain as he is. Are you bound to a wife? Do not seek to be released. Are you released from a wife? Do not seek a wife. But if you marry, you have not sinned; and if a virgin marries, she has not sinned. Yet such will have trouble in this life, and I am trying to spare you. But this I say, brethren, the time has been shortened, so that from now on those who have wives should be as though they had none; and those who weep, as though they did not weep; and those who rejoice, as though they did not rejoice; and those who buy, as though they did not possess; and those who use the world, as though they did not make full use of it; for the form of this world is passing away. But I want you to be free from concern. One who is unmarried is concerned about the things of the Lord, how he may please the Lord; but one who is married is concerned about the things of the world, how he may please his wife, and his interests are divided. The woman who is unmarried, and the virgin, is concerned about the things of the Lord, that she may be holy both in body and spirit; but one who is married is concerned about the things of the world, how she may please her husband. This I say for your own benefit; not to put a restraint upon you, but to promote what is appropriate and to secure undistracted devotion to the Lord. But if any man thinks that he is acting unbecomingly toward his virgin daughter, if she is past her youth, and if it must be so, let him do what he wishes, he does not sin; let her marry. But he who stands firm in his heart, being under no constraint, but has authority over his own will, and has decided this in his own heart, to keep his own virgin daughter, he will do well. So then both he who gives his own virgin daughter in marriage does well, and he who does not give her in marriage will do better. A wife is bound as long as her husband lives; but if her husband is dead, she is free to be married to whom she wishes, only in the Lord. But in my opinion she is happier if she remains as she is; and I think that I also have the Spirit of God."

So it is clear that God does not teach that all women need to have husbands. So if 1 Cor 14:34-35 was true, then how would any unmarried women or widows learn? If they have to ask their husbands at home to learn anything, and they have no husbands, then they cannot learn. Why would Paul advise older widows to stay unmarried in 1 Cor 7, and say she can better focus on pleasing

God if she is single, and then say that if women want to learn in the Christian faith that they should be silent in church and ask their own husbands at home? Again, there is a direct contradiction, and it is found in the very same letter from Paul of 1 Cor. He makes clear that there are differences between single and married women in 1 Cor 7, but completely ignores the existence and situation of single women, especially widows, in 1 Cor 14. There is no getting around this complete contradiction and inconsistency in Paul's letter.

Silence shows submission

In what is one of the most submissive scenes of a woman in the Bible, we see Mary, visited by the angel Gabriel, told that though a virgin betrothed, that she will bear a son, conceived by the Holy Spirit. In this scene of total submission to God's will, what does Mary do? She speaks.

"And in the sixth month the angel Gabriel was sent from God unto a city of Galilee, named Nazareth, To a virgin espoused to a man whose name was Joseph, of the house of David; and the virgin's name was Mary. And the angel came in unto her, and said, Hail, thou that art highly favoured, the Lord is with thee: blessed art thou among women. And when she saw him, she was troubled at his saying, and cast in her mind what manner of salutation this should be. And the angel said unto her, Fear not, Mary: for thou hast found favour with God. And, behold, thou shalt conceive in thy womb, and bring forth a son, and shalt call his name JESUS. He shall be great, and shall be called the Son of the Highest: and the Lord God shall give unto him the throne of his father David: And he shall reign over the house of Jacob for ever; and of his kingdom there shall be no end. Then said Mary unto the angel, How shall this be, seeing I know not a man? And the angel answered and said unto her, The Holy Ghost shall come upon thee, and the power of the Highest shall overshadow thee: therefore also that holy thing which shall be born of thee shall be called the Son of God. And, behold, thy cousin Elisabeth, she hath also conceived a son in her old age: and this is the sixth month with her, who was called barren. For with God nothing shall be impossible. *And Mary said, Behold the handmaid of the Lord; be it unto me according to thy word.* And the angel departed from her."

Among all women to bear His son, God chose Mary, a woman who when showing her submission, is not silent, but instead she speaks. In this, I believe God shows us that a woman's submission is not defined by silence.

Women are to be submissive to men

The women are to keep silent in the churches; for they are not permitted to speak, but are to subject themselves, just as the Law also says. If they desire to learn anything, let them ask their own husbands at home; for it is improper for a woman to speak in church.
The implication here is that, while not all women have husbands (widows for instance) that nevertheless all women must be silent and cannot speak.

The Bible only ever states that a woman should submit herself **to her own husband**. Every time it is mentioned it is only to her own husband. Even if was true that submission was defined by silence, who would the widows be being submissive to, in keeping silent in the churches? A widow could not be showing submission to her dead husband, because in the same letter of 1 Cor 7:39 the Bible says a widow is not bound, but free: "A wife is bound as long as her husband lives; but if her husband is dead, she is free to be married to whom she wishes, only in the Lord." If silence shows submission, and ALL women have to be silent in church, whether they are married or single, then this contradicts itself and has no internal logic.

This describes women being silent in submission to all men, even though they don't have a husband. But nowhere in the Bible does it say anywhere that all women are to submit to all men, let alone by showing silence. Nowhere does it say women need to be silent in church, except for here. In several blatant ways, these verses contradict the rest of the Bible. As shown above, neither Paul nor Jesus Himself required women to be silent in their presence, when learning, nor during church service, and both taught women who were not their wives! The statement "it is improper for women to speak in church" could not be based on showing submission to church elders. Especially as Jesus is the head and husband of the entire church!

As such, the most logical conclusion is that the widows would be showing submission to the men in general, on the basis purely of them being women, and not because of "wives submit yourselves to your own husbands" or even any misconstruing of the many places where the Bible says that wives should submit to their own husbands. This concept of women in general submitting to men in general does not originate elsewhere in the Bible, and any notion of this belief as some may teach it, I would argue originates right here in these exact verses of 1 Cor 14:34-35. Elsewhere in many places wives are told to submit to their own husbands, but women in general are not ever told to submit to men in general. Nor in the Bible anywhere is a wife told to submit to men in general. There is no second witness to this idea that women are to submit to men in general.

I would think such an important concept as women submitting to men in general should be covered in other places in the Bible if it was genuine, but the rules here of what is expected of women and men in this way are left vague and not covered anywhere else in the Bible, very unlike the submission between wives and husbands, which is covered in great detail in Eph 5, and in lesser detail in other parts of the New Testament. Why the silence elsewhere about women in general submitting to men in general? It is arguable that a woman cannot be submissive to both her own husband and to all men in general in this vague undefined way because the two would conflict. I think that is a reasonable argument.

As much as no man can serve 2 masters (Matt 6:24), no woman can submit to 2 heads of an equal sort. A woman cannot submit herself both to her husband, and to every other man who comes along. Such would lead to terrible confusion!

And the verse prior, 1 Cor 14:33 states,
"For God is not the author of confusion, but of peace, as in all churches of the saints."

In and of itself, how could such a true statement, that God is the author of peace and not confusion, in truth be immediately followed by 2 verses of such confusion, contradicting the rest of the Bible, and the rest of this book of 1 Cor, and thus even this chapter of 1 Cor 14 itself? Nowhere in the Law does it say that a wife or woman is to be submissive. The rest of the New Testament contradicts this teaching that women are to be silent and not speak in church. A woman who held church in her house surely spoke in her own house. Many women learned from Jesus, who never had a wife. The logic that women must all learn from their husbands is ridiculous as many women don't even have husbands. The lack of internal consistency with the rest of the Bible is the best proof to my mind that these verses are a gloss, besides the historical evidence I mentioned first. But the greatest proof to my heart that these verses are a gloss, is the truth I feel and peace I feel from the Holy Spirit in my heart, when I say what I know is true: that 1 Cor 14:34-35 is a gloss.

How should it truly read?

"But if a revelation is made to another who is seated, the first one must keep silent. For you can all prophesy one by one, so that all may learn and all may be exhorted; and the spirits of prophets are subject to prophets; for God is not a God of confusion but of peace, as in all the churches of the saints. Was it from you that the word of God first went forth? Or has it come to you only? If anyone thinks he is a prophet or spiritual, let him recognize that the things which I write to you are the Lord's commandment. But if anyone does not recognize this, he is not recognized. Therefore, my brethren, desire earnestly to prophesy, and do not forbid to speak in tongues. But all things must be done properly and in an orderly manner."

Chapter Three
Genesis 3 Desire

We are going to move on to the word "desire" in Genesis 3:16. "To the woman He said, I will greatly multiply your sorrow and your conception, In pain you will bring forth children; Yet your desire will be for your husband, And he will rule over you."

What is the word here that is usually translated as "desire"? What does "Your desire will be for your husband" mean?

This word translated as "desire" in Hebrew is "teshuqah". "Teshuqa" is an interesting word because it is only used 3 times in the entire Old Testament, and in 3 very different contexts. These instances are not without conflict. The first instance is as "desire" in Gen 3:16 above. The second instance is in Gen 4:7.

"If you do well, will not your countenance be lifted up? And if you do not do well, sin is crouching at the door; and its desire is for you, but you must master it."
The third and final instance is in Song of Solomon 7:10.
"I am my beloved's, And his desire is for me."

There is a word in Hebrew which means "desire" in the normal sense of the word in English. It is used to mean "desire, incline, covet, wait longingly, wish, sigh, want, be greedy, prefer". That word is "avah" (0183). There are other words translated as desire sometimes as well. But "teshuqa" is translated desire all 3 times and is only used those 3 times in the entire Hebrew Old Testament. There is no further context from which to use to define it from.

On the surface, there doesn't seem to be much of interest here to study. But lately Bible translations have started to translate "teshuqa" as a "desire to control" or a "desire to devour". It is easy to argue against this position by pointing out that in Song of Solomon 7:10 both of those negative meanings of "teshuqa" would be so out of place that it becomes obvious those cannot be the meaning. What enamored young woman in a love song would be glad that her beloved's "desire to control" or "desire to devour" is for her? It makes no sense. Yet it still is becoming more popular in some circles to say "teshuqa" means a "desire to control" or "desire to devour".

So I went to try to figure out what the word means, and it turns out there is alot more to know about this word "teshuqa" then I originally thought. The inconsistent interpretations of these 3 instances were nothing but the tip of the iceberg.

Since the time of the apostles, the Greek Christians have kept for us the Septuagint, the Greek Old Testament. It was a primary translation directly from the Hebrew, which was done about 285-500 BC. It was also the first translation of the Hebrew Old Testament into any other language, and is thus the oldest translation available. In the Greek Septuagint, Gen 3:16 reads: καί τη γυναικί είπεν πληθύνων πληθυνω τάς λύπας σου καί τόν στεναγμόν σου έν λύπαις τέξη τέκνα καί πρός τόν ανδρα σου η αποστροφή σου καί αύτός σου κυριεύσει

The word that is the translation of "teshuqa" is "αποστροφή". This is the word apostrophe in Greek, (654). It means "to return, or to turn back, or to turn away" here in Gen 3:16. The same word is used of Hagar returning to Sarai in Gen 16:9, where the word is translated into English as "return". "Then the angel of the LORD said to her, "Return to your mistress, and submit yourself to her authority."

In the Greek, Genesis 4:7 reads, "ούκ εάν όρθως προσενέγκης όρθως δε μη διέλης ημαρτες ησύχασον πρός σε η αποστροφη αύτου καί συ αρξεις αύτου".

Again "teshuqa" is translated into the word "αποστροφη", or apostrophe. In the Greek <u>translation</u> this part reads "Be still, its return is to you and you shall rule over it". In this case "it" is the sin offering, Cain's sacrifice of vegetables, which will return to Cain and he must master it, or begin again on it. His sacrifice will return to him, and he must try again to get it right, as his first attempt of what he gave as a sacrifice wasn't acceptable.

What the Greek says in Gen 4:7 is rather different from how the Hebrew is usually translated, which usually reads "sin is waiting at the door and its desire is for you". But, I want to make the Greek of 4:7 clear to you. Sin here is seen as a sin offering, as a basket of vegetables and grains, not as an entity. This also matches the Hebrew meaning of the word used here for sin, which is often used to mean a "sin offering". Looking at it that way, it would be difficult to read in the Hebrew "Your sin offering is desiring you". Surely that would be quite the case of personification, like your car desires you, or your shoes. Later, after covering more, coming back to this you may see that the Hebrew could line up with the Greek much more closely in its translation into English, that the sin offering would return to him until it was mastered, done right and made acceptable.

In Song of Solomon 7:10 the Greek reads, "ἐγω τω αδελφιδω μου καὶ ἐπ' ἐμε η ἐπιστροφη αὐτου".
The word "apostrophe" means to "turn away" while the word "ἐπιστροφη" or "epistrophe" means to "turn towards". Despite this slight variance, it is still very clear that "teshuqa" was translated as some sort of turning all three times it is used, as per the Septuagint.

I have heard, though not seen for myself, that the Ethiopic secondary translation from the Septuagint made in 400-600 AD also says "turn" of some sort, in all three verses as well. This would serve to verify the Greek OT did in fact used to say "turning" in the past, as well as still saying it now. I cannot verify this as I don't have a copy of the Ethiopic or a concordance for Ethiopic. Nonetheless, the Greek Orthodox Bible used by the Greek Orthodox Christians of today says "return". The number of Greek Orthodox Christians who use the Septuagint worldwide is estimated to be at least <u>300 million people</u>. So hundreds of millions of Christians located all over the world today do not read Genesis 3:16 as "desire" at all, but read it as "return". It is a thought worth spending some time contemplating.

Besides the Greek, I have seen a second primary translation which was made directly from the Hebrew which also uses "turn". The Syriac Peshitto was translated directly from the Hebrew about 200-485 AD by Palestinian Jews. It is said to be a very literal translation. In Gen 3:16, and 4:7 the word used in Syriac means "turn" or "return". I could not find Song of Solomon 7:10. Still, 2 out of 3 verified is pretty good.

You can verify this yourself online.
From here http://cal1.cn.huc.edu/ search the textual databases, then text browse, pick Syriac and submit, then scroll down to 62001 P GN for Genesis. Find chapter 3, verse 16 and click on the link for the lexiconed words, and the same for chapter 4 verse 7. Or directly, go here, http://cal1.cn.huc.edu/cgi-bin/analysis.cgi?voffset=62001%2029822 and http://cal1.cn.huc.edu/cgi-bin/analysis.cgi?voffset=62001%2036052 the same for Gen 4:7. Then scroll down to "pny V" which is defined as "to turn" in Gen 3:16. Compare "pny V" here http://cal1.cn.huc.edu/concord.php?text=62001 and the verses of Gen 3:16 and 4:7 which are listed if you follow the link for "pny V" to here http://cal1.cn.huc.edu/cgi-bin/kwictest.cgi?lemma=pny&pos=V&lth=10&charset=S&texts=62001.

Between the Septuagint translated in 285-500BC, and the Syriac Peshitto translated from 200-485 AD, this means that at least for a length of time somewhere between about 485 and 985 years, the Hebrew was translated as "turn, return, or turning". This is starting from the beginning of the time of any translations at all, because the Greek Septuagint was the first translation, at least it is the oldest I know of. At the very least from 285 BC to 200 AD and at most from 500 BC to 485 AD, "teshuqa" was being translated as "turning" of some sort when the Hebrew was translated. At a minimum this is 485 years, and at maximum this is 985 years, almost a millennium, in which translations from the Hebrew rendered "teshuqa" to mean "returning". That is quite a long-term precedent to be set on the meaning of the word "teshuqa".

Another interesting primary translation is the Latin Vulgate, which renders 3:16 as "power", 4:7 as "appetite" and 7:10 as "turn". It was written about 380 AD, under noted rabbinical influence, and still has one instance of "turn" in it. (Of course this was after the Christian faith already had gained much popularity and growth.)

It seems likely to me that the Syriac Peshitto was an earlier translation than the Latin Vulgate, though their estimated datings overlap, on the basis that the Syriac holds to a translation that matches the earlier primary translation to the Greek. The point of mentioning the later translation above is that "teshuqa" did not start to be translated as "desire" nor "lust", or anything except "returning" until at least 380 AD. (This is important, because it indicates that at the time of Jesus, the apostles, and the early church, the word in Gen 3:16 was read in Greek as a "return" or "turning".)

Also I want to note that in the Latin Vulgate translation, the same Hebrew word is translated as "power", "appetite", and "turn". Does that sound to you like the translators had a firm grasp on what this singular word "teshuqa" meant? Do you think its possible that personal interpretations of the meanings of the passage as a whole were getting pushed into the translation, so that the words were not being translated very precisely? It sure seems to me like that is possibly the case in this instance.

Some people argue about the same problems in translations today. Some translations are known to be focused on translating each word with precision, while other translations are more focused on a culturally understandable reading of the passage as a whole. While some translations may do this well, others may not, completely mistranslating words or even corrupting the meaning of a passage in the process. Take for instance the translation reviewed in <u>this article</u>:
"Since it professes to be in contemporary language, The Message abounds in modern expressions: "stuck up" (Pro. 30:13), "clean house" (1 Pet. 2:1), "get lost" (Gen. 19:9), "moonlighting" (1 Thes. 2:10), "said our piece" (1 Thes. 2:2), "slept with" (Gen. 4:1), "have sex with" (Lev. 18:6),

"hanging out" (Pro. 7:12), "lock, stock, and barrel" (Mat. 4:9), "sponging" (1 Thes. 4:12), and "six feet under" (Isa. 38:18). Although such language is to be expected from a Bible that makes such a profession, the result is a Bible that does not read like a Bible at all."

I find the idea that a Bible uses the phrase "lock, stock, and barrel" to be particularly outrageous, funny if it wasn't so sad, because the muskets this phrase refers to were not invented until about 1400 years after the last of the Bible was written! So you can see, some translations are more accurate than others. To me it seems possible that the Latin Vulgate was, for whatever reason, not the most accurate translation, because the same 1 word is translated into 3 very different words with different meanings.

Jumping from the Latin Vulgate in 380 AD to almost 1300 years later; in 1610 AD the Douay translation was made, which was mainly based off of the Latin Vulgate, as well as the Hebrew. And it reads for Gen 3:16, "under husband's power", for 4:7 "lust thereof under thee", and once again for Song of Solomon 7:10 "turn". Here again, there is no real consistency, and the meaning of "turn" still remains.

Around the same time the Geneva Bible came out. It was based off of the Hebrew and Greek, reading "desire" for 3:16, "sin's desire" for 4:7 and "desire" for 7:10. This marked the first time ever that a Bible translation consistently read "desire" for all instances of usage for the word "teshuqa". So it was not until 1610, over one thousand five hundred years since the end of the writing of the Bible, before a translation was made which consistently read "desire" in all 3 instances of the usage of the word "teshuqa". A little later came the original KJV, of much longer lasting popularity, which also read "desire" in all 3 instances, which was taken to mean a sexual desire at the time in Gen 3 and Song of Solomon 7. And thus began a snowball effect, by which every modern translation that I know of renders "teshuqa" as "desire", a trend which has been going on <u>only for the last 400 years</u>.

By merit of precedent, and of longevity, the rendering of "returning" for "teshuqa" not only dates back to at least 285 BC with consistency in all 3 instances, but also had a longstanding run of being the proper translation for 485-985 years. This is not counting that the rendering of "return" did survive in part until at least 1610 in the Douay Bible, preserved in Song of Solomon 7:10, and that the Greek Septuagint still renders the word "teshuqa" as "return" to this day in the still active Orthodox church.... but if one were to count Douay, it gives 1895 years of precedent for translating "teshuqa" as "return".

Not counting the Douay, this compares (at worst) 285 BC to 1610 AD, and 85 years more precedent, to (at best) 500 BC to 1610AD, and 585 years more precedent for "returning" rather than "desire" as the champion contender for accurate translation of the original that God intended and did originally write. Based on this historical evidence over the millennia, it seems that there is more weight that "returning" is how "teshuqa" should still be translated today, rather than "desire".

Teshuqa or Teshuba?

If one looks at "teshuqa", the Hebrew word in question, the Strong's says that it is derived from the word "shuwq" (7783) which means to "to overflow". Strong's says "teshuqa" means "from 7783 in the original sense of stretching out after, a longing, desire".

The Browns-Drivers-Briggs has a very different reading. To put in longhand,
"longing in all 3 cases (In the Greek OT its apostrophe in Genesis and epistrophe in SOS, whence E. Nestle Id. Marginalien u. Materialien 6 proposed "teshuba" in Gen 3:16, which Ball (?), Paul Haupt (possibly in Scared Books of the OT or the Polychrome Bible) reads in all instances; but how explain the unusual and striking word in Masotoric text?)"

This basically notes the conflict, and explains that at least 2 biblical scholars by the names of Paul Haupt and E. Nestle use the Hebrew word "teshuba" instead of the word "teshuqa". Why would they use a different Hebrew word? What is the word "teshuba"?

In my own studies I have spent some time looking at the Strong's, and I noticed "teshuba" sitting nearby to teshuqa in the Strong's. There is only 1 letter different between the 2 words. So what does the Hebrew word "teshuba" mean?

Browns-Drivers-Briggs says this (longhand):
"*return, answer* 1. 1 S 7:17 *and his return was to* (= he returned) *to Rama* 2. *at the return of the year, i.e. of spring,* 2 S 11:1, 1 K20:22,26, 2 Ch 36:10, 1 Ch 20 :1, 2 S 11:1 3. *answer Jb 34:36, 21:34.*)"

The Hebrew word "teshuba" can mean a "return", or an "answer". It has both a literal action meaning, and a more figurative verbal meaning. What a remarkable thing it is that this word "teshuba", only one letter different than "teshuqa", means a "returning"! In light of all we covered above, do you think this is just a coincidence?

When teshuba means an actual literal physical return, the word itself replies a repetitive returning, like the seasons coming back every year, or a person repetitively going back home. Here are some examples of this:

1 Sam 7:17 (NIV)
'But he *always went back* to Ramah, where his home was, and there he also judged Israel. And he built an altar there to the LORD.'
1 Sam 7:17 (NASB)
'Then his *return* was to Ramah, for his house was there, and there he judged Israel; and he built there an altar to the LORD.'

1 Kings 20:22 (NASB)
'Then the prophet came near to the king of Israel and said to him, "Go, strengthen yourself and observe and see what you have to do; for at the *turn* of the year the king of Aram will come up against you."

When teshuba means figuratively "an answer", how it would literally read is "a returning", in a verbal sense. For instance, you talk to me, and my "returning" to you is my "answer"; a verbal returning. Figuratively "teshuba" is used in the long heated dialog between Job and his friends to means "answering".

Job 34:36 (NIV)
"Oh, that Job might be tested to the utmost for *answering* like a wicked man!"
Job 21:34 (NIV)
"So how can you console me with your nonsense? Nothing is left of your *answers* but falsehood!"

Teshuba is only used 2 times to mean "answers", and is only used 8 times total in the OT. The other 6 times "teshuba" refers to a repetitive physical returning. I find it to be easy to understand the development of the word "teshuba". Its root word, the verb "shuwb" is the primary word used in Hebrew for a "return" or turning back, etc., and it is used 1066 times in the OT. It is the word "shuwb" that is a more common word for a simple "return", whereas in "teshuba" the emphasis in meaning is on the repetitive nature of the leaving and returning. The word "teshuba" is a noun formation of the verb "shuwb". Like in English, I can say "I will return" and I can say "I will have a returning". Return and returning are 2 different words; return is a verb, and a "returning" would be a noun formation of the verb "return". The distinction in the meaning of the word "teshuba" is the repetitive or cycling qualities of the returnings, like seasons returning every year. They are repetitive, like repetitive verbal replies in a long discussion or argument, which is how the additional figurative meaning of verbal "returnings" or "answers" must have developed.

Now let's take a closer look at this word "teshuqa". I do not find the development of the word "teshuqa" to be as clear-cut as the word "teshuba". "Teshuqa" is a noun that comes from the verb form of "shuwq" (7783) which is only used 3 times in the OT, and is translated in all 3 instances as "overflow", or "water it".

Joel 2:24
"The threshing floors will be filled with grain; the vats will *overflow* with new wine and oil."
Joel 3:13
"Swing the sickle, for the harvest is ripe. Come, trample the grapes, for the winepress is full and the vats *overflow*— so great is their wickedness!"
Psalms 65:9
(NASB) "You visit the earth and cause it to *overflow*;"
(NIV) "You care for the land and *water it*; you enrich it abundantly. The streams of God are filled with water to provide the people with grain, for so you have ordained it."

The meaning of "shuwq" is well-established to mean "overflow" or "running over" in the sense of liquid overfilling a space. How does a verb, "shuwq" which means "overflow" develop into a noun "teshuqa" which means "desire"? I can understand a verb "shuwb" which means "return", developing into a noun "teshuba" which means "a returning". But how a verb that means "overflow" develops into a noun that means "desire" is harder for me to understand. My point is I think the word "teshuba" has a stronger establishment of meaning relating to its root word than "teshuqa" does. As to what that might imply, it is hard to have any definite answers. I can only echo the question of the scholars Browns, Drivers, and Briggs: *how to explain the unusual and striking word "teshuqa" in the Masotoric text?*

This is how I think things are supposed to work. A word in Hebrew gets translated to a word with the same meaning, or a phrase with similar meaning, in another language.

Unfortunately, this is not the case for "teshuqa". As I have pointed out, in the Greek OT "teshuqa" 3 times is translated as a turning, either a return or a turning towards. Also in the Syriac translation, in 2 instances I can verify, "teshuqa" was also translated as a returning. Both the Greek Septuagint and the Old Syriac Peshitto were translations directly from the Hebrew, fresh primary translations. They were made at least 485 to at most 985 years apart.

Yet the meaning of "teshuqa" today is not return, turning to, or any sort of turn. The meaning of "teshuqa" today is "desire" which has been said to mean: lustful desire, hungry desire, destructive desire, a desire to control; all sorts of different desires. The same meaning just doesn't seem to hold still for more than a few hundred years.

The word "teshuqa" should in some way have a meaning that fits the word "turning", somehow, but it doesn't. Yet the word "teshuba" does fit this meaning, and is only 1 letter away from being "teshuqa".
Which makes me wonder, which word best fits the context of the three instances in which teshuqa is used in the OT?

So I'm going to go through them for you, one at a time.
Teshuba can mean a repetitive returning, or a verbal answering.
Teshuqa can/has meant a lustful desire, a desire to destroy, and a desire to control.

Teshuqa:
3:16 And you will have *lustful desire* for your husband, and he will rule over you.
4:7 And the sin offering will have a *lustful desire* for you, but you must master it.
7:10 (enamored young woman saying of her man in joy) His *lustful desire* is for me!

This doesn't make sense because a sin offering of grains and vegetables cannot have lustful desire.

3:16 And you will *desire to destroy* your husband, and he will rule over you.
4:7 And the sin offering will *desire to destroy* you, but you must master it.
7:10 (enamored young woman saying of her man in joy) His *desire is to destroy* me!

This doesn't make sense because a young woman in love is Not going to rejoice that her man wants to destroy her, nor would the

39

young man in these verses want to destroy his beloved in the first place. Nor do I think women want to destroy their husbands, though there are some men out there that claim so. And women who claim their husbands want to destroy them also. But in any case, this doesn't make sense.

3:16 And you will *desire to control* your husband, and he will rule over you.
4:7 And the sin offering will *desire to control* you, but you must master it.
7:10 (enamored young woman saying of her man in joy) He *desires to control* me!

This doesn't make sense because Solomon was already king, and at that time and culture, already had control, because he was the king, it makes no sense. He wouldn't be desiring a control he already has. And that is the least wrong with it. What enamored young woman is joyous about that? Nor could an offering of vegetables and grains actually desire to control you.

All of these translations do not match the Greek OT, and 2/3 do not match the Syriac. There is no reconciling them that I can see.

Now for Teshuba:
3:16 And your *repetitive returning* will be to your husband, and he will rule over you.
4:7 And the sin offering will *repetitively return* to you [as is], and you must master it [till you get it right].
7:10 (enamored young woman saying of her man in joy) He is *repetitively returning* to me!

3:16 And your *answering* will be to your husband, and he will rule over you.
4:7 And your sin/sin offering's *answering* will be to you, and you must master it.
7:10 (enamored young woman saying of her man in joy) He is *answering* to me!

This doesn't seem right, in that sin and sin offerings don't give verbal answers, and the young woman likely wouldn't be glad to have her man answering to her, especially if "answering" is considered negative arguing.

This I feel is the best cut for Teshuba:
3:16 And your answering will be to your husband, and he will rule over you.
4:7 And your sin offering will repetitively return to you, and you must master it.
7:10 (enamored young woman saying of her man in joy) He is repetitively returning to me!

In this translation, 4:7 matches the Greek OT, and 7:10 has an intriguing new meaning that I think better fits something a woman would find praiseworthy and enamoring about her man- that he always keeps returning to her.

And so there you have what I think Genesis 3:16 may mean:
A woman will have answers to, have repetitive verbal returnings to, her husband. This can also include that she will have verbal "comebacks" to him, "answering" in arguments or discussions, as the word "teshuba" is used in Job. And that she may be prone to repetitively come back to him, if she leaves.

Now, can I prove all this is correct? No. But I think I can and have proven that there is a reasonable amount of evidence to consider it a realistic possibility. Two ancient primary translations from the Hebrew both say the word should mean "turning" in some sense. <u>I also believe that evidence does not exist to prove what I have said here to be incorrect, either.</u> That being the case, it is up to you to make up your own mind, but I think If the original Hebrew said "teshuba", it would make so much more sense!

<u>The implications of teshuba - a returning</u>

The above being said, I want to look at the meaning of Genesis 3:16 more closely.
3:16 And your (teshuba) will be to your husband, and he will rule over you.

This can read:
And your repetitive physical returning will be to your husband;
and your repetitive answers will be to your husband;
your repetitive arguments will be to your husband,
your repetitive comebacks will be to your husband.

In context, Genesis 3:16 is God listing the negative consequences of the fall.
One negative consequence, "He will rule over you" we have already covered. It used to have a meaning of domination, but now is a rule satisfied voluntarily by the woman through submission. Perhaps there is a parallel to be drawn here, of the sinful nature tendency, and a replacement under New Testament instructions to believers.
What is the sinful nature tendency of wives since the garden? A wife arguing with her husband, or having a heated ongoing dialog with him is commonplace in marriage, and I think always has been to some extent with us sinners. These may be the "answers", like "teshuba" is used is Job, in argument, that Gen 3:16 is referring to with "your answering will be to your husband".

A woman arguing with her husband is so natural and commonplace, a nagging and contentious wife so stereotypical, that the same is even mentioned in Proverbs.
Prov 21:19 "It is better to live in a desert land than with a contentious and vexing woman."
Prov 27:15-16 "A constant dripping on a day of steady rain And a contentious woman are alike; He who would restrain her restrains the wind, And grasps oil with his right hand."
Prov 25:24 "It is better to dwell in the corner of the housetop, than with a brawling woman and in a wide house."

This tendency of wives may be what Gen 3:16 is referring to by "your answering will be to your husband". As such these statements in Proverbs are not verses on women put out in isolation, but rather they tie into the negative effects of the fall pronounced by God in Genesis 3.

(And to balance these Proverbs out, while the Bible does not record the words of a wife speaking on how terrible it is to be ruled by her husband, per "he will rule over you", the Bible is rife with absolutely horrifying stories, time and time again, of how men have mistreated their wives and women, even in a criminal manner, all throughout history. If anyone is upset that these few verses in Proverbs seem to unfairly target the sinful nature of women or wives, just keep in mind that overall, a far more numerous number of verses cover the sinful nature of men or husbands.)

So it may be that these negative "answerings" of a wife to her husband describe part of the negative consequences of the fall. What then would be the New Testament replacement in Christ? In the New Testament, it says a wife should submit herself to her own husband. Eph 5:33 also mentions the wife respecting the husband. I would think that when a Christian wife submits herself, that this is what counteracts the tendency for "answering", as well as her respecting him.

Eph 5:25-33 Husbands, love your wives, just as Christ also loved the church and gave Himself up for her, so that He might sanctify her, having cleansed her by the washing of water with the word, that He might present to Himself the church in all her glory, having no spot or wrinkle or any such thing; but that she would be holy and blameless. So husbands ought also to love their own wives as their own bodies. He who loves his own wife loves himself; for no one ever hated his own flesh, but nourishes and cherishes it, just as Christ also does the church, because we are members of His body.
FOR THIS REASON A MAN SHALL LEAVE HIS FATHER AND MOTHER AND SHALL BE JOINED TO HIS WIFE, AND THE TWO SHALL BECOME ONE FLESH.
This mystery is great; but I am speaking with reference to Christ and the church. Nevertheless, each individual among you also is to love his own wife even as himself, and the wife in order that she respects her husband.

On a wife respecting her husband, the "in order that" here is "ina" in the Greek, which means "in order that" or "so that". The meaning is that of a cause and effect relationship. Like a few verses earlier, the same word is translated "so that" in the phrase "and gave Himself up for her so that He might sanctify her".

While most women enter into a marriage showing respect for their husband, I believe what maintains that respect is the love of the husband, inspiring the wife to respect her husband. This is much like a wife's submission is supposed to replace a husband's domination. If the husband loves his wife as these verses say, then he will facilitate the wife to respect him, and this will help the wife's negative "answerings" to be replaced with respect. But this respect needs to be helped and facilitated by the husband showing her love. He loves her in order that she respects him. This cause and effect relationship is how the Greek in Eph 5:33 seems to read. It might benefit a couple to know the husband's love towards his wife is part of how to facilitate replacement of this tendency with one of respect.

There is one admonition made to women in the New Testament that I believe relates to the "repetitive returning" of Gen 3:16, in a literal physical sense.
That is 1 Cor 7: 10-11: But to the married I give instructions, not I, but the Lord, that the wife should not leave her husband (but if she does leave, she must remain unmarried, or else be reconciled to her husband), and that the husband should not divorce his wife.

It is striking to me that the wife is given more lenient instructions. She is told not to leave, but instructions are given for what she is to do if she does leave her husband anyway. The husband is given no contingency plan, and is more firmly told to not leave his wife. This difference could be reflective of God's consistency in His Word. If "teshuba", a "repetitive returning", was how Genesis 3:16 read in Paul and Jesus' time, then 1 Cor 7:10-11 would have some added meaning, tying these verses to Gen 3:16.

In closing, I think this information could be very beneficial to women, men, and married couples. In this Christians very well may have been deprived of an important insight into a successful Christian marriage. If God originally intended for the Word to contain this information, and these insights (and more ones yet unknown) to be drawn from it, then this information is still as important for people today as it ever was. Might a couple benefit from knowing that a tendency for negative verbal "answerings" is in the Bible as a consequence of the fall? That the husband loving his wife, facilitates her to respect him, which in part will help this tendency for "answerings" to him that a wife may have? That another way to see it is she will have a tendency to repetitively return to him? If this is how the original read, then I could not begin to list the importance of this understanding for Christians who trust the Word of God as their guide in life.

But if you cannot accept this

But if you cannot accept this, perhaps believing in the KJV-only, or for whatever reason are still convinced the word in Gen 3:16 means "desire", then let me suggest something to you.

Let the word "desire" mean just that. There is no basis, on the context of its 3 uses in the Bible, to say it means "desire to control" or "desire to destroy" etc. The verse in Song of Solomon 7:10 clearly counterbalances any argument for such a definition based on Gen 4:7. So the word "desire" should be taken as have a neutral meaning, and should be understood to just mean "desire".

From looking at the entire Bible, there is context to identify what sort of desire (in "your desire will be to your husband") is being meant in Gen 3:16. What is a woman's greatest desire concerning her husband? We are told: Delight thyself also in the LORD; and he shall give thee the desires of thine heart. Psalms 37:4

And for those who are Christians, God has given instructions to us in marriage. What the husband is told to do by God, more times than anything else in marriage, is to love his wife. He is told to love his wife so much it is as even as much as his own body, even as himself. See Eph 5 above. And in telling the husband to do this, God is giving the wife her greatest desire towards her husband: that he would love her. And so her desire towards her husband in Gen 3 is her desire that he would love her.

Chapter Four
1 Corinthians 11:1-16 Heads and Coverings

Another set of verses that need to be looked at are 1 Cor 11:1-16,

1 Corinthians 11: 1-16:

"Be imitators of me, just as I also am of Christ. Now I praise you because you remember me in everything and hold firmly to the teachings, just as I delivered them to you. But I want you to understand that Christ is the head of every man, and the husband is the head of a wife, and God is the head of Christ. Every man who has something on his head while praying or prophesying disgraces his head. But every woman who has her head uncovered while praying or prophesying disgraces her head, for it is one and the same as the woman whose head is shaved. For "if a woman is not covered, let her be shorn". But if it is disgraceful for a woman to be shorn or her head shaved, let her cover her head. For a man indeed ought not to have his head covered, since he is the image and glory of God. But the woman is the glory of man! For man does not originate from woman, but woman from man; for indeed man was not created for the woman's sake, but woman for the man's sake. For this reason the woman ought to have authority over her head: because of her angels. Moreover, in the Lord, neither is woman independent of man, nor is man independent of woman. For as the woman originates from the man, so also the man through the woman; and all things originate from God. Among you choose yourselves. It is proper for a woman to pray to God with her head uncovered. Nature itself does not teach you that if indeed a man has long hair that it is a dishonor to him, but if a woman wears her hair long it is a glory to her. For her hair is given to her for a covering. But if one thinks to be contentious, we have no other practice, nor have the churches of God."

What does this mean? Let's take it piece by piece.

> "Be imitators of me, just as I also am of Christ. Now I praise you because you remember me in everything and hold firmly to the teachings, just as I delivered them to you."

The teachings here are the things that Paul had taught them, and they are still following his teachings that he gave them, and haven't changed them. He praises them for this. As taught in the rest of the New Testament, included in these teachings was that women were to participate in the church, and were saved just like the men were, by grace through faith in Jesus Christ. They were encouraged to use their spiritual gifts given to them by the Holy Spirit, and to pray and prophecy, just like the men. They were to be included in the church, and participate, and both converted Jewish women and converted Gentile women were in church together.

> "But I want you to understand that Christ is the head of every man,"

Here the word used as "man" in "Christ is the head of every man" is "andros", which is exactly the same word used in James 1:20.

"For the anger of man does not achieve the righteousness of God". It goes without saying that the anger of woman does not work the righteousness of God either.

Also this is the same word used in,
"But as many as received him, to them gave he power to become the children of God, [even] to them that believe on his name: Which were born, not of blood, nor of the will of the flesh, nor of the will of man, but of God." Jn 1:12-13

Here, it is obvious that those who become born-again are not born again of the will of a man, nor the will of a woman, but only by the will of God. It is clear that this word "andros" can have the meaning of either gender; it can be all-gender-inclusive. This is confirmed in the Strong's Concordance which reads *"used generically of a group of both men and women"* and the Thayer's Lexicon, which reads *"when persons of either sex are included, but named after the more important"*.

The phrase "every man" is "pantos andros" in Greek. The word "pantos" means "all" or "any" or "every". In this verse, both "andros" and "pantos" are in the singular case, not the plural. In English, the plural would read as "all men", but this is not the case used. The case used is singular, and so a more correct reading would be "all man". This means all mankind, or all humans.

Christians as a whole, male and female, each individually do have Christ as their head. As such, this verse states that Christ is the head of every Christian person, male and female. And this is true for every Christian, male and female, equally, for we each call Jesus Christ our personal Lord and Savior, and each of us individually were called by God, and convicted, and had to choose to take Jesus Christ as our personal individual Lord and Savior.

Jesus Christ is not the lord of Christian men only. Christian women should not see Jesus as their husband's lord, as some people misread this verse, but rather each Christian woman, married or not, should see Jesus Christ as their personal and direct lord, for this is the truth the Bible teaches. (Even among non-Christians, the Bible teaches that eventually every knee shall bow and every tongue shall confess that Jesus Christ is Lord… women included…. although this passage does seem to specifically be addressed not to non-Christians, but to Christians in this life who do accept Jesus Christ as their Lord.)

"and the husband is the head of a wife,"
In addition to this, the man is the head of the woman. The words here for man and woman in the Greek are usually translated as husband and wife, and should be in this passage as well. There is no precedent for translating the words here as "the man is head of a woman", but there is precedent in Eph 5 for translating this as "the husband is head of a wife" as Eph 5:23 clearly states this. There is no other statement in the Bible which states that the head of every woman is a man, and in the case of widows and orphaned girls this would make no sense at all.

There is nothing so complicated about the dynamic described here, and there is no conflict that a wife has Christ as her head and a husband as her head. An employee in a company may have both a manager and a president over him, and both are his head in this sense, yet there is no conflict. The same is true here in that the head of every Christian wife is both a man, and is Jesus Christ.

"and God is the head of Christ."
This is an interesting statement, because Jesus Christ is God. Here, the meaning is that God the Father is the head of Jesus Christ, who is the Son of God. But at the same time, Christians know the Bible teaches the doctrine of the Godhead, or the Trinity, which contains that God the Father, Son, and Holy Spirit are one, and are all God. This raises the question as to what "head" actually means in this passage. Leaving aside assumptions in English usage, let's look at the Greek and the context to make clear the meaning of this word "head". How is God the Father the "head" of Christ, in the same way that a husband is the "head" of a wife, and Christ is the "head" of all Christians?

The word here for "head" is "kephale" in Greek. The same word "kephale" is used in all instances. It is used 76 times in the New Testament. It means the head of a body 60x. It refers to Jesus as the head or corner-stone (first stone of a building) 5x, and to the head of the table Jesus was laid on in the tomb (versus where His feet laid) 1x. Of the other 10x it is used, 4 are in this passage, 1x is of husbands in Eph 5, and the other 5x speak of Jesus Christ.

Taking these 5x speaking of Jesus in order, I have underlined the word in question, and also the word "body". First in the letter to the Ephesians,

"And hath put all [things] under his feet, and gave him [to be] the head over all [things] to the church, which is his body, the fulness of him that filleth all in all." Eph 1:22-23

"But speaking the truth in love, may grow up into him in all things, which is the <u>head</u>, [even] Christ: From whom the whole <u>body</u> fitly joined together and compacted by that which every joint supplieth, according to the effectual working in the measure of every part, maketh increase of the <u>body</u> unto the edifying of itself in love." Eph 4:15-16

"For the husband is the <u>head</u> of the wife, even as Christ is the <u>head</u> of the church: and he is the saviour of the <u>body.</u> Therefore as the church is subject unto Christ, so let the wives be to their own husbands in every thing. Husbands, love your wives, even as Christ also loved the church, and gave himself for it; That he might sanctify and cleanse it with the washing of water by the word, That he might present it to himself a glorious church, not having spot, or wrinkle, or any such thing; but that it should be holy and without blemish. So ought men to love their wives as their own <u>bodies</u>. He that loveth his wife loveth himself. For no man ever yet hated his own flesh; but nourisheth and cherisheth it, even as the Lord the church: For we are members of his <u>body</u>, of his flesh, and of his bones. For this cause shall a man leave his father and mother, and shall be joined unto his wife, and they two shall be one flesh.." Eph 5:23-31

In Ephesians, the analogy or metaphor is used that the church is the body of Jesus Christ, and Jesus is the head of that body. In all of the above references to Jesus, the usage of the word "kephale" is like that of a physical head of a physical body; the head versus all the other body parts.

Next, the letter to the Colossians,
"Who is the image of the invisible God, the firstborn of every creature: For by him were all things created, that are in heaven, and that are in earth, visible and invisible, whether [they be] thrones, or dominions, or principalities, or powers: all things were created by him, and for him: And he is before all things, and by him all things consist. And he is the <u>head</u> of the <u>body</u>, the church: who is the beginning, the firstborn from the dead; that in all [things] he might have the preeminence. For it pleased [the Father] that in him should all fulness dwell." Col 1:15-19

"For in him dwelleth all the fulness of the Godhead bodily. And ye are complete in him, which is the <u>head</u> of all principality and power: In whom also ye are circumcised with the circumcision made without hands, in putting off the body of the sins of the flesh by the circumcision of Christ: Buried with him in baptism, wherein also ye are risen with him through the faith of the operation of God, who hath raised him from the dead. And you, being dead in your sins and the uncircumcision of your flesh, hath he quickened together with him, having forgiven you all trespasses; Blotting out the handwriting of ordinances that was against us, which was contrary to us, and took it out of the way, nailing it to his cross; And having spoiled principalities and powers, he made a shew of them openly, triumphing over them in it. Let no man therefore judge you in meat, or in drink, or in respect of an holyday, or of the new moon, or of the sabbath days: Which are a shadow of things to come; but the <u>body</u> is of Christ." Col 2:9-17

In Colossians, the analogy is again used that the church is Jesus' body, and Jesus is the head of that body.

The analogy is furthered and expanded, to show that because the church is Jesus' body, that as when He was circumcised, and as He was buried, so are we, and as He rose from the dead, so shall we, and that as he triumphed over principalities and powers (evil spirits) that he also freed us from them as well, because "the (church, His) body is of Christ", who is the head of His body. It is a great analogy explaining how, because we are now the body of Christ, the Bride of the Lamb who will be as one with Him, whose Spirit is in us, His righteousness can be counted to us, in all He has done in order to redeem us, and how His victory is being applied to include us. Praise the Lord!

Summarily, every time "head" is used in referencing to Jesus and the church, it is with the analogy that Jesus is the head in a body, which is His church. This apparently was an analogy that the early Christians heard Paul use often, and were acquainted with. Like Jesus often explained deeper concepts with parables, here Paul explains a deeper concept with an analogy, which is God-breathed.

Take note of Ephesians 5:23 again, "For the husband is the <u>head</u> of the wife, even as Christ is the <u>head</u> of the church: and he is the saviour of the <u>body.</u>"

In context, it becomes clear that the same analogy is used between the husband and wife, as between Jesus and the church, which is that of the head of a body. In this analogy, the wife is every part except for the head; she is the shoulders, the torso, the arms, and the legs, of the body. The husband is the head; the eyes, ears, hair, mouth and nose of the body. In this they are two in one flesh, one body, but the husband is the head, and she is all the rest of the body. They are meant to work together, like one person, in which the head is intent of the safety of the body, and moves as the body needs to care for itself, while the body generally does what the head wants it to do, as long as it is able. Keeping this in mind, let's take a look at this verse in 1 Cor 11 again,
"But I want you to understand that Christ is the head of all man, and the husband is the head of a wife, and God is the head of Christ."

Jesus Christ and all believers, male and female, form a body, and Jesus Christ is the head of this body, while all believers make up the rest of the body. In the same analogy, the husband composes the head of a body, and his wife composes the rest of the body parts. In the same analogy, God is the head of Christ, "For in him dwelleth all the fulness of the Godhead bodily"(Col 2:9)
We know God the Father is Spirit, for "God is Spirit, and those who worship Him must worship in spirit and truth." (Jn 4:24)
And we know that Jesus said, "a spirit hath not flesh and bones, as ye see me have." (John 24:39) And the Holy Spirit is spirit also. And so while God the Father is Spirit, without flesh and bone, in His Son Jesus Christ dwells all the fullness of the Godhead bodily.

So in every instance in which "kephale" is used so far in 1 Cor 11, it is used in the figurative way of this analogy of a physical body: of a single body composed of the head, in contrast to the rest of the body parts.

A little history, a little culture

"Every man who has something on his head while praying or prophesying disgraces his head."
To understand this verse it is necessary to know the custom of a Jewish man's head covering. Jewish men would put a head covering on their heads as part of Jewish custom, to show their shame before God, as a way to show they were pious. As Christians, we can stand before God without guilt or shame, for we have been reconciled to him through Jesus' shed blood on the cross. Therefore it is a disgrace to Jesus for a man to continue to carry on the Jewish tradition of wearing a head covering to show his guilt before God. That is pretty easy to understand.

Men were not required to wear a head covering all the time in Jewish culture, but only while praying or prophesying, especially in the synagogue. The average Jewish man did not wear a head covering while fishing, or farming, or laboring, etc. However, it was a different situation entirely for Jewish women.

"But every woman who has her head uncovered while praying or prophesying disgraces her head, for it is one and the same as the woman whose head is shaved. For "if a woman is not covered, let her be shorn". But if it is disgraceful for a woman to be shorn or her head shaved, let her cover her head."
A Jewish woman wore a head covering similar to a Jewish man's, whenever she was out and about, and while she went about her daily work. Based on what Paul says here, a married woman found out and about without a head covering was considered to be a disgrace. And based on what Paul says here, it seems part of the extra-biblical Jewish traditions which had developed included that a woman found out and about without her head covered could be forced to have her hair cut short or shaved off completely. This is fitting with the culture of the community, and the laws and practices of the Jewish Pharisees at that time.

At this time a tradition had developed because of the Jews twisting the verse in Num 5:18 that says "And the priest shall set the woman before the LORD, and uncover the woman's head..." which states that a woman whose husband felt jealous but had no proof of adultery was to take her to the priest, who performed a ceremony, which included the priest uncovering her head, and her drinking some dirty water. This was a solution for a spirit of jealousy coming on a husband. The Jews added to this verse, and developed a custom of Jewish women having their heads covered, which became part of their Oral Law, which Jesus call "the traditions of men". Some of these traditions of men were later written down in such books as the Mishnah, the Talmud, etc.

The history of this Jewish custom included the right of a husband to divorce his wife for simply going out without wearing a covering on her head. And a divorce under these circumstances included that she forfeited all marital property (her Ketubah) if she was divorced from going out uncovered. (The Ketubah was a mandatory standard practice that was part of getting a marriage, essentially a mandatory prenuptial agreement, and encompassed the concepts of paying her dowry as well as today's concepts of maintenance or alimony.)

"*In Ketubot (72a) we read as follows:*

These are to be divorced without receiving their Ketubah: A wife who transgresses the law of Moshe (Dat Moshe) of Jewish practice (Dat Yehudit). And what is [regarded as transgressing the] law of Moshe? Feeding her husband with untithed food, having intercourse with him during the period of her menstruation, not setting apart her dough offering (challah), or making vows and not fulfilling them.

And what is [regarded as transgressing] Jewish practice? **Going out with uncovered head,** *spinning in the street, or conversing with every man.*"

"The married woman who uncovers her hair is transgressing assorted laws besides those involving Dat Moshe and Dat Yehudit. A woman's hair is to be considered a "form of nakedness". Thus, one is forbidden to utter words of prayer or Torah study while facing it. It is also forbidden to stare (histaklut) at a woman's erva (nakedness). Therefore, many authorities conclude that it is prohibited for a married woman to uncover her hair because she would be the transgressing the prohibition of lifnei iver ("not placing a stumbling block before a blind man" – referring to any action which leads another to sin). Also, there are authorities who see uncovered hair as a violation of the prohibition of "not going in their statutes" which refers to any non-Jewish custom adopted for reasons of immodesty. According to this analysis, since hair covering was at one time accepted by non-Jews, we must view the move away from this practice as one calculated to lesson the bounds of modesty and, therefore, a gentile practice which Jews may not imitate."

- "The Obligation of Married Women to Cover Their Hair" by Rabbi Mayer Schiller

In this case, the Jewish traditions of men developed into the cultural view that only an immodest, lewd, adulterous woman went around with her head uncovered. This is why Paul says that a woman without a head covering disgraces her husband, though Paul is just making a statement of a cultural fact at the time. In saying, "But every woman who has her head uncovered while praying or prophesying disgraces her head", Paul was not himself stating this cultural view was correct (as we will see later) but just stating that this was a fact in the culture of the time. This view that a wife having her head uncovered meant she was an immodest woman later expanded into the husband being pressured or required to divorce his wife if she went out uncovered.

"You have a man who, when a fly falls into his plate, takes [the fly], sucks on it, and then throws it away and eats what is on it. ***This is an evil man, who saw his wife go out with her hair uncovered****; or go out with her sides revealed; or acting crudely with her male or female slaves; or spins in the market; or bathes and sports with any man;* ***it is a mitzvah to divorce her."*** – Tosefta Sotah 5:9
http://www.jhom.com/lifecycle/marriage/modest_wife.htm

The word "mitzvah" has the meaning of "*A commandment of the Jewish law, The fulfillment of such a commandment, A worthy deed*". In other words, a husband was considered to be obligated to divorce his wife for going about uncovered, or he himself would be considered an evil man by the community. As a wife going uncovered was considered a form of nakedness and lewd, a wife going out without a head covering was viewed the same as her being an adulterous immoral woman. This is why Paul states that "for it is one and the same as the woman whose head is shaved". From history, we know that a wife who went out with an uncovered head was viewed as being an immodest, lewd, adulterous woman, and that this was disgraceful in the Jewish culture of the time. Paul says that this disgrace is the same disgrace as a woman whose head has been shaved, so we know that having one's head shaved is tied to a woman uncovering her head, and tied to the same disgrace of immodesty, sexual immorality, or adultery.

And so based on what Paul states, it seems that in that time and place, all that was needed for a woman to be accused of immodesty and to be divorced, was witnesses that she had been seen out and about without a head covering. This implied that she had been letting others "see her nakedness" by letting them see her hair, and implied she was an immodest, lewd, or adulterous woman. And based on what Paul states, "For 'if a woman is not covered, let her be shorn'", if her husband either accused or did divorce her for going out with her head uncovered, then the custom followed would be the violence of her forcibly having her hair cut or shaved off. This matches what history tells us, and of course was an unbiblical uninspired tradition of men, of terrorizing women that did not follow custom.

"Indeed, it was the custom in the case of a woman accused of adultery to have her hair "shorn or shaven", at the same time using this formula, "Because thou hast departed from the manner of the daughters of Israel, who go with their head covered;... therefore that has befallen thee which thou hast chosen."
-Sketches of Jewish Social Life in the Days of Christ,
by Alfred Edersheim pg. 154

At this time a divorce for a woman accused of adultery was handled by the Jewish priests, who it seems would use the above formula and cut off the woman's hair. What may be a confusing point here is why a woman would be accused of adultery for going about with her head uncovered. But to reiterate, in this time the Jewish culture was such that a wife letting others see her hair was considered the same as her letting others see her "nakedness". In itself having an uncovered head was viewed as a serious enough action for her to be divorced over this single issue. And it seems this perceived immodesty of uncovered head was understood as reasonable grounds by which a Jewish husband could accuse his wife of adultery, and seek a divorce on these grounds. And as we have seen Jewish husbands were encouraged to do so by the culture, so as to separate her disgraceful actions from himself, lest he be seen as an evil man to be looked down upon. However, an accusation of adultery without more solid proof automatically led into a ceremony conducted by the priests called Sotah. Before getting to that, it is important to note that it may have been that in order for a husband to get a divorce, in this time and place, he may have only been able to do so on the grounds of adultery or sexual immorality.

*"In the Mishnaic period the theory of the law that the husband could divorce his wife at will was challenged by the school of Shammai. It interpreted the text of Deut. xxiv. 1 in such a manner as to reach the conclusion that **the husband could not divorce his wife except for cause, and that the cause must be sexual immorality** (Git. ix. 10; Yer. So☐ah i. 1, 16b). The school of Hillel, however, held that the husband need not assign any reason whatever; that any act on her part which displeased him entitled him to give her a bill of divorce (Gi☐.ib.). The opinion of the school of Hillel prevailed. Philo of Alexandria ("Of Special Laws Relating to Adultery," etc., ch. v.; English ed., ii. 310, 311) and Josephus ("Ant." iv. 8) held this opinion. Jesus seems to have held the view of the school of Shammai (Matt. xix. 3-9).*

Although not overthrown, the ancient theory of the husband's unrestricted right was still further modified by the Mishnah. To the two restrictions mentioned in Deuteronomy the Mishnah, adds three others… The Mishnah furthermore modified the right of the husband indirectly by making the divorce procedure difficult, and bristling with formalities in ordering, writing, attesting, and delivering the get. The matter required the assistance of one learned in the law (☐id. 6a), whose duty it became to attempt to reconcile the parties, unless sufficient reason appeared for the divorce.

Another check on the exercise of the theoretical right of the husband to divorce his wife was the law compelling him to pay her the dowry or the amount of her Ketubah..."
-The Jewish Encyclopedia, Divorce, Solomon Schechter
www.jewishencyclopedia.com/view.jsp?artid=398&letter=D

It seems that at this time the Jewish priests would not grant a divorce easily, making the divorce difficult, unless there was an accusation made of adultery. In order to get a divorce, without proof of adultery, an accusation had to be made of adultery, and the woman needed to be taken to the Jewish priests to carry out the ceremony called Sotah. This ceremony was loosely based on the Numbers 5 ceremony for what to do in the case of a jealous husband, but the Pharisees had modified it greatly and its purpose. By this time, it had become a ceremony not of dealing with a husband's jealousy, but of accusing a wife of adultery, and was used for more easily divorcing a wife.

The practice that was in place at the time of Jesus and the apostles for a woman accused of adultery was this ceremony called Sotah; a Pharisaical ceremony that was a tradition of men. This ceremony was performed by the Jewish priests, and attempted to force a woman to confess to adultery. If a woman did confess to adultery, then her husband could easily divorce her.

"The Mishnaic Tractate Sotah, which appears in the Order of Women (Nashim), between Tractates Nazir and Gittin, deals mainly with the trial by ordeal undergone in the Temple by a sotah, a woman whose husband suspected her of adultery...

... At the end of the tractate the Mishnah returns to the subject of the sotah, stating: "Since adulterers have proliferated," the sotah ceremony has been abolished (9:9). Following that declaration, the tractate ends with a description of acts that were abolished during the Second Temple period and after its destruction.

The ceremony described in the Mishnah differs in several respects from that in the Pentateuch. The following are some examples of such differences.

1. *The rules of evidence:* The scriptural ceremony is performed solely on the basis of the husband's suspicions. The Mishnah, on the other hand, mentions an entire system of legal evidence – warnings and testimony – which are prerequisites for bringing the woman to the Temple.

2. *Increased severity in dealing with the sotah:* The Torah describes only one act that may be interpreted as humiliating: unbinding the woman's hair. The Mishnah develops the humiliation even further, adding the rending of the woman's garments and inviting the public to witness the ceremony, stating explicitly that the goal of these acts is to "make her repulsive."

3. *Measure for measure:* The Mishnah adds commentary to the acts described above which presents them as punishment, measure for measure, for the erring wife. Thus, the woman who took off her clothes in order to sin is forcibly stripped in public.

4. *Confession:* There is no attempt in the Torah to establish the woman's guilt via the woman herself, since the ceremony is intended to do precisely that. In the Mishnah, there are attempts to make the woman confess voluntarily. If she does so, the ceremony is stopped immediately.

5. *Death and the postponement of punishment:* While the Torah describes the results of the test, if the woman is guilty, as harm to her fertility, the Mishnah describes a theatrical death that occurs in the Temple before the onlookers. The Mishnah, however, immediately adds that if the woman has merit, the punishment may be delayed for a long time.

All these changes combine to depict the ceremony in the Mishnah as something closer to the punishment of an adulteress than a divine trial by ordeal. The laws of evidence transform the sotah from one who is merely suspected by her husband to one against whom there is solid evidence of immoral behavior (even if not of actual adultery). The increased severity of the treatment of the sotah even before the waters reveal her guilt includes various components that are more appropriate to a punitive ritual (such as the one presented in the punishment of the adulteress in Ezekiel 16, a verse of which is even explicitly quoted in the Mishnah, 1:6) than in a divine trial. The measure-for-measure principle underlying the Mishnaic commentary similarly depicts the ceremony as punishment rather than a test."

http://jwa.org/encyclopedia/article/sotah-tractate
Sotah Tractate, by Ishay Rosen-Zvi,
Jewish Women: A Comprehensive Historical Encyclopedia

In this ceremony the Priests would forcibly strip her topless to bare her breasts, inviting the public to attend and watch, to humiliate her. This had changed from the simple dignified ceremony prescribed by God in Numbers 5, to a perverted trial-by-fire that attempted to force a woman to confess to adultery, or else she would be publicly and forcibly stripped topless by male priests. She was also forced to drink not a glass of the dusty water, but forced to drink the water until *"She will not be done drinking until her face turns green and her eyes protrude and her veins become filled and they say 'Take her out,' so the enclosure does not become defiled."* (**Mishnah,** Nashim, *Sotah* 3) In other words, she was forced to drink until she had to pee so badly that they had to stop, or she would lose control and urinate, so then they took her away to urinate. These parts of the Sotah ceremony may have been abolished before the time of Jesus, or after, I do not know. As Paul does not mention it in the Bible, the stripped topless part of the ceremony may have been abolished by that time, or simply wasn't in practice in Corinth.

It would make sense that Sotah is the same ceremony where a woman who went with her head uncovered would end up having her hair forcibly cut or shaved off. This shaving of the head seems to be an addition that was added at the time and place of Paul's writing. It seems if a Jewish/Christian woman went with her head uncovered, then her husband would be obligated to divorce her by the Jewish community. Likely because of strict divorce requirements at the time making divorce difficult to obtain aside from an accusation of adultery and the Sotah ceremony, or just because going uncovered and suspicion of adultery were equated, her husband would need to put her through Sotah, even was expected to, in order to divorce her. And it makes sense that this ceremony could conclude with her hair being forcibly cut or shaven off. This practice of shaving the woman's head as part of Sotah may have varied by region, but it seems likely that this was the practice of the Jewish priests and Pharisees in Corinth. In fact this Jewish practice seems to be what Paul is quoting when he says "For 'if a woman is not covered, let her be shorn'". And so if witnesses saw her out with her hair uncovered and reported this, that was likely all it took for events to conclude with Sotah happening to her. And whether her husband was Jewish, or a Jewish-Christian convert, there would be great pressure from the Jewish community for him to divorce her for being out with her hair uncovered. Otherwise he would be looked down upon by the Jewish community also. The Sotah ceremony that an accused wife had to undergo was not what God had prescribed in Numbers 5 to deal with jealousy, but had turned into trial-by-fire of public humiliation, and intended torture, with the goal of making her confess under duress to adultery, so a husband could have a divorce easily.

Considering that we know that the Jewish priests at the time were so malicious towards women so as to rip her clothes, strip her topless publicly to humiliate her, and force her to drink this dirty water until she would have to urinate… there is really no reason to doubt that the Jewish priests would have been capable of forcibly shaving or shearing off a woman's hair. Considering how much violence had already been added to the Numbers 5 ceremony, and the twisting of the ceremony's actual purpose (to deal with a husband's jealousy) there is no reason to argue that this additional violence of cutting off the woman's hair could not have been added to the Sotah ceremony. And again, at least one historian confirms this was the case,

"Indeed, it was the custom in the case of a woman accused of adultery to have her hair "shorn or shaven", at the same time using this formula, "Because thou hast departed from the manner of the daughters of Israel, who go with their head covered;… therefore that has befallen thee which thou hast chosen."
-Sketches of Jewish Social Life in the Days of Christ,
by Alfred Edersheim pg. 154

Additionally, this is in total keeping with the attitude of the Jewish priests about the Sotah ceremony as they performed it,

"…we are told that the accused wife (sotah) is treated "with the measure that she measured out." Accordingly, "She spread the sheet before him, therefore the priest takes her hat from her head and spreads it underfoot.

She braided her hair for him, therefore the priest loosens it." Tosefta, Sotah 3"

"The Obligation of Married Women to Cover Their Hair"
by Rabbi Mayer Schiller

It is easy to see with this attitude about the ceremony, how the ceremony may have been further amplified by the Jewish priests in Corinth, to the effect of: "She let him see the nakedness of her hair, therefore the priests shaves or shears off her hair." And in fact based on what Paul says, the Bible seems to confirm this is precisely the case of what was occurring at the time in Corinth; that during Sotah accused women were having their heads forcibly shaved at the hands of the Jewish priests.

And all this information about Sotah brings new meaning to Matt 1:19, of Mary the mother of Jesus,
"Because Joseph her husband was a righteous man, and did not want to expose her to public disgrace as an example, he had in mind to divorce her quietly."

God chose a man to be step-father for Jesus who was righteous, which meant he would not force Mary to go through such a thing as Sotah. And as Mary had not been caught in adultery, this ceremony of Sotah is exactly the one Joseph would have taken Mary to the priests to undergo. This tells you what God thought about this ceremony and tradition of evil men: it was evil, not righteous. God chose a righteous man to be the step-father for Jesus, the sort of man who would not make Mary go through this, even though he noticed she was pregnant and thought she must have committed adultery during the betrothal phase of their marriage. Yet Joseph wanted to go through a more difficult and likely costly "no-fault" divorce procedure, rather than force Mary to undergo the Sotah ceremony.

The converted Jewish woman lived in a culture in which she would bring disgrace on herself and her husband if she stopped wearing a head covering. The above is what we know from historians, and Paul states here in 1 Cor 11 that a married women had a high risk of having her head shaved or shorn as a repercussion of going uncovered, and that the disgrace of having the head shaved and being uncovered were equated. If she went uncovered, Paul implies she was quite possibly going to get shaved or shorn by the Jews, and would be seen as disgraceful and disgrace her husband, all confirming what the historians say about this.

In light of this historical information, these verses need to be understood in the context of Paul referencing Jewish customs, to the Jewish converts to Christianity. Paul is clearly referencing to well known customs and common events that happened at the time he wrote to the Corinthians. Where he says *"For if a woman is not covered, let her be shorn"*, Paul is actually quoting portions of the Jewish Oral Law held by the Pharisees, the traditions of men, that the Corinthian Jewish converts were already very familiar with. Paul is quoting this, not saying this himself, nor does God say this.

Think on this: it would make no sense if it is just a coincidence that Paul is summarizing or quoting the historically documented Jewish cultural practices of the time. This cannot be a coincidence. The reason this cannot be a coincidence is because this era of history, in which these practices were common as we know from historians, is the era Paul grew up in, living for many years as a Christian-persecuting Pharisaical Jew, before his conversion to Christianity. As such Paul was well familiar with the 'traditions of men' of the Pharisees. There really is not any wiggle room on this: Paul is <u>not</u> recommending "For if a woman is not covered, let her be shorn" but rather, <u>Paul absolutely must be quoting a summary of what was already a common practice of the Jewish priests and Pharisees at the time</u>. Neither is Paul stating that it is true that it should be disgraceful for a woman to have her head uncovered, but rather <u>Paul absolutely must be stating what was a cultural fact among the Jews at the time</u>.

The historical evidence given here clearly shows at the very least that a married Jewish woman, even converted to Christianity, could be accused of adultery, divorced and left with nothing, and undergo a humiliating tortuous public trial-by-fire, just for going out with her head uncovered. Keeping this in mind, it should make more sense when Paul in the Bible seems to add that she could have her hair forcibly shaved off for going out with her head uncovered. The Jewish priests and Pharisees had and enforced traditions of violence against women routinely, as an every day matter. Even if it may remain a little uncertain whether Sotah was the ceremony Paul was referring to, the historical evidence indicates this could have been, and this is possible, and is even likely. But even if Paul was not referring to Sotah in specific, it is completely in keeping with the practices of the Jewish priests at that time to do this sort of thing, to conduct a violent ceremony publicly against a woman who was accused of violating custom. There is also the possibility that in Corinth at this time the Jewish priests and Pharisees had developed their own custom of enforcing head coverings, by accusing any women of the Jewish community who were seen with their heads uncovered, and forcibly cutting their hair. It is also possible that Jewish priests and Pharisees were intentionally targeting women who were Jewish-Christian converts, on the basis of their Christianity, to persecute them and the church, and using head coverings as an excuse to do so.

But whatever the particulars, the evidence definitely weighs in favor that Paul was commenting on unbiblical traditions of the Jewish priests and Pharisees and Jewish culture at the time. It cannot be a coincidence how closely what Paul refers to matches what is known historically about the practices and culture of the Jews. And we can see that these Jewish practices were clearly unbiblical "traditions of men" not founded on scripture. As such we can know Paul was not prescribing these practices as correct for Christians!

Paul is advocating that the culturally Jewish women that had become Christian should remain covered if they want to avoid getting their hair forcibly cut by the Jewish priests. If they don't want to get end up being violated, they should simply cover up to avoid this. (Though Paul may additionally be addressing a harsh reality, that if a Jewish Christian-converted woman does go uncovered, that the church cannot help by taking action to stop the ordeal she might have to go through.)

What is discussed here in particular is a woman "praying and prophesying", which while sometimes was done in the privacy of a believer's home, the church in those days also met out and about. It seems likely that Jewish women who were converts were encountering trouble if they uncovered their heads to pray and prophesy during worship services which were held in more public areas. Like the men, they also must have wanted to not symbolically show shame or guilt before God by wearing a covering, but rather uncover their heads to symbolize they had been reconciled to God through Jesus Christ's shed blood on the cross. But in a public area, Jews and Jewish authorities might be around, who could disrupt the Christian church meetings, and could start attacks against the Christian female Jewish converts if they had their heads uncovered.

Of course, this same problem did not apply to Gentile women. They were Romans in many cases, which had no such customs demanding women use head coverings. Many women did, but there was no law forcing such, nor punishment for not doing so.

Some detail can be found in "Life in the Roman World of Nero and St. Paul" by T. G. Tucker:
"The hair alone was subject to innumerable vagaries either of fashion or of individual taste. It might have a parting or no parting; it might be plaited over the head and fastened by jewelled tortoise-shell combs, or by pins of ivory, silver, or bronze with jewelled heads, as varied and ornamental as the modern hatpin; it might be carried to the back and rest in a knot on the neck, where it was bound with ribbons; it might be piled into a huge pyramid or "towers of many stories," so that a woman often looked tall in front and appeared quite a different person at the back; it might be encased in a coloured cloth or in a net of gold thread, for which poorer people substituted a bladder. But in all cases it was preferred that the hair should be wavy, and this was a matter which was attended to by a special coiffeur kept among the slaves. "

Obviously in the Roman empire, women generally could wear their hair uncovered, and did so elaborately. And so in the Christian churches, there was a mixture of women, both Jewish and Gentile converts. The Gentile women were not under the same cultural traditions as the Jewish converts. For some instructions targeted to Gentile women, see 1Pet 3:3 "outward plaiting of the hair", or 1 Tim 2:9 "broided hair", admonishing women to adorn themselves with modesty, not elaborately styled hair, gold, pearls, and costly array. <u>And please note, if the women being addressed had been being forced to wear head coverings, as a rule of the Christian church, no one would have been seeing their elaborately styled hair in the first place. As such giving these instructions would have been totally unnecessary.</u> Obviously, if the Bible is taught consistently, looking at it as a whole and not verses in isolation, it shows that Christian women were not being required by the church to wear head coverings as a practice of the church, as women are addressed in other sections about their publicly viewable elaborate hairstyles, of their publicly viewable hair.

In 1 Cor 11, Paul is addressing a mixed group of Christians, from both Jewish and Gentile cultures, looking for a solution to a difficult problem. As we continue, you will see Paul's conclusion is clearly a radical departure from his Pharisaical background, as he advocates for women to be able to make their own choice on what to do, and gives the Corinthians a revolutionary final word on the matter.

"For a man indeed ought not to have his head covered, since he is the image and glory of God."
To the Jewish converts of this time, this was a strong statement against everything they had been raised to follow and believe as Jews. To Jewish men, wearing a head covering in worship was normal. But if they would accept it, they not longer should, because in Christ they were now free from the guilt before God that the head covering represented. As such, they should let go of this Jewish custom whose symbolism conflicted with their new-found Christianity, and worship to God with their heads

uncovered. Additionally, Paul gives them the reason that they oughtn't have their heads covered because they are the image and glory of God; a reason he uses leading into the next case he is going to make...

"But the woman is the glory of man! For man does not originate from woman, but woman from man; for indeed man was not created for the woman's sake, but woman for the man's sake."
Here Paul confronts the Corinthians with a similar line of reasoning, that as men should go uncovered because they are the image and glory of God, that the same reason should apply to women. He is drawing a consistent point of argument out for them.

Eve was made from Adam, and for his sake, and in this she was created as the glory of mankind. The word for glory here is "doxa". It means glory, praise, honor, splendor, brightness, or magnificence. It is used to describe the bright light of the sun. The Greek here for "man" in "woman is the glory of man" is "andros" again, and Paul is saying that women are the glory of both genders of humanity. He is referencing back to the Creation account, in which the last creature God made was mankind, the pinnacle of God's creation. And the woman was the last to be made, as God's grand finale to the pinnacle of creation. What Paul is implying here is, that like men should be uncovered to show the image and glory of God, women are the glory of mankind, and should be uncovered to show the glory of mankind. (It is implied, in women being the glory of mankind, man who is the image and glory of God, it is implied that woman is also made in the image of God, as Genesis teaches. Nothing here denies that fact.)

"For this reason the woman ought to have authority over her head: because of her angels."
Here we are told that a woman ought to have authority over her own bodily head. The word here is "exhousia" and it means "power of choice". Paul is clearly stating here, making the case to the Corinthians, that a woman should have power of choice to do what she wants with her own head. The reason given is because of

her angels. This references to the common belief, which is true because Jesus Himself said so, that we all have Holy angels assigned to us that are always in the presence of God the Father. This is said in Matt 18:10,
"See that you do not despise one of these little ones, for I say to you that their angels in heaven continually see the face of My Father who is in heaven."

To read the Greek as "her angels" instead of the common "the angels" is a perfectly valid translation of the Greek. Here in 1 Cor 11:10 it reads "tous aggelous". In Phil 3:21 it reads "tou dunasphai" which is translated "his ability" even though "tou" means "the". This is because "tou" is sometimes possessive, and looks the same used possessively as non-possessively; the meaning has to be understood from context. An even better example is 1 Cor 15:25 "tous exphpous" which is translated as "his enemies". In the same way "tous aggelous" should be translated "her angels" and not "the angels".

Although I do not fully understand this, it is my understanding that just as Jesus said to not despise the children because of their angels, that women also should not be despised because of their angels. That men, women, and children all equally have angels is a representation of their equality before God. Surely a woman should have the right to choose what to wear on her own body, and it would be despising of women for the church to take a stance to force Gentile women into an unbiblical "tradition of men", or force upon women one worldly custom over another, or just to force women to wear something on their body because they are women.

Speaking of the true author of the Bible, God knew very well that the Jewish converted women were following a custom which was a Jewish "tradition of men" as Jesus often disparaged. He would not force Gentile women to take up this ridiculous custom of the Jews. God also knew that if Jewish women were to adopt the custom of the Gentile women converts, in which pretty much anything went, that the Jewish converts would face persecution by the local Jews and Pharisees. As such, women were left to choose for themselves what they thought was best for them, taking into account their own situation and the potential ramifications. God here defended the right of women to make their own choice about this.

"Moreover, in the Lord, neither is woman independent of man, nor is man independent of woman. For as the woman originates from the man, so also the man through the woman; and all things originate from God. Among you choose yourselves."

Then, in continuing the list of reasons, Paul points out that men and women are interdependent, and equal, both coming from God. Then Paul tells the Corinthians to "krinate" (2919) this themselves. This word means to *"resolve, have an opinion, select, choose, pick, or make a decision"*. What Paul is saying is that the Corinthians need to decide, each woman for herself, and each couple for themselves, whether or not she should wear a covering.

"It is proper for a woman to pray to God with her head uncovered. Nature itself does not teach you that if indeed a man has long hair that it is a dishonor to him. But if a woman wears her hair long it is a glory to her. For her hair is given to her for a covering. "

Since Paul has already heavily presented the arguments for why Jewish converted women might be prudent to wear a covering in their culture, he balances here by simply stating as a fact that it is fine for a woman to pray to God uncovered. This is as relevant for women in their own homes, as well as for women at church or in public. Most Bible translations render this statement as a question, and often people take the answer as a rhetorical "no". <u>This is done by adding a question mark into a verse which in the Greek contains no such question mark.</u> A rendering which is just as correct in Greek is "It is proper for a woman to pray to God with her head uncovered. " Paul was stating a fact, not asking a question.

He then makes the lovely statement that although there is nothing dishonoring about long hair on a man, that long hair on a woman is a glory to her. Her hair can be her covering, given by God. It is obvious that long hair on a man is not a dishonor to him. One need only think of Samson, and the Nazarenes in general, to see this. Most Bible translations render this "Does nature itself not teach you that if a man have long hair it is a dishonor to him?" <u>Again, this is done by adding a question mark into a verse which in the Greek contains no such question mark.</u> A rendering which is just as correct in Greek is "Nature itself does not teach you that if indeed a man has long hair that it is a dishonor to him", and this actually makes more sense. By nature, God made us so hair just grows longer and longer, and it is NOT a dishonor to a man, nor a woman. Again, Paul was stating a fact, not asking a question. There is nothing wrong with a man having long hair. But still, long hair on a woman is a glory to her.

…."For her hair is given to her for a covering.

But if one thinks to be contentious, we have no other practice, nor have the churches of God."

Here, Paul gives any Jewish converts, who may be insisting on women wearing head coverings, a very strong statement of policy: he tells them that the churches of God have no other practice than for a woman's hair to serve as her God-given covering. The church of God is stated to have no other practice but a woman's hair being her head covering, if one is needed. This is Paul's final word on the matter, which at the time, looking at the historical context, was quite a revolutionary statement.

Next, he says if anyone is thinking to debate or argue, that they are being contentious. That is not a compliment. The word is "philoneikos" and it means "fond of strife" or "eager to contend". So the conclusion here is that the matter is settled by his previous statement, that "her hair is given to her for a covering." He makes it clear that it is those who do not try to require head coverings that would be right, and it is those who insist women need head coverings that would be contentious and fond of strife, and wrong.

How should it be understood?

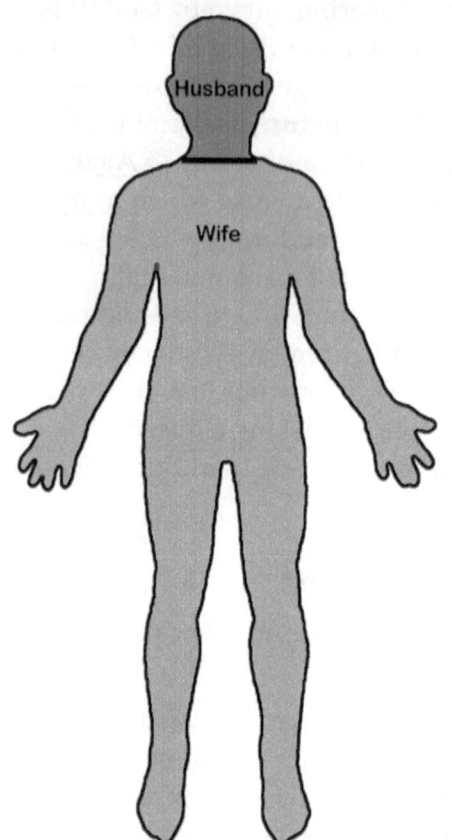

I am going to paraphrase and give expanded meaning below, and summarized commentary, of how I think 1 Cor 11 should be understood.

[The Dark/Light here represents either:
Dark Gray- God the Father / Light Gray- Jesus Christ the Son

Dark Gray - Jesus Christ / Light Gray - All Christians

Dark Gray - a husband / Light Gray - a wife]

Be imitators of me, just as I also am of Christ. Now I praise you because you remember me in everything and hold firmly to the teachings, just as I delivered them to you. But I want you to understand several things:

1. Christ is the head of every Christian, who are His body, and the husband is the head of a wife, who is like his body, and God is the head of Christ, who is the fullness of the Godhead bodily.

2. Every man who has something on his head while praying or prophesying disgraces his head, Jesus. (You men who are Jewish converts need to change your custom if you are still doing this).

3. And, as to your problem there, I know every woman who has her head uncovered while praying or prophesying in public worship disgraces her husband, for in this culture it is one and the

same as the woman whose head is shaved, (viewed in the Jewish culture as an adulteress), For in this Jewish culture they say "if a woman is not covered, let her be shorn", and we can't stop this attack from happening to her if she goes uncovered. But here is the solution: if it is disgraceful for a woman to be shorn or her head shaved, let her cover her head.

4. For indeed a man ought not to have his head covered, and a reason for this is since he is the image and glory of God. (see 2 above) Moreover, the woman is the glory of mankind. For man does not originate from woman, but woman from man; for indeed man was not created for the woman's sake, but woman for the man's sake. Mankind was the last of all that was created, the pinnacle of creation, and she was the finale, made to show the glory of men, being made from a man. Therefore, same as men shouldn't have their heads covered, so as to show the glory of God, by the same reasoning women shouldn't have to have their heads covered, to show the glory of mankind.

5. For this reason the woman ought to have the power of choice over her own head: because of her angels. Like the children, women's angels continually see the face of God and are in His presence, so do not show you despise women by the way you treat them. Do not think little of them or be mean to them, because like the children, they are important enough to God to each be represented by an angel in His presence.

6. Moreover, in the Lord, neither is woman independent of man, nor is man independent of woman. For as the woman originates from the man, so also the man has his birth through the woman; and all things originate from God. You are equal.

7. Among you choose yourselves. It is proper for a woman to pray to God with her head uncovered. You women, you couples, can figure this out yourselves, but everyone, just know if a woman chooses to pray uncovered, it is fine.

8. For nature itself does not teach you that if indeed a man has long hair that it is a dishonor to him. But if a woman wears her hair long it is a glory to her. Because her hair is given to her for a covering.

She is fine just as God made her. If you have to feel she needs a head covering, then her hair is her covering, given by God. But if one thinks to be contentious, wants to cause strife and argue, know that we have no other practice, nor have the churches of God.

Chapter Five
Eph 5 Marriage – Part 1 – Submit Yourself

Wives are told to submit to their husbands, what does the word "hupotasso" mean?
Husbands are told to love their wives, what does the word "agapao" mean?
How should Ephesians 5 look when being played out in a marriage?

Eph 5:21-33
Submitting yourselves one to another in the fear of God:
Wives, submit yourselves unto your own husbands, as unto the Lord. For the husband is the head of the wife, even as Christ is the head of the church: and he is the saviour of the body. Therefore as the church is subject unto Christ, so let the wives be to their own husbands in every thing.
Husbands, love your wives, even as Christ also loved the church, and gave himself for it; That he might sanctify and cleanse it with the washing of water by the word, That he might present it to himself a glorious church, not having spot, or wrinkle, or any such thing; but that it should be holy and without blemish. So ought men to love their wives as their own bodies. He that loveth his wife loveth himself. For no man ever yet hated his own flesh; but nourisheth and cherisheth it, even as the Lord the church: For we are members of his body, of his flesh, and of his bones. For this cause shall a man leave his father and mother, and shall be joined unto his wife, and they two shall be one flesh. This is a great mystery: but I speak concerning Christ and the church. Nevertheless let every one of you in particular so love his wife even as himself; and the wife in order that she respects her husband.

To answer these questions, we are going to look at the word for "submit yourself" which is "hupotasso" and the word for "love" which is "agapao", in Greek.

Submit yourself to your husband

Now, there is the word "hupotasso" in Greek. This is translated as "subject yourself", or "submit yourself". I find looking at all the verses in which a word is used is a good way to better understand its meaning. When I looked up hupotasso (5293) in the Strong's, it says the word is used 40x in the New Testament. There is another word which is translated the same as hupotasso, that word is hupotage. The Strong's says Hupotage (5292) is used 4x in the New Testament.

Is the Strong's correct? Not really. Actually the word hupotasso is used 19x in the New Testament, not 40x. The word hupotage, as far as I can tell, is used 13 times, plus one time with the spelling as hupotetage, bringing it to 14 times, generally, not 4x. There are also a couple new words introduced that are not mentioned in the Strong's, but are categorically lumped together under hupotasso in the Strong's.

The first word is hupotaxis. It is a combination of the word hupo (5259) and the word taxis (5010). It is used 8 times in the New Testament. The Strong's lumps all this under hupotasso.

The second word is hupotaktos, which is a combination of hupo (5259) and taktos (5002). It is used twice, once in Hebrews 2:8. There is another spelling of this, which is hupotetaktos, which is a combination of hupo (5259), te (5037) and taktos (5002). It is used once in 1 Cor 15:27.

Tasso (5021), tagma (5001), taxis (5010) and taktos (5002) are individual words that each earn their own number in the Strong's Concordance. That is because they are 4 different words. In the same way, Hupotasso (5293), hupotage (5292), hupotaxis, and hupotaktos seem like they should each have their own separate number, but do not. Almost every instance of usage is lumped under hupotasso, even when hupotasso is not the word used. Not only that, but many instances in which hupotage is used, hupotasso receives the entry, even though hupotage actually has its own separate Strong's number and entry!

Why does this matter? Well, besides simply the inaccuracy involved being a bad thing on principle, the meaning of the words are confused as a result. The words have slightly different meanings in the tone and context in which they are used.

Hupotasso is used as follows: Luke 2:51, 10:17, 10:20, 1 Cor 14:32, 14:34, 16:16, Rom 8:7, Rom 13:1, 13:5, Eph 5:21, 5:24, Tit 2:5, 3:1, 2:9, 1 Pet 2:18, 3:1, 3:5, Col 3:18.
Hupotasso means "under"+ "to set, to appoint", in a way that implies something being chosen from above, ordained, or appointed.

Hupotage is used as follows: Rom 8:20, 10:3, 1 Pet 2:13, 3:22, 5:5, 2 Cor 9:13, Gal 2:5, 1 Tim 2:11, 3:4, 1 Cor 15:28 (2x), Heb 2:8, 12:9, James 4:7. (Heb 2:8 is hupotetage).
Hupotage means "under" + "arranged in order, series" in a way that implies a time series, or ordered by highest rank first, in an order of group such as a class or troop.

Hupotaxis is used as follows: Phil 3:21, Rom 8:20, Heb 2:5, 2:8 (2x), 1 Cor 15:26, 15:27, 15:28. Hupotaxis means "under" + ordered" as in a time order, one after another. Examples would be lunch, then dinner, or prophecy then tongues at church meetings. Generally the word usage shows or demonstrates the existence of such order. Also it can show a group of a certain type or order.

Hupotaktos is only used twice, in Heb 2:8, and 1 Cor 15:27. Hupotaktos means "under" + "decided or fixed (time)". Some examples might be a set holiday, or a set time in general.

As you can see there is some difference here in the meanings of these words. This difference is significant in the quest to find out just what "submit" means in the context of wives and marriage, as well as in other areas. Sometimes the meaning of words is best understood from contextual clues. We can better understand the meaning of hupotasso by looking at all the places in the Bible where the word hupotasso is actually used.

An essential question is: Do those instances of hupotasso include all the verses applying to wives in particular? The answer is: Yes! Hupotasso is the word always used in relation to wives in marriage. Actually these instances cover all the verses aimed especially at women, with one exception. That is 1 Tim 2:11, which is hupotage, and refers to a class or learning setting, which is why the different word makes more sense, as the women are submitting to an ideal orderly situation for learning, the students ranked under the teacher.

So we should be able to understand better what hupotasso means by looking at the other places in which it is actually used in the New Testament. These all happen to be in the passive middle voice and therefore reflexive form. They are as follows:

Luke 2:51 And He went down with them and came to Nazareth, and He continued submitting himself to them; and His mother treasured all these things in her heart.

Luke 10:17 The seventy returned with joy, saying, "Lord, even the demons submit themselves to us in Your name."

Luke 10:20 "Nevertheless do not rejoice in this, that the spirits submit themselves to you, but rejoice that your names are recorded in heaven."

1 Cor 14:32 and the spirits of prophets submit themselves to prophets;

~~1 Cor 14:34 The women are to keep silent in the churches; for they are not permitted to speak, but are to subject themselves, just as the Law also says.~~

1 Cor 16:16 that you also submit yourself to such men and to everyone who helps in the work and labors.

Rom 8:7 because the mind set on the flesh is hostile toward God; for it does not subject itself to the law of God, for it is not even able to do so,

Rom 13:1 Every person is to subject themself to the governing authorities For there is no authority except from God, and those which exist are established by God.

Rom 13:5 Therefore it is necessary to submit yourself, not only because of wrath, but also for conscience' sake.

Eph 5:21-22 Submitting yourselves one to another in the fear of God, wives unto your own husbands, as unto the Lord. (The Strong's counts this verse as 2x, but in the Greek it is 1x)
Eph 5:24 But as the church submits itself to Christ, so also the wives ought to their husbands in everything.
Tit 2:5 to be sensible, pure, workers at home, kind, submitting themselves to their own husbands, so that the word of God will not be dishonored.
Tit 2:9 Urge bondslaves to subject themselves to their own masters in everything, to be well-pleasing, not argumentative,
Tit 3:1 Remind them to submit themselves to rulers, to authorities, to be obedient, to be ready for every good deed,
1 Pet 2:18 Servants, submit yourselves to your masters with all respect, not only to those who are good and gentle, but also to those who are unreasonable.
1 Pet 3:1 In the same way, you wives, submit yourselves to your own husbands so that even if any of them are disobedient to the word, they may be won without a word by the behavior of their wives,
1 Pet 3:5 For in this way in former times the holy women also, who hoped in God, used to adorn themselves, submitting themselves to their own husbands;
Col 3:18 Wives, submit yourselves to your own husbands, as is fitting in the Lord

Looking over these verses, something sticks out at me. In every instance, the word hupotasso has no odd implied meaning in usage, except in 1 Cor 14:34. <u>What a strange coincidence, as we have already established that 1 Cor 14:34 is a gloss.</u> 1 Cor 14:34 implies that the practice of hupotasso means to "not speak", but this meaning is not to be implied from any of the other verses. 1 Cor 14:34 is a gloss, and I think for years has skewed and twisted the understanding of what hupotasso means. But now the meaning of hupotasso can be re-examined afresh.

There is also one, and only one place, in which hupotasso is used in the Septuagint, which is the Greek Old Testament. Psalm 144:2, "My lovingkindness and my fortress, My stronghold and my

deliverer, My shield and He in whom I take refuge,
Who <u>subdues</u> my people under me."

The word here that is hupotasso is "subdues". Here, unlike all the other verses, the word hupotasso is used in the active form, making it not reflexive. The speaker is David, speaking of God. David is saying that God subdues his people under him. It is interesting to note that David's people are under him already, as he is king, but it is God who subdues them under him. This implies the people could be under him, but not be subdued.

Most clearly in Eph 5, and other verses, we see the woman is to submit herself to her husband. <u>This is meant to replace the "he will rule over you" of Gen 3:16, which lists the negative consequences of the fall.</u>

We also see the same concept reflected in the use of hupotasso in Rom 13:1. Obviously the Christians of the time were under the governors at that time, but being under them was different from submitting to them. This is also seen in slaves and masters as in 1 Pet 2. The slave is owned by the master, there is no doubt the slave is "under" the master, but to be "under" the master is a Different thing than for the slave to "submit himself" to his master.

And this brings me to my next point: all of the time it pertains to wives, hupotasso is used reflexively. What is reflexively? Well, I can wash the car, or I can wash myself. Washing myself is reflexive. If I say "Go wash the car." I am using the word "wash" in an active sense. If I say "Go wash yourself" to a child, I am using the word "wash" reflexively. Other examples might include the word "shave", "groom", "clean", and generally words that can be used to describe an action one does to themselves, but could also possibly be done to something else as well.

An important point in the reflexive nature of hupotasso is that the wives are told to submit themselves. It is something they do to themselves. Nowhere in the Bible are the husbands told to submit their wives. The husband is not told to hupotasso his wife, or to try to force her to submit. In other words the husband is not told to dominate her. No where is he told to try to make her hupotasso, or submit, to him. The wife is to submit herself.

<u>The word hupotasso does not mean obey.</u> In the very next chapter, Eph 6, the word in Greek for "obey" is used twice. This is the word "hypakouo" which means obey. And so it becomes clear that if the word for "obey" had been intended of wives in Eph 5, it would have been used. It is used of children obeying their parents, and slaves obeying their masters in Eph 6.

Of hupotasso, the Strong's says, *"In non-military use, it was "a voluntary attitude of giving in, cooperating, assuming responsibility, and carrying a burden".* This means is in keeping with a simple English definition of the words "submit" and "subject".
What do those words mean?
Submit means: *To yield or surrender (oneself) to the will or authority of another. To subject to a condition or process. To commit (something) to the consideration or judgment of another. To offer as a proposition or contention.*
Subject means: *To submit for consideration. To submit to the authority of. To expose to something.*

Well, it certainly seems self-explanatory. It means to choose to do what someone else wants to do, to go with another's judgment, and in this case for the wife to decide to do, to go with, what the husband wants to do. Hupotasso never means a man forces his wife to submit, rather the wife must submit herself, as the word is reflexive. Truly, these verses nowhere give a husband any right or authority to try to force his wife to submit to him. The husband is given no authority by God to force her to submit. God instructs the wife to submit herself to the husband. The wife is submitting because of the authority of God. In every case of a wife submitting herself, she is actually submitting to the authority of Jesus Christ when she does so.

Submitting herself is a simple instruction, but it entails much from the wife. The Bible does not say, "submit yourself to your husband if you think he is correct about this" or "if you feel like it". The

Bible does not say "except for if you think this is a terrible idea" or "except if you think he is being totally selfish".
The Bible says, "submit yourself to your husband". The emphasis here is for a wife to bring herself under control, to control herself, to get herself in line with her husband and what he wants.

The verses above also clarify this further in some detail. Wives are instructed to submit themselves to their own husbands, "in everything" (Eph 5:24). The Greek here is "en panti". This means in "each, every, any, all, the whole, everyone, all things, everything" according to the Strong's. In the Thayer's, it says in this usage it means, "in every particular". So there is no way to say, "well, that doesn't apply to where we eat dinner because this is just about spiritual things", etc. etc.

Wives are also instructed to submit themselves to their own husbands "as unto the Lord" (Eph 5:22).
The Greek here is "hos o Kyrios", and the word "hos" here means *"as, like, even as"* (Strong's) and *"according as, in the same manner as"* (Thayer's). In this context I think the clearest meaning is wives submit yourselves to your own husbands "in the same manner as the Lord". Which means, as I have covered elsewhere, that it is like the wife has 2 people as heads over her, like a president and a manager. The president-head is Jesus Christ, and the manager-head is her husband. She submits herself to Christ, and in like manner she should submit herself to her husband because Christ has said she should.

Of course, there are some limits to submission, as Col 3:18 says, "<u>as is fitting</u> in the Lord".
In the Greek this is "hos aneko en kyrios". The phrase "en kyrios" is used many times in the New Testament, the same as we use the term today, "in Christ" or "in the Lord".
Such as in Rom 16:8 "Greet Amplias my beloved in the Lord." or Eph 6:10 "Finally, my brethren, be strong in the Lord, and in the power of his might."
The term "hos aneko" is the same hos as meanings are above, with "aneko", which means, "as was fitting". The same word "aneko" is used in Eph 5:4 and Phil 1:8, "and there must be no filthiness and

silly talk, or coarse jesting, which are not <u>fitting</u>, but rather giving of thanks."…"Therefore, though I have enough confidence in Christ to order you to do what is <u>proper.</u>"
The word in contextual use means what is proper or appropriate, in a moral sense.
So the instruction to wives here in Col 3:8 is, Wives, submit yourselves to your own husbands, as is proper or appropriate in a moral sense in the Lord.

This does put some limitation on what a wife should submit to, as to whether it is morally proper behavior or not. Many instances come to mind, like Abigail and Nabal, but foremost is the example in Acts 5:1-11,
"Now a man named Ananias, together with his wife Sapphira, also sold a piece of property. With his wife's full knowledge he kept back part of the money for himself, but brought the rest and put it at the apostles' feet. Then Peter said, "Ananias, how is it that Satan has so filled your heart that you have lied to the Holy Spirit and have kept for yourself some of the money you received for the land? Didn't it belong to you before it was sold? And after it was sold, wasn't the money at your disposal? What made you think of doing such a thing? You have not lied just to human beings but to God." When Ananias heard this, he fell down and died. And great fear seized all who heard what had happened. Then some young men came forward, wrapped up his body, and carried him out and buried him. About three hours later his wife came in, not knowing what had happened. Peter asked her, "Tell me, is this the price you and Ananias got for the land?" "Yes," she said, "that is the price." Peter said to her, "How could you conspire to test the Spirit of the Lord? Listen! The feet of the men who buried your husband are at the door, and they will carry you out also." At that moment she fell down at his feet and died. Then the young men came in and, finding her dead, carried her out and buried her beside her husband. Great fear seized the whole church and all who heard about these events."

Here, a wife went along with her husband wanting to lie and keep some money for himself. She went along with a plan to lie to the Apostles. And she received the same sentence as he did for her shared crime. And the point of the story is that a woman does not have to, and never should do what her husband wants when she knows it is morally wrong or a sin.

This is because we are each individually accountable to God as Rom 14:10-12 says,
"But why dost thou judge thy brother? or why dost thou set at nought thy brother? for we shall all stand before the judgment seat of Christ. For it is written, [As] I live, saith the Lord, every knee shall bow to me, and every tongue shall confess to God. <u>So then every one of us shall give account of himself to God.</u>"
God's commandments and laws take priority and precedence over what the husband might want. The husband is only caused to have the wife submit herself to him because God has declared it so to her, and so nothing from the husband can supersede God's authority, and His moral laws.

There are commandments and instructions which are given to all believers, male or female, of things to do, and things to not do. If the husband wants only things that are fitting in the Lord, as a Christian, then it is good for the wife to submit herself Christ and to him. But if the husband's will is for her to not do the things she should, or to do the things she shouldn't, before God, then she is not to submit to her husband, but to Christ. She should not do anything that would not be proper or appropriate in the Lord, as a Christian.

Included in the instructions given to all believers are things such as, "Therefore, to one who knows the right thing to do and does not do it, to him it is sin" James 4:17
"Holding on to faith and a good conscience. Some have rejected these and so have shipwrecked their faith."1 Tim 1:19
"Hold the mystery of the faith in a pure conscience." 1 Tim 3:9
A wife submitting herself to her husband should not ever involve her doing something she believes is wrong or violating her conscience, nor did God ever intend for it to.

"Pursue love, yet desire earnestly spiritual gifts, but especially that you may prophesy." 1 Cor 14:1

"Do not neglect the gift that is in you, which was given to you by prophecy with the laying on of the hands of the eldership."
1 Tim 4:14

"for the gifts and the calling of God are irrevocable." Romans 11:29

A wife submitting herself to her husband should not ever involve her having to neglect her spiritual gifts given by the Holy Spirit, nor her calling from God.

And concerning the bedroom, this is an area in which equal authority is specifically given to both the husband and the wife, as 1 Cor 7:2-4 spells out, "Nevertheless, to avoid fornication, let every man have his own wife, and let every woman have her own husband. Let the husband render unto the wife due benevolence: and likewise also the wife unto the husband. The wife hath not power of her own body, but the husband: and likewise also the husband hath not power of his own body, but the wife."

If there is not mutual agreement in the bedroom, then logically spouse A can tell the other with authority "Don't do that with your body" while spouse B says "Yes do this with your body" and in effect, if the two spouses are not in agreement, then they cancel each other out. So unless there is mutual agreement in the bedroom, nothing should happen. This is an area that the Bible specifies as not falling under the general instruction of a wife to submit herself to her husband. If it were not so, then the verses above would read differently, here where this topic is specifically addressed by God.

And there are many other applicable verses that place limitation on what God expects a wife to submit herself to her husband about. Hopefully it is at least clear that a wife submitting herself does not mean obedience to her husband, and especially not her doing anything that is outside of God's will. If the husband's will is in line with God's will, then there should be no conflict in this. If there is conflict, to quote Acts 5:29,

"But Peter and the apostles answered, "We must obey God rather than men.""

Chapter Six
Eph 5 Marriage – Part 2 – Love Your Wife

Wives are told to submit to their husbands, what does the word "hupotasso" mean?
Husbands are told to love their wives, what does the word "agapao" mean?
How should Ephesians 5 look when being played out in a marriage?

Eph 5:21-33
Submitting yourselves one to another in the fear of God:
Wives, submit yourselves unto your own husbands, as unto the Lord. For the husband is the head of the wife, even as Christ is the head of the church: and he is the saviour of the body. Therefore as the church is subject unto Christ, so let the wives be to their own husbands in every thing.
Husbands, love your wives, even as Christ also loved the church, and gave himself for it; That he might sanctify and cleanse it with the washing of water by the word, That he might present it to himself a glorious church, not having spot, or wrinkle, or any such thing; but that it should be holy and without blemish. So ought men to love their wives as their own bodies. He that loveth his wife loveth himself. For no man ever yet hated his own flesh; but nourisheth and cherisheth it, even as the Lord the church: For we are members of his body, of his flesh, and of his bones. For this cause shall a man leave his father and mother, and shall be joined unto his wife, and they two shall be one flesh. This is a great mystery: but I speak concerning Christ and the church. Nevertheless let every one of you in particular so love his wife even as himself; and the wife in order that she respects her husband.

To answer these questions, we are going to look at the word for "submit yourself" which is "hupotasso" and the word for "love" which is "agapao", in Greek.

Love your wife

What does it mean to love your wife? The word used in Eph 5 of husbands loving their wives is "agapao". This sort of love is an unconditional love, and is the same word used of God's love for us. It is used in John 3:16 "For God so loved the world that he gave his only begotten Son, that whosoever believeth in him should not perish, but have everlasting life."

Here are some more uses in the Bible, from Thayer's lexicon:

ἀγαπάω, -ῶ; [impf. ἠγάπων]; fut. ἀγαπήσω; 1 aor. ἠγάπησα; pf. act. [1 pers. plur. ἠγαπήκαμεν 1 Jn. iv. 10 WH txt.], ptcp. ἠγαπηκώς (2 Tim. iv. 8); Pass., [pres. ἀγαπῶμαι]; pf. ptcp. ἠγαπημένος; 1 fut. ἀγαπηθήσομαι; (akin to ἅγαμαι [Fick, Pt. iv. 12; see ἀγαθός, init.]); *to love*, to be full of good-will and exhibit the same: Lk. vii. 47; 1 Jn. iv. 7 sq.;   with acc. of the person, *to have a preference for, wish well to, regard the welfare of*: Mt. v. 43 sqq.; xix. 19; Lk. vii. 5; Jn. xi. 5; Ro. xiii. 8; 2 Co. xi. 11; xii. 15; Gal. v. 14; Eph. v. 25, 28; 1 Pet. i. 22, and elsewhere; often in 1 Ep. of Jn. of the love of Christians towards one another; of the benevolence which God, in providing salvation for men, has exhibited by sending his Son to them and giving him up to death, Jn. iii. 16; Ro. viii. 37; 2 Th. ii. 16; 1 Jn. iv. 11, 19; [noteworthy is Jude 1 L T Tr WH τοῖς ἐν θεῷ πατρὶ ἠγαπημένοις; see ἐν, I. 4, and cf. Bp. Lghtft. on Col. iii. 12]; of the love which led Christ, in procuring human salvation, to undergo sufferings and death, Gal. ii. 20; Eph. v. 2; of the love with which God regards Christ, Jn. iii. 35; [v. 20 L mrg.]; x. 17; xv. 9; Eph. i. 6. When used of love to a master, God or Christ, the word involves the idea of affectionate reverence, prompt obedience, grateful recognition of benefits received: Mt. vi. 24; xxii. 37; Ro. viii. 28; 1 Co. ii. 9; viii. 3; Jas. i. 12; 1 Pet. i. 8; 1 Jn. iv. 10, 20, and elsewhere.   With an acc. of the thing ἀγαπάω denotes *to take pleasure in the thing, prize it above other things, be unwilling to abandon it or do without it*: δικαιοσύνην, Heb. i. 9 (i. e. steadfastly to cleave to); τὴν δόξαν, Jn. xii. 43; τὴν πρωτοκαθεδρίαν, Lk. xi. 43; τὸ σκότος and τὸ φῶς, Jn. iii. 19; τὸν κόσμον, 1 Jn. ii. 15; τὸν νῦν αἰῶνα, 2 Tim. iv. 10, — both which last phrases signify to set the heart on earthly advantages and joys; τὴν ψυχὴν αὐτῶν, Rev. xii. 11; ζωήν, 1 Pet. iii. 10 (to derive pleasure from life, render it agreeable to himself); *to welcome with desire, long for*: τὴν ἐπιφάνειαν αὐτοῦ, 2 Tim. iv. 8 (Sap. i. 1; vi. 13; Sir. iv. 12, etc.; so of a person: ἠγαπήθη, Sap. iv. 10, cf. Grimm ad loc.). Concerning the unique proof of love which Jesus gave the apostles by washing their feet, it is said ἠγάπησεν αὐτούς, Jn. xiii. 1, cf. Lücke or Meyer ad loc. [but al. take ἠγάπ. here more comprehensively, see Weiss's Mey., Godet, Westcott, Keil]. The combination ἀγάπην ἀγαπᾶν τινα occurs, when a relative intervenes, in Jn. xvii. 26; Eph. ii. 4, (2 S. xiii. 15 where τὸ μῖσος ὃ ἐμίσησεν αὐτήν is contrasted; cf. Gen. xlix. 25 εὐλόγησέ σε εὐλογίαν; Ps. Sal. xvii. 35 [in cod. Pseudepig. Vet. Test. ed. Fabric. i. p. 966; Libri Apocr. etc., ed. Fritzsche, p. 588] δόξαν ἣν ἐδόξασεν αὐτήν); cf. W. § 32, 2; [B. 148 sq. (129)]; Grimm on 1 Macc. ii. 54.

On the difference betw. ἀγαπάω and φιλέω, see φιλέω. Cf. ἀγάπη, 1 fin.

You can, and maybe should, spend some time studying the above context behind this word for love. But at least understand, "agapao" is the word for God's unconditional love for us, and the word for Christ's love for us. This is the kind of love that God shows us. Moreover, husbands are called to a self-sacrificial love towards their wives, as they are to love them just as Christ loved the church.

John 15:12-13 My command is this: Love each other as I have loved you. Greater love has no one than this, <u>that he lay down his life for his friends</u>.
Eph 5:25-33 Husbands, love your wives, just as Christ loved the church and <u>gave himself up for her</u> to make her holy, cleansing her by the washing with water through the word, and to present her to himself as a radiant church, without stain or wrinkle or any other blemish, but holy and blameless. In this same way, husbands ought to love their wives as their own bodies. He who loves his wife loves himself. After all, no one ever hated his own body, but he feeds and cares for it, just as Christ does the church — for we are members of his body. "For this reason a man will leave his father and mother and be united to his wife, and the two will become one flesh." This is a profound mystery — but I am talking about Christ and the church. However, each one of you also must love his wife as he loves himself, and the wife so that she respects her husband.

That being said, rather than saying more on what love is, I want to talk about what love is not.

<u>What Love Is Not</u>

1 Cor 13:4-7 Love is patient, love is kind and is not jealous; love does not brag and is not arrogant, does not act unbecomingly; it does not seek its own, is not provoked, does not take into account a wrong suffered, does not rejoice in unrighteousness, but rejoices in the truth; bears all things, believes all things, hopes all things, endures all things.

Love is patient,
The word here for "patient" is also translated as "suffereth long" and the Strong's says it means
"1) to be of a long spirit, not to lose heart
a) to persevere patiently and bravely in enduring misfortunes and troubles
b) to be patient in bearing the offenses and injuries of others 1) to be mild and slow in avenging 2) to be longsuffering, slow to anger, slow to punish."
The emphasis here is on waiting, through troubles, hence the term "suffereth long".

The word impatient means:
"Having or showing a tendency to be quickly irritated or provoked (an impatient motorist blaring his horn, she was impatient with any restriction); Intolerant of (a man impatient of bureaucracy); Restlessly eager (they are impatient for change, he was impatient to be on his way)" -Google Dictionary
And so, if a husband is impatient with his wife, he is not loving her.

love is kind
The word here for "kind" means "1) to show one's self mild, to be kind, use kindness"
According to Google Dictionary, being "kind", "mild", and use "kindness", mean:
kind: "Having or showing a friendly, generous, and considerate nature; affectionate"
mild: "Gentle and not easily provoked"
kindness: "The quality of being friendly, generous, and considerate"
If a husband is unkind or inconsiderate to his wife, he is not loving her.

love is not jealous
The word here for "jealous" is also translated as "envieth not", and is the verb form of the noun which means the same, "jealousy" or "envy".
The Bible makes clear that being jealous or envying is not acceptable for Christians.

"Now the deeds of the flesh are evident, which are: immorality, impurity, sensuality, idolatry, sorcery, enmities,
strife, <u>jealousy,</u> outbursts of anger, disputes, dissensions, factions, <u>envying</u>, drunkenness, carousing, and things like these, of which I forewarn you, just as I have forewarned you, <u>that those who practice such things will not inherit the kingdom of God.</u>"
Gal 5:19-21

"Who among you is wise and understanding? Let him show by his good behavior his deeds in the gentleness of wisdom. But if you have bitter <u>jealousy</u> and selfish ambition in your heart, do not be arrogant and so lie against the truth. This wisdom is not that which comes down from above, but is earthly, natural, <u>demonic</u>. For where <u>jealousy</u> and selfish ambition exist, there is disorder and every evil thing." James 3:13-16

Above, Gal 5 compares jealousy right alongside idolatry and sorcery, and for a good and valid reason.
That jealousy is demonic is confirmed in Num 5:14, "the <u>spirit</u> of jealousy come upon him".
As Christians, what are we to do when a demon attacks us? We are to reject it, have nothing to do with it, and rebuke it in the name and authority of Jesus Christ.

If a husband is envious of his wife, or jealous about his wife, he is not loving her.

love does not brag
The word here for "brag" means: *"1) to boast one's self 2) a self display, employing rhetorical embellishments in extolling one's self excessively"*
If a husband brags about himself to his wife, he is not loving her.

love is not arrogant
The word here for "arrogant" means *"a) to puff up, make proud b) to be puffed up, to bear one's self loftily, be proud"*
If a husband is being proud, prideful, or arrogant with his wife, he is not loving her.

love does not act unbecomingly
The word here for "act unbecomingly" means just that. Many modern translations render the word as "rude" or "behave rudely". If a husband is rude to or behaves rudely to his wife, he is not loving her.

The only other context "unbecomingly" is used is 1 Cor 7:36, where a father might think he acts unbecomingly towards his virgin daughter if he does not let her get married. The Thayer's defines the word as *"ie contextually, to prepare disgrace for her"*. The idea here is one of the welfare of the daughter, that the actions of the father keeping his daughter from marrying could lead her into a bad situation in her life overall. This might be because she could fall into temptation, but more likely relates to her having a full life, having a marriage, having children, a home of her own, etc. This was normal in the culture of the time for a virgin woman to marry around a certain age, and the idea here is that preventing her from marrying is abnormal. Paul advised people to not marry, because of a crisis present then, and to devote themselves better to the Lord. But it is quite possible a father could feel he is depriving his daughter of what is a normal life, if he were to refuse to let her marry. A father could feel she might end up single, and barren, and thus have a cultural stigma, if he waits too long to let her marry, waiting until the crisis is over that is the basis for Paul's advice to not marry in the first place. If she waits too long to marry, she might have a harder time doing so, and might never. A father could be concerned it is a window of opportunity that might pass by unused, and later be regretted.

And so to act "unbecomingly" is to act without regard towards the overall welfare of a person's life and happiness longterm. In context, the word is full of implication of a fatherly unconditional love. And so, if a husband acts unbecomingly towards his wife, he is not loving her.

love does not seek its own

The word here for "seek its own" means *"to seek i.e. require, demand a) to crave, demand something from someone"*. This phrase is also translated as "self-seeking" or "seeking its own way" or "demand its own way". The emphasis is on self-centeredness, and being self-satisfying. So if a husband is seeking or demanding his own way, with his wife, he is not being loving to her.

This concept deserves further exposition, as it is **important**. While a wife is told to submit to her husband, at the same time the husband is told to love his wife. To love his wife a husband has to not seek or demand his own way. Which means he should be seeking not his way, but another's way, his wife's way.

On the one hand, the wife is told to submit to her husband, which means she should try to do what he wants, let him have his way. On the other hand, the husband is told to love his wife, which means he is to not seek or demand what he wants, not to seek or demand his own way, but to seek her way. Therefore, he is to be seeking his wife's way, which means he should try to do what she wants, let her have her way. This truth about love is echoed in 1 Cor 10:24, "Let no one seek his own good, but that of his neighbor."

So when it comes to decision making in a marriage, in loving the wife, the husband is told to seek what the wife wants, and not demand what he wants. And the wife is told, in submitting to her husband, to try to do what he wants. What does this mean?

<u>The wife is supposed to do what the husband wants to do, but the husband is supposed to do what the wife wants to do.</u> **As such, there is meant to be equality in decision making in a Christian marriage, which means there should be compromise.** <u>Another way to put this, is "If he's loving her as much as she's submitting to him, then they should meet somewhere in the middle." And of course, both should be seeking what it is that God wants of each of them.</u>

love is not provoked
The word here for "provoked" means "to irritate, provoke, arouse to anger". Love therefore is not provoked to get irritated, or angry. The Greek here does not read "easily provoked" as the KJV reads, but simply states "love is not provoked". It may seem a high bar to reach for, but love does not get provoked to anger or irritation. Truly, the Bible teaches that anger is unacceptable for Christians. It is something to be overcome, and learn how to receive God's grace to not get angry.

Gal 5 (above) lists anger as a work of the flesh, comparable to idolatry and sorcery.
Col 3:8 states, "But now ye also **put off all these**; <u>anger</u>, <u>wrath</u>, malice, blasphemy, filthy communication out of your mouth."
Eph 4 states, "Be ye angry, and sin not: let not the sun go down upon your wrath, neither give place to the devil… Let all bitterness, and <u>wrath</u>, and <u>anger</u>, and clamour, and evil speaking, **be put away from you**, with all malice".
The tense here for "be ye angry" would be better translated as "be ye angered" as by some external force trying to act upon you. When temptation comes to be angered, we are told to not sin, and we are told to put anger away from ourselves, and quickly, the same day, <u>or we give place to the devil.</u>

If a husband is angry or irritated with his wife, then he is not loving her. Even more so, if he even lets himself start to get angry towards his wife, then he is not loving her, as love is not provoked.

love does not take into account a wrong suffered
The phrase "does not take into account a wrong suffered" is also translated as "thinketh no evil" in the KJV. The word in Greek for "thinketh" is "logizomai". The word logizomai means, "*1) to reckon, count, compute, calculate, count over, 2) to reckon inward, count up or weigh the reasons, to deliberate, 3) by reckoning up all the reasons, to gather or infer*".
This leaves us with several possible meanings, including not taking into account wrongs suffered. One meaning is to deliberate no evil, or think of evil things to do. Another meaning is to infer no

evil, to not assume or infer evil. So there are several contexts here within a marriage.

If a husband takes into account wrongs suffered from his wife, then he is not loving her. This can include if he counts up all her faults, then he is not loving her. If he thinks of evil towards her, to do evil to her, then he is not loving her. If a husband infers evil about her, then he is not loving her.

love does not rejoice in unrighteousness but rejoices in the truth
The phrase "does not rejoice in unrighteousness, but rejoices in the truth" has a broad range of meanings, and I would like to just touch on a few. "Rejoice" here is also rendered "glad". If a husband is glad (for whatever reason) if his wife does something wrong, is glad about her faults, rejoices over her faults or failures (perhaps in bitterness using them against her, pointing them out to her), then he is not loving her. And if a husband is glad when he does something wrong or evil to his wife, then he is not loving her.

And very important: the opposite of being glad in the truth is being glad in lies. A husband should be glad in the truth, not lies, and so should be honest and tell the truth to his wife. Truly God loves us perfectly, for He is Love, and God never lies to us, or deceives us, but always speaks the truth, for He is Truth.

<u>If a husband deceives his wife, he is not loving her.</u>

<u>**If a husband lies to his wife, he is not loving her.**</u>

love bears all things, believes all things, hopes all things, endures all things.
To bear means to cover or protect, and to endure means to remain. And so a husband who is loving his wife will protect his wife, believe his wife, have hope for his wife, and remain with his wife. And a husband who will not protect her, not believe her, has no hope for her, or won't remain with her, is not loving his wife.

More On What Love is Not

Moving on to our next set of verses on what love is not,
Lev 19:18 "Do not seek revenge or bear a grudge against one of your people, but love your neighbor as yourself. I am the LORD."
Luke 10:27 "He answered: " 'Love the Lord your God with all your heart and with all your soul and with all your strength and with all your mind' ; and, 'Love your neighbor as yourself.' "
Galatians 5:14 "The entire law is summed up in a single command: 'Love your neighbor as yourself.'"
James 2:8 "If you really keep the royal law found in Scripture, "Love your neighbor as yourself," you are doing right."
Matt 7:12 "So in everything, do to others what you would have them do to you, for this sums up the Law and the Prophets."

Here the Bible makes 2 points on what love is. In Leviticus, the Bible contrasts loving your neighbor as yourself, with seeking revenge or bearing a grudge against your neighbor. Which means seeking revenge or bearing a grudge against someone is the opposite of loving them.
So, if a husband is seeking revenge (or to "avenge" himself) against his wife, he is not loving her. And if a husband is bearing a grudge against his wife, he is not loving her.

The second point made is that "loving your neighbor as yourself" is defined as "doing unto them what you would have them do unto you".
If a husband is doing anything to his wife that he wouldn't want done to himself, then he is not loving her. To put another way, if a husband is doing something to his wife that he wouldn't want her to do to him, then he is not loving her.

Col 3:19 "Husbands, love your wives, and be not bitter against them."
Here the Bible shows another opposite of a husband loving his wife, which is bitterness against her. This verse deals specifically with husbands and wives.
If a husband is bitter towards his wife, then he is not loving her.

1 Peter 3:7

There is no contradiction in the Bible. Any other positive commands to husbands must not conflict with the positive command for husbands to love their wives. As such this verse is also applicable:

Likewise, ye husbands, dwell with [them] according to knowledge, giving honour unto the wife, as unto the weaker vessel, and as being heirs together of the grace of life; that your prayers be not hindered. 1 Peter 3:7

dwell with [them]

Looking at the Greek, and the context in which the words in this passage are used, it becomes clear that this is a powerful verse. The word "dwell with" here is "synoikeo" which is only used here in the Bible. It is a compound of 2 words, "syn" and "oikeo". If Peter had wanted to mean "live with" in a way that referred to just 2 people living together, he more likely would have used a term like "oikeo meta" which means "dwell with", and is the very phrase used in 1 Cor 7:12-13 for a husband or wife dwelling with each other in some residence. But Peter uses an unusual composite word, which is used only here in the Bible.

"Syn" is used as a prefix to describe people equally doing something together. For instance, "syn-odia" is "a company of travelers", "synthapto" is "to bury together with" and "synistemi" is to "stand with". These compositions all imply participants that are each equally part of some activity. The Greek prefix "syn" has the same meaning as the Latin prefix "co". In English, we use terms like co-chair, co-pilot, co-author, or co-worker. In the verb form, we might say co-authoring, co-chairing, co-piloting, or co-working. In 1 Pet 3:7, "dwell with" would be more correctly translated "co-dwelling".

according to knowledge

The word knowledge here is "gnosis" and in the New Testament, its meaning in use is one of the knowledge of truth of God, Jesus Christ, salvation, and understanding of the Christian faith or religion. This is not just a general word for "knowledge", as in "I have knowledge about cars". If it were it would make sense that a more broad Greek word for knowledge would be used, "epignosis", which is used more this way. But "gnosis" is used speaking of the deeper understanding of what is true and good in the Christian faith. The Strong's reads:

1) knowledge signifies in general intelligence, understanding
a) the general knowledge of Christian religion
b) the deeper more perfect and enlarged knowledge of this religion, such as belongs to the more advanced
c) esp. of things lawful and unlawful for Christians
d) moral wisdom, such as is seen in right living

As such, husbands are instructed "co-dwelling with deep knowledge of the Christian religion and moral wisdom from such…"

giving honour

The word here for "give" is only used here in the New Testament. Again, it is a unique composite word, "apo-nemo". The word "apo" used as a prefix indicates *"separation, liberation, cessation, departure… finishing and completion… refers to the pattern from which a copy is taken… or to him from whom the action proceeds"*. (Thayer's) The word "nomos" (-nemo) means "law" and is translated as such in every instance in the KJV (197x). It can refer to the Mosaic Law, or any rule or law. But in the context of the word "gnosis" above, referring to an understanding of the Christian faith and religion, the "law" referenced to here must be one of the Christian faith. In the Thayer's under "nomos" it says, " *3. Of the Christian religion… the law demanding faith, Rom 3:27… the moral instruction given by Christ, esp. the precept concerning love, Gal 6:2…"* What does Gal 6:12 say? "Bear ye one another's burdens, and so fulfil the law of Christ."

Gal 5:12 better defines this for us: "For all the law is fulfilled in one word, [even] in this; Thou shalt love thy neighbour as thyself." And note that in this letter something is pre-established in Gal 3 which says, "For you are all sons of God through faith in Christ Jesus. For as many of you as were baptized into Christ have put on Christ. There is neither Jew nor Greek, there is neither slave nor free, there is neither male nor female; for you are all one in Christ Jesus."

Yet the only specifically "new commandment" Jesus gave is in harmony with this one, and is found in John 13:34-35: "A new commandment I give unto you, That ye love one another; as I have loved you, that ye also love one another. By this shall all [men] know that ye are my disciples, if ye have love one to another." The Thayer's defines the word "apo-nemos" based on extra-biblical usage in the works of Josephus and others, as meaning *"(nemo to dispense a portion, to distribute), to assign, portion out"*.

With a unique word that literally means "from-law", which means "to assign, portion out" (Strong's) the translation of "give" is not accurate. The word would better read "apportioning" or "apportion". What is being apportioned?

The word here for "honor" is "time" and the Strong's defines it as, *"1) a valuing by which the price is fixed a) of the price itself b) of the price paid or received for a person or thing bought or sold 2) honour which belongs or is shown to one a) of the honour which one has by reason of rank and state of office which he holds b) deference, reverence"*

This is not the same word that Jesus uses for "honor thy father and they mother" (Matt 19:19) which is "timeo", and it is also not the same word for "honor widows" (1 Tim 5:3). Nor is it the same word as "honor all men" or "honor the king" as is used in 1 Pet 2:17, which is earlier in this same book. "Timeo" denotes a meaning of *"to estimate, fix the value a) for the value of something belonging to one's self"*. With "timeo" the value is estimated for something belonging to one's self.

This is not the case with "time". Rather, this word "time" is used again and again in a way that means a fixed value to God, a value fixed by God, as something which is valuable or worth something great, or honor to a rank or position (of value). Peter uses this word earlier in the same letter in,

"That the trial of your faith, being much more precious than of gold that perisheth, though it be tried with fire, might be found unto praise and honour and glory at the appearing of Jesus Christ" 1 Pet 1:7

"Unto you therefore which believe [he is] <u>precious</u>: but unto them which be disobedient, the stone which the builders disallowed, the same is made the head of the corner" 1 Pet 2:7
And also in 2 Pet 1:17, "For he received from God the
Father <u>honour</u> and glory, when there came such a voice to him from the excellent glory, This is my beloved Son, in whom I am well pleased."
This word "time" therefore refers to a value or price that God will set or has set on something.
It is the same word used twice in 1 Cor (6,7) repeated in "Ye are bought with a <u>price</u>".
This price is not left to be determined by men, but has been determined by God.

Therefore, in 1 Pet 3:7 the word "honor" means an honor which reflects value, and the value of a price that has been fixed by God, not by men. It implies a set value God has put on someone, not the value a man puts on something that is his. So far, the verse reads, "Likewise, ye husbands, co-dwell with deep knowledge of the Christian religion and moral wisdom from such, apportioning honor from value set by God…"

unto the wife
The word here for "unto the wife" is "gynaikeios". Again, this word is only used here in the Bible.
It means, *"of or belonging to a woman, feminine, female"*. This word is an adjective, not a verb.
Again, the translation "unto the wife" is not accurate, as this word is referring to something which <u>belongs</u> to the woman or to the female. Nor does the word imply this belongs to the "wife" in particular, but rather implies this belongs to the "woman, feminine, female".

The verse so far should read, "Likewise, ye husbands, co-dwelling with deep knowledge of the Christian religion and moral wisdom from such, apportioning the honor (from her value or price as set by God) belonging to the woman/female…"

as unto the weaker vessel
The next phrase here is "as unto the weaker vessel". The word here for "as" is "hos" which means "as, like, even as, etc". There are no words contained in the Greek here to be translated "unto the". The word for "weaker" is "asthenes" and it means weaker as it is spelled here for comparative use. The word here for "vessel" is "skeous". This word is used one time with the same spelling in Luke 8:16 which reads, "Now no one after lighting a lamp covers it over with a container, or puts it under a bed; but he puts it on a lampstand, so that those who come in may see the light."
The same word "skeous" is used in 2 Cor 4:6,
"For God, who commanded the light to shine out of darkness, hath shined in our hearts, to [give] the light of the knowledge of the glory of God in the face of Jesus Christ. But we have this treasure in earthen vessels, that the excellency of the power may be of God, and not of us."
and in 2 Tim 2:20-21
"But in a great house there are not only vessels of gold and of silver, but also of wood and of earth; and some to *honour*, and some to dishonour. If a man therefore purge himself from these, he shall be a vessel unto *honour*, sanctified, and meet for the master's use, [and] prepared unto every good work." (Note: the word *honour* here is "time" in Greek, as above, both times.)
This meaning, this illustration, has the weight of how the Epistles use the word vessel when referring to Christians. Christians are vessels of God, as the Holy Spirit lives in us, and through God's power we are enabled to do good works.

The same meaning is also inherent in 1 Thes 4:3-6
"For this is the will of God, your sanctification; that is, that you abstain from sexual immorality; that each of you know how to aquire his own vessel in sanctification and honor, not in lustful passion, like the Gentiles who do not know God; and that no man transgress and defraud his brother in the matter because the Lord is the avenger in all these things, just as we also told you before and solemnly warned you."
In this verse on how men should go about acquiring a wife, she is called a "vessel". This can have 2 references and meanings.

The first is that as a Christian, she is a vessel of the Holy Spirit, and God's power. The second, as we covered in Chapter 4, is the usage of the word vessel in referring to a body, as in marriage the husband is the head, the wife is the rest of the body, and they are one flesh. So here the reference is how the husband is to go about getting "his own body" to be the head of; without fornication, in sanctification and honor.

Back to 1 Pet 3:7, the same 2 meanings are inherent. The wife is a vessel of the Holy Spirit, empowered by God. At the same time she is the "weaker vessel", which begs the question, weaker than what? A woman's physical body generally is weaker than that of a man's. And the repeated analogy in the Bible is that the wife is like the body, and the husband like the head of that body, in being one flesh. He is the head, and she is all of the other body parts, metaphorically. Nevertheless, in physical practicality, she is the weaker body. So this part should read "as a (weaker) vessel".

(Note: This does not mean that the Bible teaches that women are physically weak, but rather in addressing husbands God seeks to remind them that generally she is physically weaker than him. The term is only used comparatively, and only when God is addressing husbands. Obviously some women are stronger than some men, even stronger than their husbands. But this also is said especially in the context of a husband of a married woman, in which there is the issue of pregnancies. Even the most strong body-building athletic wife is likely to experience some physical disabling from pregnancy and also during labor, which a husband doesn't have to go through. So at least on average for a time she is bodily weaker than her husband, and God wants him to be understanding of this. Even doctors today recommend women not lift as much weight while in late pregnancy, not stand for long periods, must not overheat, must stay well hydrated, etc. or risk damaging herself or the baby.)

as being heirs together of the grace of life; that your prayers be not hindered.

The word for "heirs together" is "sygkleronomos" (also from the prefix syn-) and would better be translated as co-heirs. The emphasis is on an equality of sharing. This word is also used of the Gentiles, in Eph 3:6
"That the Gentiles should be <u>fellowheirs</u>, and of the same body, and partakers of his promise in Christ by the gospel". The word here for "life" is "zoe", which in context almost always refers to eternal life. The word for "that" is "eis" and would better read "so that" or "towards that".

When this is all put together, the meaning should read as thus: "Likewise, you husbands, co-dwell with deep knowledge (of the Christian religion and moral wisdom from such), apportioning the honor (from her value or price as set by God) belonging to the woman/female, as a (bodily weaker) vessel of the Holy Spirit and God's power, and as being co-heirs of the grace of eternal life; so that your prayers will not be hindered"

Wow. Who knew that Peter was such a feminist? Knowing about the culture he came from, this was a radical teaching and perspective. But for anyone who does know what the culture was like back then for women, that Peter was a feminist should be no surprise. Jesus was also a radical, going against cultural norms in the way He treated women. So it should be no surprise that if Jesus was a feminist that His disciples were also.
(See here <u>http://www.religioustolerance.org/cfe_bibl.htm</u>)

Back to talking about what love is and is not, this verse is part of how husbands are told to love their wives. If a husband co-dwells with his wife with this understanding, then he is loving his wife.

But: If a husband does not apportion to woman the honor that belongs to her of being an equal co-heir of eternal life, then he is not loving his wife.
If a husband does not honor woman as having a value set by God which is the same as his value, as they equally are vessels housing the Holy Spirit, who Christ died for, then he is not loving his wife.

If a husband does not co-dwell with woman with understanding of the equality male and female have in Christ, then he is not loving his wife.

If a husband does not co-dwell with understanding that he and woman are both equal vessels of God, though she is the weaker one, then he is not loving his wife. And inherent in all this is that a husband needs to treat a wife as he would want her to treat him; to love her as his neighbor, as he loves himself.

love your wives, even as Christ also loved the church, and gave himself for it

As with submission, the instruction for a husband to love his wife should never involve the husband breaking God's Commandments, violating his conscience, or doing something he believes is morally wrong. He is also individually accountable to God. On to gifts and callings…. While a husband should not neglect his spiritual gifts or be prevented from his calling any more than a wife should, there is a difference that makes his situation unlike that with wives and submission. That difference is between the black and white, and the many shades of grey, and is the difference between Love and Submission.

A husband is told by God to have a self-sacrificial level of love for his wife. If a husband has to sacrifice himself, sacrifice his life, his work, his works for God, whatever he has, in order to love his wife, then he does well. He is instructed to love his wife with a type and level of love that is self-sacrificial. In fact, without self-sacrifice, a husband cannot fulfill his orders:

"Husbands, love your wives, even as Christ also loved the church, and gave himself for it".

If a husband never sacrifices anything of himself in order to love his wife, then he is not loving her like he has been instructed by God to do. I have never heard of a wife having the power to prevent a husband from serving God in his gifts and calling, to force him to completely abandon his calling and completely neglect his spiritual gifts.

I know of no Christian woman who would want such a thing as a husband to completely stop all of his works for God. I also know no Christian woman who has the power to do this, to force him to stop. But if a wife was able to do so, she would be fighting against God, and be working evil. This is the black.

In so much as a husband has the power to not let his wife stop him or prevent him from pursuing his gifts and calling, even if she tried, and she truly has no power to stop or prevent him, this is his freedom to choose, and this is the white. But in between are many shades of gray.

When we use our gifts and pursue our calling, what we do is good works for God.
If a woman has to submit herself to a husband who prevents her from good works, then he is not being loving, nor should she submit to him rather than God, for he is contrary to God's will. If her manager wants her to do contrary to what the president has told her to do, then she must do what the president wants.

But if a man obeys God to love his wife self-sacrificially, and this prevents him from good works, because of self-sacrificial love, then there is no conflict. He is not obeying his wife rather than obeying God, but rather either way he chooses, whether to do good works, or to show self-sacrificial love to his wife, he is still obeying God. In any given situation, he is choosing between a positive instruction to good works, and a positive instruction to love his wife self-sacrificially, and both of these instructions come to him from the same authority which is God.

This is the difference between men and women, between Submission and Love in action. And the Bible speaks on this problem of pleasing the Lord versus pleasing your wife:
1 Cor 7:32-34 "I would like you to be free from concern. An unmarried man is concerned about the Lord's affairs—how he can please the Lord. But a married man is concerned about the affairs of this world—how he can please his wife— and his interests are divided."

A husband's interests may feel divided, between pleasing the Lord and pleasing his wife, and God acknowledges this; God knows this. But in self-sacrificially loving his wife, a husband is also is pleasing the Lord. Really, there is no conflict here.

But if it feels like there is a conflict, then husbands should know that God recognizes this division even in His Word, and surely understands. If a husband whose interests are divided were to spend even up to half, or even up to 49%, of the time choosing to please his wife when faced with this conflict, do you think God would not understand? As God acknowledges this conflict in His Word, I do think God understands.

Over the course of a year, or a month, how many times does a husband choose to sacrifice "something he is doing for God" in order to show love to his wife? Is this picture balanced? Is it 60/40? 95/5? As God has told a man both to love his wife self-sacrificially, and to do good works, then the picture should be balanced. If a husband feels there is conflict, and this picture is not balanced, then there is a problem.

And to say again, when husbands self-sacrificially love their wives this is pleasing to God. This is a good work a husband does for God as much as any other good work, so in truth there really is no conflict here between the two. Either way is obeying God. And in these decisions made by husbands are the many shades of gray: the husband has freedom to choose among a good work of one kind or a good work of another kind.
Still, if a husband never sacrifices anything of himself in order to love his wife, then he is not loving her like he has been instructed by God to do.

Chapter Seven
Eph 5 Marriage – Part 3 – Love and Submit

Wives are told to submit to their husbands, what does the word "hupotasso" mean?
Husbands are told to love their wives, what does the word "agapao" mean?
How should Ephesians 5 look when being played out in a marriage?

Eph 5:21-33
Submitting yourselves one to another in the fear of God: Wives, submit yourselves unto your own husbands, as unto the Lord. For the husband is the head of the wife, even as Christ is the head of the church: and he is the saviour of the body. Therefore as the church is subject unto Christ, so let the wives be to their own husbands in every thing.
Husbands, love your wives, even as Christ also loved the church, and gave himself for it; That he might sanctify and cleanse it with the washing of water by the word, That he might present it to himself a glorious church, not having spot, or wrinkle, or any such thing; but that it should be holy and without blemish. So ought men to love their wives as their own bodies. He that loveth his wife loveth himself. For no man ever yet hated his own flesh; but nourisheth and cherisheth it, even as the Lord the church: For we are members of his body, of his flesh, and of his bones. For this cause shall a man leave his father and mother, and shall be joined unto his wife, and they two shall be one flesh. This is a great mystery: but I speak concerning Christ and the church. Nevertheless let every one of you in particular so love his wife even as himself; and the wife in order that she respects her husband.

To answer these questions, we are going to look at the word for "submit yourself" which is "hupotasso" and the word for "love" which is "agapao", in Greek.

Love and Submission in Marriage

One good analogy I have heard for a healthy Christian marriage, is that it is like a dance. The husband leads, indicating where he wants to woman to go, and she chooses to follow his lead. At the same time, the husband is careful to lovingly keep her from bumping into walls, and his desire is for her to enjoy the dance and to feel loved and close to him. The bottom line is that you both are supposed to be enjoying this dance, this marriage.

The instructions to Christians in the Bible on marriage are meant to help a marriage to be a healthy and happy one which is pleasing to God. The key to this beautiful dance of marriage is to know how to dance. It is quite a sight when he is trying to tango, and she is trying to waltz, neither knows the proper moves anyway, and God wanted you to jitterbug in the first place. But thankfully, those steps we need to learn to do this God's way are laid out for each of us in the Bible.

The main theme of those steps are how to lead (Love) and how to follow (Submit Yourself). If you do not know how to love or submit, then learn how and practice, and seek God to help you in this. Until you get these basic steps down, you will not experience marriage the way that God intended it to be.

But sometimes, intentionally or unintentionally, someone steps on somebody else's toes. Two different people, sharing one life and one home, are bound to have disagreements. Regardless of if your spouse seems to be following their instructions from God, each of us as Christians are under our own instructions from God to follow.

If your husband is all-around unloving to you, you still need to try to submit to him.
If your wife is all-around not submitting herself to you, you still need to try to love her.

We are each accountable to God for our own actions, and really it is our relationship with God that is the reason we know we should submit or love. The commitment to love your wife or submit to your husband cannot be based on their actions towards you, but rather must be a commitment based on your desire to show God you love Him by obeying Him. These instructions are given to husbands and wives by God, so this is all a matter of obeying God. While your spouse is imperfect, God is perfect, and will never let you down. And when you try to submit, or try to love, because you want to obey God, this is what God will help you to do. Like many things, if you want to please God, to show Him you love Him by obeying Him, then He will help enable you and change you so you can do so, for we cannot do anything apart from Him. And it remains the job of each husband to love his wife, and the job of each wife to submit herself to her own husband.

Eph 5:21-33
Submitting yourselves one to another in the fear of God:
Wives, submit yourselves unto your own husbands, as unto the Lord. For the husband is the head of the wife, even as Christ is the head of the church: and he is the saviour of the body. Therefore as the church is submits unto Christ, so let the wives be to their own husbands in everything.
Husbands, love your wives, even as Christ also loved the church, and gave himself for it; That he might sanctify and cleanse it with the washing of water by the word, That he might present it to himself a glorious church, not having spot, or wrinkle, or any such thing; but that it should be holy and without blemish. So ought men to love their wives as their own bodies. He that loveth his wife loveth himself. For no man ever yet hated his own flesh; but nourisheth and cherisheth it, even as the Lord the church: For we are members of his body, of his flesh, and of his bones. For this cause shall a man leave his father and mother, and shall be joined unto his wife, and they two shall be one flesh. This is a great mystery: but I speak concerning Christ and the church.
Nevertheless let every one of you in particular so love his wife even as himself; and the wife in order that she respects her husband.

Understanding what "head" means in this verse, as was explained in Chapter 4, the term "head" here is part of an illustration of the head of a body, and the rest of the parts of the body. In summary: Christ is the head of every Christian, who are His body, and the husband is the head of a wife, who is like his body, and God is the head of Christ, who is the fullness of the Godhead bodily.

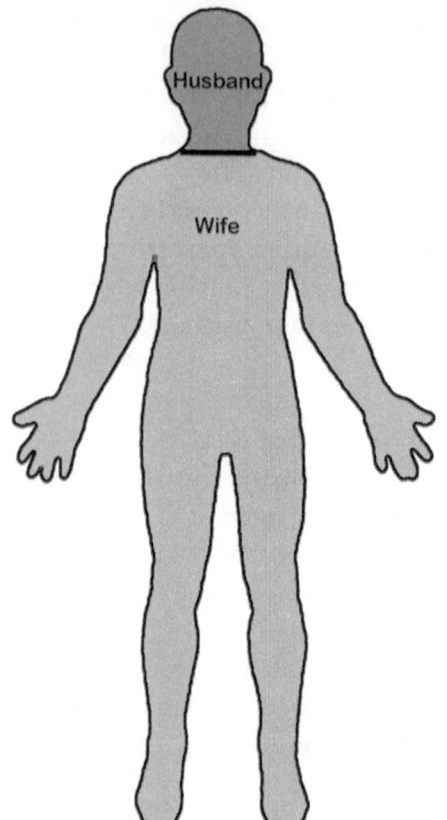

[The Dark/Light here represents either:
Dark Gray- God the Father /
Light Gray- Jesus Christ the Son

Dark Gray - Jesus Christ /
Light Gray - All Christians

Dark Gray - a husband /
Light Gray - a wife]

Now let's go through this section of Ephesians 5, and its symbolism. This is the best analogy for marriage, as it is God's analogy for marriage, as given in the Bible. The husband is like the head of the body, he is the eyes, the ears, the nose, and the mouth. The wife is like the rest of the body parts, the arms, the hands, the feet, and the torso.

Now, the head thinks on where to go, and the head wills the body to go there, and the body is to follow. (submission) The head protects, cherishes and nourishes the body and takes care of the body. (love) This is partly so the body feels alright and is fit and able to do what the head wants it to do. (One flesh: interdependent needs)

The head uses the eyes and ears, and the brain, to watch out for the body. The head uses the eyes, ears, the nose even, to look out for danger, to guide the body through life, carefully protecting it, so it will not be injured: for it is the head's body. (The head is like the savior of the body, protecting it.)

The head also spends a large amount of time giving the body instruction to care for itself. The head tells the body to prepare food and eat it, to care for any wounds it might have on the skin, and to lay down to rest, etc. Because, if the body is weak, sick, or injured, then the body may not be able to do what the head wants it to do. Also, if the body is in need or in pain, the head will feel this need or pain also, from the body. (No one hates his own flesh but lovingly takes care of it)

Beyond the head taking care of the needs of the body so it is fit to follow the head's leading, the head also wants its body to look nice. Beyond necessity, is taking satisfaction in that the body is clean, dressed nicely, is well-kept, at least presentable, but beyond this, the head wants to look in the mirror and see itself and its body as beautiful. When the head sees the body, the head wants to be pleased and feel good about the view. (This is a moral beauty, to be glorious, holy, without spot or blemish, washed in the Word of God. For those who say the husband has an obligation to be a spiritual leader to his wife, this is how, by washing with the Word).

The body, conversely, feels a large amount of sensation from inside itself, and from the skin outside, and automatically sends this information to the head. The body has needs, for care, for energy and food, for rest, and tells the head how it is feeling. The body tries to follow what the head wants, trusting the head. But the body cannot follow the head if it cannot find the strength to, or if the head wants the body to do something it is not capable of doing. Like the head might tell the body to do a chin-up, and though the body tries to, it cannot. So if the head wants the body to be able to change to do a chin-up, then the head will have to patiently work to change the body gradually, to enable the body to be able to do a chin-up.

If the head does not care for the body, neglecting its needs, causing it pain, or instructing it to hurt itself, taking poor care of it and not loving it, then the body will not respect the head. But if the head takes care of the body and lovingly cares for it, then the body will respect the head. (Husbands love your wife as yourself, in order that the wife respects her husband.)

And that is the gist of Ephesians 5 on husbands and wives, and on love and submission. The fact is that a husband and wife are one flesh, like 2 people in one person. God joined them together when they became married. They affect each other automatically, need each other implicitly, and must work together in order to be healthy, happy, and at peace. And while they are different, and have different roles, neither one is much without the other. What is a head without a body? What is a body without a head? Surely they were designed to be joined together as one flesh, and function as one.

As for problems in marriages.... I wonder if we could see couples as one body, what would we see?

Perhaps... bodies bruised in places, dirty, dressed in something old and worn, and weak, but still trying to carry on to where the head wants to go, or a body with a head that seems to be straining desperately, reaching and jerking, trying to decapitate itself, by sheer will. Perhaps the hands feel their way up and try to pull the head off, finding the task impossible, as we see the closed eyes of a head lost inside itself trying to block out reality, or perhaps a body feeling its way around aimlessly, like the head has no control over where the body goes, or like the head is blind... Is this what some Christian marriages look like to God?

To carry the illustration further, the head seems to contain the mind, as the term is used in the Bible, and the body seems to contain the heart, as the term is used in the Bible. (As well as the head literally contains the brain, and the body literally contains the heart, as organs.) I feel this is balanced, as God writes,

"This [is] the covenant that I will make with them after those days, saith the Lord, I will put my laws into their hearts, and in their minds will I write them" Heb 10:16
"And the peace of God, which passeth all understanding, shall keep your hearts and minds through Christ Jesus." Phil 4:7
God works equally in the minds and in the hearts of Christians, so there is balance in this illustration.

"But when Jesus perceived their thoughts, he answering said unto them, What reason ye in your hearts?" Luke 5:22
"And he said unto them, Why are ye troubled? and why do thoughts arise in your hearts?" Luke 24:38
Some people don't know this, but the Bible teaches that 1. thoughts arise in the heart and 2. that the heart can reason. Nevertheless, the mind also reasons with thoughts. So this is balanced. But while both the heart and mind can reason with thoughts, the heart is known more for feelings.

I don't know about you, but I find that feelings can be deceptive and misleading at times. Emotions can cause pain, and sometimes it takes thinking something through in order to get emotions under control. In other words, that sometimes the mind needs to settle down the heart, thinking of hopeful things to comfort it with, and battling misperceptions or lies with thoughts of truth. While the head perceives situations and the mind draws conclusions about what is happening, the heart soon reacts with feelings and emotions about the conclusions the mind has drawn, and situations the head has perceived.

This same interaction may be another part of being one flesh in marriage. And if so, then if the heart of a wife is in emotional pain, then it is good for a husband to try to calm her heart, the same as if it was his own heart feeling pain and in need of attention. Along the same lines, if a man's mind is tired and needs a rest from busyness, then a wife should give him rest, same as if her own mind was exhausted. Also at times the mind may have consider thoughts or ideas of possible actions which conflict with what the heart needs, wants, or feels is right, and so a person may have to weigh out their thoughts against their feelings to make a decision.

This same sort of interplay and balance also can occur between a husband and wife in marriage. For they are one flesh, one person.

And so slowly, this illustration draws closer to a better understanding of "love your neighbor as yourself" and "love your wife as yourself" and "love your husband as yourself", as in this illustration, your spouse is in fact also your own self, as you are one flesh.

When things go wrong in a marriage

One of the worst problems in marriage is when people get their instructions confused. Especially if a husband decides it is his job to make his wife submit, or a wife thinks it is her job to make her husband love her. (Though for the most part, I do not think many Christians today, male or female, understand what they are doing.)

While some women may try to force their husbands to love them, generally this does not work, because the ability to love unconditionally comes from God, so it is futile for a wife to enable or make an unloving man to love her. The best thing she can do so he finds it easier to love her is to submit to him. When women don't try this, they often resort to arguing verbally, which is just a negative consequence of the fall, and comes from her sin nature. (See Chapter 3) Also mentioned in that Chapter, is the topic of men dominating women, another negative consequence of the fall into sin, and when men try to dominate their wives, or women, this is also out of his sin nature. (See Chapter 1)

Some men seem to think it is their job to make sure their wife submits to them, by forcing her by various means to do what he wants, whether by violence, force, threat, fear, manipulations, deceptions, trickery, etc. This is called dominating, and it is something a Christian husband has no authority before God to do to his wife. It is this sort of behavior, out of the sinful nature, which is physical, emotional, psychological, even sexual abuse of women: and what is recognized as the legal crime of Domestic Violence (in the United States anyway). And a review of the literature on

Domestic Violence will tell you that it revolves around one thing, which is a man seeking to control his wife, to rule over her. "He will rule over you" of Gen 3 has been as much of a curse for all of humanity, in every culture, in every time period, as has mankind's tendency to break the 10 Commandments, to sin, and need a Savior. The fact that much of history, and many cultures today, still are rife with men unjustly dominating women, does not mean that this is not a sin. It is surely not men treating women as men would like to be treated, and so violates the command to love your neighbor as yourself.

The longevity with which this sin has been carried out in the world in no way changes that it is a sin. That a man can succeed to get and keep control over his wife, to her detriment, in no way changes that it is a sin. Success at a sin does not prove any morality to the task, any more than a well-planned bank robbery. That women are weaker only shows that yes, they can be dominated, not that they should be dominated, nor that God ever wished for them to be.

If there is one major theme in the New Testament, even in the whole Bible, it is of Christ, and His Bride. What do you see in the story of Christ and the church?

Following the Jewish custom of betrothal, we are a bride betrothed to Christ, who will wed with Him at the marriage supper of the Lamb. The Son has the bride drawn to Him by the Father. But never does the Son force anyone to become betrothed to Him, nor does the Father, it remains the choice of the girl to become a bride. We each feel drawn and convicted by the Holy Spirit, but to accept Jesus as our Savior remains our choice, we have free will, and God does not force us.

When Jesus was here with His disciples, He did not force them to follow Him. When He was with them, He was understanding, patient, and a servant to them, even washing their feet. And He gave his life so that they could live. He let them know what He wanted them to do, but He never forced them to do what He wanted.

In our relationship with Jesus today, as Christians, He still never forces us to do anything. We choose to follow Him and to try to obey what He wants of us. Why?

It is because He loved us. He loved us enough to pay the greatest price anyone could pay, His life, to have us. And all this for us, while we were still sinners, while we were not deserving of love, He loved us anyway, accepting us for how we were. We were evil, and perishing in our depravity and disobedience, but He still loved us. He loved us, first, before we ever came to understand His goodness. And because of His love for us, He made a way for us where there was no way.

And does the Holy Spirit take us over like robots, forcing us to do His will, even if it is still against our own faulty mind and understanding? No!

Slowly but surely, with patience and love and forgiveness upon forgiveness many times over, He teaches us, talks to us, shows us love, correct us gently with mercy, takes care of us and provides for all our needs, and comforts us when we sorrow. And all this, while we still sin, many times, in ignorance or even sometimes really knowing better. Does He ever give up on us? No!

Does He get angry and yell at us about our many faults and imperfections? No, instead He is full of patience, and corrects us gently. And does the Lord ever lie to us, deceive us, or manipulate us so as to do what He wants? No!

And despite that He is infinitely powerful and stronger than us, as He is God, and could "hit" us with physical harm, does He ever? No! Next time you sin, and Jesus does not use the power at His command to throw you across the room or hit you, remember that. Because He could, but He will not, because He is Good. And because of His goodness and His righteousness, His love and His mercy, our Lord does no such thing.

I have heard it said that the point of the entire creation was to make a bride for Christ, who would choose of free will to love God, and obey Him. How can it be that the choice of free will is any less what Jesus wants in our earthly marriages, if it is His Will in His own marriage to us? And because free will of the bride is what we know is true in our marriage to Christ as His Bride, in how each of us came to know Him and choose Him, and in how He treats us now as His betrothed... then shouldn't the church follow Jesus' example and try to do as He is doing?

If Christian men want to be like Christ, then they should also be like Him in their marriages. He does not dominate, but rather leads and rules through servant-leadership. We follow Him because He loved us, and He came as a servant. To be like Christ, Christian men need to do the same.

Servant-leadership is the only Biblical and righteous option which Christian men have been given for how to lead their wives. And as Christ as our leader made us to have freedom to submit to Him or not, Christian men must do the same with their wives. This is what is Godly in a Godly marriage. Anything that involves the husband forcing the wife to submit, dominating her, is from the sin nature, and is not what God has instructed Christian husbands to do.

And in the same way that Christ first loved us, and now we learn to submit to His will, as He continues to love us as we make mistakes... there is much merit in Christian men first loving their wives, and as wives learn to submit to their husbands, for husbands to continue to love them even as they make mistakes. In the beginning, God made 2 intelligent orders of beings. First God made the angels, more powerful than mankind, who were meant to serve God by being ministers to mankind who would receive salvation. Second God made mankind. While the angels were more powerful than mankind, and were made first, a big part of their job for God revolved around helping mankind, who was the weaker order of beings, who was made second. And we know it is the fallen angels, the evil spirits, who now hate and war against mankind. They were not content to be ministers to mankind, but instead seemed to have sought power over mankind, and wanted this more than to obey God. They abused and still abuse their power, as the stronger order God created them to be.

Is it dissimilar to the history of men and women?

From the beginning, woman was made as the second and weaker gender of mankind. For first God made Adam, and then from Adam, God made Eve. And the history of mankind since the fall, since mankind gained a sin nature, has been for men to dominate women. That a husband would "rule over" his wife is listed as a clear negative consequence of man's fall into sin. That men have dominated and abused women all throughout history, has shown that men have seemed to want power over women, more than to obey God by loving their neighbor as themselves. Men were made by God as the stronger gender, but have abused and still abuse their strength.

In both cases, the stronger and inherently more powerful was made first, and the weaker was made second. In both cases, in disobedience to God, the first-made has abused their power as the stronger.

But today, God has told Christian husbands that their job is to love their wives, and to be servant-leaders, a job of helping the weaker kind of mankind, who was made second. God has shown Christian men that women are equal heirs of salvation, vessels of the Holy Spirit, and to be apportioned honor, the same honor that God has apportioned to men. God has told us to love our neighbors as ourselves, and that there is no male nor female in Christ Jesus.

As for Jesus Christ and His Bride, the church, He also was the first among many brethren. The only begotten Son of God, Jesus was the first of many adopted brothers and sisters, who make up his Bride. And He came not to be served, but to serve. He accepted God the Father's will, to do for us what no one else could do, and obeyed God. He sacrificed Himself for us, and did not use the power He had thinking of His own life, to save Himself from death, but rather was selfless and thought of us, suffering for us in love. And by His love for us, and all He has done to help us, He

has saved us. And now He enables us to help Him, as His body, to do His work. And even right now, He sits at the right hand of God the Father, hearing our prayers and advocating for us as our high priest, for our welfare. Surely where all of creation, of every created order of being, has failed, God came to us and showed us His Perfection, that He could do what we all failed to do. He has shown His perfect love towards the weaker, the Bride, who was made second. And most importantly, God made a way for us to be able to become like Him. He enables us to do what we cannot do without Him. He put His Spirit in us, and gives us His power, so we can become like Him and carry out His perfect will.
Glory to God, and the Lord Jesus Christ!!!

Chapter Eight
Genesis – The First Marriage

The concepts of love and self-submission in a Christian marriage date back to God's original design for marriage. The illustration of the husband as the head, and the wife as the body, which are together one flesh (as was seen in Eph 5), also originated with Adam and Eve. This all was part of God's original design for marriage, which was corrupted with Adam and Eve, but now can be restored for Christians to God's original design, through Jesus Christ.

The 6th Day (in chronological order) Gen 1:24-31, Gen 2:1-3,14-25

On the 6th day the first thing that God did was make the animals. Before this day He already made the birds and fish and plants. It is interesting to note that the plants, flying life, and swimming life are all masculine nouns, which are made after "his kind". Yet elsewhere in the Bible, some birds, etc. are feminine nouns. For instance in Lev 11:19 it says "and the stork, the heron, after *her* kind". So while the birds are said to be made after "his kind" in Gen 1, some individual types of birds are mentioned "after her kind" elsewhere.

The Hebrew language itself is not gender-neutral, same as in Spanish most words are themselves feminine or masculine, but it can be understood that God created both male and female of plants, birds, and swimming life at the same time. If the gender is understood as all-inclusive and equal, this makes sense. If "his kind" is understood as reflective of the importance of the masculine over the feminine in Gen 1:1-23 then there will be problems. The problem of seeing the gender in the term "his kind" as showing the male was more important than the female, can be seen when the actual gender in the Hebrew is used in Gen 1:24, with the creation of the animals:

(see this for yourself at
http://www.ancient-hebrew.org/genesis/index.html)

"Then God said, "Let the earth bring forth the living creature according to *her* kind: cattle and creeping thing and beast of the earth, each according to *her* kind"; and it was so. And God made the beast of the earth according to *her* kind, cattle according to *her* kind, and everything that creeps on the earth according to *his* kind. And God saw that it was good." Gen 1:24-35

Here the kinds of animals are brought forth each according to her kind, excepting the creeping thing which are made according to his kind. As such, if the specified gender of the pronoun (based on the inherent gender of the animal's noun) denotes more importance, or if the specified gender "owns", or is the model for the species, then it should be understood that the language indicates the female of most species of animals is the primary model of the species, the more important, as it is "her" kind.

But the same problem arises, which is elsewhere in the Bible, "living creatures after her kind", is shown to include "the weasel…and the mouse…. after his kind" (Lev 11:29). So like the masculine term includes the feminine, also the feminine term includes the masculine. Hebrew is not a gender-neutral language, but other verses in the Bible show that gender should be considered equal and all-inclusive in these verses in Genesis. As such the correct term in all instances of the creation of life would properly be "their kind". Neither the male nor the female gender is considered more important, but both are equal in importance, in the case of all plants, birds, fish, and animals. And they were each created together, male and female together, in all these verses. And as it is not specified that one was made before the other, and as neither gender is more prominent, it makes the most sense that God made the male and female of each kind at the exact same time. It is not "his kind" nor "her kind", but is equally "their kind".

For the next section I am including notes of the Hebrew specifics seen in this passage.
Then God said, "Let Us make the man (humankind) in Our image, according to Our likeness; let them (masculine plural) have dominion over the fish of the sea, over the birds of the air, and over the cattle, over all the earth and over every creeping thing that creeps on the earth." Gen 1:26

Because God said "let them (plural) have dominion" about that which He planned to make, the "man" here God planned to make was not referring to 1 man, but refers to the other use of this word in Hebrew, which is referring to all humankind. As the Strong's says of this word, *"man, mankind (much more frequently intended sense in OT)"*.

In this case we know God made a man and a woman. It is important to note in the above verses that a masculine plural pronoun is shown by God to specifically include both the male and the female genders. We know the plural God was speaking of was a man and a woman, and so we know that "man" here refers to both men and women, as humankind.

Unless there is some reason to know that only males are being specified, in the rest of the Bible the baseline assumption should be that a masculine plural pronoun can also include women.

As such, it is clear that God's original purpose for creating humankind, male and female, was for them to have dominion over the earth. Which means God created the male for the purpose of him to have dominion over the earth, and God also created the female for the purpose of her to have dominion over the earth. God's stated intent before He made humans was for them both to equally have dominion over the earth. Male and Female were each created equally for the purpose of having dominion over the earth. God also says, "Let Us make the humankind in Our image, according to Our likeness" and so both the male and the female were equally made by God in His image and according to His likeness.

The next verse, Genesis 1:27, tells what God did, summarized in order, without much detail,
"So God created man (humankind) in His own image:
(1) in the image of God He created him (masculine singular);
(2) male and female He created them (masculine plural)"

God made man and woman equally in His image, and both genders of humankind are equally image-bearers of God. Next we are told a little detail of the creation order. First God made the male in His image, and then God made the female in His image.

And truly, as Jesus is the image of God (Col 1:15), who we were created to look like, who Himself made us, women also were made in His image, after His likeness. The differences between how human men and women look are trivially minor when compared to the image of any other thing God made. And some women can be mistaken for men, and some men mistaken for women, minus a couple different parts of the body. Truly, woman was also made in the image of and after the likeness of Jesus Christ. You could not say women were not made in the image of and likeness of Jesus, anymore than you could say Jesus did not have the likeness or image of his mother Mary. And we know all children have the likeness of their parents. And how could anyone say Jesus looked like His Father, not His mother, when Jesus Himself is already the image of God? God is Spirit (Jn 4:24), but Jesus Christ is the fullness of the Godhead bodily (Col 2:9), and Jesus is the image of the invisible God (Col 1:15), which leads to an infinite regression. So He 'looked like Himself'. But also He looked like his mother, and had her image and her likeness. So both men and women were made in the image of God, who is Jesus Christ.

The Bible teaches in Genesis that there is a male-man and a female-man. Just as there are white-people and black-people, and Gentile-people and Jewish-people, the first real dichotomy was of the male-man and the female-man. But God considers them all equally "man", and neither one is more human than the other. They are equally made in the image of God. Again, it is not "his kind" or "her kind" but is equally "their kind". Which Jesus confirms in

Matt 19:4 "He answered, "Have you not read that he who made them from the beginning made them male and female".

The details of God's creation of humankind, male and female, are given in the next chapter. In Genesis 1:27 we are given a brief summary, which includes the order of creation of the male and then the female. But in Genesis chapter 2 we are given the details of God's creation of the first male-man and the first female-man on the 6th day, as was summarized in the single verse of Gen 1:27.

So these are the details of the creation of humankind on the 6th day: "And the LORD God formed man of the dust of the ground, and breathed into his nostrils the breath of life; and man became a living being. The LORD God planted a garden eastward in Eden, and there He put the man whom He had formed." Gen 2:7-8

Here the first male-man, we call Adam, is made outside of the garden, which has not been made yet. God breathes life into Adam, and he becomes a living being. God then makes the garden of Eden and moves Adam into it.

"And out of the ground the LORD God made every tree grow that is pleasant to the sight and good for food. The tree of life was also in the midst of the garden, and the tree of the knowledge of good and evil. Then the LORD God took the man and put him in the garden of Eden to tend and keep it." Gen 2:9,15

We are told here about the garden. God's purpose for putting Adam in the garden was for him to tend and keep the garden.

"And the LORD God commanded the man, saying, "Of every tree of the garden you may freely eat; but of the tree of the knowledge of good and evil you shall not eat, for in the day that you eat of it you shall surely die." Gen 2:16-17

Here God commands Adam to not eat of the tree, or Adam will surely die. When God says "you may eat", "you shall not eat", and "you shall surely die" to Adam, the Hebrew shows that "you" here is a masculine singular pronoun. The instructions God gave here were instructions to Adam, and were not said as a plural "you".

"And the LORD God said, "It is not good that man should be alone (separated); I will make him a help comparable." Gen 2:18

God determines and says that is not good for the male-man to be separated. The word here in Hebrew (905) means "something separated, a part" (Gesenius Lexicon). This is not a word that implies the male-man Adam was ever complete on his own, but would get lonely. No, this word actually implies that the male was incomplete and separated from something, in this case the male was separated from the female. The Genesius says this properly reads "in his separation". Also this could read "apart".

All of the other life, birds, animals, God made male and female together, at the same time. From God's perspective, having a male without a female was an incomplete creation. And as God was right there with Adam, having just told him to not eat from this tree, we know that Adam was right there to hear what God said outloud.

One major point of this verse is that God was right there with Adam, and said outloud in front of Adam "it is not good that the man should exist in his separation". God was letting Adam know that there was something missing, that he was separated from. What God said may have also carried the understanding, "It is not good that humankind exists separated, apart, incomplete."

Then God said, again in front of Adam, "I will make him a help comparable". This is sometimes translated as "help meet", not the best translation, and incorrectly also said to read "help mate" which is not what the words mean or say at all.

The words here in Hebrew are "ezer kenegdo".
The word "ezer" does not mean a servant or helper, and does not even imply such. This word is used predominantly of God's help. In fact, while 2x it refers to a meet help, and 3x any person who is a help, a total of 16x out of 21x total, this word refers to help coming from God.

"Our soul waiteth for the LORD: he [is] our help and our shield." Ps 33:20

"I will lift up mine eyes unto the hills, from whence cometh my help. My help cometh from the LORD, which made heaven and earth." Ps 121:1-2

"But I [am] poor and needy: make haste unto me, O God: thou art my help and my deliverer; O LORD, make no tarrying." Ps 70:5

As such, this word contains absolutely no connotation of a "helper" or "servant". Rather this word implies a help that is sufficiently great and strong to competently fulfill some need of help.

The word "kenegdo" literally translates as "as-corresponding-him". It could also read "alike to him" or simply "matching him". If you put this all together, Adam heard God's thoughts that God spoke aloud, announcing what He would do, "It is not good for the man to be separated, I will make him a (great) help alike to him." There is no implication here of "mating" whatsoever. There is not any implication of a servant.

Also note here that per the Hebrew the verse should read "I will make him a help" and not "I will make for him a help". This is a subtle difference, with not-so-subtle implications. The point is that while God did make Adam a help alike to him, this was done out of the need for Adam to not be separate, which was not good. The man was in a problematic imperfect situation and God would fix it by making the woman. And this is the only way in which God implied she was made for his sake. This had nothing to do with possession. The verse does not imply that God gave the woman to the man as a possession, as in "I will make for him a help alike to him". Woman was not made for man. Rather, woman was made for man's sake, as is specified in 1 Cor 11:9, "for indeed man was not created for the woman's sake, but woman for the man's sake."

What God said here in front of Adam was an entire thought, that he wanted Adam to hear so as to understand what God was about to do next.

That thought was, "It is not good for the man to be separated (a part, only a piece), I will make him a (great sufficient) help alike to (matching) him."

This verse also carries with it the meaning that the "help matching him" would in fact be his equal. An "alike to him" help, "comparable to him" help, means an equal help. Turn the words around in English, as is common with Hebrew translation to English, and this becomes the emphasis, "It is not good for the man to be separated, I will make him an equal help."

Another point to be made is that God was speaking to Himself here, but letting Adam hear what He said. It may be that the "help" mentioned here had to do more with God's task for humans, having dominion over the earth, tending to the garden, as God's stated task for the man was to tend to the garden, and later said, to subdue the earth, be fruitful, and multiply. As such, God may well have been emphasizing He was about to make an equal-to-the-man help for whatever tasks God had for them. In any case, God's point to Adam in what Adam heard, was to let Adam know that he was separated and this was not a good thing, and God was about to fix that by making a help equal to himself.

"Out of the ground the LORD God formed every beast of the field and every bird of the air, and brought them to Adam to see what he would call them. And whatever Adam called each living creature, that was its name. So Adam gave names to all cattle, to the birds of the air, and to every beast of the field. But for Adam there was not found a helper comparable to him." Gen 2:19-20

Here God brings one animal after another to Adam. It is possible these were all females of the different species of life God made, from birds, to mammals, to reptiles, etc. Again, the nouns here are a mix of male and female according to the kinds of animals, so there is no telling. But as the point of this exercise was Adam looking for that help equal to himself, it is possible they were female. God has let Adam know what He was up to in this exercise. Adam knew this was about him finding a help alike to him. He was looking for this help matching himself as he called each animal something.

Can you imagine, as God brought a dog to Adam, and Adam looked at it, could see it was not alike to him, and named it a dog? Next a horse, not alike to Adam either, and a turkey, not alike Adam and no apparent help, here is an elephant, not alike to Adam… Adam could see with each animal that it was not like him, and not the one God must have been talking about making. The suspense must have been killing Adam, but it also sounds like he was having fun. He was surely amazed at all the animals God had made.

But it should always be noted, the purpose of Adam naming the animals was that he was looking for that which was a help equal to him. And among all the animals, none were. While Adam did name the animals, all of this was done not because "he was the man" but was done because he was looking for the woman and had need for her to exist so things could be good, as they were not good. In doing this, God helped Adam to gain understanding that his equal help was special, and was not just some animal. When Adam did finally meet the woman, he knew right away this was who he had been waiting to meet.

"And the LORD God caused a deep sleep to fall on Adam, and he slept; and He took one of his ribs, and closed up the flesh in its place. Then the rib which the LORD God had taken from man He made into a woman, and He brought her to the man." Gen 2:21-22

Some people say this was a rib, but I have also heard people saying Adam was originally a hermaphrodite who had a uterus and female genitalia. That is because this word can also mean a side chamber. I really don't know, though I think this makes some sense. But if it was a rib, based on the symbolism of Jesus on the Cross, I would guess it was the rib over Adam's heart. Whatever it was, I will refer to it as a rib.

"And Adam said: "This is now bone of my bones And flesh of my flesh; She shall be called Woman, Because she was taken out of Man. Therefore a man shall leave his father and mother and be joined to his wife, and they shall become one flesh. And they were both naked, the man and his wife, and were not ashamed."
Gen 2:23-25

Immediately, Adam recognizes the help alike to him that God had spoken of. And he notices his missing rib, and understands God had to make her from him, and that in fact she was made of his own body. And he calls her woman, as she was taken out of man. The word here for "taken" is the same word used repeatedly later in the Bible for "take a wife".

Here we find the same illustration as in Eph 5, which is that a woman is like a man's own body. While she is a separate soul and has a separate living spirit, and a separate body, it is like a wife is made out of a piece of the man which was taken from him by God. Once God had taken his rib, it was no longer his, but belonged to God. As Adam belonged to God, who made him, this was not stealing something that belonged to Adam, but rather it was God rearranging something that belonged to Him. And so God built woman out of the rib. God could have built the woman from the ground, but God wanted Adam and the woman to gain understanding that they belonged to each other. God wanted them to have a relationship, and see they were related. God did things this way so as to show them this clearly, both Adam and the woman. So they could see, in a way, she is like his own body. And this is why they are one flesh when they are joined together in marriage, because it is like she was made from his rib. So they are one body, in two, and joined together to make one flesh.

In Eph 5, the man is said to be like the head of this one body, whereas the woman is like all the other body parts. This same picture is seen here in the first marriage, where all of the woman's body comes from a piece of the man's body. Her head, came from his rib, all of her body was formed of his body, which is why she is like his body. And having his head intact, while his body is not intact, as she was taken from his body and not his head, he is her head. Her head is made out of his body. But in this dichotomy of dividing the body into the head vs. every other body part, he is the intact head, with his body missing something, and she is the piece of body that he is missing. Neither one of them is a whole body without the other. This is where the analogy or illustration in Ephesians 5 comes from.

Note in all of this, that the woman fit the requirements of being a great help alike to Adam, just as God made her. God made her to be this, just as He created her to be. This was not a job description, or something for her to strive for, or a job to fulfill. This was what she was, just as God made her.

Nor was she created for the purpose of being Adam's help meet. She was created primarily to have dominion over the earth, including tending the garden. The other reason why she was created was because without her the human race was incomplete, which was not good. She was not created to help a complete Adam with his aloneness, rather she was created because this was God's will to make humankind, male and female, from the beginning. But God wanted to make the point clear to Adam that it was not good for him to be a part, separated from the whole which should be, both male and female, and God did things this way so Adam could learn and understand this truth.

God also wanted Adam to understand very clearly that the woman was made of the same stuff that he was. As she was built from the bone and flesh of a man, she also was the same as him. God wanted Adam to see that she was just as human as he was.

"Then God blessed them, and God said to them, "Be fruitful and multiply; fill the earth and subdue it; have dominion over the fish of the sea, over the birds of the air, and over every living thing that moves on the earth." Gen 1:28

After God had made both the man and the woman, He gives them both dominion over all life, jointly, and jointly tells them to be fruitful and multiply. God gave a command on what to do and gave dominion to the man, and God gave a command on what to do and gave dominion to the woman. And they are jointly given the task to be fruitful and multiply. And they are jointly blessed.

"And God said, "See, I have given you every herb that yields seed which is on the face of all the earth, and every tree whose fruit yields seed; to you it shall be for food. Also, to every beast of the earth, to every bird of the air, and to everything that creeps on the earth, in which there is life, I have given every green herb for food"; and it was so." Gen 1:29-30

Here God gives both of them all the plants for food. Jointly they own all the plants for food. He has been given all the plants, and she has been given all the plants. Note here that God does not repeat His command to not eat the fruit of the tree of life to the woman. She does not know about this, and only hears from God that she may eat all the fruit there is.

"Then God saw everything that He had made, and indeed it was very good. So the evening and the morning were the sixth day. Thus the heavens and the earth, and all the host of them, were finished. And on the seventh day God ended His work which He had done, and He rested on the seventh day from all His work which He had done. Then God blessed the seventh day and sanctified it, because in it He rested from all His work which God had created and made." Gen 1:31-2:3

And this is all we are told that happened on the day that God made humankind.

Now, after making all the animals male and female at the exact same time, God made the humans with the male first and the female second. Why did God choose to make humankind differently?

The way that God did this seemed to be for 2 reasons, which were to instill the concepts of a man loving a woman, and a woman loving and respecting a man, trusting him, and willingly following him.

Adam was shown how special Eve was, and had to wait with some anticipation to meet her. He also became aware that his existence was not complete without her, and without her it was not good. Without her, his existence and the existence of humanity was not complete. He knew her right away as being a help alike to him, matching him, his peer, his equal. He also knew that she was made from his very body, his own flesh. He knew that she was equally human as he was, and just as essential. He knew that God made her, and she was designed by God, the Creator. This all was meant to foster an understanding that she was equally as human, a help matching him, who also had dominion over the world, and the same shared instructions as he had to be fruitful and multiply. All of this was meant to foster feelings of love, acceptance and appreciation for the woman.

On the other side of things, the woman opened her newly made eyes, saw the Lord, and then was led by Him, to a man. Overwhelmed by sensations, colors, things she could see all around, not knowing what anything was, having just been created, the man immediately exclaims to her,
"This is now bone of my bones And flesh of my flesh! She shall be called Woman, because she was taken out of Man."

And so the first thing this woman hears is acceptance and belonging. She is told that she will be called woman by the man, a word which in itself relates her to the man in front of her. And no doubt, the man seemed to be very happy to see her, and friendly towards her. Everything about her first moments conveyed to her total acceptance, belonging, and that she was liked, in other words, she felt loved.

Then the Lord told both of them to be fruitful, to multiply, and have dominion over the earth and subdue it. He told them He had given them both all the plants to eat, and also for the animals to eat.

Then the story leaves off. But it is easy to imagine that soon Adam started telling her about what had happened before she got there. He started showing her all the animals, and telling her of his quest to meet her, and what he had called each of them while looking for her. But how none of them were a help alike to him, that God said He would make. This probably made Eve feel very special. As she met the animals, in all their amazing colors and shapes and personalities, wondering over them, all this was wrapped up in a story about how she was more special to this man than any of them. He told her he had been looking for her all day, and she was the only creature God has made which would do, to fix what was not good, to be a help alike to him. She surely felt very special, and appreciated. He was probably enjoying her company very much. And as she heard of all the names he had given all the animals, in his quest to meet her, she felt respect for him, that he had done all this which was impressive, but even more so that he had done it out of love for her, which is likely what she would have done too she imagined if she had been in the same situation. And as he loved her, she responded by feeling love for him, and respect as well. And so God designed the first day so that the man and woman would easily begin to love each other, and then she would feel respect for him.

We also can gather, from the next chapter, that Adam told the woman about the commandment God had spoken to him prior to her creation. It is not specified in the Bible that God repeated this command to the woman, so her knowledge of it must have come from Adam. And until the serpent got involved, the woman did not eat of the tree, apparently for some time.

From this we can see that the woman, feeling loved by Adam, trusted him in what he told her. She had not heard this herself from God, but trusted the man when he told her about it. And, she submitted herself to what he said, by not eating of the tree. That is until the day the serpent interfered.
It is important to note that this speaks of a woman's nature, which is that she was designed to trust a man when she feels loved by him, and naturally follow him or naturally submit herself to him. The woman was naturally trusting and had a natural tendency to follow, or submit herself. And we will cover this chapter of Gen 3 on the fall in more detail later.

But the point is that in the creation story, we see that (in order):
1. God led Adam to love the woman and appreciate her, and see her as his equal
2. God led Adam to show acceptance of her, appreciation, and love to her
3. God led her to feel loved even from her first moments
4. God put both of them in a situation so that the things Adam told her about, naming the animals, would also make her feel loved by him, which made her feel respect for him
5. God designed the woman to then be trusting and naturally inclined to follow the man, or submit herself to him

And so the creation story contains the same elements that we see in Eph 5 of God's design for a Christian marriage. Love and self-submission were not a matter of authority, but of the nature God designed men and women to naturally have. They were meant to naturally respond this way to each other. God designed them to get into this groove of behavior naturally, and led them into things starting off well. And it was disobedience to God that disrupted this bliss, leading to the corruption and destruction of God's original design for marriage.

A Little Q & A

1. Woman was made from Adam's rib, his body. Does this mean that a woman is a man's property?

No. God took the rib from Adam, and once God took it, it no longer belonged to Adam. God made Adam, and so the only ownership implied here is that God owns everything that He made. Adam did not create the woman, God did. If anything, God just rearranged part of a person He owned, and transformed it into another person God owned. God made the woman for Adam's sake, because it was bad for him to be apart from her; for the male to exist without the female. However, God did not make the woman for Adam, as in a gift to be owned and a possession. She was made for <u>his sake</u>, not <u>for him</u>. The point of making her out of Adam's rib was to show Adam that they were made of the same stuff, and completed each other together, as humankind.

Look at this another way, as the Bible clarifies in
1 Cor 11:8-9, 11-12:
"For the man is not out of the woman, but the woman is out of the man; for indeed man was not created for the sake of the woman, but woman for the sake of the man… Moreover, neither is woman separate of man, nor is man separate of woman, in the Lord. For just as the woman is out of the man, in this manner also the man is through the woman; but all together from God."

Here what is understood from Genesis is recapped. This is a correct translation of the Greek. Woman was created for the <u>sake</u> of man, not for the man himself. Also, that men exist because they are birthed through women is directly compared to woman having been made out of a man's rib. This means that the woman being made from Adam's rib in no way implies ownership anymore than a mother owns her son. In the same way grown adult sons own themselves and are not owned by their mother, a woman is not owned by her husband. This direct comparison is made by God in His Word to make this point clear. Husbands do not own their wives, and a wife is not property. And as such, neither did Adam own his wife, even in the beginning and in the first marriage. The woman was not Adam's property. Neither a woman being made out of man's body, nor a man being made out of a woman's body, equates to the one who was made being the property of the one that person was made out of.

It is interesting to note that the word God used for "make" in "make an alike- to-him help" is the same Hebrew word "asah" which God also uses for "make" when it comes to a child in his mother's womb:
"Thus saith the LORD that <u>made</u> thee, and formed thee from the womb, [which] will help thee; Fear not, O Jacob, my servant; and thou, Jesurun, whom I have chosen." Isa 44:2
"Did not he that <u>made</u> me in the womb <u>make</u> him? and did not one fashion us in the womb?" Job 31:15
As 1 Cor 11:12 states, woman out of man, and man through the woman, but ALL are made BY God.

2. God brought the woman to Adam, and let Adam choose what to call her, just like God did with the animals, who God gave Adam dominion over. Does this mean that God gave Adam dominion (or authority) over the woman?

No. God specifically told both the man and the woman that He was giving them both dominion over the animals. God brought the animals to Adam to see what Adam would call them, but the woman was also given equal dominion over all the animals. Therefore, naming something does NOT give a person authority over it. The authority was, and has to be, specifically given by God. Adam naming the animals was not an act of Adam showing his dominion over them, as God had not yet told Adam or the woman that He was giving them dominion over the animals. Adam was just naming the animals in the process of God letting Adam figure out for himself who this alike-to-him help was, that God said He would make. While the woman did not name the animals, she also had dominion over them, because God gave it to her. In the same way, Adam calling her a "woman" did not in any way establish that he had authority over her.

If God had wanted the man to have authority over the woman, it would be specified. To make this very clear, if God had given dominion over the woman to the man, in keeping with the rest of the chapter, in keeping with God's actions, in keeping with consistency and logic, God would have said, and the Bible would read:

Then God blessed them, and God said to them, "Be fruitful and multiply; fill the earth and subdue it; have dominion over the fish of the sea, over the birds of the air, and over every living thing that moves on the earth." And then God said to the man, "Have dominion over the woman also...." No!

God didn't say that, because God didn't do that, which is why it's not in the Bible! It could easily be there, if it had been what God intended, but it is not there, because it is Not what God intended. Naming things does not give you authority over them, either you have authority already, or you don't. A different dynamic and purpose was taking place here.

Men and women both need to feel loved and respected (as in the meaning of esteemed or honored). While the man looked for God to make a meet help, the time of God letting the man name the animals, was a special time together for God and the man, in which God made him feel special to God, which made him feel respected and loved by God. Later, as the woman accepted that the animals were named as Adam had called them, as he told her the story of his first day, Adam also felt respected by the woman, and loved by the woman. But the reason Adam was the one to call her woman was so he would make her feel special and accepted by him, and loved, right from her first moments. Also the woman's later moments made her feel loved by Adam, as she heard all about her back-story. She came to feel special to Adam and to God, and loved by God also in hearing this. And in hearing this story about Adam naming the animals, she felt respected by Adam that what he called her reflected that she alone was his peer. And as she was given dominion over the world and given the plants to eat by God, she also felt special to God from this, and respected and loved by God. This first day was all about Love and Respect, that both the man and woman felt special to God, loved by God, and respected by God, and also felt special to the other, and loved and respected by the other. It seems the man's need was more for respect, and the woman's need was more for love, and this difference is reflected in how God set up this first day to progress. But nevertheless, it is clear that both the man and woman needed both to feel loved and respected by the other, and by God.

God designed marriage to be a naturally symbiotic relationship, and led the first man and woman to align to each other in this natural groove. The man was meant to naturally lead, and the woman was meant to naturally follow, they both were designed to need love, and respect. On their first day God naturally led them into him loving her and her respecting him, and they both felt loved and respected by God. And we see it was also her nature to trust and follow him. And God met each of their needs, and also met their needs in providing each one for the other to meet the other's needs.

Neither the man nor the woman were given authority over the other. They were designed by God to naturally get along, without any rules on them to do so. God made men and women different, but complimentary, like two clock gears interlocked together, each one turning the other with each spoke progressing the other around. And God is the one who powered this and set it in motion originally, with how He carefully planned the first day of the man and woman. This is what marriage is supposed to be, and without sin, this is what man and woman were designed to do naturally, as God made them to be. Without sin, a woman is designed to need love and respect from him, and to love him, and respect him because he loves her, and to trust him and therefore be naturally inclined to follow her husband. Without sin, a husband is designed to need to feel love and respect from her, and to give her love and respect. This is the nature of man and woman which God designed them to have when He made them.

And it is sin, disobedience to God, a temptation of the Devil, which threw a wrench in the works and messed all this up, and still does today. And we see this in the next chapter of Genesis 3.

Some of what we have learned here, in summary:
1. Men and women were created equal. They are equally humankind.
2. They were both equally created for the purpose of having dominion over the earth.
3. They were both equally created in the image of God.
4. The man and the woman were designed to have a naturally symbiotic relationship,
that God guided him to accept her, love her, respect her, and guided her to love him, respect him, and trust him.
5. God made the rules and was in charge, not the man nor the woman, and neither was given authority over the other. But she was designed to be naturally inclined to follow him.

Chapter Nine
Genesis – The First Marriage Problems

We are going to start by looking at just a few aspects of this story of the Fall.

The MAN
walked away from the 6th day having been told by God:
"And the LORD God commanded the man, saying, "Of every tree of the garden you(si) may freely eat; but of the tree of the knowledge of good and evil you(si) shall not eat, for in the day that you(si) eat of it you(si) shall surely die."
(in the Hebrew all the "you" are singular) Gen 2:16-17
(See all these singular/plurals for yourself at
http://www.ancient-hebrew.org/genesis/index.html)

"Then God blessed them, and God said to them, "Be fruitful and multiply; fill the earth and subdue it; have dominion over the fish of the sea, over the birds of the air, and over every living thing that moves on the earth. And God said, "See, I have given you(pl) every herb that yields seed which is on the face of all the earth, and every tree whose fruit yields seed; to you(pl) it shall be for food. Also, to every beast of the earth, to every bird of the air, and to everything that creeps on the earth, in which there is life, I have given every green herb for food"; and it was so."
(in the Hebrew all the "you" are plural) Gen 1:28-30

The WOMAN
walked away from the 6th day having been told by God:
"Then God blessed them, and God said to them, "Be fruitful and multiply; fill the earth and subdue it; have dominion over the fish of the sea, over the birds of the air, and over every living thing that moves on the earth. And God said, "See, I have given you(pl) every herb that yields seed which is on the face of all the earth, and every tree whose fruit yields seed; to you(pl) it shall be for food. Also, to every beast of the earth, to every bird of the air, and to everything that creeps on the earth, in which there is life, I have given every green herb for food"; and it was so."
(in the Hebrew all the "you" are plural) Gen 1:28-30

Here we see that God told the man he could freely eat of all the trees, but also commanded the man to not eat of the Tree of the Knowledge of Good and Evil, before the woman was made.
God is not recorded as having given the woman this command. The woman was told by God that all the fruit-bearing trees had been given to them for food, without any exception mentioned in what God told her. It should be noted that God telling her she could eat from all the fruit-bearing trees was one of the few interactions the woman had with God on her first day, and probably made her feel special, respected, and loved by God that He told her He gave her dominion over the animals and the herbs to eat and fruit trees to eat from.

From the woman's perspective: God told her she could eat from all the trees.

From the man's perspective: God told him that he could eat from all the trees except for one. There was one tree he was commanded not to eat from, and if he did he would surely die. Then the man saw God told the woman she could eat from all the trees.

Which leads up to the next events, of Genesis Chapter 3:
"Now the serpent was more cunning than any beast of the field which the LORD God had made.
And he said to the woman, "Has God indeed said,
'You(pl) shall not eat of every tree of the garden'?"
And the woman said to the serpent, "We may eat the fruit of the trees of the garden; but of the fruit of the tree which is in the midst of the garden, God has said, 'You(pl) shall not eat it, nor shall you(pl) touch it, lest you(pl) die.'"
(in the Hebrew all the "you" are plural)

"Then the serpent said to the woman,
"You(pl) will not surely die. For God knows that in the day you(pl) eat of it your(pl) eyes will be opened, and you(pl) will be like God, knowing good and evil."
(in the Hebrew all the "you" are plural) Gen 3:1-5

Here the woman knows of something similar to the command God gave Adam, before she was made. It contradicts what God told her directly, which was that she could eat from all the trees. The most logical conclusion, as the Bible does not record God repeating this command to her, is that the man told the woman about what God had commanded him. As such, the most logical conclusion is that she heard this command second-hand from the man, not from God directly.

"So when the woman saw that the tree was good for food, that it was pleasant to the eyes, and a tree desirable to make one wise, she took of its fruit and ate. She also gave to her husband with her, and he ate. Then the eyes of both of them were opened, and they knew that they were naked; and they sewed fig leaves together and made themselves coverings." Gen 3:6-7
Note: the woman's eyes are not recorded to have opened until after the man ate the fruit, and no time delay is mentioned between her and his eyes opening.

"And they heard the sound of the LORD God walking in the garden in the cool of the day, and Adam and his wife hid themselves from the presence of the LORD God among the trees of the garden. Then the LORD God called to Adam and said to him, "Where are you(si)?" (In Hebrew this "you" is singular)

"So he said, "I heard Your voice in the garden, and I was afraid because I was naked; and I hid myself." And He said, "Who told you(si) that you(si) were naked? Have you(si) eaten from the tree of which I commanded **you(si)** that **you(si)** should not eat?"
(in the Hebrew all "you" are singular) Gen 3:8-11

God confirms that He said to Adam singularly that "you should not eat." God could have said, "Have you eaten from the tree I commanded you(si) that 'you(pl) should not eat'?"
But this is not what the text says. When God says "you should not eat", He is repeating his command given to Adam in Gen 1, which reads in the singular, and here also is repeated in the singular. <u>God makes it clear and confirms here that the command to not eat was solely given to Adam.</u>

"Then the man said, "The woman whom You gave to be with me, she gave me of the tree, and I ate." And the LORD God said to the woman, "What is this you have done?"
The woman said, "The serpent deceived me, and I ate."

So the LORD God said to the serpent: "Because you(pl) have done this, (the "you" here is plural) Gen 3:12-14

The "you" here is plural. As such this "you" seems to be directed at the serpent and the woman. What did they do together?
Tempt the man to eat from the tree.

"You are cursed more than all cattle, And more than every beast of the field; On your belly you shall go, And you shall eat dust All the days of your life. (the other "you" are singular)
And I will put enmity Between you and the woman, And between your seed and her Seed; He shall bruise your head, And you shall bruise His heel."
To the woman He said:
"Multiply, I will multiply your pains, and your conception in pain you shall bring forth children;
Your desire will be for your husband, And he will rule over you." Gen 3:14-16
(Note: "he will rule over you" is a negative consequence of the fall told to the woman, not a permission or instruction given to the man.)

"Then to Adam He said, "Because you(si) have heeded the voice of your wife, "she ate from the tree" of which I commanded **you(si)**, saying, '**You(si)** shall not eat of it':"
The "you" here is singular in all instances. <u>God confirms a second time that He said to Adam singularly that "you shall not eat of it."</u> God could have said, "I commanded you saying 'You(pl) shall not eat of it." But this is not what the text says. It is singular and God's command was just addressed to Adam. This is a 2nd witness by God of what His original command was, even specifying what He said most precisely, and so there are 2 witnesses of God's original command being to Adam alone.

"Cursed is the ground for your sake; In toil you shall eat of it All the days of your life. Both thorns and thistles it shall bring forth for you, And you shall eat the herb of the field. In the sweat of your face you shall eat bread Till you return to the ground, For out of it you were taken; For dust you are, And to dust you shall return." (in Hebrew all the "you" are masculine singular) Gen 3:17-19

"And Adam called his wife's name Eve, because she was the mother of all living. Also for Adam and his wife the LORD God made tunics of skin, and clothed them. Then the LORD God said, "Behold, the man has become like one of Us, to know good and evil. And now, lest he put out his hand and take also of the tree of life, and eat, and live forever" — therefore the LORD God sent him out of the garden of Eden to till the ground from which he was taken. So He drove out the man; and He placed cherubim at the east of the garden of Eden, and a flaming sword which turned every way, to guard the way to the tree of life." Gen 3:20-24

Let's look at the cause and effect in this story, of what was done, and what God said as a result.

The woman is not specifically told that she will die because of eating from the tree, but the man is told he will die because he ate from the tree. If the woman would die because of eating from the tree, what would make sense is that God would have mentioned she would die for eating from the tree in what God told her were her punishments. But God does not.

Instead the only reason given for her punishment is found in the statement directed to the serpent in the plural "you". As this you is plural, it seems that God was addressing both the serpent and the woman. It would better read "because you two have done this". What had they done together? They had tempted the man to eat from the tree. So the most straightforward reading of the text is that what God says to the woman as punishments or consequences are because of her participation with the serpent in tempting the man to eat from the tree that was forbidden to the man.

Here God forces man to leave the garden, for the stated reason to prevent the man, just the man, from eating of the tree of life. God specifies much to the man. Included is that the man will return to the dust from which he was taken. It is not specified that the woman will die, only that the man will die.

Without making any assumption, based just on what God says, it seems that if the man dies, then the woman will die also, which is implied as a cause and effect.

All this raises the question, as to whether the woman would have died if only she had eaten the fruit of the tree. Most people seem to think the woman was set to die once she ate from the tree. But is this actually what the Bible teaches?

1. God commanded the man alone to not eat, and God confirms this twice after they ate.
2. Man is told he (singular) will die because he ate.
3. Woman is never told she will die because she ate, and she was not commanded to not eat. Despite 2 opportunities to confirm she had been commanded not to eat also, God only says that He had singularly commanded the man to not eat, and God twice confirms this is the case.
4. Apparently God telling the man he (singular) will die also means the woman will die.
5. The woman's eyes are not recorded as having been opened until <u>after</u> the man ate the fruit.

What might this mean? Is it possible that the woman did not die because of eating from the tree? While she did face negative consequences and punishment from the fall, the only time she is addressed as to why she is being punished, seems to be as the serpent is addressed.

The serpent is told "because you(plural) have done this" Or another way to put it would be "because you two have done this". What did the serpent and the woman do together? The serpent deceived the woman into tempting the man to eat, and as such they both tempted the man to eat the fruit that God had commanded him to not eat. And after God is done addressing the serpent, without any "because you did...." to the woman, God then addresses her. As such, just based on what the Bible actually says, it makes the most sense that her crime was participation in tempting the man to eat from the tree which God had commanded him to not eat from. This argument has more going for it, based on what God's Word actually says, than the argument that she was punished for eating the fruit herself.

That she is punished for eating the fruit is never specified. Rather, it is specified that her punishment is for participation with the serpent, in what they both did together.

Is it possible that the man was the only one who was forbidden to eat the fruit? Is it possible that the woman would not have died, nor had her eyes opened, if she alone had ate the fruit? Based on the punishments specified to her, which does not include anything about her dying, and based on that her eyes were not opened until after Adam ate the fruit, this does seem to be at least a possibility that the Bible indicates. The most straightforward reading of the causes and effects in the story shows this to be a possibility.

Most people have been taught, and assume, that the woman died because she ate, and the man died because he ate. But this is not specified in the Scriptures. Rather, as Adam is the only one told that he will die, and the woman is not told her punishments are for eating from the tree, and because twice God confirms His command was singularly to Adam, this all points to the possibility that the woman died because Adam died.

And you may be surprised to learn there is additional corroboration and support for this argument in the rest of scripture. And I found these as I looked for further references to the story of the first man and woman:

1 Cor 11:8 "For the man is not out of the woman, but the woman is out of the man"

1 Tim 2:13-14 "For Adam was first formed, then Eve. And Adam was not deceived, but the woman being deceived became in the transgression."

Rom 5:12-21
Wherefore, as by one man sin entered into the world, and death by sin; and so death passed upon all men, for that all have sinned: For until the law sin was in the world: but sin is not imputed when there is no law. Nevertheless death reigned from Adam to Moses, even over them that had not sinned after the similitude of Adam's transgression, who is the figure of him that was to come. But not as the offence, so also is the free gift. For if through the offence of one many be dead, much more the grace of God, and the gift by grace, which is by one man, Jesus Christ, hath abounded unto many. And not as it was by one that sinned, so is the gift: for the judgment was by one to condemnation, but the free gift is of many offences unto justification. For if by one man's offence death reigned by one; much more they which receive abundance of grace and of the gift of righteousness shall reign in life by one, Jesus Christ. Therefore as by the offence of one judgment came upon all men to condemnation; even so by the righteousness of one the free gift came upon all men unto justification of life. For as by one man's disobedience many were made sinners, so by the obedience of one shall many be made righteous. Moreover the law entered, that the offence might abound. But where sin abounded, grace did much more abound: That as sin hath reigned unto death, even so might grace reign through righteousness unto eternal life by Jesus Christ our Lord. (KJV)

Therefore, just as through one man sin entered into the world, and death through sin, and so death spread to all men, because all sinned– for until the Law sin was in the world, but sin is not imputed when there is no law. Nevertheless death reigned from Adam until Moses, even over those who had not sinned in the likeness of the offense of Adam, who is a type of Him who was to come. But the free gift is not like the transgression. For if by the transgression of the one the many died, much more did the grace of God and the gift by the grace of the one Man, Jesus Christ, abound to the many. The gift is not like that which came through the one who sinned; for on the one hand the judgment arose from one transgression resulting in condemnation, but on the other hand the free gift arose from many transgressions resulting in justification. For if by the transgression of the one, death reigned through the one, much more those who receive the abundance of grace and of the gift of righteousness will reign in life through the One, Jesus Christ. So then as through one transgression there resulted condemnation to all men, even so through one act of righteousness there resulted justification of life to all men. For as through the one man's disobedience the many were made sinners, even so through the obedience of the One the many will be made righteous. The Law came in so that the transgression would increase; but where sin increased, grace abounded all the more, so that, as sin reigned in death, even so grace would reign through righteousness to eternal life through Jesus Christ our Lord. (NASB)

1 Cor 15:21-22, 45
For since by man came death, by man came also the resurrection of the dead. For as in Adam all die, even so in Christ shall all be made alive. And so it is written, The first man Adam was made a living soul; the last Adam was made a quickening spirit.

What these verses state is that by Adam's sin, death passed to all men, including women. This is something assumed to pass genetically from the parents to child, and many assume that mortality passed from *both* Adam and Eve to all of their children. However, this is not what the Bible actually teaches. It teaches that death passed to all men from the sin of 1 man, which is specified to be Adam. There are 2 witnesses to this in the New Testament as being the true. And we know that death passed to all of Adam's male and female children, and that "all men" thus includes women as well.

Not only that, but the balance of Jesus' righteousness being given to many, is directly compared to Adam's condemnation being passed on to many. Jesus is specified as one originator of forgiveness and life, and so is Adam one originator of condemnation and death, in this direct comparison.
Just taking the Bible as God's Word, God states that death passed to all people, the children of Adam, because of Adam's sin.
It is believed that the death caused by eating from the tree was a spiritual death, and many people teach this. It makes sense

because Adam did not immediately physically die from eating the tree. As such it is thought that he spiritually died, and because he spiritually died, his body started dying as well.

Also it should be noted that eating from the tree of life is what would cause immortality:
"Then the LORD God said, "Behold, the man has become like one of Us, to know good and evil. And now, lest he put out his hand and take also of the tree of life, and eat, and <u>live forever</u>" — therefore the LORD God sent him out of the garden of Eden to till the ground from which he was taken. So He drove out the man; and He placed cherubim at the east of the garden of Eden, and a flaming sword which turned every way, to guard the way to the tree of life."

If Adam was already immortal, the tree of Life would not have been necessary, and it is specified that eating from it is what would cause immortality, to live forever. This also may have referred to a spiritual living forever. It may be that when it came to the trees in the garden, that a spiritual death caused a physical death, and a spiritual immortality caused a physical immortality. This seems to make sense and be likely. Neither tree referred to physical death or life directly, but rather to the life or death of the spirit, leading to the life or death of the body. But if this is the case, then why does the verse saying he must leave the garden so he won't eat from the tree of life, indicate that the tree of life would only affect Adam, and not Eve?

Gen 2:7 says, "And the LORD God formed man [of] the dust of the ground, and breathed into his nostrils the breath of life; and man became a <u>living soul</u>."

1 Cor 15:45 And so it is written, The first man Adam was made <u>a living soul</u>; the last Adam was made a quickening spirit.

The word here for "soul" is "psyche" and it means "life" and "soul". It is also used in Matt 10:28
"And fear not them which kill the body, but are not able to kill the soul: but rather fear him which is able to destroy both <u>soul</u> and body in hell."

And so we know that the soul lives on past physical death as something spiritual, and that therefore what God breathed into Adam was something spiritual, when God breathed into Adam and he became a "living soul".

Now, granted, it is difficult to tell sometimes when the Bible is referring to the soul, and to the spirit. We know they are different, but sometimes the words used for each leave us with slightly fuzzy definitions. Why this is so seems to be alluded to in Heb 4:12, "For the word of God [is] quick, and powerful, and sharper than any two-edged sword, piercing even to the dividing asunder of soul and spirit, and of the joints and marrow, and [is] a discerner of the thoughts and intents of the heart."

The soul and spirit are so tightly joined together, that it takes something like a very finely sharpened instrument, to divide them apart. That being said, it still seems that the death or life from the trees in the garden had an effect upon the soul or spirit of man, which would then have an effect on the body.

From what is recorded in the Bible, God breathed the "breath of life" into Adam and he became a living soul. Then God formed the woman out of Adam's rib. What is the "breath of life"? The Bible indicates that the "breath of life" is the "spirit" of life.

"The Spirit of God hath made me, and the breath of the Almighty hath given me life." Job 33:4

"All the while my breath [is] in me, and the spirit (ruach) of God [is] in my nostrils" Job 27:3

"And the LORD said, My spirit (ruach) shall not always strive with man, for that he also [is] flesh: yet his days shall be an hundred and twenty years." Gen 6:3

And so it seems that in Genesis, God made Adam's body, and then breathed the spirit of life into Adam, also called the "breath of life", and then Adam became a living soul.

The Bible teaches that the life of the body is found in the blood, as seen in Lev 17:11,
"For the life of the flesh [is] in the blood: and I have given it to you upon the altar to make an atonement for your souls: for it [is] the blood [that] maketh an atonement for the soul."
At first Adam had a body, but it was not alive, and he was not a living soul, until God breathed into him a spirit, which gave him life. Then Adam became a living soul. And once Adam became a living soul, then his body also had life. This implies that the life in the body comes from the life of the soul, and the life of the soul comes from the spirit which is the breath of life. So the life of the spirit gives life to the soul and gives the body life. And the life of the flesh is in the blood. Which must mean the spirit is tied to or in the blood somehow.

Now, when God formed the woman of Adam's flesh and bone, Adam then said she was flesh of his flesh and bone of his bones. The blood is in the flesh, and also blood is in the marrow of the bone of a rib, and the life is in the blood, and the spirit gives life, so the spirit must be in the blood or tied to it somehow. Which would mean that whatever the spirit or "breath of life" is made of, I'll call it "spirit-matter", was in or tied to the flesh and bone God took from Adam and used to make the woman. Adam's blood was in the rib God took from Adam and made the woman with. She then had her individual soul, and he had his individual soul, but they both had a soul made alive from the same substance of spirit or "breath of life", like "spirit-matter", which came from Adam. Just like they had two bodies, both made of the same skin and bones and blood, they were separate, but each was made of the same stuff. And in the same way, they each had a separate soul, but their souls were both made alive of the same stuff, the same "spirit" giving life or "breath of life". And the individual body and spirit of the woman was formed out of the substance of the body and spirit of the man; and the combination of both body and spirit of life is what made each of them to be individual living souls.

As the Bible does not specify that God again breathed life into the woman, but only into the man, then this must mean that her living spirit came from Adam's living spirit, the same as her body was built from a rib taken from Adam. And as the spirit is tied to the blood, and a rib contains blood, that all adds up very well. Her spirit was built from the "spirit-matter" taken from Adam.

The spirit is the "breath of life" which gives life to an individual soul. As Adam was the one who was given the original living spirit, could this mean he was effectively the guardian of it, and all human spirits? The woman's spirit in her, giving her life, had been built from Adam's spirit that God had breathed into him. Could it be if his spirit died spiritually, that her spirit would die spiritually also? And if his spirit died, and his body began to die as a result, could it be that the woman's spirit would die, and her body would begin to die also?

Well, in the case of children, the Bible always lists lineage by the father. There is some reason to think that the spiritual condition of the father is what defines the spiritual condition of the child. For instance, Jesus Christ is the Son of God, and spiritually He also IS God. He is as His Father is. He did not inherit just a normal sinful spiritual state from his mother, He was human, but He was not just human, He was also God. (*And some people argue there is another case, in Gen 6, having to do with the origin of demons, for anyone familiar with the example, the argument also shows that the spirit of the father determines the type of spirit of the child.)

We also see in Ex 20:5 that God says, "Thou shalt not bow down thyself to them, nor serve them: for I the LORD thy God [am] a jealous God, visiting the iniquity of <u>the fathers</u> upon the children unto the third and fourth [generation] of them that hate me"

And the terms here do refer to paternal ancestors, but not maternal ancestors (though it could refer to paternal ancestors on the mother's side). The Bible seems to indicate strongly that the paternal line passes on the spiritual state of the child.

Also the Bible directly says that men come THROUGH a woman, in the same manner that the first woman came out of the first man. This word does mean to "pass through" as in motion through.

1 Cor 11:8, 12 "For the man is not out of the woman, but the woman is out of the man; For just as the woman is <u>out of</u> the man, in this manner also the man is <u>through</u> the woman; but all together from God."

And as such, the Bible teaches that children come <u>from</u> their father, <u>through</u> their mother, to having life. And this is specified as in the same manner as the first woman came out of the man, to life. What is spoken of here is not just the body, but as the life is from the spirit, and the life is in the blood, this also is referring to the substance of the spirit coming through the body and the flesh and the blood. Children gain a living spirit from their father, through their mother, and also in this manner the first woman gained her spirit out of the man. It is not just the flesh and bone spoken of here, but the blood, which contains the life, and the spirit is what gives life, so this speaks of the substance of the spirit also. The spirit of life of a child comes from the father as its origin, passing through the mother. The spirit of life of a child does not originate from the child's mother, but the child's father. Nor does the Bible teach that God breathes the "breath of life" or life-giving "spirit" into a child at conception. Many people believe this, but the Bible does not read this way. God builds from the materials already in place, which are "<u>multiplied</u>".

The first man and woman were told to "multiply". Now, multiplying implies something is copied, thus becoming more, a self-generation. We can know what the Bible means by the term "multiplied" from the example of the first "multiplication" which is recorded for us. God did the first multiplication of 1 into 2, multiplying Adam into being both Adam and Eve. One body became 2, one spirit became 2, one soul became 2. And then by the children they were multiplied into many more. But Adam was the original, and both the first woman, and all the children, were multiplied from Adam. We procreate children by multiplying, not adding, though each new child and new soul is still a miracle from God. And this is how it has been since the beginning, and is taught in Genesis. The man had his own body, spirit and soul, and the woman had her own body, spirit, and soul, just like a father and a son each have their own body, spirit, and soul. But the woman's spirit was multiplied from the man's, as a child's spirit is still multiplied from the spirit of the child's father. Ultimately all of humanity has the origin of its spirit (giving life, the "breath of life") as multiplied from Adam's one spirit, which came from God when God breathed into Adam. This is similar to how all of us are bodily related to Adam.

So when Adam sinned, and died spiritually, because the original spirit had changed, therefore the other multiplied spirits changed, and all sinned and died because Adam sinned and died and had his eyes opened. This is what Romans 5 and 1 Cor 15 actually say. All die because Adam died, all sin because Adam sinned.
And in a way, Eve was a multiplication of Adam like all Adam's children. The same spiritual change that affected all Adam's children (which we know is true) also affected Eve. And as such, the reason Eve's eyes were opened, and the reason Eve died, was because Adam ate from the tree. And this is in the same way, for the same spiritual reason, that all of his children have had their eyes opened, and died, ever since. The spiritual reason that all of Adam's children would die and sin and have their eyes opened, is the exact same spiritual reason that Eve would die and sin and had her eyes opened.

1 Cor 15:21-22, 45 "For since by man came death, by man came also the resurrection of the dead. For as in Adam all die, even so in Christ shall all be made alive. And so it is written, The first man Adam was made a living soul; the last Adam was made a quickening spirit."

Romans 5 "Therefore, just as through one man sin entered into the world, and death through sin, and so death spread to all men, because all sinned– for until the Law sin was in the world, but sin is not imputed when there is no law. Nevertheless death reigned from Adam until Moses, even over those who had not sinned in the likeness of the offense of Adam, who is a type of Him who was to come. But the free gift is not like the transgression. For if by the transgression of the one the many died, much more did the grace of God and the gift by the grace of the one Man, Jesus Christ, abound to the many. The gift is not like that which came through the one who sinned; for on the one hand the judgment arose from one transgression resulting in condemnation, but on the other hand the free gift arose from many transgressions resulting in justification. For if by the transgression of the one, death reigned through the one, much more those who receive the abundance of grace and of the gift of righteousness will reign in life through the One, Jesus Christ. So then as through one transgression there resulted condemnation to all men, even so through one act of righteousness there resulted justification of life to all men. For as through the one man's disobedience the many were made sinners, even so through the obedience of the One the many will be made righteous. The Law came in so that the transgression would increase; but where sin increased, grace abounded all the more, so that, as sin reigned in death, even so grace would reign through righteousness to eternal life through Jesus Christ our Lord." NASB

In any case, however it worked, Romans 5 clearly states that all died because of Adam's sin. If my thoughts above on this are incorrect as to how this worked, nevertheless the Bible does state that everyone (Eve included) died from Adam's sin. Because of the comparison used of Jesus Christ, saying Eve did not die because of Adam's sin would be like saying someone could be forgiven and have eternal life without Jesus Christ's gift to them of salvation. If you doubt this, I suggest you read Romans 5 again, as I am only saying as its logic dictates.

Now, some people might protest that it is not fair for the woman's eyes to have been opened and for her to have died, because of Adam's sin. How is it any more or less fair than every child born from them, and their children's children, etc, to have had their eyes opened and to have died? Babies die while still innocent, and have ever since the fall. Their eyes are not yet opened in that way, but they still die. This understanding I am teaching actually gives more of a reason as to why this is like it is, than the idea that God breathes "the breath of life" into each child at conception. Yes, God does a miracle to multiply. But God does not add anew. God builds an individual child, and that child's spirit, from what is already there, pre-existing materials, in the case of each child, just as in the case of Eve.

And others might say that the children were like both their parents, born to have their eyes opened, born to die someday. And would say that it was the sin of both the parents, Adam and Eve, in eating the fruit, that caused this upon the children. But this is not what the Bible actually teaches. The Bible teaches that in Adam all die, and that through the sin of Adam, just 1 man, sin passed to all humanity. The Bible even states it was just 1 sin that took place, done by 1 man, and does not state it was 2 sins done by a man and a woman.

"So then as through <u>one transgression</u> there resulted condemnation to all men, even so through one act of righteousness there resulted justification of life to all men. For as through the <u>one man's disobedience</u> the many were made sinners, even so through the obedience of the One the many will be made righteous." Romans 5

And the same spiritual rules of how things work also seem to apply to men, not women, when it comes to the sins of men. The Bible specifies it is the sins of the fathers that are visited on the children to the 3rd and 4th generation. And then there is the example of Jesus, who was one with His Father, but not of the same spiritual nature of His human mother, because He Himself was and is also God.

1 Jn 5:1 "Whosoever believeth that Jesus is the Christ is born of God: and every one that loveth Him that <u>begat</u>, loveth him also that is begotten of Him."

Jesus Christ was begotten of God the Father. The same word for "begat" is used in Matt 1:2 "Abraham <u>begat</u> Isaac; and Isaac <u>begat</u> Jacob; and Jacob <u>begat</u> Judas and his brethren"

A child being begat is intrinsically tied to the father and the spiritual paternal line. There is more to being begat than being sired physically, because also there is a spiritual heritage and line. There is a physical multiplication, but also there is a spiritual multiplication, which gives the body life and makes someone to be a living soul. In some way, the spirit of the father also passes to the children, as multiplied to them. And children come through their mothers, but they are not spiritually given life from her, but from their father. This also explains why lineages in the Bible often leave women out entirely. It is not without a cause, or some sexist thing, but rather the Bible speaks the truth, and it tells a truth of how the spiritual heritage, the life of a living spirit, is passed down, being multiplied. Fathers alone beget their children, and this term is never used of mothers. This proves that the Biblical truth is that there is something fathers contribute that mothers do not, a bottom line which makes it true that fathers should ultimately be understood as generating the child. What the fathers solely contribute cannot be the body, as all modern knowledge of reproduction precludes this. Therefore, it must be the "breath of life" or "spirit" that is multiplied solely from the father of the child, and this "breath of life" is the essential ingredient for the child to become alive and become an individual "living soul".

And the same as if Eve had been Adam's daughter or son, because she came from him, and her spirit was multiplied from his original spirit, death passed from Adam to Eve, by his sin. In a way, God only did ever make 1 human spirit giving life, which then multiplied into more spirits giving life to all men and women. But it was the male, Adam, who carried both the power and the responsibility of the well-being of both of the first 2 humans, and their children, and he was the one given a commandment, to not eat the fruit. Whatever he did that affected his spirit, would affect all other spirits that had been multiplied from his original. He was the original, and all multiplications of his spirit were still tied to him, by spiritual rules of how things work.

So could this be possible, which I think is what the Bible actually teaches and is true:

The reason the woman died and her eyes did open was not because she sinned in eating of the tree, but because Adam sinned in eating of the tree, and because his eyes were opened from eating. And in sinning, his spirit died, so his body died (over time). And because of this, the woman's spirit, multiplied from his, also died, and so her body died (over time). And this is also why all the children of Adam would sin, die, and would have their eyes opened. (The spiritual death here caused an immediate separation from God spiritually, but apparently even the presence of the spirit in a "dead" state was already tied to the body and blood, and continued to give the body and soul life for some time, though eventually the "dead" state of the spirit would catch up to the body, and people would die.)

This also would explain why the woman's eyes were not recorded to have opened until after Adam ate of the tree. If the woman alone ate of the tree, she would not die, because she had not been commanded by God to not eat of it, so it was not sin to her. Therefore, if she ate of it, she had done no sin, and so would not die. She would have been unchanged. And because her spirit was multiplied from Adam's, it's likely she <u>could not</u> have her eyes opened, a spiritual matter of the soul, unless Adam ate. If so, then the reason would be because if she ate she would not know good from evil, from sinning in disobeying God, because it was not a sin for her to eat from the tree.

If Adam had eaten of the tree and sinned, but she had not eaten of the tree, her eyes would still have been opened, and she still would have died. The same as would her children, because he was their father, and he would be the original of their spirits (giving life), and was the original of her spirit also, as all spirits were multiplied from his.

This is why Adam was commanded to not eat of the tree, but the woman was given no such command. Adam had the original spirit giving life, who all spirits were multiplied from. What he chose to do had power to affect the woman and all the children, real power, and so he carried the responsibility of not eating from the tree.

This idea has the weight of the verses included above, and also is entirely allowable by what is said in Genesis, and what is not said in Genesis.

Looking at Romans 5, some might argue that the one sin is "accounted" to Adam, as he was originally given the command to not eat, and making sure the woman did not eat was his responsibility, as he was in charge. But this is not what the Bible actually says, anywhere. Adam was never charged by God to keep the woman from eating from the tree. God only commanded Adam to not eat, <u>but God told the woman directly that she could eat from all the trees</u>. (Gen 1:29)

Many people claim to take the Bible literally. A "day" is a "day", and so on. But in Romans 5, people take the statements as not being literal. But if you want to take the Bible as literal, it literally does say Adam singularly sinned, and by this one sin, death passed to all of humanity. It is not a figurative responsibility, it is a literal one.

We will look in detail at Genesis 3 in more detail next.

Chapter Ten
Genesis – The First Marriage Problems Continued

We have already covered that the reason all sin and die was because Adam sinned and died, as Romans 5 and 1 Corinthians 15 state. We have covered that the woman did not sin in eating from the tree, but rather she was told by God she could eat of all the fruit trees. We already covered that her spirit and body were multiplied from Adam's, like any child, and that this is the case with children also. And so why she died, and could sin, and had her eyes opened was the same reason why the children of Adam would also inherit this same spiritual state. The woman died because Adam died, as was the case with their children. Taking Romans 5 and 1 Corinthians 15 literally, let's look in more detail at what the Bible says happened:

The MAN
walked away from the 6th day having been told by God:
And the LORD God commanded the man, saying, "Of every tree of the garden you(si) may freely eat; but of the tree of the knowledge of good and evil you(si) shall not eat, for in the day that you(si) eat of it you(si) shall surely die.
(in the Hebrew all the "you" are singular) Gen 2:16-17

(See all these singular/plurals for yourself at http://www.ancient-hebrew.org/genesis/index.html)

Then God blessed them, and God said to them, "Be fruitful and multiply; fill the earth and subdue it; have dominion over the fish of the sea, over the birds of the air, and over every living thing that moves on the earth. And God said, "See, I have given you(pl) every herb that yields seed which is on the face of all the earth, and every tree whose fruit yields seed; to you(pl) it shall be for food. Also, to every beast of the earth, to every bird of the air, and to everything that creeps on the earth, in which there is life, I have given every green herb for food"; and it was so.
(in the Hebrew all the "you" are plural) Gen 1:28-30

The WOMAN walked away from the 6th day having been told by God:
Then God blessed them, and God said to them, "Be fruitful and multiply; fill the earth and subdue it; have dominion over the fish of the sea, over the birds of the air, and over every living thing that moves on the earth. And God said, "See, I have given you(pl) every herb that yields seed which is on the face of all the earth, and every tree whose fruit yields seed; to you(pl) it shall be for food. Also, to every beast of the earth, to every bird of the air, and to everything that creeps on the earth, in which there is life, I have given every green herb for food"; and it was so.
(in the Hebrew all the "you" are plural) Gen 1:28-30

Here we see that God told the man he could freely eat of all the trees, but also commanded the man to not eat of the tree of the Knowledge of Good and Evil, before the woman was made. God is not recorded as having given the woman this command. In fact, the woman was directly told by God that all the fruit-bearing trees had been given to them for food, without any exception mentioned in what God told her. At the same time this was reiterated to Adam, but without the exception mentioned.

From the woman's perspective: God told her she could eat from all the trees, and told the man that he could eat from all the trees.

From the man's perspective: God said she could eat from all the trees, but that he could eat from all the trees except for one. There was one tree he was commanded not to eat from, and if he did he would surely die. In front of him, God told the woman she could eat from all the trees.

This is all the man knew at the time. On one hand, he was told to not eat from the tree. On the other hand, God hadn't commanded the woman this, and told her she could eat from all the trees. This was what he knew, and all he knew. Adam knew that he knew something that the woman did not know, and also he had to figure out what to do with it.

As God's command was not repeated, it seems clear that Adam told Eve about what God had said to him before she was made. If we are to assume that God repeated this command to Eve, then we would be putting words in God's mouth, adding to the Bible Words of God that God is not recorded to have spoken. Such is dangerous. If God said it, then it would be recorded, and we must not add Words from God that He is not recorded to have said. Therefore, we can only conclude from God's Word the Bible that we are to understand that Adam relayed information to the woman about what God had said before she was made.

Adam had this most accurate option:
He could have just told her the truth, that while God told her she could eat from any tree, that God told him, before she was made, that he could not eat from 1 tree or he would die. And he didn't know why.

But when we read what the woman believed, which she told the serpent, it becomes clear that the facts of what God said were not relayed to her accurately by Adam.

"Now the serpent was more cunning than any beast of the field which the LORD God had made.
And he said to the woman, "Has God indeed said, 'You(pl) shall not eat of every tree of the garden'?"
And the woman said to the serpent, "We may eat the fruit of the trees of the garden; but of the fruit of the tree which is in the midst of the garden, God has said, 'You(pl) shall not eat it, nor shall you(pl) touch it, lest you(pl) die.'"
(in the Hebrew all the "you" are plural) Gen 3:1-3

The woman believed that God said they both should not eat of the tree, nor touch it, or they will die.

God goes on to twice confirm that His command was singularly to Adam:
Have you(si) eaten from the tree of which I commanded you(si) that you(si) should not eat?" Gen 3:11
(in the Hebrew all "you" are singular)

God confirms for the first time that He said to Adam singularly that "you should not eat."
God could have said, "Have you eaten from the tree I commanded you(si) that 'you(pl) should not eat'?"
But this is not what the text says. When God says "you should not eat", He is repeating his command given to Adam in Gen 1, which reads in the singular, and here also is repeated in the singular. God makes it clear and confirms here that the command to not eat was solely given to Adam.

Then to Adam He said, "Because you(si) have heeded the voice of your wife, "she ate from the tree" of which I commanded you(si), saying, "You(si) shall not eat of it" Gen 3:17

The "you" here is singular in all instances. God confirms a second time that He said to Adam singularly that "you shall not eat of it." God could have said, "that I commanded you(pl) saying 'You(pl) shall not eat of it." But this is not what the text says. It is singular and God's command was just addressed to Adam. Also it is confirmed here that it was spoken only to Adam. This is a 2nd witness by God of what His original command was, even specifying what He said most precisely, and so there are 2 witnesses of God's original command being to Adam alone.

God confirms twice that His command was given to Adam singularly, and was not given to them in the plural. All three times are recorded in the Hebrew, for us to see this. All three times as it is recorded in the Bible, God gave the command to Adam alone, with a singular-tense "you", and not the plural-tense "you" that would show God gave the command to both of them. It is also recorded that <u>God directly told the woman that she could eat of all the trees</u>, and that Adam was also there when this was said.

The woman seemed to sincerely believe what she told the serpent, and had no reason to lie to the serpent. She could have told the serpent, "Well God said he couldn't eat of it or he would die, but I think that applies to me too, and I suggested, and we both agreed to not even touch it." But she didn't say that. Truly, she seemed to believe what she said to the serpent, which is that God said They must not eat of it, and that God said They must not touch it, or They would die. And because she believed what she said, it seems most likely that she was told this, and did not make it up herself. To me, what she said to the serpent shows that she was not the originator of this information. It was told to her, and she believed it, and she did not herself make it up.

And so,
1. because Adam knew God had told the woman she could eat of all the trees (Gen 1:27-29)
2. because she had not existed when God gave him this command to not eat
3. because God spoke the command to the man singularly, in singular tense
4. because the most simple explanation that does not add to the Words of God in the Bible is that Adam told Eve about this command
5. because Eve's understanding clearly was not correct, yet this is what she believed
6. because "not touching" is an obvious addition to what God said which Adam told her about
7. because saying God said "they" when He said "you" in singular, is an obvious addition to what God said which Adam told her about

My conclusion is that Adam lied to Eve.

The most simple and logical explanation is that Adam took a different option than the simple truth, which was to tell her this instead:
He told the woman that despite what God had told her directly, which was that she could eat from all the trees, that there was more that God had said only to him, before she was made. He told her that God had said that they could not eat of this 1 tree, or touch it, or they would die.

Whereas Adam had this most accurate option of the simple truth:
He could of just told her the truth, that while God told her she could eat from any tree, that God told him, before she was made, that he could not eat from 1 tree or he would die. And he didn't know why.

The argument of the man lying to the woman has much weight to it, as when God reiterates his command to Adam twice more, God always addresses Adam in the singular "you" and quotes His command as "you" in the singular and never in the plural. This shows a conflict between what God said which remained consistent, and what Adam was told and what Eve reported. God twice confirms that the instructions to the man were singularly to him.

And let's just be clear on one thing: the Bible calls this the Tree of the Knowledge of Good and Evil. It is not called The Tree of the Knowledge of Using Logic to Tell Truth from Lies. The fact is that both the man and the woman were made to have working logical faculties from the beginning. The man used logic to name the woman, and she used logic even in knowing which tree it was she had been told they could not eat from. Logic and reasoning to tell contrast between truth and lie was already inherent in both of them. They did not gain the ability to use logic from the Tree. But what they did not know was Good and Evil, and they did not understand that the Truth is Good and that Lies are Evil.

And some people might say this was a misunderstanding, perhaps that the woman heard the man wrong or was confused about what he meant. Well, he was with her a while, even with her as she ate. If in her words to the serpent she revealed that she had misunderstood Adam's words to her, why didn't Adam speak up and correct her misunderstanding? Also, how difficult is it to understand the difference between "I'm telling you not to eat or touch this or you will die" and "God said not to eat or touch this or we will die". Do you have a hard time understanding the difference between these statements? Then why would she? Was she dumb?

Or on the other hand, was the man dumb? Was he incapable of finding the words to explain the situation accurately? Really, how hard is it to say the truth accurately, when it is this simple? It is the difference between "God said" and "I say". How hard it that?
If God had not made them capable of understanding words, they wouldn't have been able to understand anything He said to them, so surely they understood the words that they heard. Their brains worked fine in this regard. And I would think anyone smart enough to call a woman a wo-man, "because she was taken out of man" would be smart enough to know the proper words to use to accurately tell the woman what God had said to him. There really seems no room for a misunderstanding.

More evidence is that, in Hebrew, you and you are spelled differently, which I would like you to see.
The *singular* you will (not) eat is תֹּאכַל which seems to be pronounced "tahell".
And the plural you will (not) eat is תֹּאכְלוּ which seems to be pronounced "tahelloo" or "tahelv".

The point being that:
1. they are clearly written differently, and
2. pronounced differently,
Both of which indicates the Bible leaves no room for misunderstanding between God and Adam and Eve.

Is there any reason so far to object that the man could have lied to her about what God said?
If you can believe Eve did wrong by misquoting God before eating of the tree as she spoke to the serpent, then you can believe they both were capable of speaking a lie, a wrongdoing even before they committed a known sin. Eating from the tree was the only known sin. So they would have been innocent of all else. But if you can believe she spoke a lie before the first sin, then you can and do believe they were both capable of wrongdoing before the fall, both able to speak lies, even if they were innocent and God did not account it to them. Then you should have no problem with conceiving that Adam could have spoken a lie, based on principle. If the woman could do wrong, so could he. If she could add to God's Word, so could he, they were both capable of speaking lies and making things up.

And Romans 5 also says, "for until the law sin was in the world, but sin is not imputed when there is no law."
This speaks that there was sin in the world, before the law of Moses showed it to be sin.

As for Eden, I make this analogy:
The law here was a command, to not eat from the tree. So, in analogy, wrongdoing was possible in Eden, even before there was technically a sin committed because of breaking the command. Some people say that Adam and Eve were perfect, sinless, capable of no wrong-doing in Eden. But then how did sin ever get committed in the first place? Also if this was the case, then why were they made so innocent as to not even be ashamed of their nakedness? They were like young children. It's not that they could do nothing wrong, but rather they were innocent of any and all wrongs they did, except for the only thing God had commanded. They were not incapable of doing wrong (as we know it), but God did not account any wrongs to them because they were innocent, completely innocent of them. Where does the Bible say they were incapable of wrongdoing before the first actual disobedience of God's command, the first sin? And if they were incapable of anything wrong, then how did sin occur? And if they were both incapable of speaking a lie out of their mouths, then why is it

recorded that Eve did say that God said "not touch it"? The idea that they were incapable of any wrongdoing or speaking any lies is inherently flawed.

But the Bible speaks the truth:
"When tempted, no one should say, "God is tempting me." For God cannot be tempted by evil, nor does he tempt anyone; but each person is tempted when they are dragged away by their own <u>evil desire</u> and enticed. Then, <u>after desire has conceived, it gives birth to sin</u>; and sin, when it is full-grown, gives birth to death." James 1:13-15
And so before there is sin, there is an evil desire. And so before there was the first sin, there was the first evil desire. And so there was evil, is evil, before sin occurs. And if there can be an evil desire, then there can be wrongdoing, like a lie, even if it was not disobedience to the 1 command God gave.

Is it possible that a good desire led him to lie? This seems unlikely. Someone might argue that he lied to her because he wanted to protect her from the tree. The problem with this is that Adam saw God Himself tell her she could eat of all the trees. As such, Adam had every reason to think that the tree was safe for the woman to eat from. He would have had to assume that he knew more than God, in order to be trying to protect her. But as he saw God Himself tell her she could eat from all the trees, there is no reason he would have assumed that he knew more than God, or the tree was unsafe for her. And he was faced with not knowing why he would die if he ate from the tree, as God did not tell him why. Which would have made it crystal clear in his mind that God knew more than he did, and would contradict the thought that he knew more than God. He knew that God knew more than him, and so there was no way he would have assumed he knew more than God, like assuming a tree would hurt the woman when he saw God told her she could eat freely of all the trees.

Bottom line, if he had a good desire, wouldn't he have just told her the truth of what God said? If he had no other agenda, then it seems he would have just told her the truth. But as he lied, it makes the most sense that he had an evil desire. And if James 1 is correct, then Adam must have had an evil desire before he sinned by eating of the tree, which was the evil desire that conceived and gave birth to the sin of eating from the tree. So as we can know Adam did have an evil desire that was present, that existed and led him to eat from the tree, it makes the most sense to assume that he also had an evil desire which led him to lie.

So what was this evil desire the man had which led him to lie? Truly, he knew that God had given her all the trees to eat from. He was there when God told her this. Which meant he knew that this tree was hers to eat from. It was something she had been given by God, that he had not been given by God. She had a tree given to her by God which he did not have. She had power to eat from it, which he did not have. In a way, she "owned" it, and he did not. So she had a possession that he did not have, and a power that he did not have, and it seems if he could not have this, then he wanted to make sure she would not either. At least effectively, this is what his lie attempted to accomplish. This brings to mind concepts of envy, and of covetousness. Otherwise, why would it bother him if she ate and he did not?

And how might he have felt towards God about all this? Could he have felt insecure in God's love for him, thinking God loved her more, because God would let her do something he could not do? If so, could he have over-compensated, telling himself that God loved him more, and he was more important than she was? If so then this would be pride. Could pride and envy have led him lie to the woman, portraying his own words to her as the Words of God? To me this idea is very reminiscent of Isa 14:14, "I will be like the Most High."

And is this possible because, not knowing right or wrong, good from evil, people still had emotions? Emotions like envy, like anger, or like pride. Without knowing right from wrong, emotions rule. As even now, knowing right from wrong, emotions still rule people's thinking and can be hard to control. What went through Adam's mind and heart? ***It is impossible to know.***

Nevertheless, while we cannot know what went through his mind and was in his heart, I think that he lied to Eve is clear, and in effect assumed a role over her in falseness that was similar to the role God in truth had over him (and her).

And what should have been this:
He could of just told her the truth, that while God told her she could eat from any tree, that God told him, before she was made, that he could not eat from 1 tree or he would die. And he didn't know why.
Somehow became this:
He told the woman that despite what God had told her directly, which was that she could eat from all the trees, that there was more that God had said only to him, before she was made. He told her that God had said that they could not eat of this 1 tree, or touch it, or they would die.

But it is very important to note, that at this time neither the man nor the woman knew the difference between Good and Evil. The man was completely innocent of understanding that bearing false witness about what God had or hadn't said was evil. We know this, as Christians, and as our eyes are open, but their eyes were not yet open, and they were innocent of any wrong they did, like young children. This does not mean they could not do wrong or sin (as we know what is sin), but rather that they were innocent and didn't know when they sinned (as we know it). They did not know right from wrong, and so most likely just went with their emotions and desires.

So what happened from the woman's perspective?
"And God said to them, "Be fruitful and multiply; fill the earth and subdue it; have dominion over the fish of the sea, over the birds of the air, and over every living thing that moves on the earth. And God said, "See, I have given you(pl) every herb that yields seed which is on the face of all the earth, and every tree whose fruit yields seed; to you(pl) it shall be for food." Gen 1:28-29

God told the woman was that she could eat from all the trees, and God told her this directly and Himself in person to her. God also said this to the man along with her. This is one of the few interactions she had with God on her first day. Shortly after she was made, God told her He was giving her dominion over the world and all the animals, and all the plants to eat, and also gave her commands to be fruitful, multiply, and subdue the earth.

Then she was told by Adam that God had told Adam, but not her, about a life-or-death command to not eat or touch 1 tree, or she would die. God tells her one thing, and the man then tells her another. The man seems to reveal that God doesn't bother to warn her about something that will kill her, but the man does warn her. God leaves it to the man to tell her, if he wants to.

What do you think it made her feel when Adam told her that God had not bothered to give her a life or death warning about the tree? How do you think it made her feel when, on top of not eating from the tree which God told her personally she could eat from, she also learned that if she had touched it that it would have killed her? Did she feel that God, her maker, cared if she lived or died? Could she have felt hurt, like God does not love her as much as the man?
Could she have felt like she could not trust God? Could she have felt like God kept important things from her that were essential for her to know? Could she have felt bad that she was made second, and was not as important to God as the man whom God warned about the deadly tree? Could she have felt God cared if the man died, but not her?
Would she have seen the man as being more trustworthy than God, because he warned her and God did not? Could she have come to feel that God must love her through the man, not directly? Did she see the man as protective of her? Did she have doubts in her mind, wondering if the man might be lying to her, as she was not yet made and was not there? If she believed God in what He told her, and chose to not believe the man, could this have made her feel bad, because then she would have felt hurt like the man did not love her, as he lied to her?

It is hard to know how she felt or what she thought, as the Bible does not specifically record how she felt or what she thought, so there is no way to know for sure.

But what we can know for sure is that she was faced with a contradiction between what God told her, and what the man told her. And based on what she told the serpent, it seems that she chose to believe the man, even though what he told her directly contradicted what God had told her.

Why would she do that?
I would describe her as trusting and even somewhat gullible. By nature, she was designed to be trusting and follow the man. She loved the man, and felt he loved her, and so she trusted him in what he told her, for it to be truth. Also, as Adam was there before her, it was believable that something had happened before she was made. In any case, it is clear that she believed Adam, as this is reflected in what she told the serpent.

It also would make sense that her trust in God was somewhat damaged, as God had told her she could eat safely, and then she found out second-hand that no, in fact one tree was deadly to her, and that God could have personally warned her about this, but did not. This seems to have likely damaged her feeling that God loved her, and her trust in God.

Now, she could have chosen to believe what God told her, and believe the man was lying to her, because what he said seemed to contradict what she saw God tell both her and him. But apparently for some reason, she chose to believe God had not told her something of life-or-death importance, rather than believe the man was lying to her. This is probably because she loved him, so she assumed he was telling the truth, but also because she really wanted to believe that the man loved her. But in believing him, she had to also believe that God had left her in the dark, and passed a loving command of protection through the man, instead of giving it to her directly.

And so the man, in lying to her, would have served to have her believe that the way things were was that God loved her through the man, and protected her through the man, instead of God just loving her and protecting her directly. And he also served to have her believe that God let instructions he gave her take precedence over what God told her directly! And she seems to have rather believed all this than to believe that the man lied to her, which probably would hurt her. So she trusted the man in what he said, and believed him.

And so she did not eat of the tree, until after her conversation with the serpent, and what he told her.
"Then the serpent said to the woman,
"You(pl) will not surely die. For God knows that in the day you(pl) eat of it your(pl) eyes will be opened, and you(pl) will be like God, knowing good and evil."
(in the Hebrew all the "you" are plural) Gen 3:4-5

The serpent, who was also made before her, directly contradicted Adam, and thus claimed that what she heard from Adam was not true. She knew the serpent also was around before she was, just like Adam. Both the serpent and the man were made before her, and were both around when this command from God was given, that she had only heard about second-hand.

Adam said that God said they could not eat it nor touch it or they would die.
The serpent said they would not die. But he did not deny that God had said to not eat from the tree.
And so Eve was faced with a direct contradiction. Both Adam and the serpent had been around before her, and she was hearing 2 different stories. She didn't know who to believe.

She knew what God had told her directly face-to-face was that she and Adam could eat freely from all the fruit trees. What would you have thought? Having 2 contradictory second-hand claims, versus what she had heard from God herself, it seems she defaulted to what God had told her first-hand.

She did choose to eat from the tree, and from this it is possible to gather that she believed the serpent that they would not die if they ate, and stopped believing Adam that they would die if they ate. God had told her she could eat freely, directly, and so the serpent seemed to be a second witness to what God had told her. Both God and the serpent indicated she and the man could eat safely, and so this made what Adam told her seem to be a lie. Because she ate, it seems clear that she no longer believed what Adam had told her, but rather believed the serpent, and also what God had told her.

This was likely because what the serpent said more closely confirmed to her what God had told her personally. God said she and the man could eat freely. Adam said they would die if they ate from this one tree, or touched it. The serpent said they would not die. This probably made her think that Adam had lied about them dying if they ate from the tree, and even that Adam had lied about the whole thing he said that God had said. Although, the serpent did not deny that God had said something.

The serpent also said if they ate they would be like God, knowing good and evil. Which she saw as gaining wisdom. With all this confusion, between what God had told her, and what Adam told her, and what the serpent told her, with direct contradictions, it makes sense she would want some wisdom. She probably felt she was lacking something, as what others said was confusing to her.

With the man telling her one thing, and the serpent telling her another, did she decide to fall back onto what she knew God had said to her, which was that she could eat of all of the trees freely? I would think the answer to this is yes. She was hearing 2 contradictory stories second-hand, but God had personally told her that she could eat from all the trees. It seems clear that she defaulted back to what God had personally told her, which was that they could eat freely.
And so she touched the fruit,
"So when the woman saw that the tree was good for food, that it was pleasant to the eyes, and a tree desirable to make one wise, she took of its fruit and ate." Gen 3:6

And in that moment when she touched it, she would have known for sure that what Adam had told her was a lie, because when she touched the fruit, she did not die. And so she ate the fruit, and did not die, and now she might have believed again what God had told her originally, that she could eat from all the trees, and she knew God had told Adam the same thing in front of her. Which would have meant that Adam must have been making all of this up, about them 'not being able to eat or they would die'. She knew God had told her and him at the same time that they could eat freely from all the trees, and she was there when God said this to Adam, after she was made. So she very well might have thought that Adam made all this up, and that what God told her was the entire truth of the matter, which was that they could both eat freely.

So it seems likely that Eve no longer believed Adam, and believed he had lied to her about not eating or touching this one tree. And then perhaps as the serpent seemed to have told the truth, where Adam had lied, and had helped her to stop being fooled, whereas Adam had fooled her, she felt more trust in the serpent than in Adam. The serpent had said they would not die if they ate, and she did not die. And this matched what God had told her and the man, which was they could eat freely. She seemed to totally believe that the fruit was harmless to both of them and would not kill them. The serpent said it would make them both wise, and she seems to have believed the serpent. It would make sense that she wanted wisdom because she was finding things confusing, as those older than her told her contradictory stories. But why did she give the fruit to Adam, why did she want him to eat?

Now, because her husband had just lied to her, and been caught in this lie, that she would die if she touched or ate from the tree… and she now knew he had lied to her…
Do you think that she might have at least felt hurt that he had lied to her? Do you think this made her feel unloved? As this was the first time she had ever felt her trust had been betrayed, that someone she loved and who she thought loved her, had lied to her, fooled her… do you think she might have felt hurt? Do you think she might have thought he was kind of foolish?

I mean, do you think that she thought that maybe he could use some wisdom, because he wasn't all that smart? Do you think that she might have thought if he was a little wiser, that he might not hurt her by doing stupid things like lying to her, and getting proven a liar? That he was foolish to lie to her about things even a mere snake could call him on, as the snake and animals had been there too, before her? Do you think she might have assumed he had no malice, but had just been acting stupid or foolish to lie to her?
These are possibilities…. all possibilities… but it is impossible to say for sure. Yet this seems a likely reason she gave him the fruit: she thought the fruit would make him wiser, and she had a reason to think he needed more wisdom, so she gave him the fruit.

"She also gave to her husband with her, and he ate. Then the eyes of both of them were opened, and they knew that they were naked; and they sewed fig leaves together and made themselves coverings." Gen 3:6-7

Apparently she wanted him to have more wisdom, and in this was trying to help him. It's possible her trust in him, and feeling that he loved her, had been broken by her knowing he had lied to her. Maybe she thought her trust would be repaired, and he would be better, and would change, so she could feel like he loved her again, if he ate and got wisdom. It may be that she did not assume any malice on his part for lying, but rather thought he was just stupid, and thus needed wisdom.
It is impossible to say for sure what she felt or thought, as the Bible does not say. All we know is that she ate, and gave to Adam also.

And while we are here, it is completely in contradiction of the text for anyone to say that the woman wanted to eat of the tree in order to gain power over the man. The serpent told her that in the day both of them ate, both of their eyes would be opened, and both would be like God, knowing good and evil. But it is obvious the woman wasn't wanting power over the man, but rather thought that the tree would benefit them both. She was trusting and gullible. In fact, her trusting nature that caused her to believe what Adam told her, which seemed to be for her benefit, is the same trusting gullibility that made her more vulnerable to the serpent's lies, as this information was also couched as being for her benefit. And she believed it was for her benefit, which is why she offered to her husband also, cause she thought it would be good for him as well. So she could not have wanted to gain power over her husband by being wiser than him, as she offered him the thing that she believed would give wisdom to him, so he could have it also.

So the woman ate. And in truth, God never told her she could not eat, and it was completely allowed by God for her to eat the fruit of this tree. It would cause her no change or harm or death. It was not a sin for her to eat.

But then she gave to her husband who was with her.
Note that based on what God actually had commanded, which was that the man not eat, this is where the woman actually does go against God's commandment, by tempting the man to eat. That she tempted him to eat was her "becoming in the transgression". The word transgression here in Greek is singular, as in 1 transgression, that she was "in"; Not that she committed.
1 Tim 2:13-14 "For Adam was first formed, then Eve. And Adam was not deceived, but the woman being deceived became in the transgression (singular noun)."

This verse does not say she herself transgressed, but that she was IN THE (1) transgression. THE transgression was Adam eating from the tree which he alone had been commanded by God to not eat from. As the woman had been lied to by the man, and deceived by the serpent, she was confused, and did not understand that what would have been right for her to do was to help the man to not eat the fruit, instead of the opposite which was tempting him to eat. Which she might have known, if the man had just told her the truth.

Note that God had not told her that her job was to be a "help meet" and so therefore she should help the man to obey God's command to him. If this was so, God would have told her of the command to Adam, and that she should help him to not eat.

But does anyone doubt that if the man had told her the truth, that he must not eat from the tree or he would die, that the woman's natural response would have been to do what she could to help him to not eat from the tree? And had she been given the truth from the man, which would have been consistent with God's Word she knew He gave to her, it seems doubtful she would have believed the serpent that "they would not die" if "they ate" nor that "their eyes would be opened".

But in any case, does anyone doubt she would have tried to help the man to not eat, if she had known the truth? Every action she took shows her desire to feel loved and to love others. Especially even in handing the fruit to her husband to eat after she ate, showed <u>she wanted to help him</u>. All of this is confirmation that it is in her nature to be helpful, just as she is, just as God made her. Just as she is naturally inclined to be, she is helpful, just as God made her.

The fact that God never charged her with helping the man to not eat from the tree shows that her being a help meet is NOT her job description, or something she has to try to do for the man. It is not a job she was ordered by God to do, to help him not eat from the tree. But rather, this is just a description, an apt one, of what a woman is by her very nature that God designed her to have. If it was her job to be a helper to the man, if this was her purpose in being created was to be the man's helper, then God would have instructed her to help the man. God would have told her of the command of Adam to not eat. But God did not, because she was not created with the job to be his helper, servant, or to serve him. But rather, by her nature, she simply was a great help alike-to-him, matching him, that by nature would help him, not put there to serve him, but who just in being who she is would try to help him for his benefit.

And if it is in a woman's nature as some say, as some make the argument that she "saw and couldn't help but touch", this should be understood as the way she was made by God, and was not a flaw in His design of her. There is nothing wrong in that it looked good for food and was pleasant to her eyes. God completely made her safe and acceptable in the world He put her in. If she wanted to touch and eat from the tree, if it looked good, it was ok, God made her in such a way that she would perhaps like to, and God made the world in such a way that this was entirely fine for her to do so. There was nothing wrong with her in this. It was not a flaw in her design. God made her to naturally feel these things, and put her in a world where it was no trouble to her. And if there truly is some difference here "see and can't help but touch" between a woman and a man, it is not a flaw in the woman, but just a difference, as she was not designed to have to not eat from the tree, and God never told her not to. That's if anyone would want to say this is a flaw that is in a woman's nature.

Note that the woman's eyes are not recorded to have opened until after the man ate the fruit. It is not recorded that he experienced any time delay, as some argue she might have experienced. We do not read here that the woman said "oh my, I'm naked!" before the man did. Nothing indicates any time difference. In fact the verse seems to try to indicate that HE ate THEN both their eyes were opened, as a cause and effect. And then their view of the world suddenly changed. This is in keeping with the spiritual change in Adam's original spirit, affecting a change in Eve's spirit which had been multiplied from his. (See Last Chapter.)

As many have commented, it seems that the man witnessed the entire interaction between the serpent and the woman, and was right there as the woman ate the fruit. And said and did nothing. Why? The Bible does not say explicitly, so it is hard to know for sure. But we will get back to this a little more in the next chapter, after a more detailed look at what the serpent said.

And why did Adam choose to eat when she handed him the fruit? All we know is that "Adam was not deceived" and that he believed eating the fruit would kill him, and therefore he did want to die.

Why did he choose to kill himself?
He knew that God, with his command to him alone, had put him in this position where he could not eat, but she could. He also

knew he had just been proven a liar by the woman as she touched and ate, and that a snake had showed the man he had no real power to keep the woman believing his lie about her long-term. And somehow, all this together, prompted him to knowingly choose to eat something that he believed would kill him.

Might he have been upset that the woman could eat safely, but God had made him so he would die if he ate, and was upset enough about this seeming unfairness that he did not want to live, if she would now eat freely whenever she wanted to, and he could not? Maybe he was overcome with envy, and could not stand that she could eat and he could not, so took the fruit not caring if he died? Maybe he felt it was better to die than to have to live with her knowing that he had lied to her? Maybe it was better to die than to have been shown a liar by one of the animals? Maybe he didn't care what God had told him because he was mad at God that He had told her she could eat, and him that he could not? Might he have wanted to express his anger towards God about this? Maybe he wanted to spite God by killing himself, in pure rebellion? Maybe if she wouldn't obey what he told her like he was a god, then he wouldn't obey what God told him? Maybe he thought if he died there in front of the woman that it would prove she should have listened to him?

And is it possible he didn't care how she would feel, not believing him about any of this dying if they ate stuff, if she were to hand him the fruit and he was to die there in front of her, or how she would feel later, having handed him his death, her not believing there was any danger to him, and leaving her all alone with him dead?

And it makes sense that Adam was aware that she did not believe him, and had been deceived into thinking that the tree was safe for both of them. It makes sense that Adam knew when she handed him the fruit, that she did not believe it would kill him, but that she had been deceived by the serpent.
However, he believed it would kill him, and had not been deceived, as "Adam was not deceived" (1 Tim 2:14).
But to Adam's surprise, he did not die like he thought he would.

Chapter Eleven
Genesis – Setting a Pattern of Marriage Problems

Continuing…
"And they heard the sound of the LORD God walking in the garden in the cool of the day, and Adam and his wife hid themselves from the presence of the LORD God among the trees of the garden. Then the LORD God called to Adam and said to him, "Where are you(si)?"
(In Hebrew this "you" is singular) Gen 3:8-9
(See all these singular/plurals for yourself at http://www.ancient-hebrew.org/genesis/index.html)

Here God calls to Adam and asks him "where are you" which is singular. God was addressing the man, not the woman. As neither one was in sight, why was God not speaking in the plural, to both of them? Maybe God knew if weird behavior was afoot, that Adam was the one to look for.
God was looking for Adam in the garden, because if God couldn't find either of them it meant it was possible that both their eyes had been opened, which meant Adam must have eaten from the tree. It wasn't that God preferred the man over the woman, and that is why God called for the man instead of the woman. Rather, just that if they were hiding, He knew Adam was the one He needed to address.

"So he said, "I heard Your voice in the garden, and I was afraid because I was naked; and I hid myself." And He said, "Who told you that you were naked? Have you(si) eaten from the tree of which I commanded you(si) that you(si) should not eat?"
(in the Hebrew all "you" are singular) Gen 3:10-11

God asks the man if he ate of the tree that God has commanded him (singular) to not eat from. Here God confirms that His commandment was to the man, for the man to not eat from the tree, and this command was meant to the man singularly. This is God's 1st confirmation that His command was to the man only.

The questions here are also interesting. Now, if the woman had her eyes opened, and he did not, do you think he would have understood even if the woman told him he was naked? Would he have hid? I would venture not! No matter who told him, he would have felt no need to cover himself unless he himself had his eyes opened. Look at infants and children, and you can see this, they have no awareness of it when they are naked. Telling a young child that they are naked, will not produce the desire to cover. Until they are old enough that their eyes open this way, they do not understand this themselves. As such, I would argue the question "Who told you that you were naked?" is rhetorical as to who told him, as no one else could have told him and had it produce him hiding. He must have eaten himself, and this is why God then immediately asks him if he ate of the tree.

Note that God does not ask the woman if she ate of the tree, at any point. And God did not ask her why she was hiding, because God knew that if she was hiding it was probably because the man had eaten from the tree and had his eyes opened, so therefore her eyes had opened also. And so God does not ask her if she ate from the tree, first off because she was allowed to, and secondly because God knew that whether she ate or not, she would only know she was naked if the man had eaten from the tree. The woman is not overlooked here at all, but rather God knew that the man's sin would have affected her in a cause and effect way, and so God needed to ask if the man had broken the command God gave him. Which is why God looked to the man in all of this, asking him these questions, and did not ask the woman if she ate from the tree nor who told her she was naked. This was not because she was overlooked or less important to God, or because Adam was His favorite.

"Then the man said, "The woman whom You gave to be with me, she gave me of the tree, and I ate." And the LORD God said to the woman, "What is this you have done?"
The woman said, "The serpent deceived me, and I ate."
Gen 3:12-13

Here we see the man admits he ate from the tree, and implies fault on the part of the woman and even perhaps fault on the part of God who gave her to be with him.
From what he says here to God, Adam makes it out to seem like this was some sort of accident that he ate, like the woman brought him the fruit and he didn't notice which kind of fruit it was.

After having lied to her (perhaps out of envy towards her because she could eat and he could not), and having his lie found out, then knowing the woman handed him the fruit believing it was harmless to him, not wanting to admit his lie, not wanting to live if she could do what he could not, then eating the fruit believing he would die by her hand in front of her, and then surprisingly not dying, it was in keeping with his previous actions that the man then tried to blame her and God for his actions, and act like his eating was an accident and more the woman's fault.

The woman gives the reason that the serpent deceived her. This is also translated as thoroughly deceived, beguiled or tricked. The woman here has just heard moments prior, for the first time clearly, that God told Adam he could not eat from the tree, Adam alone.
And then she hears the man blame her for him having ate, that she ate and gave it to him. She does not deny that she gave it to him. But what was the reason she gave it to him? She believed the serpent, and was deceived by the serpent that 1. Adam would not die and 2. Adam would gain wisdom by eating. She IS NOT saying here that she ate because the serpent deceived her. <u>She IS saying here that she gave the fruit to Adam because the serpent deceived her into giving the fruit to him.</u>

And she also mentions that she ate. There was nothing wrong with her eating, in and of itself. But she had been deceived into also giving the fruit to Adam. And that she gave the fruit to him is what she did wrong, and would be punished for by God.
"The serpent deceived me, and I ate."

As to why she gave the fruit to Adam, she says the serpent deceived her. She also adds that she ate herself, which God and her and Adam knew God had told her she could eat from all the trees. Although she may have been expressing feeling some doubt about eating, based on her self-admission, from feelings of guilt, fear, and shame… these feelings were truly were coming from her participation in tempting Adam to sin… and the death in her spirit caused by the death in Adam's spirit from him having sinned and ate. After he ate and she felt the change of her eyes opening, she realized that there had been some truth to what the man had told her. While the man had lied to her that she could not eat or she would die, and she could gather that God had in fact not said this to him about her… at the moment Adam ate she had felt a change in herself that told her what Adam had said was true for him, that he could not eat. And she saw that it affected her. And so feelings of fear and guilt for tempting him to eat would have made sense. But also her self-admission of eating may have possibly been expressing to God confusion as to why it seemed she could eat, and Adam could not eat, and even irritation that God had not given her the whole picture here, preventing her from being lied to or deceived.

Though the truth was, she made a choice of what she wanted, which was Adam over God. To Eve, at no point had the possibility been removed from the table that God had told the man that he could not eat. And in fact, the serpent did not deny that God had said something to Adam. The serpent only contradicted that they both would die if they both ate, but not that God had said something to Adam about not eating.

The reason she ate from the tree was because it seemed good, to make one wise, pleasant to touch and eat, and because what the serpent said matched what God had told her, unlike what Adam had said. In her defaulting back to what God had told her (with the serpent as a second witness) it seemed there was no longer a reason not to eat from the tree. God said she could eat, the serpent seemed to agree she could eat, only Adam had said she could not. But however, this implies that she likely had always had some doubt and reservation about what Adam had "relayed" to her, which was rightly based on the Fact that God had told her she could eat from all the trees, with Adam right there as a witness. (Gen 1:29)

But she could have guessed, sorting through all this confusion, that Adam might have been telling the truth that God had said he could not eat, before she was made, and the serpent had not denied that God said something to Adam, before she was made. So in a way, she had had one active witness telling a partial truth, and one passive witness who did not deny this same truth: that God might have told Adam to not eat from the tree before she was made. Even with her believing Adam would not die, this was still the case.

Once he had eaten and their eyes were open, Eve realized that Adam had told her some truth along with the lie. And she may have realized that what the serpent told her did not deny that God had said something to Adam before she was made about him not eating.
<u>And so when she gave him the fruit, she was ignoring a possibility that God had told him to not eat.</u> Even though she believed he would not die from eating, as the serpent had deceived her, she still was aware there was some possibility that God had told him (for some reason) to not eat from the tree. And because she ignored this possibility and, in wanting him to have wisdom, gave the fruit to him, this is why she was culpable and punished, even though she had been deceived by the serpent.

The woman states that the serpent deceived her, not that he "lied" to her. So what was the "deception"?
When the serpent said 'you(pl) will not die' Eve made the assumption that Adam had lied about everything he had said, and that they both would not die, as what the serpent told her implied such. However, the serpent was deceptive. The serpent said "you(pl) will not die", but this was only true if she alone ate.

Changing you(plural) to "you both", let's see how this reads:
(the serpent) "And he said to the woman, "Has God indeed said, 'You both shall not eat of every tree of the garden'?"
(the woman) "God has said, 'You both shall not eat it, nor shall you both touch it, lest you both die.'"
Then the serpent said to the woman, "You both will not surely die"…

What is the "deception" here? In his answer to the woman, the serpent is negating her claim that if they both eat or touch, they will both die. What the serpent said could be taken 2 ways, one of which was true and the other which was false. The truth was that they both would not die if she ate or touched the fruit.

The truth was that if "you both" ate it or touched it, they would not both die. If Adam ate, they would both die, and if she ate, neither of them would die. Another way to put this is that if "either" of them ate of it, they would not both die, in her case. And this was the deception. What the serpent said to Eve led her to believe that he was denying that either of them would die if either of them ate. What Eve understood by "you both will not surely die" was "if either of you eat, that individual will not die." In fact, what the serpent said was that it was not true that they would both die if either one of them ate, if the one was her. Also, the serpent said the truth that they would not both die if either one of them touched the fruit. The part which the serpent left out, was that they both would die if Adam ate, and neither one would die if she ate. This may seem a minor point… but it is not! Eve must have later understood that the serpent tricked her, as there was a double meaning to his words, and she had understood the wrong meaning. She thought he meant that neither would die if either one of them ate, her or Adam. We know this because she states that he "deceived" her. Not that he "lied" to her. <u>The deception, in context, is that what the serpent said was partially true, and had a double meaning.</u>

And so this is how what the serpent said was a deception, not a just a blatant lie. What happened here was NOT that the serpent spoke a lie and the woman believed him. She was, in fact, thoroughly deceived, by the double-meaning of the words the serpent chose.

Oftentimes it seems people look at this chapter of Genesis and ponder, "How is it that Eve is so gullible that all you have to do is tell her a lie, and she will jump at believing it?" And I think this implies to people that the woman was just evil, or incredibly stupid. This is not the case. If you understand how complicated all of this actually was, it becomes clear that the woman was thoroughly deceived by a very intelligent deceiver, Satan. And that, in the midst of probably being confused and emotionally hurt by a lie from the man. She really was thoroughly deceived, not just lied to, as 1 Tim 2:14 and 2 Cor 11:3 also confirm,

"And Adam was not deceived, but the woman <u>being deceived</u> became in the transgression(singular)". 1 Tim 2:14

"But I am afraid that, <u>as the serpent deceived Eve by his craftiness</u>, your minds will be led astray from the simplicity and purity of devotion to Christ." 2 Cor 11:3

Another question is did Adam understand what the serpent actually meant? Yes, as "Adam was not deceived" (1Tim2:14), it seems likely that he did understand to a far greater extent. When the serpent said what he said, in context, it is likely that Adam understood that the serpent meant they would not both die if they both ate, but rather that just he would die if he ate. However, it seems very likely that Adam did not know that he and Eve both would die if he ate, but rather just that he would die if he ate.

And so what would seem to be the likely reason Adam said and did nothing as the serpent deceived the woman? <u>Because if he spoke up to contradict the serpent, he was going to have to admit that he lied to the woman. He could not contradict the serpent's statement without getting caught in his own lie to the woman.</u> This seems the most likely reason he said and did nothing. And if this is the case, then it is an important piece of proof that Adam's lie to the woman was intentional, and done knowingly, which he was fully aware of, and not a misunderstanding.

(And the story seems to imply that Satan carefully chose words which were not fully lies, but still were tricky and misleading with double meaning, perhaps so as to claim innocence and not be punished for lying to these innocent humans who were like children. God is just, and it is possible that the woman would not have been held culpable if in fact Satan had clearly told her that "if either of you eat, that individual will not die". Satan's ability to deny malicious intent "oh, she just misunderstood me" may explain why he was still entering the presence of God even in the time of Job, as he still had not gotten caught in outright rebellion against God by that point in time.)

Being deceived, Eve trusted the serpent, who she seemed to think was helping her to stop being fooled by Adam, telling her and him how to get wisdom. And her desire for them to have wisdom, outweighed the possibility that she knew existed, that Adam had been told to not eat of the tree. She didn't believe he would die, but still knew there was some possibility that existed that God had told him to not eat before she was made. Which means it must have mattered to her more for Adam to get wisdom, than the possibility that God might have told him to not eat. The question is, why was it so important to her that the man get wisdom, so much so, that she would disregard a possibility that God might have said the man should not eat of the tree?

I would think the answer is in what Eve did <u>not</u> say to God.

"The serpent deceived me, and I ate."
She does not say that the man lied to her, confusing her, before the serpent deceived her. Why does she not mention that the man lied to her, which set her up to be tricked? The man seemed more than happy to blame her for why he ate. Why does she not tell God that the man lied to her and this confused her? Why does she, knowing the man lied to her, which set her up to be deceived by the serpent, why does she not say anything to God about it? She could have said, "The man lied and confused me, the serpent deceived me, and I ate." But she does not.
She could have said, "I wasn't told by Adam that only he couldn't eat, he lied and said neither of us could eat, and then the serpent used that to deceive me, and also I ate." But she does not.

If the reason she gave the fruit to the man was because she wanted him to have wisdom, because he hurt her, because he lied to her, so she thought he was foolish to lie, so he needed more wisdom so he wouldn't hurt her, so she could feel loved… then it would make total sense that she would tell God, if she was being honest, that she wanted the man to gain wisdom, so he wouldn't hurt her, so she would feel loved by him. Why does she not tell God this? Because in fear she did not want to admit the reason she ignored the possibility that God had commanded him to not eat, in which she now knew was true, was because of her desire to be loved by the man, and towards this she wanted him to have wisdom. She cared more about him gaining wisdom, so he wouldn't do dumb things like lie to her (and get caught in it by a snake) than she did about the possibility of disobeying God. She was guilty of that wrong choice, and seems to have known it. Like the man, she does not admit her guilt. But she does more than this, she does not admit the man's guilt either, or blame him for deceiving her. Why? She does not tell God this because she STILL wants the man to love her. He is blaming her, and she is taking the blame he lays on her, like she thinks if she does that he will love her for it.

Why does she take the blame the man puts on her?
She assumed that he lied to her because he was dumb, which is why she wanted to give him the fruit so he could get wisdom. So last we checked, she believed he lied to her about her dying from eating and touching the tree, because he was dumb. She gives him the benefit of the doubt. But even after hearing that God had only given the original command just to the him, the man... the woman now assumes that he was dumb and didn't understand God right when God gave this command to Adam the first time, instead of assuming he lied out of any malice. She goes from believing he lied to her, just making it all up cause he was dumb, to believing he was dumb when he heard God the first time, and that he misunderstood God. She really just assumes he meant her no malice, and that he ate of the tree having been deceived like she was, thinking it was harmless. And so rather than trying to tell God about the man's part in confusing her by lying to her, rather than tell God that the man never told her clearly that he alone had been told that he could not eat, the woman accepts the man's blame on her and does not defend herself... because she STILL really wants to believe the man loves her, and is not intentionally lying to hurt her, but is just dumb. He lied to her, and she was confused, but as he only partially lied to her, she blames herself and gives him the benefit of the doubt, as to why he is blaming her before God for what he has done.

In giving him the benefit of the doubt... it seems she thinks that the man was also deceived, and that he thought the tree would not harm him. It seems the idea does not cross her mind that the man was trying to kill himself in front of her, for any malicious reasons. It seems the idea does not cross her mind that envy or pride or anger are why he ate, knowing he would die. Remember, WE know "Adam was not deceived", but SHE did not know this (1 Tim 2:14).

She likely thought that he also believed it was safe, because she did not die. When he blames her, she thinks he is being honest, that he really did just eat because she wanted him to, to gain wisdom, in innocence of any danger, and that he originally bungled sharing with her God's original command because he must have been dumb and just misunderstood God in the first place. The idea that he would kill himself in spite of God, and out of envy or resentment towards her being able to do what he could not do, doesn't seem to cross her mind. It seems she really cannot fathom that he resents her, let alone enough to kill himself and leave her alone, and at that, alone and having handed him the instrument of his death.

So she accepts his blame, and does not defend herself. Again, she probably just thinks he was dumb, and misunderstood what God told him when God originally commanded him, and therefore probably never meant to intentionally lie to her in the first place. And so she believes she should have not stopped trusting him, and was wrong to have trusted the serpent instead. The man was dumb and didn't hear God correctly, but he did try to warn her, so she goes right back to believing he is just dumb, and does blame herself for not believing him when he lied to her, because he at least tried to warn her, even if he was dumb and relayed the message incorrectly. She gives him the benefit of the doubt. She believes it would have been better to have followed his half-truth, and faults herself for just not understanding he was dumb. It seems she is in absolute denial that he lied intentionally, and insists on believing he is just dumb and got confused, but meant her well!

And so instead of putting blame back onto the man for confusing her and lying to her, in what she says to God, she assumes he did not mean to lie to her, but being dumb misunderstood God's original command to him in the first place, and only accounts blame to the serpent, giving the man the benefit of the doubt. Again, because she really wants to believe that he loves her, she assumes he is stupid, not that he had evil intent towards her. This seems very likely.

And so this is what can be seen in what she did <u>not</u> say to God.

And then God punishes the serpent, not asking the serpent if this was true or not, because God knew what the serpent had done. Just to pause a moment on this, if anyone wants to know where marriage problems came from, this is it. It was not from the man or the woman, but from the Devil. The book of Revelation teaches that Satan was that serpent of old. (Rev 12:9, 20:2) Before the serpent came along and attacked this marriage, it had been surviving and neither had eaten from the tree. It was a precarious balance but it was functioning. The problem was that once this marriage was attacked, it did not defend itself. Nor, being innocent of Good and Evil, that the truth was good and lies were evil, were they understanding of this attack. They were clueless that their own internal beliefs, lies to themselves, self-delusions, were evil. They were clueless that believing what makes you feel good, if it is a lie then it is evil. Even though it may not be disobedience to God, a sin, it is still evil. That your emotions, your heart's beliefs, and the thoughts of your heart, the thoughts of your emotions, can lie.

And Jesus Christ taught this concept repeatedly: that what is in the heart and mind does matter, not just your actions (Mt 5), and that out of the heart (Mt 15:9) come evil thoughts and all evil actions. And this all explains why the Bible repeatedly says "thoughts of the heart" and not "thoughts of the mind", because since the beginning, people's thoughts and logic have come from the heart, from emotion.

Still, neither man nor woman had fallen of their own accord up to this point in disobeying God's command. It was only the interaction with Satan which brought about the fall. Without that interaction, there is every reason to think the marriage and innocence would have continued on in bliss and peace, and with no one eating from the tree. It may have been an accident waiting to happen, like a house of cards, but it took an outside influence which was the serpent, like a hand lifting a foundation card piece, in order for it all to fall down and for sin to be committed.

Yet, God knew the marriage would come under attack, and had forearmed them to be safe from it, if they obeyed God. And in Adam eating from the tree, and in the woman tempting him to eat from the tree, neither of them obeyed God's singular command for Adam to not eat from the tree.

"So the LORD God said to the serpent: "Because you(pl) have done this"
The "you" here is plural. As such this "you" seems to be directed at the serpent and the woman.
What had they done together? Tempted the man.

Next comes the consequences to the serpent and the woman,
"You are cursed more than all cattle, And more than every beast of the field; On your belly you shall go, And you shall eat dust All the days of your life. (the other "you" are singular)
And I will put enmity Between you and the woman, And between your seed and her Seed; He shall bruise your head, And you shall bruise His heel."
To the woman He said: "Multiply, I will multiply your pains, and your conception in pain you shall bring forth children; Your desire will be for your husband, And he will rule over you." Gen 3:14-16

The only place in which the woman seems to be told "because you did this, then this" is in the plural "you" directed to the serpent in God's opening statement. The woman's crime is not stated to be eating from the tree, rather her only crime was specifically in her participation in tempting the man to eat the fruit of the tree. While she was gullible, deceived, she should not have offered the fruit to the man, even if she had eaten it herself already. In the consequences of the fall, the woman is not specified to have been in trouble for eating from the tree, and the consequences on her are not specified as from disobedience to a command God gave her, but rather for what she did with the serpent in tempting the man.

Now, God knew everything that had been taking place in both of their hearts, and all that had happened. And God found it fair to punish the woman for tempting the man. Why? Because Adam said God had ordered them to not eat from the tree, or they would die, before she was made. The serpent who was also around before she was made said they would not die, and the serpent did not deny that God had said they should not eat of the tree. God told her and him directly that they could eat from all the trees, so it is understandable that she believed God and thought Adam to be a liar when she touched, and ate, and did not die. But Adam said God had told him not to eat it before she was made, and the serpent did not deny this. She had two witnesses that seemed to confirm something happened before she was made, and it's not like she was unwilling to believe something had happened before she was made.
Even believing that she was permitted to eat, Adam still might have been told to not eat it, and even the serpent did not deny this. She knew it was possible Adam had been told not to eat from the tree, even though she believed the serpent that he would not die from it. And so on one hand she knew there was
a <u>possibility</u> that God had told Adam to not eat before she was made, and on the other hand it seems she wanted him to eat, likely to gain wisdom, so he would not do dumb things like lie to her, which hurt her, and made her feel unloved, so he would change, so she would feel like he loved her. So she was culpable because she chose wanting Adam's love over God and obeying Him.

So then why was the woman punished? It was not because she ate of the tree, but because she participated in tempting Adam to eat of the tree, she was deceived/tricked into doing so, but still she tempted Adam to sin against God, <u>and aware this is what she *might* have been doing</u>.

As Jesus said, in Matt 18:7
"How terrible it will be for anyone who causes others to sin. Temptation to do wrong is inevitable, but how terrible it will be for the person who does the tempting."
This is why the woman was punished, and God said he would multiply her pains and cause her to have pain in childbirth. As for the rest, He did not say that He would do these things, nor was He advocating them, but rather just said they would happen, as negative consequences of the fall.

As to the woman's punishments, note that the "he will rule over you" is not God giving permission, but rather just a statement of what will happen. And this is in a list of the negative consequences of the fall, a list of bad things, not good things. <u>And God never gives Adam any authority here to rule over the woman, as He is not even speaking to Adam, but to her.</u> Nor is God saying that He will do this or cause this to happen. God specifies that He will multiply her sorrow and cause her pain in childbirth, and that is all God says that He will do. The rest are just natural consequences that God tells her will follow. Which also include that she will keep returning to her husband, leaving and returning, or that she will argue and debate with him (teshuba), or as some may see it, that she will desire for him to love her (desire). And this while he dominates her, rules over her, which is a <u>negative</u> thing.

So, what was likely her Achilles heel? She wanted the man to love her. She chose the possibility of something that would help him love her, over the possibility God had said he must not eat the fruit.

What was likely his Achilles heel? Pride and power. He wanted control over the woman like God had over him, and to be the most important of the two. He chose to disobey God in envy and rebellion and to die, over her being able to do 1 thing he couldn't do, and not wanting to have to admit it to her.

And it seems likely it was pride, because of the hypocrisy inherit in it, because he already had been shown what might have seemed (to him if he was proud) like some preferential treatment, being made first, naming the animals…. yet could not bear another to even seem to receive any preferential treatment. It was like he had to be the most important and in control, like God was. So I think it was pride, and also power.

Then to Adam He said, "Because you have heeded the voice of your wife, "she ate from the tree" of which I commanded you, saying, 'You shall not eat of it':
(In the Hebrew all the "you" are singular) Gen 3:17

A couple of notes on this verse. First, the word "you" here is singular in all instances. God did not say that "they" could not eat from the tree, but here confirms a <u>second time</u> that He said that the man, masculine singular, must not eat of it. On this final occasion, God even makes it very specific that what He commanded He did so by <u>saying</u>: "I commanded you(si) <u>saying</u> "You(si) shall not eat of it." For those that seek "2 witnesses" in God's Word, here you have them. God Himself witnesses twice as to what He accurately said the first time He said it.

The second point is that the verb "eat" here in "she ate from the tree" is in a third person feminine singular form. This means that it is referring to the woman eating. Most translations render this as the man "hath eaten" from the tree. This is not correct. The verb is in the feminine form and must be referring to the woman. The way it is written above is more accurate. (See and compare esp. 1 Sam 1:18, also 2 Kin 1:10,12, Jud 9:20, וַתֹּאכַל) Or perhaps "heeded the noise of your wife as she ate from the tree, of which I commanded you…"

What seems to have happened here is that when the woman ate, she may have told the man "I ate from the tree" and handed him the fruit. Or it could be that Adam only heard the sound she made as she ate from the tree, as this word "voice" also just means sound or noise, and "heeded" it. And once he heard her, the man decided to eat also.

God's emphasis here is not that it was evil for Adam to listen to his wife, as a matter of principle, but rather that what she said or did should not matter if it directly conflicted with what God had commanded him.

Next we see the consequences of the man eating the fruit of the tree, including death:

"Cursed is the ground for your sake; In toil you shall eat of it All the days of your life. Both thorns and thistles it shall bring forth for you, And you shall eat the herb of the field. In the sweat of your face you shall eat bread Till you return to the ground, For out of it you were taken; For dust you are, And to dust you shall return." (in Hebrew all the "you" are masculine singular) Gen 3:17-19

As already discussed in the first part of this series of articles, because the man's spirit dies, and the woman's spirit was multiplied from his, she died because he died. And for the same reason her eyes were opened. And for the same reason all his children would die and have their eyes opened to know good from evil. The woman did not die because she sinned, but because the man sinned and died, spiritually. And because of this she, and all the children, would die, sin, and have their eyes opened.

If the woman had tempted Adam, and he had said no… neither of their eyes would have been opened, and neither would have died in their spirits. So this is how Adam could have actually protected her: by obeying God and sticking to His precise Word.

And the woman was designed by God to be as she was… the same trusting nature that led her to follow Adam's instructions to her in the first place, to not eat from the tree, unfortunately also made her gullible and vulnerable to evil, to eat from the tree. God knew the way that woman had been made could prove to be a double-edged sword, she would trust her husband, and follow him. But maybe also God knew she might trust anything else that might come along. This maybe is why God set things up so that even if she did eat of the tree, it would not do anything to her. In fact, she was entirely safe from death, as long as Adam obeyed God. And this is why God did not put the command on the woman that she must not eat of the tree in the first place, as there was no reason for her to not eat from it, as it would cause no harm in and of itself.

It was never up to Adam to arbitrate whether the woman would live because he warned her, or to die because he did not warn her. Adam was inherently given control by God over the situation and Eve in that If Adam killed himself, he would kill her also, and if Adam lived, she would live also. Adam could not let her die, and himself live. Either they both died, or they both lived, based on Adam's obedience. Adam had the authority to kill the both of them or protect the both of them by obeying God. But he did not have the authority to let her come to harm while he remained fine. The idea that she could eat and die, while he didn't eat and was fine, is an illusion and a lie. They were one flesh. What he did to her, he did to himself. How he loved himself, was how he loved her. And on the other hand, she could eat from the tree, and they would both be fine. What she did to herself, she did to him. They were one flesh. They were completely bound to love the other as they loved themselves, in what either one might choose to do.

The bottom line was that even before Adam knew sin, he did wrong, adding to God's word in saying the woman could not eat, saying she could not touch and putting his word on equal level as God's to her, and not caring what God had said, and then sinning. And Eve was deceived by the serpent, but also lied to by her husband. This led to her not believing what her husband had told her. He had told her she would die if she touched, but she did not die when she touched, so she ate, and did not die, nor feel any different, and so she was deceived and offered him the fruit as well. And in this she tempted him to sin.

Had he not sinned, though, even while tempted by her, it is questionable as to whether she still would have been punished as severely for tempting him. In any case her eyes would not have opened, and she would not have died. Much of her burden came about because the man had fallen into sin, if he had not, she wouldn't have had to die. And what the man did before he knew of sin, like adding rules to control her, and adding his rules to God's Word making his rules equal to God's Laws… after the man had sinned and knew of sin, the man continued to do the same things…. dominating her, ruling over her, the very same things that had eventually led to his own temptation by her, and his sin.

And women still can be easily deceived and gullible, in wanting to be loved.

What was the first way the man "ruled over her"? The first way he dominated her? He called her a new name, actually a nickname, which he insisted on calling her.
"And Adam called his wife's name Eve, because she was the mother of all living." Gen 3:20

Now, just think about this. God has just said that He will cause her pain in childbearing, terrible pain, as a punishment for tempting the man to sin. This of course sounds frightening, something you would dread. The man starts to call her a word that literally means "makes known life" or "life-giver", a term that the Bible even says he called her because she would be the "mother of all living".

Her name was already "Woman" which meant "taken out of man" and was a term of endearment and love for her. There was no need whatsoever for her to have a new name, **She already had a name!** But now he start to call her "life-giver".

What he did here was to give her a nickname, that he insisted on calling her, as an act of dominating her. It was mean for him to do this, as the name had a double meaning, and he might as well been calling her "child-birther-in-terrible-pain" every time he addressed her. This nickname he gave her was designed to make her think about God's punishment of painful childbirth that she would endure, every single time he addressed her. And as there was no one else around to call her anything, no doubt the name did stick, and he probably insisted on the children calling her that as well.

Excuse me? His name was "man", what if she turned around and started calling him "ground-tiller"? So every time she addressed him he was reminded of his punishment of having to work the land?

So Adam went from lying, seemingly to try to control her, likely in envy, to make sure she wouldn't have something he couldn't have, wouldn't do something he couldn't do, likely making her feel like he was between her and God, without caring how that might affect her, effectively making his rules into God's commands to her, likely feeling sure in pride that all this was A-OK because he was the first one made and the more important one, even deciding to kill himself in front of her, knowing she handed him his death deceived that it would not hurt him, not caring how him dying at her hand right in front of her might affect her either, and all that was BEFORE he actually sinned.

And after he sinned, God warned the woman "he will rule over you". And as soon as God is done telling Adam his punishment for his sin, Adam turns around and let's Woman know that he is going to address her as "life-giver", her painful punishment, from then on out. And so the "rule over" her began that God had warned her about.

And I think that at this point, when Adam tried to rename her "life-giver" Eve may have finally realized something. I think this was so obviously mean a name, so obviously cruel a name, that all of her delusions that the man was just dumb fell away. Prior she had been giving him the benefit of the doubt, accepting the blame he placed on her, assuming he had just misunderstood God's command to him, believing he had no malice towards her. But when he turned around and called her a name, designed to remind her of her dreaded punishment, I think her self-delusions broke down. She could see clearly that the man really just did not love her, and really did have malice towards her. There simply was no other explanation for why he would choose to call her that name, or give her a new name in the first place. She could see clearly that he in fact really did have malice towards her... and whereas she had never felt completely heartbroken before, now she did. She could no longer give him the benefit of the doubt.

"Also for Adam and his wife the LORD God made tunics of skin, and clothed them.
Then the LORD God said, "Behold, the man has become like one of Us, to know good and evil.
And now, lest he(si) put out his hand and take also of the tree of life, and eat, and live forever" — therefore the LORD God sent him(si) out of the garden of Eden to till the ground from which

he(si) was taken. So He drove out the <u>man</u>; and He placed cherubim at the east of the garden of Eden, and a flaming sword which turned every way, to guard the way to the tree of life."
Gen 3:21-24

Now, let's not make the same mistake twice. Who does God kick out of the garden of Eden?
Here we see God, in His Mercy, kicks the man out of the garden. Why? So that Adam cannot take from the tree of life and eat, and live forever in this sinful state. And also, so the woman would not also be trapped forever in this sinful state, because if Adam became immortal in sin, so would she also. And the Hebrew here also singularly points to Adam. It does not say "them" and is not plural. It just says Adam got kicked out, as if he the man Adam singularly had eaten, then they both would have become immortal, and in a state of sin, perhaps meaning they could never be redeemed. And conversely, if the woman ate from the tree of life, it would not affect her. As such there was no reason why it was a danger for her to be allowed to remain in the garden. Nothing here indicates that God kicked the woman out of the garden of Eden. From this passage, the clear meaning is that God let the woman remain in Eden, and kicked the man out. Not only that, but God placed a cherubim there with a flaming sword to keep Adam out of the garden.

And so the word in Genesis 3:16, which is "teshuba", now has new meaning in context. The word means a repetitive returning. God told the woman that her return would be to her husband, and that he would rule over her.

And so we can picture from this verse that the man was driven out of the garden, and the woman was left alone in the garden. She could eat from all the trees, and had the garden to herself. And as long as she was there, the man could not reach her. It is unknown how long she stayed there, perhaps crying and lonely. After Adam had just nicknamed her "life-giver" which was a name which referred to her punishment of pain in childbirth, she may have not wanted to see the man for a while. She was likely heartbroken, and now had to face many painful truths about why Adam had done the things he had done. She was taking time to pick up the pieces of these recent events, and piece it all together.

God had told her, taking the Hebrew most literally, that "multiply, I will multiply your pains". But now it becomes clearer as to what was meant. It seems that God meant if she chose to multiply, that He would multiply her pains. In fact, she was alone in the garden soon after, the man kicked out, shows that there was a choice involved here. If she stayed in the garden, the man could not reach her, and so she was effectively given the choice to not multiply. God did not force her to decide to have children with Adam, or leave her unprotected from Adam if he chose to force himself upon her. Adam was gone, and she was protected. She had the choice to stay in the garden, with all her needs provided for, and to not have children, and even to never see Adam again, but it seems she would also eventually die there in the garden. God's punishment to her was actually only partially a pronouncement, but also partially a warning. If she chose to multiply, then God would multiply her pains. Although it is likely she did start to have pain with menstruation even still while in the garden.

Also, it seems that God was warning her that if she returned to the man, that he would rule over her. Not that she had to return to him, it was her choice. But that if she did, that he would rule over her, and would dominate her. And with her new nickname, his parting blow, she had already had a taste of what that meant.

Alone in the garden, protected, food well-supplied, Eve had everything that she needed to survive physically. She was safe from harm, even if she did have periodical pains. But if she returned to the man, she was warned he would rule over her. And she knew it was also likely or possible if she returned to the man, that she would multiply, and if she did so, that God would multiply her pain. In fact, the woman had many reasons to never leave the garden, and never return to the man. So why did she?

There are several reasons that seem possible, and one I believe is the most likely.

One could say she was hopeful that Adam would change and be nicer to her. On the other hand, she knew God had warned her that he would rule over her, and so far that seemed like a painful thing. She may have still wanted Adam to love her, and have had hope that he would if she returned to him. But she also knew God had said he would rule over her, which she did not think she would like at all, based on what she had already seen.

One could say she hoped to have children and to not be alone and take comfort in love between her and them. This is a possibility. And depending on how long she stayed in the garden, the woman may have seen animal mothers in nature give birth, and have babies, and come to decide she wanted this. On the other hand, she had been warned it would be very painful, and that God would multiply her pain if she chose to multiply. She likely already had menstruation pain, and probably did not like the idea of that pain being multiplied if she multiplied. And she had never seen a human child before, nor did she know what it might be like to have a baby, as she had never seen one. Really, neither the man, nor children, were necessarily a strong enough motivation for her to leave the garden, as both motivations had major drawbacks of pain and being dominated.

I believe the reason she chose to leave the garden was this:
"And I will put enmity Between you and the woman,
And between your seed and her Seed,
He shall bruise your head, And you shall bruise His heel."

Woman knew that God had said she would have a seed that would defeat the serpent. She probably wondered about this, and thought about this word that God had spoken. God had said it would happen, that her seed would be victorious over the serpent. God had said it would happen, and she wanted it to. She hated the serpent, and wanted her seed to defeat the serpent. And so I believe this is the reason why she chose to leave the garden. If she did not return to Adam, even though he would rule over her, and if she did not leave and multiply, even though God would cause her pain if she did, then her seed would not live to defeat the serpent, whom she hated.

And so she left the garden, and returned to Adam.
"And Adam knew Eve his wife; and she conceived, and bare Cain, and said, "I have gotten a man from the LORD."

There is proof that this may have been her primary reason for leaving the garden and having children. She did seem to be looking for her seed that God had spoke of who would defeat the serpent. Unlike how most translations read, the Hebrew here does not say "I have gotten a man from the LORD". The verse in Hebrew does not contain the word "from". (Compare Josh 24:15, 2x, Deut 6:13)
Rather, the woman said,
"I have gotten a man – the LORD(!)"
She was anticipating the one whom God had spoke of, her seed who would crush the head of the serpent. And at first, she thought her son was the one God had spoke of.

She came to realize this was not the case, as time progressed, and she had more children. Nevertheless I think she accepted this, while still looking out hopefully for the one, her seed, which God had said would defeat the serpent. I believe she was looking for him until the day she died, anticipating the one God had spoke of, and perhaps taught her children to look for him as well.

One more thing...
I think it is important to know the rest of the story...

For instance, in the joy of motherhood, seeing her children grow, and actually living out being the mother of all living, I think the nickname forced onto Eve stopped bothering her so much and took on a new and better meaning for her. While at first this nickname was given with meanness, as she actually became a mother of all the living, I believe she became happy with the name. It was what all her children called her. It honored that all those around her had come through her, she was the mother and grandmother and great-grandmother, etc, etc, for probably 900 years worth of generations. It became a nickname that esteemed and honored her, not hurt her.

And I would venture to say that no one blamed her for what had happened, for death or for sin. She probably told her side of the story to many, and what actually had happened, how she was deceived both by her husband and the serpent, became apparent. I think the people knew, back then, who was responsible for the fall. First off the story was told orally back then, from her to others, so there was no confusion as to the scriptures' reading. And part of why I say this with some certainty, is because of what the Bible indicates became of Adam.

Apparently people knew what had happened, while he lived.

When I first read this, understanding it, it shocked me. It might shock you too. This is what Job knew... I found this in Job 31:
"If I covered my transgressions as Adam, by hiding mine iniquity in my bosom:
Did I fear a great multitude, or did the contempt of families terrify me, that I kept silence, [and] went not out of the door?"

Adam lived for 930 years. And he had many sons and daughters. And as the people grew in number, over those 930 years.... they became a multitude. And people knew who Adam was, the first man, who tried to cover and hide his iniquity in his bosom, which comes from the word "cherish", that which is cherished, in other words, his wife. He tried to hide his rebellion and transgression in his wife. But obviously Job knew this, which means this attempt failed, and the people knew this as well. In Adam's day, the people knew who was responsible for the first sin that brought sin and death into the world, and that he was the first to speak a lie. A world of sinful people.... and they apparently hated him, blamed him for death and hardship, and he became terrified of them. So much so, that eventually in fear, he stopped talking and would not go outside of his home. Living over 900 years, he may have lived this way for over 500 years, or more.

To live in that kind of shame, feeling that much hatred, having so much regret, so very much regret, for being the one by whom death and sin came into the world…

It is sad, because he was like a child. He must have looked back at his early time in Eden like one looked back with the understanding of right and wrong of a 3 year old. He was different then, he was innocent, in so many ways he was like a little boy. He did not know good from evil, like a child, neither of them did. And no more than you would hate a 3 year old who ate a piece of fruit you told him not to eat, or envied that his friend could have some…. I mean yes, it's evil, but he was no different than a child.

You typically don't have a child, that eats a piece of fruit they were told not to eat, and as a result, everyone on the planet hates him. For someone who was like a child, eating a piece of fruit? Then the world hates you, hates you, and you grow so terrified you will not leave your house, you will not even speak…

It is just heart-wrenching. And who was his help, in this time? Who was the one who probably still loved him, while the rest of the world hated him? That would be Eve. And so I think eventually, he came to appreciate her like God had wanted him to, and they made up. At least I hope so.

But for thousands of years, what became of Adam, has been what women have endured. Today in some countries, women hardly speak nor leave their homes. I imagine women covered in burkas, beaten, isolated, having no rights. Even in Jewish history, this was the case to a large extent. And Adam set the nature of men, all men, that his iniquities would be visited upon men, that they would also try to dominate and rule over their wives, and in many cases, women have been forced into silence and being homebound, and abused, and hated. And it extended from one wife, to all women.

But still… it just strikes me as true, that really, Adam was just a man. And like any man today, he had some faults, but he really was no worse. We have no grounds on which to judge him, he sinned, we sin, we are all like him. He was just a man. He made mistakes, he disobeyed God, but he was and is only responsible for his sins, not the sins of every other person.

Because the truth is that no one, no man, no woman, is capable of not sinning without God's help. You or I, without Jesus, probably could have done no better than they did, we are just like the first man and woman, we are like them, and they are like us. We are all sinners, having evil desires before actual "sin" has been birthed, doing wrongs even when we were innocent as like children, and didn't know.

Adam broke the command, not having been deceived, he just broke it, out of his evil desires. Eve was deceived by the serpent, lied to by the man, and helped him to break the command, also out of her own evil desire. Yes, she wanted to be loved, but she placed her desire for a man's love above her desire to obey God. So they both did wrong ultimately because of their own desires, that they put before God and His Word. So there's no good pointing fingers at either gender of humanity, because like we today would fail, any man or woman, so he also failed, and she failed. Because none of us are good enough on our own account. The Glory is God's.

Truly, Eden should not be looked at as something that "might have been" but was lost, but rather was a lesson for everyone to learn from. So we could all learn that even if God told 1 person to not do 1 thing, and all else was overlooked, that not 1 person could do this and be good enough. No one could. No one is good but God. That's why we all need grace, and mercy, and Jesus Christ.

Eve believed in the Savior first, and I think Adam did too, and while they did not know His name, they knew of the 1st prophecy of the Savior who was to come, who would crush the head of the serpent. And Adam and Eve were the first told of him, and I think they believed He would come, and would defeat the one who attacked them and their marriage so that they fell into sin, who was the serpent, Satan. And this Savior to come who would defeat their enemy was and is the Lord Jesus Christ.

And the same is true today, the enemy of all marriages, and all people, is not the man, nor the woman, but Satan, who is our mutual enemy. And it is Jesus Christ who has and does defeat him.

Chapter Twelve
Lessons from the First Marriage

In the story of Adam and Eve, we can see that truly, each of them chose their desire, whether desire for love of a man, or desire for God-like control over others, they chose their desires over obeying God and His Word. And truly "Your desire/return/argument (teshuba) will be to your husband and he will rule over you" has been played out in history ever since, that she wants him to love her, argues with him, leaves and returns to him, and he does all sorts of things to control and dominate her.

God said this would happen as a fact. The reason why is because they would continue on as they had, choosing their desires that they wanted more than Him. This was their choice, and He was not going to stop them from their choice, as they had free will. And by their nature, by their choices they made, of their desires that were more important to them than God's Word and obeying God, it all was only going to continue.

And again, the ultimate reason why the fall into sin happened was because the serpent, Satan, interfered and intentionally attacked the man and the woman and the first marriage. They, in innocence, were in good standing with God. And they likely would have continued on that way indefinitely, except for outside interference from the enemy.

A Christian man is not the enemy, nor a Christian woman, but rather the Devil is the enemy. And using their desires, sins and weaknesses to pit one against the other is exactly what happened in Eden, and exactly what Christians today should be wary of, within marriage or without. The story of the fall is one that helps us to better understand the nature of men and the nature of women in their weaknesses and faults. It can help us to better understand ourselves, other people, and humanity around us, including the fallen world that is lost.

It is a sad story. And I cannot say I am 100% sure I have gotten it all right. But I do think the view I have presented has as much or more Scriptural backing, based on what is actually there in the

Bible, than the other ones I have heard. It is a sad story, and for most of the world, and some of the church, the lessons that should be learned from this story have not yet been learned.

But today, we are saved by grace through faith, and God has made a way. Today, in Jesus Christ, there is redemption for people and for marriages. For God gives the fruit to us of self-control, to overcome sin, temptations, and gives wisdom to us to make good choices. We have been forgiven in Christ Jesus. And God has restoration for what has been broken for so long, which is marriage.

And in this time, God has told husbands to love their wives as their own bodies, to love them self-sacrificially, to honor them as equals, and to not be harsh with them, so they will respect their husbands. And God has told wives to submit themselves to their own husbands. But none of it will work without obeying God's Word, and trusting God, as without loving Him more than anyone else, ourselves included, and it never did work without God and His Word being of the most importance. And as we are sanctified in each of our lives, and as the sin nature grows ever weaker in its hold on each our lives, and as we obey God, there can be restoration for marriages.

I believe this version I have presented is the more accurate based on what the Bible does and does not say. It certainly has one thing going for it more than any other I have heard, which is lessons to be learned from it, which match the heart and spirit of the Lord's words in the New Testament. (And also the Old Testament, "Every word of God [is] pure: he [is] a shield unto them that put their trust in him. Add thou not unto his words, lest he reprove thee, and thou be found a liar." Prov 30:5-6)

What **should** have happened? What did God want to happen with Adam and Eve?
The un-chosen option:
He should have just told her the truth, that while God told her she could eat from any tree, that God told him he could not eat from 1 tree or he would die. And he didn't know why.

What would she have done?
What she would have done is completely reflected in how she responded to what he did tell her. She trusted him, and followed him, and believed him. She would have believed what he told her was all true, and from God, and with as much love as she had for him, she would have tried to help him to not eat from the tree. And if he didn't want her to eat either, in her compassion, she probably would not have either. And when the serpent came a knocking, they wouldn't have been home.

And likely someone would have thought to ask God why this difference was so. And God (I think) would have explained that children are begat by the father, and born through the mother, and that if the man ate, as he was the one with the original living spirit or "breath of life", that all spirits multiplied from his, whether that of the woman, or of any children, all spirits would die if he ate, and his own would die. And this is why the man could not eat of the tree. But the woman had no such responsibility, so she could eat and nothing would happen, it was harmless, and so this is why she could eat.
And both would have felt loved by God, with no doubts, no pride or lies, coming in between them.

Honesty. Treating others as you would like to be treated. Honoring, respecting, and loving the woman. Loving, respecting, and honoring the man, and naturally trusting and following him. Two people working together to carry out the will of God. Cooperation. Equality, among differences. Peace.

Something to note... How could it be fair for God to give the man a command to not eat from the tree, but allow the woman to do this? How is that balanced or fair?

Consider this: the man was given a command to not do something, and he had no choice over this. He was not allowed to do this, and he had no choice. He had no decision and no control.

On the other side of this scale, God made the woman to have to go through pregnancy, and she had no choice over this and no control. Even if it originally would not have been painful, prior to the fall she had no choice over this. She would get pregnant, her body would enlarge, and even without pain, it still would be an uncomfortable thing to go through, and she had no choice over it. God gave her something she had to endure, pregnancy, which she had no choice but to do. The only way she wouldn't is if she died, as long as she lived she had no choice but to go through pregnancy, as long as she obeyed God's command to multiply. And she herself had no way she could choose to die. So she had no choice but to endure pregnancy.

And so also God gave the man something to endure, a command, which he had no choice but to not do, or die. This is balanced and fair. Neither gender was given preferential treatment. Knowing one absolutely must do something and that they have no choice, how is that any more or less stress than knowing one absolutely must not do something and that they have no choice? And so God's command to not eat from the tree was balanced by the fact that God made her so she would have to go through pregnancy and childbirth over and over again. So it was fair and balanced. Just as she could eat from the tree, he did not have to carry and bear children. Just as he could not eat from the tree, she had to go through pregnancies, there in Eden.

And the woman was going to bear most of the load of the multiplying, as her body itself would require her to do. This was her main job, but there was more beyond this, as there was breastfeeding. And this is interesting, because Adam's main job was to tend and keep the garden. This was their food supply, which God prepared and grew, and the man essentially just needed to keep it pretty and prune it. And it was like they lived in a grocery store, a beautiful all-organic smorgasbord, which he was to tend and keep. And as he was tending to their food, she was going to be tending to the food for the infants. And so you know, with nursing the baby, breastfeeding the baby, the woman might have helped with the garden, but comparatively she was going to minor in it, while the man majored in it. And visa versa, the man was going to minor in feeding the infants, and major in the garden. They were both told to be fruitful and multiply, but the loads for each were different, even though they overlapped, and were balanced.

This is how things would have been had they not fallen, that the grocery store remained stocked without much work, and the pregnancies would be easy without much to any pain at all, and with plenty to eat to feed infants through breastfeeding, and children through tending the garden. The man taking care of the food, the gardening, was balanced not by only the pregnancies, but by the breastfeeding of the babies. This breastfeeding likely would have continued on for over 2 years for each child, with one child potentially coming up to replace the other for nursing. And it probably would have been nursing-on-demand, whenever the child was hungry. (Which is actually quite a lot of work, for those who don't know much about that.) And after this period, soon the child could find and get food for themselves, or for others. So as the man helped the woman with food, the woman helped the babies with food, and as the child got older the child helped the man and with food. And so the workload was easy and balanced when it came to everyone getting fed. Truly, I would say him not eating from the tree was completely balanced by her going through pregnancy, with some left to spare, and the principle is the same and fair. And his working the garden was balanced by her pregnancies also, and by her breastfeeding the infants.

This explains why God's punishment to each of them was what it was. Truly, he was charged to not eat from the tree, and she I do believe would have helped him to not if she had known the truth. But because he ate, and because she tempted him to eat, they both were punished. Her light load, became heavy and painful, terribly painful especially her time of labor, and also likely became painful during menstruation. And his light load also became heavy and more painful.

They both participated in what God told them not to do, and as such God made it harder for them to do what He had told them to do. It became hard for the man to be "fruitful" and for her to

"multiply", as these they were their main tasks, even though of course they did overlap and were shared, as she helped with the fruitful part, and he helped her with the multiplying also. But of course, they needed food, and could hardly help but multiply, and they were helpless to be otherwise, as long as they lived.
But this also shows how their punishments were balanced. It is no worse for her to have pain than for him to have pain, whether from inside the body, or from outside of it. It was balanced. Of course, this is just what God did, He gave her pain, and He cursed the ground giving Adam pain, and this is specified that God did these things.

But as for her returning/arguing/desire to be to him, and for him to rule over her and dominate her, God did not do these things. Rather they were just a continuation of their original problems. Such as him acting like he was more important and trying to come between her and God, and her believing him over God because she wanted him to love her. But it doesn't work, it never did, because it is based on a lie. God loves men and women equally, He always has, and He always will. Pride, lies, self-deception, envy, whatever, between men and women will not change the truth, God made us different, but equal, and equally loved by Him, with neither one in charge of the other, or preferred over the other. He loves us equally. He always wanted a man and woman to love each other and get along as peers, accepting and enjoying their differences, which He made them to naturally function in, and that is still what He wants today.

God wanted the man to tell the woman the truth about His Word, to teach her His Word.
Not for the man to make up his own words or pass them off as God's.

God wanted the man to respect God as the authority over both the man and the woman as equals.
Not for the man to use his whatever power he had to his advantage to control the woman.

God wanted the man to be trustworthy, and honest, and love the woman as she was.
Not to lie to her, or envy her, or have malice towards her, just for being as she was.

God wanted the man to ask Him and turn to Him for answers about what he didn't understand.
Not to make assumptions that he could figure out the answers for himself.

Looking at the story of the fall of Adam and Eve, it is clear that God's intent was for the man to do quite different than he did. If the man loved the woman, as God wanted him to, then he would not have lied to her. If he loved her, he would not have sought his own way, but her way, God's way for her, used not his own words, but told her God's words. He would have honored her, as God had honored her, that she could eat from all the trees freely. He would have used his position as the first-made to show his trustworthiness, and not taken advantage of the opportunity to fool her. He would have treated her as he would have wanted to be treated, if he had been made second, and told her the truth about what had happened before she was made.

It seems the essential question, is why did Adam not do these things? What was the problem he had in how he perceived the woman? It seems he must have had a problem in how he perceived her, how he thought about her, that led him to not behave towards her as God wanted him to. How would he have had to perceive the woman, in order for him to have done what God would have had him do that would have been correct?

Well, it seems likely that he envied her, that she could eat but he could not. This conveys that he considered her to be in competition with him. He was not aware that her going through pregnancy, to bear his children multiplied from his spirit, was going to take place, and that she would not have any more choice over this than him not eating of the tree. And that in not eating from the tree, he was protecting her and the children. That was one problem, and he should have asked God about this, to see there was a reason why all this was balanced and fair. So ultimately he was not focused enough on God. But before he asked God, in the meantime, was there something else that could have held him at bay from competition with her before God, and envy? Yes. At least a lesson we could learn, even though he did not understand this fully.

Adam had seen that God had made her from him, and she would be the one through whom all his multiplied children would come, his and her children. But in a way, she also was like his child, as she was multiplied from him. Which is not to say that a woman is a child, but rather to speak a truth. The woman had great natural need for the man to love her, the same as if she was his own child. And in a very real way, she was his child! In a way, the woman was the only child of the man. And through her all of his other children, their children would come. This oddly enough, is somewhat parallel to Jesus. Jesus was the only begotten Son of God, and through Jesus Christ, all of God's other children, us His adopted children, would come. It is similar, as in much of the same way, it is like the woman was like the only begotten daughter of the man, and through the woman all of the man's other children would come. It is just a loose analogy, but it is true that the female gender is the only child the male gender ever directly begat.

This sentiment seems to be why 1 Cor 11 says,
"For a man indeed ought not to have his head covered, since he is the image and glory of God. But the woman is the glory of man! For man does not originate from woman, but woman from man."

This verse expresses than the woman is the glory of man, originating from him, in such a way that is very in keeping with the happiness and parental pride of a father about his only child. Just as Eve was the only child of Adam. She was like his only-begotten daughter, or another way to put it, is that the female was like the only child of the male. And in 1 Cor 11 as Paul writes on husbands and wives, God encourages men to see their wives this way – with a parental pride and joy of the wife, the female being like the only child of the male, a glory. And this is because a wife is like the first woman, and a husband is like the first man, it should be seen by the husband that this woman who is his wife, it was like

God made her out of his own rib, and she was like the only child begotten directly from his own body and spirit, by God.

This is what Adam did not understand, that had he perceived about the woman God brought to him, he would not have found her competition or envied. Because she was like his child in a way, and thus that he had a responsibility that she did not have was not unfair, but made sense. I am not trying to say that women are children, by any means, but rather that there is a special way that a husband was meant to view only his own wife, like she was the only begotten child made directly from his body and spirit by God. In this special way, she is not a child, but she is like his child. Which may help us to understand why over and over God instructs men to love their wives, "agapao" them, with the same kind of love that God has for His children, which is an unconditional fatherly love.

A woman is not a man, nor is she a child, but her husband is meant to love her with a fatherly sort of love. Adam did not see things this way, but instead seemed to succumb to envy of the woman, but if he had seen her more like she was his special only begotten child, how silly would it have been for him to envy her? Does a righteous parent envy their child? Does a righteous parent resent their child for any responsibility that the parent has more than the child? No.

And in the same way, Eve was naturally designed to be trusting and submissive to Adam . She was designed emotionally both to view him like a peer, but also like he was in some ways her father, especially in that she needed a fatherly sort of unconditional love from him, like a child craves from their father. This is why over and over again she seems to have given him the benefit of the doubt about him lying to her, and blaming her, because she could not conceive that he could have malice towards her, anymore than a child is naturally inclined to believe their father has malice for them. Indeed, in some ways, she was emotionally and psychologically built like she was the child of Adam.

And so from the very beginning, God intended for the man to love the woman with an unconditional fatherly sort of love, and God intended for the woman to be naturally trusting and follow the man, submitting to him. And this is the exact same thing, the same dynamic, which the New Testament describes for Christian husbands and wives, telling women to submit to their own husbands, and telling men to love their wives, not seeking their own way, even self-sacrificially, so that the woman will respect him, and for him not to be harsh with her. For what child can respect their father if he does not seem to love them, and is harsh with them? But if a father loves his child and shows it, and is not harsh with his son, then the child will respect his father. But a son cannot respect an unloving and harsh father, any more than a wife can respect an unloving and harsh husband.

Can a father love a child who shows no submission to his father, and refuses to do what the father wants him to do? What father does not love his child? This is a difference, as with a child, not a grown child but a child, a righteous father will still love a son who is ornery. But truly, how often is a ornery child the result of an unloving and harsh father, in which the child's treatment by the father has prompted a natural response of a rebellious child? This is not always the case, but with actual children it is often the case. Surely, a child is born with a predisposition to be submissive to his parents, like a woman is made with a predisposition to be submissive to her husband, but often when this is ruined it is in the same way. This is not always the case, but it often is, especially with an actual child, say under 10 years of age.

But even as God made woman to be emotionally and psychologically like a child to her husband in some ways, and meant for the man to be emotionally and psychologically like a father to her in some ways, there is a major difference. And it is the lack of understanding of this difference that is so essential in marriages. A husband was never given authority over a wife and Adam was never given authority over Eve, not to control her, not to punish her like a child for disobedience, not to give her his own orders and have them be seen like they were from God himself. Adam had 1 way in which God had given him actual power over the woman, and that was that he could choose to teach her more of God's word, or not, as she did not know what God had said before she was made. He was to show her that he heeded and respected God, in His Word, and this was his choice, to teach her God's Words, or to play god over her himself, which was wrong and led to sin, and is sin.

When it comes to authority, the man was to relate to the woman like she was his grown son, a beloved peer, not a young child. He was to teach her the Word of God like they were peers. It was like he could relate and teach the Word of God to his grown son, or he could not. But what righteous man would gain anything by presenting his own words as the Words of God to his son? And as Adam's lie was found out by Eve because of the serpent, it seems that inevitably his lie would have been found out by the woman interacting with God directly, at some point in the future, if sin had not occurred. It might have been someday, even likely, that the woman would have asked God "why will I die if I eat from the tree?" or "why did you tell me I could eat from the all the trees, and not tell me this one would kill me if I ate?"

And so, like a father lying to his grown son about the Bible's Words, while he might be believed, eventually the grown man can and likely will learn for himself, and himself see his father lied. Then he may confront or disagree with his father, same as Eve was given the power by God to disagree with Adam about what God said to her directly about what she herself could or couldn't do.

And so Adam was only ever given this particular limited power over Eve, just like that of a father over his grown son, to teach him the truth about God or to lie, to explain to her what he was doing by not eating of this tree, and what God had truly commanded him. And Eve was in balance given an equal but opposing power over Adam, to correct him in regards to God's Word in what God had told her directly, and choose to obey what God had told her directly.

And the Bible also teaches this pattern of relating in the example of Jesus and His Father God, as seen in John 5:19-20,
"Jesus gave them this answer: "Very truly I tell you, the Son can do nothing by himself; he can do only what he sees his Father doing, because whatever the Father does the Son also does. For the Father loves the Son and shows him all he does. Yes, and he will show him even greater works than these, so that you will be amazed."
In the same way, Adam should have shown Eve that he would not eat of the tree, and revealed to her God's true words. And it is likely with her submissive trusting nature, that she would have done as he did, and if nothing else, she would have also obeyed God's command to Adam, by helping him to not eat from the tree.

This is the ONLY amount and sort of power that God EVER gave to a man in a marriage over his wife. When God gave power and authority to a husband over a wife it was not in name, but in deed. We can see clearly the exact type and amount of authority that God gave a husband over his wife in marriage, in the story of Adam and Eve, and exactly the responsibility as well. It was precisely that Adam had the authority to teach her God's command, teach her what must be done to obey God, or to not, and the responsibility to protect her with his obedience to God, or to not. This is the ONLY authority, and concept of responsibility, that God ever gave a husband over a wife.

But this does not mean that the husband has more authority over the wife than she has over the husband, because she was given the authority by God over her husband, to contradict and correct him in regards to herself, and stick to what she knew God had said to her, and herself obey it. So neither one actually had more power or authority than the other. He could teach her something she didn't know, but only about his relationship with God. If he tried to teach her more about herself, interfering with her relationship with God, it was in sin, as she had her own instructions directly from God, same as he did, and she couldn't teach him more about himself without it being sinful either. The wife also had power given by God to correct her husband if he was wrong about her direct relationship with God. So their power and authority over each other was equal.

God did not give the Adam the authority to force the woman to obey him rather than God, and that the man tried to force her to obey him was his first mistake. Nor did God give the man the responsibility to make sure that she did obey God's command, as the tree was harmless to her, and she could eat of it, and was not commanded as he was. The responsibility of the man was to protect her with his obedience to God, and to teach her about God's command to himself. All the power the man had was essentially to be able to teach her a little more knowledge about God, as it related to his relationship with God. This is the only power that God ever gave a husband over a wife, and the corresponding responsibility. But again, this is balanced by her autonomy before God, and that God gave her the authority and power to correct her husband about God's Words to her, and stick to what God had told her about herself. <u>So again, neither the husband or wife had more power or authority over the other, but were equal.</u>

To step back a moment, to the punishments of Adam and Eve, there is additional insight here.

The man was forced to till a cursed ground, to provide food for himself, as he was cast out of the garden alone. And his sin against God came about first because he did not see nor behave towards God as he should of. But secondly, because he did not love or treat the woman as God intended. He was a poor husband, and as a result he had to work the ground, because he was forced to get away from his wife, so he would not further hurt himself and her by trapping them both in a state of sinful immortality. His punishment was not conditional upon being with the woman, but was for being a man who was sinful. His lot in life then became to live the rest of his life alone, and he had no choice in this, working the land to eat, and had no choice in this either unless he let himself starve.

But the woman's punishment was in part a choice. She was there alone in Eden with all her food provided. She likely had an amount of menstruation pain already. Either she could live and die alone and never bear children, or she could choose to go to the man and had been warned she would be dominated (not something God did to her as a punishment, but something the man would just continue to do), and would also be potentially choosing to multiply by choosing to return to the man, and God said he would multiply her pain if she did choose to multiply.

It seems clear that the woman's punishment by God's hand of multiplying her pain was conditional on her having children, and in this returning to the man. For if he dominated, as God warned her he would, then she might have no choice about multiplying, so her choice to not multiply meant not leaving the garden. In fact, her punishment of pain in childbirth was conditional upon her choosing to have children if she returned to the man, chose to leave the garden. Which God let her stay in. She knew that Adam did not love her right. She was like his only child in a way, and he did not love her, but was sinful. Therefore, she had every reason to think that he would not love another sort of child right either, the sort which he would father through her. It was God's command for them to multiply, but she was given the option by God to stay in the garden, and was not forced to leave as the man was. It was her choice to multiply, or to not, and God did not force her.

But her willingness to go through this pain, showed that she was committed enough to love her child, that she was willing to suffer terrible pain in order to have this child to love. Her choice to multiply and endure pain also showed God her willingness to do as He had commanded them to do, to multiply. And I believe Eve's ultimate reason to return to Adam and multiply, was to give birth to her seed who would crush the serpent.

We can see a light analogy of this choice in the sacrificial love of Jesus dying on the cross for us. We would never have been able to be born (born-again) if not for His willing choice to suffer pain, even unto death, in order for us to be able to be born. We were not yet alive in spirit, and if we were not made alive in spirit, then we never would have existed to eternal life, so we could have a loving relationship with Him. And this is somewhat like a mother who chooses to multiply is willing to suffer pain, even a risk unto death, so that she can have a child to love, and to love her.

There are more analogies to be had like this.
For instance, as all people now are made "through" a woman, the same is said of Jesus,
"He was in the world, and the world was made through Him, and the world did not know Him." Jn 1:10
Also, as now child only meets his father because of a woman, the same is said of Jesus,
"Jesus answered, "I am the way and the truth and the life.
No one comes to the Father except through me." Jn 14:6

And in the same way that Eve was like Adam's only-begotten daughter, but he would have other children with her and through her, and they were both her children and also her siblings in a way, the same is true that Jesus Christ is God's only-begotten Son, and God has us as children through Jesus Christ, and we are both like His brothers and sisters and His children, as He is God:
"God, for whom and through whom everything was made, chose to bring many children into glory. And it was only right that he should make Jesus, through his suffering, a perfect leader, fit to bring them into their salvation. So now Jesus and the ones he makes holy have the same Father. That is why Jesus is not ashamed to call them his brothers and sisters. For he said to God, "I will proclaim your name to my brothers and sisters. I will praise you among your assembled people." He also said, "I will put my trust in him," that is, "I and the children God has given me."
Heb 2:10-13

Also there is a Mystery that is revealed in the fact that as long as Adam did not sin, he and Eve were both spiritually alive and right with God. Why is this important? If the first man did not sin, but was right with God, then his wife was spiritually alright with God. We Christians are the bride of Christ. Jesus the Christ is without sin, and when we become born-again, His Spirit comes to live in us. This parallels how Adam's spirit was multiplied, giving life to Eve, and then the spirit was in her giving life. When a person believes on Jesus Christ for their salvation and becomes a Christian, they are born again, and it is like their newly born spirit is multiplied from the spirit of Jesus Christ. This happens by His Holy Spirit multiplying a new spirit into us, as a new living creature. Similar as how Adam's spirit was multiplied to give life to Eve. And the Holy Spirit, who is the Spirit of Jesus, also dwells inside the newly born-again Christian. And in becoming Christian a person becomes part of the body of Christ, and bride of Christ. In this Jesus' righteousness is accounted to that person, as a part of His body, His bride. The same as Adam's choice to not sin also affected Eve spiritually, Jesus Christ's decision to never sin affects us when we become born-again as His bride. His sinless righteousness is accounted to us. This is part of how Jesus Christ is the second Adam, who never sinned, and so we are like the second Eve, His bride who rests safely in His sinless righteousness. And the same as if Adam and Eve would have had faith in the Lord, and if Adam would have been honest with Eve, and if Eve's faith in Adam and what he told her would have been justified, we are justified by grace through faith in the Lord Jesus Christ.

"… for we say that faith was reckoned to Abraham for righteousness… he staggered not at the promise of God through unbelief; but was strong in faith, giving glory to God; And being fully persuaded that, what He had promised, He was able also to perform. And therefore it was imputed to him for righteousness. Now it was not written for his sake alone, that it was imputed to him; But for us also, to whom it shall be imputed, if we believe on Him that raised up Jesus our Lord from the dead; Who was delivered for our offences, and was raised again for our justification." Rom 4:9b, 20-25

"For by grace are ye saved through faith; and that not of yourselves: [it is] the gift of God: Not of works, lest any man should boast." Eph 2:8-9

Going back to Adam and Eve, and marriage, what was God's original intent for them as parents? Was the man to have more or less authority over the children than the woman?
In the analogy of God the Father and Jesus Christ, a foundation to understand this (and more) is that there is yet another confirmation that men and women are equally considered man. "So, because Jesus was doing these things on the Sabbath, the Jewish leaders began to persecute him. In his defense Jesus said to them, "My Father is always at his work to this very day, and I too

am working." For this reason they tried all the more to kill him; not only was he breaking the Sabbath, but <u>he was even calling God his own Father, making himself equal with God."</u> John 5:16-18
"<u>I and the Father are one.</u>" John 10:30

In the same way that Jesus is the only begotten Son of God the Father, it is like the woman Eve was the only-begotten child of the man Adam. And as Jesus is one with the Father, the woman is one with the man. And like Jesus Christ is also equal with God in this way, and we as children should view them as both being equally God, the woman is also equal with man in this way, and both should be viewed as equal.

Many times the Bible reflects equal authority when it comes to men and women as parents:
"Honour thy father and thy mother: that thy days may be long upon the land which the LORD thy God giveth thee. Ex 20:12
And he that smiteth his father, or his mother, shall be surely put to death." Ex 21:15
"For every one that curseth his father or his mother shall be surely put to death: he hath cursed his father or his mother; his blood shall be upon him." Lev 20:9
"If a man have a stubborn and rebellious son, which will not obey the voice of his father, or the voice of his mother, and [that], when they have chastened him, will not hearken unto them" Deut 21:18
"My son, hear the instruction of thy father, and forsake not the law of thy mother" Prov 1:8
"Children, obey your parents in the Lord: for this is right." Eph 6:1
"Children, obey your parents in all things: for this is well pleasing unto the Lord." Col 3:20
In fact, it is clear that the mother and the father are intended to have equal authority over the children.

And while much has been covered that the spirit of life of the child is multiplied solely from the father, the child's body and personality, as you know, is also multiplied from the mother equally as the father. The life of the soul is from the father, but even the imprint of the soul, as in mind, heart, will, is also multiplied from the mother. And the truth is that the mother alone carries and bears the child, which balances that the spirit of life in the child is multiplied from the father alone. And so the child is equally of the mother and the father, and so the authority they have over the child is equal and shared.

And even in the analogy of the husband as the head, and the wife as every other part of the body:
"But I want you to understand that Christ is the head of every man, and the husband is the head of a wife, and God is the head of Christ." 1 Cor 11:3
"God has put all things under the authority of Christ and has made him head over all things for the benefit of the church. And the church is his body; it is made full and complete by Christ, who fills all things everywhere with himself." Eph 1:22-23
God is the head of Christ, who is the fullness of the Godhead bodily, and God has put all things under Jesus' authority, and made him head over all things pertaining to the church, his body, and Jesus is one with God, and God also still has authority over all things and the church.
In the same way also the husband is the head of the wife, who is like his body, and he should have all things also be under her authority, and should also have her be head over all things pertaining to the children, which are also hers, and as she and her husband are one, while the husband also still has authority over all things and the children. And so the Bible teaches a shared authority over the children, even taking into account the analogy of the husband being the head and the wife being like the rest of the body, and them being one flesh.

And so this means that the husband has no greater authority over the children than the wife does. And again, the ONLY authority God ever gave a husband over a wife was to teach her God's Word, and this was balanced by the authority God gave a wife over a husband to correct him about God's Word in regards to herself. Does the father have more authority to teach the children than the mother does? No. In Israel, when Moses gave the law, the instructions were given to all the people for them to teach these words of God to their children, not just the fathers, but also the mothers.

"You shall teach them diligently to your children, and shall talk of them when you sit in your house, and when you walk by the way, and when you lie down, and when you rise." Deut 6:7
"Cursed is the one who does not confirm all the words of this law. And all the people shall say, Amen." Deut 27:26
Here we see that all of the people were told to teach God's Word to their children. And as they entered into covenant with God, all of the people said Amen. And so both the mothers and the fathers agreed to teach God's Law to their children, as was and is God's will.

And so while the husband does have the authority over the wife to teach her God's Word and the responsibility to protect her and the children by obeying God, the wife has equal authority and responsibility to correct him when she knows he is wrong, and over the children to teach them God's Word, and equal authority as the husband to have the children obey her. Nor does any of this preclude the wife also teaching the husband what of God's Word that he does not know or seems to have forgotten, even as Eve could have corrected Adam about what God told her.
When you add it all up, the only difference between the authority that the husband and the wife have, even taking into account the children, is that the husband has the authority to teach the wife God's true Word and about truly obeying God as per God's exact commands. But this is balanced by the fact that God gave Eve the ability to correct Adam about what God had said to her, setting the precedent that God allows for a wife to correct her husband if he contradicts God. <u>Therefore, again, the authority that a husband and wife have over each other in respect to God's Word and instructions is equal.</u>

Sometimes I hear the term "head of household" used as a church catchphrase(?) in reference to a husband, trying to reference defining some sort of authority that the husband has more than and over the wife. And also it seems to reference to the husband having more authority over the children than she does. This term is found nowhere in the Bible. (Go ahead and see for yourself, run a search for the phrase at BLB.org) This term is not in the Bible.

The term "head of the house" is in the Bible, but only refers to a representative of an entire tribe of Israel,
"And with you there shall be a man from every tribe, each one the head of his father's house." Num 1:4

There are times in which the household of a husband is referenced as "his household". But there are also times in which the household of a wife is referenced as "her household".
"She is not afraid of the snow for her household: for all her household are clothed with scarlet.
She looketh well to the ways of her household, and eateth not the bread of idleness." Prov 31:21, 27

As far as I can see having read the Bible, while the husband is the head and the wife the other body parts, they are one flesh, and the household and children equally belong to both of them. Again, the only authority the husband was given over the wife is to teach her God's Word and about how to obey God, and is completely balanced by the authority God gave the wife over the husband to correct him about God's Word and about how to obey God. Neither one has more authority over the other, than the other. Everything else in the Bible in which a husband seems to have more authority over a wife than this which God gave, is an example of him ruling over her, dominating her, as a curse passed from Adam, the same sort of sinful behavior that brought about the fall into sin and death in the first place. The story of Adam and Eve shows clearly that the opposite of a husband loving his wife is him trying to rule over her, dominate her, or abuse whatever power he has over her, even by teaching her God's Word incorrectly.

God has told Christian women to submit to their own husbands. God has told Christian husbands to love their wives. But there is no authority given by God to the Christian husband to do more than that of him teaching his wife the truth of Word of God and about obeying God, but this is balanced by the authority given to her by God to correct him if he contradicts God, and have her own knowledge of what God has told her directly. So neither ultimately have more authority over the other in regards to God's Word and obeying God. They have equal authority of their children. They are meant to function as one flesh, one body, with the husband as the head and the wife as the rest of the body parts, as Adam and Eve were also made one body together.

Their relationship is meant to be a naturally symbiotic one, in which she follows him as he loves her, and as they both obey God. A Christian marriage is meant to be a restoration to God's original design for marriage, like Adam and Eve were meant to have, and following many examples of the loving relationship between God the Father and Jesus Christ His only begotten Son. And it is only with Jesus Christ and God and God's True Words being in a marriage, and of central importance, that a Christian marriage can be restored and made to be what God intended it to be.

Chapter Thirteen
1 Timothy 2 – Female Teachers, etc.

Now we are going to take a look at 1 Timothy 2:
"I exhort therefore, that, first of all, supplications, prayers, intercessions, and giving of thanks, be made for all men; For kings, and for all that are in authority; that we may lead a quiet and peaceable life in all godliness and honesty. For this is good and acceptable in the sight of God our Saviour; Who will have all men to be saved, and to come unto the knowledge of the truth. For there is one God, and one mediator between God and men, the man Christ Jesus; Who gave himself a ransom for all, to be testified in due time."

Here Paul says to Timothy that he wants the people there to pray for all people, and lift them up to God in many ways. Included in this are those in authority, like kings. In this there is hope God will guide those in authority so that the people under them can have lives that are quiet and peaceful.
Paul makes clear that God wants all people to be saved, and come to the truth, who is Jesus Christ, who is the ransom for every person. And this truth, the Gospel message, was intended to be testified of in due time. The word here for testified "martyrion" refers to a person giving witness or testimony of Jesus Christ. It also refers to anything which is done so that a person may have a witness or proof that God has worked. One example is the lepers Jesus healed going to the priests to give the mandated offerings, as a witness to the priests that God had worked and healed them.

"Whereunto I am ordained a preacher, and an apostle, (I speak the truth in Christ, and lie not;) a teacher of the Gentiles in faith and verity."
Now, for the reason of giving testimony of Jesus Christ, Paul says he had been ordained as a preacher, apostle, and a teacher to the Gentiles. The word here for ordained is "tithemi" and in this case it also means "appointed". Paul uses the same word in Acts 13:47, in the same way, "For so hath the Lord commanded us, [saying], I have <u>appointed</u> thee to be a light of the Gentiles, that thou

shouldest be for salvation unto the ends of the earth."
When used this way the word refers to God appointing someone to do something. In this case, Paul was appointed to be an apostle, preacher, and teacher, giving the testimony of Jesus Christ, the Gospel, to all men, but the Gentiles in particular.
So here we see reference to the instructions that all Christians have to share the Gospel, the testimony of Jesus Christ. And we also see reference to the particular appointment or calling that Paul has, including being an apostle, preacher, and teacher.

The word for preacher is the noun form of the verb for "to preach". The verb is used in Luke 24:47 when Jesus said, "And that repentance and remission of sins should be <u>preached</u> in his name among all nations, beginning at Jerusalem."
And which Peter used referring to Jesus' command in Acts 10:42, "And he commanded us to <u>preach</u> unto the people, and to testify that it is he which was ordained of God [to be] the Judge of quick and dead."
And also as Jesus said in Mark 16:15-18,
"And he said unto them, Go ye into all the world, and <u>preach</u> the gospel to every creature. He that believeth and is baptized shall be saved; but he that believeth not shall be damned. And these signs shall follow them that believe; In my name shall they cast out devils; they shall speak with new tongues; They shall take up serpents; and if they drink any deadly thing, it shall not hurt them; they shall lay hands on the sick, and they shall recover."

So here is a question. Can women be preachers? Yes, all Christians are told to be preachers of the Gospel of Jesus Christ. This is the Biblical meaning of the term "preacher". And in fact all Christians, women and men, are told to be preachers by Jesus. It is not a gift of the Holy Spirit per se, but the most basic appointment given to all Christians. We are all appointed by God to share the Gospel of Jesus Christ, the same as Paul was appointed to do.

Paul also says he was appointed as an apostle and teacher. These words are all also found in 1 Cor 12:18, 28:
"But now hath God <u>appointed</u> the members every one of them in the body, as it hath pleased him. And God hath <u>appointed</u> some in

the church, first <u>apostles</u>, secondarily prophets, thirdly <u>teachers</u>, after that miracles, then gifts of healings, helps, governments, diversities of tongues."
And the same term of apostle and teacher are used in
Eph 4:4-8,11-12
"There is one body, and one Spirit, even as <u>ye are called in one hope of your calling</u>; One Lord, one faith, one baptism, One God and Father of all, who is above all, and through all, and in you all. But unto every one of us is given grace according to the measure of the gift of Christ. Wherefore he saith, When he ascended up on high, he led captivity captive, and gave gifts unto people. And he gave some, <u>apostles</u>; and some, prophets; and some, evangelists; and some, pastors and <u>teachers</u>; For the perfecting of the saints, for the work of the ministry, for the edifying of the body of Christ:"

So Paul's appointment to being an apostle and teacher comes from him receiving these gifts of the Holy Spirit. Just as he was appointed to preach, as all believers are, in his case he was also particularly appointed to be an apostle and teacher, because he received these gifts of the Holy Spirit. This was his particular "calling", a broader term for all he was appointed to do. And while Christians may each have a slightly different calling from God, we all share the same hope, each in our individual callings. And the Bible also says in Rom 11:29, "For the gifts and calling of God [are] without repentance." And so what gifts and calling of God a person has cannot be repented of nor should be repented of.

Who chooses what gifts and calling a Christian has? God chooses. The Bible also says earlier in the same chapter as quoted above,
1 Cor 12:4-14,18
"Now there are varieties of gifts, but the same Spirit. And there are varieties of ministries, and the same Lord. There are varieties of effects, but the same God who works all things in all persons. But <u>to each one</u> is given the manifestation of the Spirit for the common good. For to one is given the word of wisdom through the Spirit, and to another the word of knowledge according to the same Spirit; to another faith by the same Spirit, and to another gifts of healing by the one Spirit, and to another the effecting of miracles, and to another <u>prophecy</u>, and to another the

distinguishing of spirits, to another various kinds of tongues, and to another the interpretation of tongues. But one and the same Spirit works all these things, <u>distributing to each one individually just as He wills</u>. For even as the body is one and yet has many members, and all the members of the body, though they are many, are one body, so also is Christ. For by one Spirit we were all baptized into one body, whether Jews or Greeks, whether slaves or free, and we were all made to drink of one Spirit. For the body is not one member, but many. But now <u>God has placed the members, each one of them, in the body, just as He desired</u>."

God, the Holy Spirit, Himself chooses which gifts to give to each person. It is not the choice of any person, male of female, as to which gifts God chooses to give that person. Indeed, the language here in 1 Cor 12 "Jews or Greeks, slaves or free" is very similar to what Paul also says in Gal 3:28,
"There is neither <u>Jew nor Gentile</u>, neither <u>slave nor free</u>, neither <u>male nor female</u>, for you are all one in Christ Jesus."
And so Paul expresses the same concept in 1 Corinthians 12, that everyone in Christ has the same Holy Spirit inside of them, who gives gifts as He chooses, without any regard to the person being Jew or Greek or slave or free or male or female.

And the Bible records quite clearly that the Holy Spirit does choose to give the gift and calling of apostle to women, mentioning Junia, a woman apostle; and this name in Greek is a female name:
"Greet Andronicus and Junia, my kinsmen and my fellow prisoners, who are outstanding among the apostles, who also were in Christ before me." Romans 16:7
And the Bible says "first are apostles" which some take to mean this is the "first" gift to receive. As such if a woman can receive the gift of apostle, it would make sense she could receive any of the other "following" gifts as well.

Even in the Old Testament, both Miriam (sister of Moses) and Deborah (Judge of Israel) are called prophetesses. (Ex 15:20, Jud 4:4) And they both were servants of God. Under the same covenant, there was Anna who praised God for Jesus as a newborn baby and told people of him (Luke 2:36).

In the New Testament among Christians, in Acts 21:8-9 we read, "And the next [day] we that were of Paul's company departed, and came unto Caesarea: and we entered into the house of Philip the evangelist, which was [one] of the seven; and abode with him. And the same man had four daughters, virgins, which did prophesy." And so God's Word makes clear that Christian women can also have the gift of prophecy, the 2nd gift.

The last gift that is listed is the gift of tongues, which was the first gift given by the Holy Spirit to Christians on the day of Pentecost. Women were also given this gift on the day of Pentecost.
Acts 1:4-5,8-14; 2:1-4
"And, being assembled together with [them], commanded them that they should not depart from Jerusalem, but wait for the promise of the Father, which, [saith he], ye have heard of me. For John truly baptized with water; but ye shall be baptized with the Holy Ghost not many days hence. But ye shall receive power, after that the Holy Ghost is come upon you: and ye shall be witnesses unto me both in Jerusalem, and in all Judaea, and in Samaria, and unto the uttermost part of the earth. And when he had spoken these things, while they beheld, he was taken up; and a cloud received him out of their sight. And while they looked stedfastly toward heaven as he went up, behold, two men stood by them in white apparel; Which also said, Ye men of Galilee, why stand ye gazing up into heaven? this same Jesus, which is taken up from you into heaven, shall so come in like manner as ye have seen him go into heaven. Then returned they unto Jerusalem from the mount called Olivet, which is from Jerusalem a sabbath day's journey. And when they were come in, they went up into an upper room, where abode both Peter, and James, and John, and Andrew, Philip, and Thomas, Bartholomew, and Matthew, James the son of Alphaeus, and Simon Zelotes, and Judas the brother of James. <u>These all continued with one accord in prayer and supplication, with the women, and Mary the mother of Jesus, and with his brethren. And when the day of Pentecost was fully come, they were all with one accord in one place.</u> And suddenly there came a sound from heaven as of a rushing mighty wind, and it filled all the house where they were sitting. There appeared unto them cloven tongues like as of fire, and it sat <u>upon each of</u>

them. And they were <u>all filled with the Holy Ghost, and began to speak with other tongues</u>, as the Spirit gave them utterance."

And so here we see the women who followed Jesus, and Mary His mother, also received the Holy Spirit and the gift of tongues on the day of Pentecost.
As women can have the 1st and 2nd gifts of being an apostle and prophet, and were also among those given the original gift of Tongues, which Paul lists last, it therefore make sense that women can have any gift in between, from the first to the last, which the Holy Spirit chooses to give her.

As for the 3rd gift listed, which is to be a teacher, the Bible records of Priscilla and Aquila, a married Jewish couple. In some instances Priscilla's name is listed first when they are mentioned in Paul's letters, and in Acts, which some people say shows she was the more prominent of the two. (Acts 18:18, Rom 16:3) In any case, they both traveled with Paul to Syria in the Lord's work, after he apparently converted them to becoming Christians. Then he parted ways with them in Ephesus, and they stayed there on their own. There is reason to think they were both teachers, as they are described as teaching Apollos, a Jew who already was already well familiar with the scriptures and also the Baptism of John.

In Acts 18:24-28 we read,
"And a certain Jew named Apollos, born at Alexandria, an eloquent man, and mighty in the scriptures, came to Ephesus. This man was instructed in the way of the Lord; and being fervent in the spirit, he spake and taught diligently the things of the Lord, knowing only the baptism of John. And he began to speak boldly in the synagogue: whom when Aquila and Priscilla had heard,<u> they</u> took him unto them, and <u>expounded unto him the way of God more perfectly.</u> And when he was disposed to pass into Achaia, the brethren wrote, exhorting the disciples to receive him: who, when he was come, helped them much which had believed through grace: For he mightily convinced the Jews, and that publicly, shewing by the scriptures that Jesus was Christ."

What this says is that both Aquila and Priscilla taught Apollos. He already was "mighty in the scriptures" but they had more to teach him, as they had learned from Paul. And so they expounded to him the way of God more perfectly. In Acts 28:23 Paul is said to have "expounded" (the same word):
"And when they had appointed him a day, there came many to him into [his] lodging; to whom he <u>expounded</u> and testified the kingdom of God, persuading them concerning Jesus, both out of the law of Moses, and [out of] the prophets, from morning till evening."
Apparently, expounding includes teaching out of the scriptures in both instances. And both Aquila and Priscilla taught Apollos from the scriptures, who then went on to "mightily convince the Jews" showing by the scriptures that Jesus was the Christ. He already knew the scriptures well, but they had more that they taught him, and then he became a Christian, and he then did well, and with what they had taught him. So while it is not specified, Priscilla is described as someone who was a teacher, and likely had the gift of the Holy Spirit gift of teaching.

Getting back to Paul's words in 1 Timothy 2,
"Who gave himself a ransom for all, to be testified in due time. Whereunto I am ordained a preacher, and an apostle, (I speak the truth in Christ, and lie not;) a teacher of the Gentiles in faith and verity."
Because of God's will that the Gospel be testified of, Paul has been called to preach (as we all are) and his calling and gifts are that of an apostle and teacher.

And also for the cause of preaching the Gospel, testifying of Jesus Christ, Paul says next,
"I will therefore that men pray every where, lifting up holy hands, without wrath and doubting."
Paul wants the men, as part of testimony of Jesus Christ, to pray publicly where-ever they go, lifting up blameless or holy hands to God, without showing anger or doubt. Imagine a man in a marketplace, praying and lifting his hands to God, a man that shows no anger, nor doubt. This is a man who seems to have faith.

This is a man that perhaps other men will seek to talk to, or listen to, wondering about the peace he has. And I think this is what Paul is encouraging here, because this is public behavior that seemed likely (at least at the time, perhaps today also) to have the men be a beacon in public that others would come to, to stand out, so that the Gospel could be preached. And both men and women would likely find a man who acts like this in public interesting to talk or listen to.

And in like manner, for the same reason,
In like manner also, that women adorn themselves in modest apparel, with shamefacedness and sobriety; not with broided hair, or gold, or pearls, or costly array;
Here Paul encourages woman to stand out, for the same reason. But for them it is different. What is going to make them stand out in a crowd, so other women and men might find them interesting and talk to them or listen to them, is for them to be modest, seemly, and simple in appearance.

The word "shamefacedness" also means reverence, and refers to an internal feeling of what would make you feel shame or not, or should. In any given culture, this will vary, as to what clothing a woman feels is modest or seemly enough that she feels no shame to wear it. The word "sobriety" means "soundness of mind, self-control, sobriety". Which seems to indicate apparel that reflects these qualities.

Some examples of what is not considered modest is wearing gold, pearls, costly (very expensive) apparel. Also mentioned is "broided" hair. Note the "o". This word does not necessarily mean "braided", but is defined by Thayer's as, "woven, plaited, twisted together, a web, plait, braid, ringlets, curls". Which basically encompasses everything a woman might do to style her hair, whether a weave, twists, plaits, braids, curls, ringlets, or some complicated web design. Perming your hair would probably be included in this, as well as straightening it. And it might also include anything which takes a long time to do, like brushing it into feathers with a blow-dryer, using a curling iron, etc. Though the Greek here still places the emphasis on telling women to "modest themselves" and the apparel, hair, jewelry, and expensive apparel are all included in this. Women are indicated to do this themselves, not for anyone else to determine it for them. The emphasis is still for a woman to wear what she feels shows "shamefacedness" or "reverence" and "sobriety". And in any given culture, this may vary. What are the clothes of a rich person in one country, might be standard common wear in another, and a hair style in this time that is plain for the culture, might in another culture be considered excessive. But what women themselves are to do, is to be determined by their internal feeling of what they feel is self-controlled, sober, shamefaced or reverent, of a sound mind.

"But (which becometh women professing godliness) with good works."
But rather than adorning herself with all that above, a woman is to adorn herself with good works, which becometh women professing godliness. The terms here also means 'promising reverence toward God's goodness'. And all of this ties into Paul's previous theme of what is helpful to women preaching the Gospel or out in public with such an aim.

The next couple of verses are translated in the KJV to read: "Let the woman learn in silence with all subjection. But I suffer not a woman to teach, nor to usurp authority over the man, but to be in silence."

For anyone who is not aware, there is much debate about this verse and its meaning. First of all, people seem very uncertain as to what the word for "usurp authority" means, which is the word "authentein". It is only used here in the Bible, and rarely in extra-Biblical literature of that time, or in other time periods. Secondly, the order of the words in this verse are different in different manuscripts. The KJV uses the "Textus Receptus" from the early 1500s, a project which used various manuscripts had at the time, with a pick-and-choose process when it came to variants in the text of the copies, with some apparent influence from the Latin Vulgate, of which the earliest manuscript we have containing it is from the early 700s.

In the mid 1800s the discovery was made of the Codex Sinaiticus in a monastery in Sinai. In 1911 the New Testament of this Codex was first published. It has been firmly dated by scholars to have been written between 325-360AD. Even Wikipedia states,
"With only 300 years separating the Codex Sinaiticus and the original manuscripts of the New Testament, it is considered to be very highly accurate, as opposed to most later copies, in preserving obviously superior readings where many later manuscripts are in error.[5] For the Gospels, Sinaiticus is generally considered among scholars as the second most reliable witness of the text (after Vaticanus); in the Acts of the Apostles, its text is equal to that of Vaticanus; in the Epistles, Sinaiticus is the most reliable witness of the text."

And 1 Timothy 2 is one of those Epistles, which the Codex Vaticanus does not contain a copy of.

So I went to the "most reliable witness" of the text, to make sure I understood 1 Timothy 2:12 correctly.
I got these pictures from www.scribd.com/doc/14129399/Codex-Sinaiticus-01-Scripture-Index and checked them against the original, as the entire Codex is online to read(!),
at http://www.codex-sinaiticus.net/en/

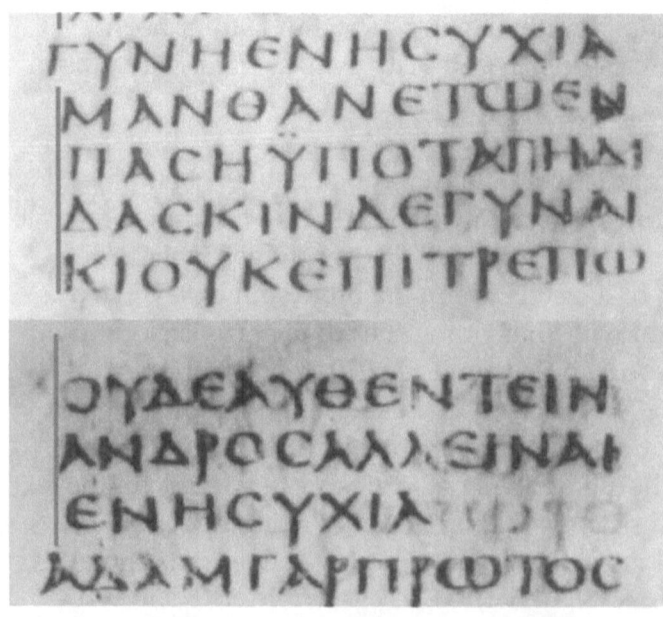

What you see here is the oldest, most ancient, copy of the original 1 Tim 2:11-12. This is the best anyone has to work from. The first thing I would like to point out to you is the lines on the left. Do you notice the letters that stick out to the left, over the line? These letters mark the beginning of a verse, as they were understood then, back in 325-360 AD. And what this says here is that verses 11 and 12 as we know them, used to all be considered one verse. Which means the Greek from these 2 verses should not be divided under critical study. Another important thing to note is that 2 words here have switched their order, versus how they are ordered in Textus Receptus (1500s) which the KJV uses.

Put into Greek type, the above equates to this:

γυνη ἐν ησυχία μανθανέτω ἐν πάση υποταγη διδάσκειν δε γυναικί οὐκ ἐπιτρέπω οὐδε αὐθεντείν ανδρός αλλ' είναι ἐν ησυχία

a-woman in quietness she-must-learn in all subjection to-teach

but the-woman not I-allow neither to-authentien the-man but to-be in quietness

Let's figure out what this means.

Based on how the Greek γυνη is usually translated, the singular woman here is best rendered "a-woman", not "the-woman".

ησυχία Means stillness or quietness and is also used in 1 Thes 3:10-12, "For even when we were with you, this we commanded you, that if any would not work, neither should he eat. For we hear that there are some which walk among you disorderly, working not at all, but are busybodies. Now them that are such we command and exhort by our Lord Jesus Christ, that with <u>quietness</u> they work, and eat their own bread."

The Strong's states, *"description of the life of one who stays at home doing his own work, and does not officiously meddle with the affairs of others"*. And it comes from an adjective which means "quiet, tranquil" and is translated as "peaceable". So this word does not refer necessarily to any level of speech, whether loud or quiet, but rather the state of life of an orderly, reserved, content to work, quiet tranquil peaceful person, and in context means that someone works without being a busybody or disorderly.

μανθανέτω here means to learn, and it is a verb in "Third Person Present Active Imperative Singular" form. As Paul is speaking to Timothy, this means Paul is telling Timothy (as a church leader) that he must have her learn. The same verb form, for a different verb, is also used twice in 1 Cor 14:28-30, and the force of the verb is well rendered in the NASB, as this is imperative, which means it is a command, for a verb that means to keep silent:
"But if there is no interpreter, he must keep silent in the church; and let him speak to himself and to God. Let two or three prophets speak, and let the others pass judgment. But if a revelation is made to another who is seated, the first one must keep silent."
And so this verb here means "she-must-learn". Another way to put it is "have her learn" And the meaning is "you Timothy (as a leader of your church there) must have her learn".

υποταγη or subjection here is Hupotage which means "under" + "arranged in order, series" in a way that implies a time series, or ordered by highest rank first. It is a word made from the combination of "upo"(under) and "tagma"(order). The type of "order" here is determined by the word "tagma", of which the Thayer's says, "*that which has been arranged, thing placed in order… a body of soldiers, a corps… a band, troop, class*". So what is being referred to here with subjection in this verse is the kind of subjection found in a class or learning situation, which is very fitting.

So what or why must she learn?
διδάσκειν means "to teach". This is the verb form of the noun which means "teacher", and is used of the gift of teaching in the prior passages referring to the gifts of the Holy Spirit.

So far this reads "A woman in quietness must learn in all subjection to teach"

The next word is δε which means "but", a conjunction that shows we are moving on to the next thought.

γυναικί means "the woman" or "the wife" based on how it is usually translated.

οὐκ means "not" ἐπιτρέπω means "allow" and is in the first person, so Paul is saying what he personally does not allow. οὐδε means "neither".
These 3 words combine together to form a construction which is a double negative negation in Greek. In English someone might say, "Badges? We ain't got no badges. We don't need no stinkin' badges!" or "We don't need no education, We don't need no thought control". The same sort of double negative negations are also present in Greek. And if one looks in the Thayer's under the word in question "oude" it reads:
"3. not even... Gal 2:3 in a double negative for the sake of emphasis, οὐκ...οὐδε... Matt 27:14; Luke 18:13; Acts 7:5."
And the same sort of double negative is used here for added emphasis in 1 Tim 2:12.

Let's look at some of the other verses which contain this same construction, so as to better understand how it works.
καὶ **οὐκ απεκρίθη αὐτω πρός οὐδε ἓν ῥῆμα** ωστε θαυμάζειν τόν ηγεμόνα λίαν
not answered to him **neither in word**
(not even a word, not never a word)
"And he answered him to never a word; insomuch that the governor marvelled greatly." Matt 27:14

καὶ ὁ τελώνης μακρόθεν εστως **οὐκ ηθελεν οὐδε τους ὀφθαλμους** εἰς τόν οὐρανόν ἐπαραι αλλ' ετυπτεν εἰς τό στηθος αὐτου λέγων, Ο θεός ἱλάσθητί μοι τω αμαρτωλω
not willing **neither his eyes** (not even his eyes, not never his eyes)
"And the publican, standing afar off, would not lift up so much as [his] eyes unto heaven, but smote upon his breast, saying, God be merciful to me a sinner." Luke 18:13

καί **οὐκ** εδωκεν αὐτω κληρονομίαν ἐν αὐτῃ **οὐδε** βημα ποδός καί ἐπηγγείλατο αὐτω δουναι εἰς κατάσχεσιν αὐτην καί τω σπέρματι αὐτου μετ' αὐτόν οὐκ οντος αὐτω τέκνου Acts 7:5
not give him inheritance in the land **neither** space-of foot
(not even a foot, not never a foot)
"He gave him no inheritance here, not even a foot of ground. But God promised him that he and his descendants after him would possess the land, even though at that time Abraham had no child." Acts 7:5

And so this double negative construction generally means "not even" or "not never", and places emphasis on the negation.

Back to 1 Tim 2:12, based on the examples above, how should it read?
οὐκ ἐπιτρέπω **οὐδε** αὐθεντείν ανδρός
not I-allow **neither** to-authentien the-man
but the woman "I allow not even" or "I allow not never" to-authentien the-man.

As such, Paul places great emphasis that he does not allow the woman to-authentien the man.
In any case, the word "neither" here does not refer to the verb teach, at all. It is part of a double negative construction centered around the verb of "I allow", referring to Paul.

So far this all reads,
A woman in quietness must learn in all subjection to teach. But the woman I allow not never to-authentien the-man, but to be in quietness.

αὐθεντείν means, according to both the Strong's and the Thayer's *"one who with his own hands kills others or himself"*. This is the primary usage listed, and as such, a large concept is built into this one compact verb.

ανδρός is usually translated "the man" or "the husband" and also means just a "person".
αλλ' is "but"
ειναι is "to be"
ἐν is "in"
ησυχία is "quietness", as was used before

All of this together reads:
"A woman in quietness, you must have her learn in all subjection to teach. But the woman **I allow not never** to be-one-who-with-her-own-hand-kills the man, but to be in quietness."
And the next verses are:
"For Adam was first formed, then Eve. And Adam was not deceived, but the woman being deceived became in the transgression."

So what does it mean?

"A woman in quietness, you must have her learn in all subjection to teach."
The first thing this says is that a woman in quietness must learn in all (classroom-type submission to authority) subjection to teach. This indicates that a woman who is going to teach, must first learn before she can teach. Timothy as a leader of the church is charged with this, that before she teaches she must first learn. So Timothy must have her learn. The woman is in quietness, stillness, *"description of the life of one who stays at home doing his own work, and does not officiously meddle with the affairs of others"*. This is the state she should be in as she learns, meaning she needs to do her work, not be meddlesome, and learn also, in all classroom-type subjection.

The main emphasis in the New Testament on teachers is that they teach the Word of God, the Bible, doctrine and concepts and truths found in the Word of God. While someone may have the gift of teaching, before they will have anything to teach, they first will have to learn the Word of God. And here Paul is telling Timothy to see to this, that she learns, so that she can teach. In short, Paul makes it clear to Timothy that a woman needs to learn so she can teach, and Timothy as a leader of the church needs to see to it that this is happening. And Timothy needs to make sure she learns before teaching.

"A woman in quietness, you must have her learn in all subjection to teach. But the woman **I allow not never** to be-one-who-with-her-own-hand-kills the man, but to be in quietness. For Adam was first formed, then Eve. And Adam was not deceived, but the woman being deceived became in the transgression."

Paul makes a clear reference here back to the story of Adam and Eve. It is in this story that we can understand why Paul used the word "authentein", as in context he is trying to convey to the reader the entire concept of Adam and Eve eating from the fruit of the tree, and what happened. Because (not having been taught the true Word of God) as Eve with her hand gave Adam the apple, with her hand she took part in the action of him eating the fruit, that both resulted in him dying, and also herself dying. In tempting him to eat she became "in the transgression" (in the one singular transgression of Adam eating). The verb "authentein" means "one who with his own hands kills others or himself". So this verb "authentein" is actually a perfect verb to use to describe this.

And here Paul (who wrote Romans 5 which explains all die because of 1 sin committed by Adam) goes into a further explanation of what he means. Which is not that the woman is responsible for killing the man, but rather that being deceived, she became in the singular transgression, became part of Adam's sin, because she tempted him. And by Adam's choice to sin, he killed himself and her. So this is balanced, as Paul recognizes their deaths were ultimately because of the 1 sin of Adam (Rom 5), and so it is fairly balanced here to reference to Eve's part in it. Paul is by no means blaming Eve by using the word this way, but rather it is referential to his points which relate the story.

Paul is making a couple of points here.
Paul is making the point that a woman is trusting, and this can make her easy to deceive, and a woman who teaches something could lead others astray. For instance, after Adam lied and did not

teach her the true Word of God, the serpent "taught" Eve a deception, which she believed, and after she ate from the tree, she thought she had something to "teach" Adam, and handed him the fruit. That is what "authentein" references to here, to convey the meaning that a woman, can be potentially dangerous if she teaches without first being taught the truth of the Word of God. (The same obviously being true of a man also.)

As such the second point he makes is that Paul is speaking of his own responsibility, leading by example, trying to convey to Timothy as a church leader that he absolutely does not allow a woman to get into the situation of the same sort of thing happening again. What happened with Adam and Eve is an important reason why it is important for her to learn before teaching, in which Paul points out to Timothy a woman must (imperative command) learn in all subjection to teach. She must be a student, of a true teacher, before she is a teacher herself. Otherwise, a situation in which she has been deceived or is incorrect might arise, and she could end up helping to hurt others or herself unintentionally.

And Paul makes it clear he as a church leader absolutely never allows this to happen, but rather for her to be in quietness, which is referencing back to her being in a state of learning, "but to be in quietness (learning)". Paul conveys to Timothy that he considers it his responsibility to make sure the women learn before they teach. In other words, he does not want women to teach until they have learned, because someone could get hurt, someone else, or herself, and he does not want any responsibility on himself for that. In essence, Paul does not want to do as Adam did, by withholding the Word of God from a woman, leaving her in ignorance, and references to the consequences.

Who she could hurt with a false teaching could be anyone else, as the "the-man" here is more likely just a word used as an example that fits the reference to the story. In other places this word "the-man" which is "andros" can refer to someone of either gender. So a woman teacher who has not learned first, potentially could hurt another woman with her teachings, and that is also a possibility which is implied here. Paul says he never allows that to happen, leading by example to Timothy with the responsibilities of a church leader, and giving instructions likewise. Paul makes sure that women do learn before they teach. Paul instructs Timothy as a church leader to make sure this happens, and also writes so the women of the church understand this themselves, that "she must learn in all subjection to teach".

And this references well back to Paul's student Priscilla, who he led to Christ, and taught her and her husband, and they both later taught Apollos. Paul himself taught a woman, and Acts recognizes this same woman taught Apollos, and there is no problem mentioned with any of this. In this story, it is in fact very clear that the Bible says it is fine for a woman to teach a man, and in this case her actions were part of how he was led to salvation in Jesus Christ.

These verses do not restrict women from teaching men, or a woman from teaching a man. These verses do not at all refer to a woman "usurping authority" over a man. Neither of these concepts are present in these verses.

These verses instruct a church leader to make sure that women learn, and specify this as a necessity in order for her to teach, and make this a church responsibility. Rather than restrict her from teaching, these verses acknowledge, affirm, and accommodate women as teachers. And this is done especially keeping in mind both that her trusting nature makes her potentially vulnerable to being deceived, and that the women in that time in general were not as educated as the men. The emphasis in this aspect is bringing her up to speed.

These verses say a woman should learn as a student, with proper respect for the teacher. These verses say she should learn co-currently with doing her work and not being meddlesome in the affairs of others, being tranquil. And so in this women are instructed by Paul, through Timothy, to themselves consider Paul's words and have the self-control and wisdom from God to acknowledge that they must guard themselves from being false teachers, and be responsible, and themselves make sure they are well-learned before they teach. These are the guidelines, pointed out to the women through his letter, that they are to follow. But having accepted the responsibility to learn first, and having learned first, they are in no way restricted from teaching after they have learned.

The women only appeared to be singled out here because firstly they needed to be brought up to speed, and reminded to guard against being gullible or being deceived, and to recognize their own need to be educated with the truth first, before they taught others. And this is as much common sense for women as it should also be for men, and is equally true for men, but the men at this time were more likely to be able to read and be familiar with the scriptures. But the heaviest emphasis in this verse is directed to Timothy or any church leader that responsibility falls upon, to facilitate the women to learn, or they will bear some responsibility for negligence.

In fact, Paul was fighting against sexism in the church, so that it would (as Jesus or he does in so many other places) open up new doors for women that were far greater than they were accustomed to in the Pharisaical Jewish culture and religion they had been in.

And Paul cautions Timothy that he never allows a woman to get into a situation of accidentally hurting herself or others because she tried to teach while being unlearned in the truth of God's Word. And Paul further emphasizes that women have a trait of being deceived due to being trusting, and so this is a very good reason for Timothy to make sure the women learn before they teach.

Furthering into a correct understanding of Genesis 3, and Romans 5, another point made here is that not teaching a woman the truth, the Word of God, was also a mistake made by Adam. So Paul further points to Timothy's responsibility to teach the women the

Word of God, lest it prove disastrous for the church. The way that Paul <u>never</u> allows a woman to potentially hurt anyone else or herself is the way of prevention. Paul makes sure that women learn before they teach, so they will know God's Word, and the situation will be prevented. Knowing God's True Word, they will not be easily deceived, and will not accidentally hurt someone else or themselves in trying to teach.

An ounce of prevention (teaching her the truth of the Word of God) is worth a pound of cure (her and others being hurt), is basically what Paul says here.

After referencing to Eve's part in the 1 transgression, which was her tempting Adam to eat, Paul then references here to the punishment she received for her part in the transgression, but in a very positive redemptive way:
"But she shall saved through childbearing, if they continue in faith and love and holiness with sobriety."
This is a most strong and excellent promise to Christian women, saying that she will be kept safe through her childbearing, if she continues in faith and love and holiness with sobriety. This is an excellent promise to claim, too.

In summary, 1 Tim 2:11-14 is actually one of the strongest passages in the New Testament that shows the church's need, and the requirement on church leaders, to recognize women as teachers and make sure to meet their needs to be taught. And while making clear that the church must make sure to accommodate and facilitate women to learn and be taught before they teach, it places no restrictions whatsoever on who women can teach once they have been taught. There is no difference here between the women and the men, both must learn to teach, but emphasis is placed on women here as many at that time were not yet educated. Ultimately, the gift of teaching is given by the Holy Spirit to whomever He wills, including women, along with any of the other gifts that comprise one's calling from God. And it is the responsibility of the church to provide for and facilitate women as students and as teachers in the body of Christ.

And besides this, women may be apostles, prophets, or have any of the other gifts of the Holy Spirit as well. And the church needs to facilitate a woman in whatever calling, whatever gifts, she may have.

In 1 Timothy 2, after covering points helpful to men and women in preaching the Gospel, Paul spends a brief but powerful time covering women as students and teachers, before a full transition into covering the qualifications for the offices of elder and deacon, in the next chapter of 1 Timothy 3.

Chapter Fourteen
A Pause for a Romans 13 Study

We are going to take a brief pause from the overall flow of this series, to take a look at Romans 13...

This is going to be a straight scripture translation study, which is foundational to understanding of the next couple of articles, and Biblical concepts. First we are going to go through a translation verse by verse, fresh from the Greek, of Romans 13. Following this will be commentary and explanation for understanding what this actually says. Then this will touch on John 19 and 1 Peter 2 in a few verses.

First shown below is a an example of a modern translation, influenced by the KJV translation from the 1500s, by those living under a monarchy, a translation commissioned by the King, James. Next the Greek is shown, with a very literal word-by-word from the Greek. Finally, underlined, is what I believe is a more correct and honest translation of what is actually said in the Greek.

Romans 13

Every person is to be in subjection to the governing authorities For there is no authority except from God, and those which exist are established by God.

πασα ψυχη ἐξουσίαις υπερεχούσαις υποτασσέσθω οὐ γάρ εστιν ἐξουσία εἰ μη υπό θεου αἱ δε ουσαι υπό θεου τεταγμέναι εἰσίν

all souls authorities to-hold-over-prominent submit-themselves not for is authority except under God the but(moreover/and) that-is(being) under God and self-appointed/arranged that-is(being)

<u>Every person is to submit themselves to the authorities having hold over them, for there is no authority except under God, but the authorities which exist are under God, and exist self-arranged.</u>

Therefore whoever resists authority has opposed the ordinance of God; and they who have opposed will receive condemnation upon themselves.

ωστε ὁ αντιτασσόμενος τη ἐξουσία τη του θεου διαταγη ανθέστηκεν οἱ δε ανθεστηκότες εαυτοίς κρίμα λήμψονται

So then whoever will not submit himself to the authority, the of God disposition resist they but themselves sentencing take

So then whoever will not submit himself to the authorities, resists the disposition of God, and themselves will take sentencing.

For rulers are not a cause of fear for good behavior, but for evil. Do you want to have no fear of authority? Do what is good and you will have praise from the same;

οἱ γάρ αρχοντες οὐκ εἰσίν φόβος τω αγαθω εργω αλλά τω κακω θέλεις δε μη φοβείσθαι την ἐξουσίαν τό αγαθόν ποίει καί εξεις επαινον ἐξ αὐτης

the for rulers not are fear/dread/terror the good business but the evil, you-want but not to-fear the/their authority the/this/that good do and you-will-have praise from the-same

For the rulers are not a fear to the good business but the evil. You want to not fear their authority? This good do and you will have praise from the rulers.

For it is a minister of God to you for good. But if you do what is evil, be afraid; for it does not bear the sword for nothing; for it is a minister of God, an avenger who brings wrath on the one who practices evil.

θεου γάρ διάκονός ἐστιν σοί εἰς τό αγαθόν ἐάν δε τό κακόν ποιης φοβου οὐ γάρ εἰκη την μάχαιραν φορεί θεου γάρ διάκονός ἐστιν εκδικος εἰς ὀργην τω τό κακόν πράσσοντι

God for servant are/is you to/into the/this/he/it good if/except but/and/also/now the/this/it evil you-do/make to-fear not for vainly(without success) the/this/he/it sword to-wear God for servant are/is avenger to/into/among/against punishment the/this/it/those the/this/that evil commit

For you are God's servant towards this good, except if now this evil you do, be afraid, it is not vainly these wear the sword, the punisher is God's servant towards punishing those that commit evil.

Therefore it is necessary to be in subjection, not only because of wrath, but also for conscience' sake.

διό ανάγκη υποτάσσεσθαι ού μόνον διά την όργην αλλά καί διά την συνείδησιν

wherefore neccessary to-submit-yourselves not only through/by/reason this/the punishment but and/also/even through/by/reason this/the conscience.

This is why it is necessary to submit yourselves, not only because of the punishment, but also because of the conscience.

For because of this you also pay taxes, for rulers are servants of God, devoting themselves to this very thing.

διά τουτο γάρ καί φόρους τελείτε λειτουργοί γάρ θεου εισιν εις αύτό τουτο προσκαρτερουντες

through/by/reason that/this(thing) for and/even/also taxes you-pay servants/ministers for God they-are to/into/towards the-same this/that(thing) they-to-continue-steadfastly(constant attention to)

For because of this [punishing of those who commit evil] you servants for God pay taxes, these [taxes] are towards giving constant attention to this same thing [punishing of those who commit evil].

255

Render to all what is due them: tax to whom tax is due; custom to whom custom; fear to whom fear; honor to whom honor.

απόδοτε πασιν τάς όφειλάς τω τόν φόρον τόν φόρον τω τό τέλος τό τέλος τω τόν φόβον τόν φόβον τω την τιμην την τιμήν

Pay-off all your debt this/your those taxes whom taxes, this/your those custom whom custom, this/your those fear whom fear, this/your those honor whom honor.

<u>Pay off all your debts, your taxes to whom taxes, your custom to whom custom, your fear to whom fear, your honor to whom honor.</u>

Owe nothing to anyone except to love one another; for he who loves his neighbor has fulfilled the law.

μηδενί μηδεν όφείλετε εί μη τό αλλήλους αγαπαν ό γάρ αγαπων τόν ετερον νόμον πεπλήρωκεν

no one nothing owe except the loving one-another this for loving the other law is-fulfilling

<u>Owe nothing! Nothing except the loving of one another, for loving one another is fulfilling the law.</u>

All together this is:
"Every person is to submit themselves to the authorities having hold over them, for there is no authority except under God, but the authorities which exist are under God, and exist self-arranged. So then whoever will not submit himself to the authorities, resists the disposition of God, and themselves will take sentencing. For the rulers are not a fear to the good business but the evil. You want to not fear their authority? This good do and you will have praise from the rulers. For you are God's servant towards this good, except if now this evil you do, be afraid, it is not vainly these wear the sword, the punisher is God's servant towards punishing those that commit evil. This is why it is necessary to submit yourselves,

not only because of the punishment, but also because of the conscience. For because of this [punishing of those who commit evil] you servants for God pay taxes, these [taxes] are towards giving constant attention to this same thing [punishing of those who commit evil]. Pay off all your debts, your taxes to whom taxes, your custom to whom custom, your fear to whom fear, your honor to whom honor. Owe nothing! Nothing except the loving of one another, for loving one another is fulfilling the law."

With expanded meaning:

A King named James commissioned the KJV, and still today so many modern translations default to it as a standard, no matter how much its translation was skewed by translators seeking approval from the King who commissioned it.

"Every person is to submit themselves to the authorities having hold over them, for there is no authority except under God, but the authorities which exist are under God, and exist self-arranged."

You are not to obey, but rather to "submit yourself", to the authorities which have power over you. There is no authority except under God, which means that unless something is in line with God's will a person has no business to be doing it. However, all the authorities which do exist in the world are in fact under God, because they exist, and He is Almighty and above them. For instance, God reigns, but Satan is still the prince of this world. This does not mean that they are on the same side. Similar, the governments and rulers exist, and are also under God. This also makes note that the authorities of this world exist self-arranged or self-appointed. Which means the people of this world arrange or appoint themselves into systems of power over others, whatever system it may be, good or bad, with consent of the people or not. But no matter what system, God is still above it, and it is under Him. There is nothing that is not under God, as He reigns supreme, and so these authorities that exist (self-arranged) are under God's power too.

"So then whoever will not submit himself to the authorities, resists the disposition of God, and themselves will take sentencing."

The disposition of God refers to God's "permissive" will, and not his explicit will. We can see that God must be disposed to allow the rulers of this earth to continue on, if they exist, because if God was not so disposed, they would all cease to exist. Therefore their existence is proof positive of God's disposition to permissively allow whatever authorities to exist which do exist. This does not mean that God ordained them, or established them or approves of all they do. This term "sentencing" refers to worldly courtrooms of the laws of the land. If you break the law of the land, and refuse to submit to the law of the land, then yes, you will receive sentencing, in the courts of the land.

"For the rulers are not a fear to the good business but the evil. You want to not fear their authority? This good do and you will have praise from the rulers."

The "good business" refers to business. This term equates very much to the usage of the terms "right and wrong" versus our modern day uses of the terms "good and evil". The law of the land defines what is right and wrong, and God in the Bible defines what is good and evil. What is right by the law of the land is called "good business" which is referenced again in the phrase "This good do", which makes clear that the good to do is "good business", which is what is "right" under the law of the land. And so if you do what the rulers consider as "good business" or right, under the laws of the land, you will not have to fear their authority. Instead you will receive praise from the rulers.

"For you are God's servant towards this good, except if now this evil you do, be afraid, it is not vainly these wear the sword, the punisher is God's servant towards punishing those that commit evil."

Again, "this good" and "this evil" refer back to "business" under the laws of the land, which is much like we use the terms "right" and "wrong" today. There is what is "right" under the law, and what is "wrong", and how much this matches what is biblically defined as "Good" and "Evil" varies, even seems to only line up coincidentally by chance at times. Here Paul makes clear that you are actually being God's servant in doing what is "right" by the law of the land. But if you do "wrong" by the law of the land, then be afraid, as those in power can hurt you. This power they have is not for no reason, but rather for a serious reason. Paul carries on this idea to explain that the authorities have power so that they can punish those who commit actual biblical evil. The evil Paul refers to here is not "this evil (business)" as in "wrong" under the law. Rather Paul refers to actual moral evil, that is really evil. So here Paul merges 2 ideas, that the punisher has power in order to punish those who do commit biblically defined evil, not just those who do "wrong" by the law of the land.

Note the verse reads "towards punishing" which implies motion towards. This makes clear that in fact the punisher is doing something towards the goal of punishing those who commit evil, his actions show effort towards this punishing those who do evil, but this does not mean that the punisher gets it correct all the time, or in any way defines moral Good and Evil by his actions.

This further explains why it is God's disposition, or permissive will, to allow these authorities to exist. They just exist, as they have arranged themselves, not ordained by God, but simply under Him and His power, as all things are. But God let's them go on, and He is disposed to, as is His disposition, at least for the reason that they do (often) punish those who commit actual Evil (in the sight of God.)

This means that for all earthly rulers do wrong, they usually at least get 1 thing right, which is to punish those who do Evil, at least in part, such as murderers and thieves. Apparently this is better than the anarchy of murderers and thieves running around making amuck free without punishment.

So we should all be able to admit, at least most governments usually do something right, in that they do punish the moral evildoers, to some extent, even if only in part. If this is enough of a valid reason for God to let them stay in existence, then we should also see this as valid.

"This is why it is necessary to submit yourselves, not only because of the punishment, but also because of the conscience."

So we need to submit ourselves to these earthly authorities, because quite factually, if we don't we can or will get punished. But also, another good reason is because of conscience. This may be because of tripping up our own consciences, violating them, and shipwrecking our faith. Or this may refer to putting a stumbling block in the way of another believer, or a lost person, by making them think a Christian is a bad/evil person, because a Christian does not do that which is thought of as right ("this good (business)") and instead does what is thought of as wrong ("this evil"); doing what is wrong and not what is right under the laws of the land. Certainly there is much in the New Testament pertaining to how important it is to not violate your own conscience, or the conscience of other people, as it can prove a stumbling block to others, and shipwreck their faith or your faith.

"For because of this [punishing of those who commit evil] you servants for God pay taxes, these [taxes] are towards giving constant attention to this same thing [punishing of those who commit evil]."

Paul seems to say here that as servants of God we pay taxes so someone will be giving constant attention to punishment of those who commit actual biblical evil. Which implies that we get something out of this, in that Evildoers are punished, so they are not as likely to do evil to us (or others).

"Pay off all your debts, your taxes to whom taxes, your custom to whom custom, your fear to whom fear, your honor to whom honor."

As those authorities do the service of punishing evildoers, who do Biblical evil, which is a service which benefits us, this seems to say that taxes are debts which we owe, and so need to pay off, along with customs. We benefit from the service of these authorities in their punishment of evildoers of actual Biblical moral evil, and so therefore we should pay them taxes for the services they have rendered to us. Fear here might be better understood as respect or apprehension of fearful potential, and so we should also pay off all our debts of respect and honor due to earthly authorities.

"Owe nothing! Nothing except the loving of one another, for loving one another is fulfilling the law."

Here "owe nothing!" is put as an imperative, which means, do it! Owe nothing! In other words, a debt is being referred to, and we should not owe a debt. Except the loving of one another is still owed, which is implied as owed continually, as this is the fulfilling of the command to love your neighbor as yourself. And this is the fulfillment of the Law.

"The commandments, "You shall not commit adultery," "You shall not murder," "You shall not steal," "You shall not covet," and whatever other command there may be, are summed up in this one command: "Love your neighbor as yourself." Love does no harm to a neighbor.
Therefore love is the fulfillment of the law.
And do this, understanding the present time: The hour has already come for you to wake up from your slumber, because our salvation is nearer now than when we first believed. The night is nearly over; the day is almost here. So let us put aside the deeds of darkness and put on the armor of light. Let us behave decently, as in the daytime, not in carousing and drunkenness, not in sexual immorality and debauchery, not in dissension and jealousy. Rather, clothe yourselves with the Lord Jesus Christ, and do not think about how to gratify the desires of the flesh."

John 19:11-12

"Then saith Pilate unto him, Speakest thou not unto me? knowest thou not that I have power to crucify thee, and have power to release thee? Jesus answered, Thou couldest have no power [at all] against me, except it were <u>given thee</u> from above: therefore he that delivered me unto thee hath the greater sin."

Here "given thee" is the word "didomi" which also means "to grant or permit". So this could also read "permitted thee from above".

And as God has permitted Pilate to be in power, those who brought Jesus to Pilate, accused as a criminal, falsely accused, those Jews who brought Jesus to Pilate have the greater sin. In other words, in keeping with Romans 13, Pilate was permitted to be in authority in order to punish evildoers. Those who falsely accused Jesus as an evildoer and brought Him to Pilate were the worse sinners, because to some extent Pilate was just trying to do one valid part of his job as a ruler. God allowed Pilate to have the power to punish evildoers, and he was just trying to do this. Those who falsely brought Jesus to Pilate, accusing him of being an evildoer, had the worse sin.

1 Pet 2:12-16

Here I have made corrections from the Greek also, but am showing them in brief, as I focused only on a number of the key words:

"Having your behavior admirable among the Gentiles: that, whereas they speak against you as evildoers, by your good business, which they having watched, they may glorify God on the day of investigation. Submit yourselves to all human institutions because of the Lord: whether it be to the king, as higher; or unto governors, as unto them that are sent by him for the punishment of evildoers, and for the praise of them that do well. For so is the will of God, that with well doing ye may put to silence the ignorance of foolish people: As free, but not as pretext for having maliciousness is your liberty, but as the servants of God."

This closely parallels Romans 13. I think especially important in this is the term "human institutions" which is in the KJV as "ordinance of man". This is misleading as "of man" is an adjective. "Human institutions" is much clearer. And this also clarifies very well that kings and governors, governments, etc. are in fact human institutions. Again, this passage mentions "good business" or what is "right" according to the laws of the land, versus what is morally Good as defined by the Bible. In this passage, it implies that Christians who follow the laws of the land, are observed to do so by the authorities, and so when ignorant people speak against the Christians as evildoers, when the matter is investigated by the authorities of the land, the authorities will glorify God on account of the upright citizens that the Christians are. And in this, the ignorant and foolish persecutors will be silenced. Understood correctly, this makes much more sense, and these are very practical instructions for Christians which give clarity about practical situations and cause and effect of living in this world, dealing with human institutions, of worldly governments and authorities.

Overall between these 3 passages, the meaning is clear that these human institutions of authority are permitted by God, and God finds them to have at least one beneficial reason to exist, so allows them. This beneficial reason is that they often do punish those who commit moral evil, if imperfectly.

But nowhere do these verses say that God has ordained these human institutions, but rather that they are human institutions, instituted by humans, and these institutions are self-arranging. Which means people have made and arranged these institutions themselves. The existence of rulers in authority, of whatever sort of government, is an arrangement of the humans, by the humans, and to some extent for the humans, which is Only permissively permitted by God, Only towards the punishment of those who commit evil. Even in this, the implication is only towards this end of the punishment of moral evildoers, and nothing specifies that human institutions do this perfectly, but rather only that they do this in part, and work towards this goal, however incompletely or imperfectly. No other reason why God permits these human institutions of governments is mentioned, nor validated. And the verses here should be noted to clearly only speak on human institutions of governance, not "authorities" in any more general of a sense.

Chapter Fifteen
Humanity's History

Before the first sin was the first evil desire, which led to the first sin. The first evil desire was that man wanted to rule over another man, a female man. A man wanted his words to another man to be equal with God's words. A man wanted to be sovereign over another man. A man wanted to be the ruler over another man, to do as he pleased, whatever he might want, without regard to God's commandment. In this desire, to be lord and master over another man, that he would have more power than another man, that he would possess as much as another man, even if it was forbidden by God, even in disobeying God's will, this is what led to the first sin.

And so it was only a continuation of the first man's evil desire which led to sin, when God told the weaker man that the stronger man would rule over him. In the beginning God made man, male and female made He them, in His image and after His likeness. And the first sin was all about the stronger man wanting to rule over the weaker man, in clear disobedience to God. God's original intent was clearly for God to rule over each man, male or female, individually and directly. And it was the stronger man's desire to rule over the weaker man, instead of God's rule, which led to the first sin.

As history progressed, this evil desire, which was the core of the first sin, took several forms. The first form was a male-man ruling over a female-man. Next, a male-man ruling over several female-men. Then soon to follow was a male-man ruling over another male-man, and then a male-man ruling over many male-men, and female-man followed suit as well. And in all cases, this is oppression.

The first sinful construct man made contrary to God's will should be the most obvious, which was the idea that a man owned his wife. Next, the man owned many "wives" or "concubines". He also owned his children, and continued to own his female children even upon maturity.

Then a man came to own another man. Then a man came to own many men.

To quote Joshua in the movie The 10 Commandments,
God made men. Men made slaves.
Indeed it is true. Male-men made slaves, first of female-men, then of other male-men.

How did this come about? We can see the immoral tactics used by Adam to rule over Eve, and how she took to this so easily, as a woman was designed to be trusting and want a man to love her. Truly, God made women to naturally follow and submit to a man, and this is God's will, but this is in fact the opposite of a man ruling over her, and was always meant to be balanced out in love and equality. But as it was not, it is easy to understand that as he took authority over her, which God never gave him, he also claimed more authority than her over the children as well. The sons grew to fill his shoes, and were like him, and the daughters he kept or gave away ultimately as he saw fit, having more say than their mother, who he oppressed in ruling over her.

And Adam's sons were like Adam. That Adam envied that Eve could eat of a single tree he could not eat of, and was willing to lie to her, disobey God, and even with his sin cause her to die, all of this iniquity was visited upon his sons, and passed down through him.

Gen 4:3-8 "And in the process of time it came to pass that Cain brought an offering of the fruit of the ground to the LORD. Abel also brought of the firstborn of his flock and of their fat. And the LORD respected Abel and his offering, but He did not respect Cain and his offering. And Cain was very angry, and his countenance fell. So the LORD said to Cain, "Why are you angry? And why has your countenance fallen? If you do well, will you not be accepted? And if you do not do well, your sin offering lies at the door. And it will return to you, and you should master it." Now Cain talked with Abel his brother; and it came to pass, when they were in the field, that Cain rose up against Abel his brother and killed him."

Who does not know the story of Cain and Abel? Cain the first-born was like Adam, and envying his brother's favor with God, like Adam envied Eve over what seemed as favor, and Cain was willing to kill his brother Abel, just as in eating from the tree, Adam caused Eve to die. The stories are very closely paralleled, showing the traits of the father passed on to his sons. And a man who could not rule over another man, or beat him in competition, would kill him.

The tactics a man used over his wife to oppress her, rule over her, and dominate her, from the beginning, are clearly seen in the words of Lamech, who was Cain's great-great-great-grandson. Lamech was the first man to mock God's construct of marriage, as God designed it to be. He was the first man to practice polygamy. How did he rule over 2 wives, as he was outnumbered?
"And Lamech took unto him two wives:
the name of the one was Adah, and the name of the other Zillah....
And Lamech said unto his wives,
Adah and Zillah, Obey my voice; <u>ye wives of Lamech,</u>
be obedient unto my speech:
for I have slain a man to my wounding, and a boy child to my hurt.
If Cain shall be avenged sevenfold, truly Lamech seventy and sevenfold." Gen 4:19,23-24

There are several things to note here. The first as underlined, is that Lamech made a big point to his wives that they were owned by him, like his possessions. They knew he was their husband and they were his "wives" that he had taken. He was not saying this to them to remind them they were married, but rather to make it clear to them that he considered them his possessions, like he owned them.

And what does he tell them? To obey him and to be obedient to his voice. Why? Because he has killed a boy child, even to his own hurt and wounding. Essentially, he makes it clear to them that he is capable of killing a child, even if later he feels pain about it. So, he tells his wives to obey him because he is capable of killing a child, even a child that it will hurt him later to have killed, a child he implies he therefore has some love for. Now what would that bring to mind but their own children? It implies 'Obey him, his owned wives, because he is capable of killing your children, even a child you think he cares for.' And after this, he makes it clear that he has killed a child, and implies he could do it again, but God will not punish him for it, and he will get away with it.

And he also adds to God's Word to his "wives", as Adam did with Eve, and passes his own words off to them like they are the words of God. Apparently he believes that God will not punish him for murdering a child, or at least he wants his wives to believe this, and he tells them this because he wants them to obey him. Though he says he has killed a child it is unknown if he actually did, or if all of this was just said to threaten his wives so they would obey him, using their love for their children as a weapon against them. The Bible does not record that Lamech killed anyone, and it is entirely possible that he lied and made all of this up just to cause his wives to fear for the lives of their children if they did not obey him.
And so, the first polygamist ruled over his "wives".

Now, were they actually both married to him? Jesus teaches a resounding NO.
"Haven't you read," he replied, "that at the beginning the Creator 'made them male and female,' and said, 'For this reason a man will leave his father and mother and be united to his wife, and the **two will become one flesh**'? So they are no longer **two**, but one flesh. Therefore what **God has joined together**, let no one separate." Matt 19:4-6
"But at the beginning of creation God 'made them male and female.' For this reason a man will leave his father and mother and be united to his wife, and the **two** will become one flesh.' So they are no longer **two, but one flesh**. Therefore **what God has joined together**, let no one separate." Mark 10:6-9,
And also see,
"For this cause shall a man leave his father and mother, and shall be joined unto his wife, and they **two shall be one flesh**." Eph 5:31

Jesus twice confirms, and also God through Paul, that marriage is the union of TWO people, 1 Man and 1 Woman. It is **God that joins them together** into one flesh. This is something God does, and that God alone is sovereign over. It is not and has never been up to the will of man to join himself to a woman in marriage, but in fact God joins them together in what is marriage before God in His sight. Marriage in the sight of Jesus, of God, is only the union of 1 man and 1 woman, and that is the same as it always has been from the beginning. And how it works has never been up to man. God joins people in marriage, according to His will, not according to the will of men. God also grants divorce according to His will, not according to the will of man. Men's laws do not matter, as to what men say marriage is or when divorce can occur. In truth, God has always retained complete sovereignty over marriage and divorce. Men's laws they have made about it have never changed a thing.

And so while the Bible often records that a man had many "wives", the truth is that men at the time called them "wives" and this was the word they used, but in truth they were never their wives. But as daughters were given in marriage, and as men took women to possess them, this is how it was, and women had little or no choice over it.

At this time, there was no custom of betrothal. Essentially, a man "took" a wife, and that is exactly what he did. At this time, men married their sisters at first, and when he had reached an age to find her attractive, he "took" her, and then she was his wife. Because men ruled over their wives, considering them "owned" in a way, so they also "owned" their daughters, and gave them away in marriage as well. This was the time before the flood, and the custom of Jewish betrothal was not yet around. But of course, if a man laid with a girl and wronged her, he would have to deal with her father, especially if a father loved his daughter and was offended. So surely they worked it out amongst themselves, but a girl had no recourse or real choice about who she married, beyond what love her father had for her, that he might wish her to be happy and protect her or give her some choice in the matter.

The next instance of polygamy mentioned is in Gen 6:2
"That the sons of God saw the daughters of men that they were fair; and they took them wives of all which they chose."
In this case, they each took many wives, of all which they chose. Shortly thereafter, God destroyed the world with a flood. No matter what you think of the strange phrase "sons of God" as to who they were, the fact is that they took multiple "wives", and likely set an example for other men around them to do the same, making polygamy more common in that time. Along the lines of "Hey, the sons of God, who sure have an important title, are taking lots of wives, let's be like them and do that too."

And it is interesting to note that Noah had one wife, a man of whom God says in Gen 6:9,
"These are the records of the generations of Noah. <u>Noah was a righteous man, blameless in his time;</u> Noah walked with God."

Not that Noah was without sin or perfect, but in his time, he was a righteous man. And he had one wife. All the more interesting is that in a culture which allowed and accepted polygamy, each of Noah's sons had 1 wife each. And these 4 married couples were saved from the flood, only 8 souls, one man and one woman each.

After the flood, God said, in Gen 9:6,
"Whoso sheddeth man's blood, by man shall his blood be shed: for in the image of God made he man."
And so the threat of Lamech to his "wives" was made void, as no longer could a man threaten to kill a woman's child and get away with it, or say God was protecting him, in trying to rule over her. Surely, there was more good reason for God to say this, but noting the words of Lamech, it is interesting.

After the flood is the first time we see both kings, and slaves. The first time that a servant is mentioned in the Bible, of one person being over another person, is in Gen 12:5,
"He took his wife Sarai, his nephew Lot, all the possessions they had accumulated <u>and the people they had acquired</u> in Haran, and they set out for the land of Canaan, and they arrived there."

In this case this is a broad term. In Gen 13:8 some of these people are specified to be herdsmen, as Abraham owned many cattle. And so some of these people may have been his employees, who worked for him with pay. But not all were: some were servants or slaves who were essentially owned.

In Gen 14:1 there is the first mention of kings of a particular city, and the kings of various cities banding together to make war against other bands of kings of little cities. In the fighting, Abraham's nephew Lot is taken captive, to be made a slave. In some extreme irony, Abraham takes his slaves who were born in his house, and they all go with him to rescue his nephew Lot from the fate of slavery. This is a very informative passage,

Gen 14:11-24: "And they took all the goods of Sodom and Gomorrah, and all their victuals, and went their way. And they took Lot, Abram's brother's son, who dwelt in Sodom, and his goods, and departed. And there came one that had escaped, and told Abram the Hebrew; for he dwelt in the plain of Mamre the Amorite, brother of Eshcol, and brother of Aner: and these were confederate with Abram. And when Abram heard that his brother was <u>taken captive</u>, he armed his trained <u>slaves, born in his own house 318</u>, and pursued them unto Dan. And he divided himself against them, he and his slaves, by night, and smote them, and pursued them unto Hobah, which is on the left hand of Damascus. And he brought back all the goods, and also <u>brought again his brother Lot, and his goods, and the women also, and the people.</u> And the king of Sodom went out to meet him after his return from the slaughter of Chedorlaomer, and of the kings that were with him, at the valley of Shaveh, which is the king's dale. And Melchizedek king of Salem brought forth bread and wine: and he was the priest of the most high God. And he blessed him, and said, Blessed be Abram of the most high God, possessor of heaven and earth: And blessed be the most high God, which hath delivered thine enemies into thy hand. And he gave him tithes of all. <u>And the king of Sodom said unto Abram, Give me the persons, and take the goods to thyself.</u> And Abram said to the king of Sodom, I have lift up mine hand unto the LORD, the most high God, the possessor of heaven and earth, That I will not take from a thread even to a shoelatchet, and that I will not take any thing that is thine, lest thou shouldest say, I have made Abram rich: Save only that which the young men have eaten, and the portion of the men which went with me, Aner, Eshcol, and Mamre; let them take their portion."

We can learn several things from this passage. Abraham was horrified enough about his nephew being taken captive, to be made a slave, that he takes over 318 of his own slaves to go rescue him. These 318 men had been born in his house, and essentially were under his rule, and he owned them. By definition, a slave is a slave when they are born into slavery, and so there is no confusion here that these 318 men were in fact slaves, not servants by choice or indentured. There were also likely ones that had not been born in his own house that went too, that he likely had purchased. He did not want this fate to become a slave to befall his nephew Lot. Lot also owned many people, and when Abraham rescues Lot, he also brings back Lot's women, possessions, and people. Those would be the people that Lot had as servants or slaves. Later the king of Sodom tells Abraham to take the goods, but to give him the people, which means he would take them as slaves. Abraham insists that he does not want the possessions, agreeing for the king to take the slaves. But Abraham insists that the 3 men who went with him should take their portion, who are Aner, Eshcol and Mamre.

Funny, it seems like at least 318 men went to battle with Abraham, but yet he only asks for 3 men to have a portion of the spoils. Why? Because those 3 men were free men, and leaders of their own estate of slaves and servants. The rest of the men, the 318 slaves, were not considered to be equally as men, because they were slaves, born into slavery. Now, there is every reason to think that they were treated well, more like servants than slaves, but nevertheless they were not considered equally men as Abraham, Aner, Eshcol, Mamre, and Lot, who all had slaves under them.

And so we see both kings of cities, and also rich free men of power like Abraham who had many servants or slaves under them. Were these slaves all male? No. They were also women. And the first time we see the concept of a "concubine", a female slave that a man has sex with, although she is not his wife, is in the case of Hagar, Sarah, and Abraham. And while men invented polygamy, of many "wives", and women had no choice about it, Sarah was the first person recorded to have made a slave into a "concubine".

"Now Sarai, Abram's wife, had borne him no children. But she had an Egyptian slave named Hagar; so she said to Abram, "The LORD has kept me from having children. Go, sleep with my slave; perhaps I can build a family through her." Abram agreed to what Sarai said. So after Abram had been living in Canaan ten years, Sarai his wife took her Egyptian slave Hagar and gave her to her husband to be his wife. He slept with Hagar, and she conceived. When she knew she was pregnant, she began to despise her mistress(owner). Then Sarai said to Abram, "You are responsible for the wrong I am suffering. I put my slave in your arms, and now that she knows she is pregnant, she despises me. May the LORD judge between you and me." "Your slave is in your hands," Abram said. "Do with her whatever you think best." Then Sarai mistreated Hagar; so she fled from her. The angel of the LORD found Hagar near a spring in the desert; it was the spring that is beside the road to Shur. And he said, "Hagar, slave of Sarai, where have you come from, and where are you going?" "I'm running away from my mistress Sarai (owner)" she answered. Then the angel of the LORD told her, "Go back to your mistress(owner) and submit to her." The angel added, "I will increase your descendants so much that they will be too numerous to count."

And so while it is entirely possible that men did sleep with their female slaves before this, the problem is that then the owner has sons and daughters by the female slave, who stood to inherit. Which is a likely reason why men did not have actual intercourse with their female slaves. There was a class system of owners and slaves in this society, and the two did not mix so that a man's heirs were from a slave. Sarah gives Hagar to be Abraham's second wife, but when it doesn't work out as Hagar hates Sarah, Abraham makes clear that she is still Sarah's slave. She was not given her freedom at any point. When Sarah her owner then mistreats her, she runs away. And then God tells Hagar to go back to her owner and submit to her, and comforts her that He will bless her.

And this is the concept of a concubine… she is not a wife, and does not have the rights of a wife, but she is used for sex and/or offspring, and is essentially a female slave. As women could not prevent a husband from taking a second "wife" of the status of a "wife", it seems women were themselves willing to mistreat other women, making them "concubines" or sex slaves, so that they could retain more power. And some of it had to do with whether a woman was free or a slave to start with.

But it should be understood that the sin of Adam to rule over others did not just pass to men, but also to women. Where they could, women also were sinful, and wanted to rule over others, slaves, even female slaves, even in this case to have her be used for sex, and then in Sarah imagining to steal Hagar's child as her own. Which of course did not work, and was proven a foolish idea, as she could not nurse nor bond with this child like his mother could. But make no mistake, the nature of women was also to sinfully rule over others, slaves, and women. They learned to mistreat their own gender and others, but truly it was men who first set this example for women to follow in.

For many people, it might be upsetting that God seems to condone slavery here, in telling Hagar to return to her master and submit to her. God does not condone slavery. But what would you have had God do? Send multitudes of angels to rule over man, forcing them not to enslave each other and treat each other right? God gave people free will, and with it men made slaves of women and other men, and women followed suit, and men ruled over other men. God has always wanted people to choose to love Him and obey Him and be righteous as He is, by choice. God could not allow for people to have free will to be good or bad, love Him or not, obey Him or not, and at the same time force the sinful world to turn upside-down so as to abolish all sin. That is an important thing to understand when reading the Bible, especially the Old Testament, that God worked with people where they were. God tried to help people to be moral, within systems that they insisted upon and were stuck in.

And keep in mind also, that as a few people accumulated wealth and land, soon it was all owned. A person without anything in many cases might want an owner or master, to be their slave or servant, much like today a person needs an employer to earn a living. Back then, why would a man pay another man for work, when he could take him captive and force him to work or die, or even find men who would beg him to take care of them as they had nothing, if they committed to obey him and be his slave. People were slaves and servants by choice in some cases, because they could not feed themselves nor have shelter any other way, as the land and food was owned by others. But others were born into slavery, considered subhuman from birth by class, and had no choice over this at all.

Still, all this was rooted in the same desire for a man to rule over other man, as Adam first tried to do with Eve, and all of this in complete contradiction of God's true law for men to love their neighbors as themselves, and for God's clear desire seen in Eden, for God to directly rule over each person.

And Sarah eventually regretted her decision to do this to her slave Hagar, as she found it of no benefit to herself, but not out of compassion for Hagar. And so she sent her away with her son, after Sarah had her own son Isaac. What a terrible thing, to be a female slave, forced to have sex, forced to bear a child, and then cast out of her home with no husband, and only with a water bottle and a little food. (Gen 21) But because God's hand was on her and her child, and God told Abraham he would take care of them, Abraham did all this, and sent her away with God's reassurance. But if anyone wants to think that women back then were considered to have much rights, or thought of as mattering in how they felt or were treated, please have no illusions. Male slaves were seen as less than men, and so were wives and daughters seen as less than men and even as little as almost nothing, but a female slave was seen as less than nothing.

And this is Sarah and Abraham, whom God chose to bless the world through! Were they the cream of the crop, the most righteous couple around? Apparently so. If they were "good people", the best humanity had to offer, while all else were in blindness and sin, how terrible were the bad ones?
If even the "good" people who had no law and had not been taught of sin, owned slaves and would do this to a female slave, what were the bad people like?

The Bible teaches that Lot, Abraham's nephew, was a just man, but was oppressed and his soul was vexed because he was living in Sodom, and thus was in temptation to be evil like those around him, and struggled not to be.
"And delivered just Lot, vexed with the filthy conversation of the wicked: (For that righteous man dwelling among them, in seeing and hearing, vexed [his] righteous soul from day to day with [their] unlawful deeds;) The Lord knoweth how to deliver the godly out of temptations, and to reserve the unjust unto the day of judgment to be punished:" 2 Pet 2:7-9

Lot is said to have been delivered out of temptation, by the angels that destroyed the city. And he was vexed or oppressed by the evil all around him, which did lead him to be tempted to do evil. Lot is an example of a good man, but who under oppression and in blindness, was tempted and willing to do something terribly wicked, but the angels delivered him and his daughters out of Sodom.

"The two angels arrived at Sodom in the evening, and Lot was sitting in the gateway of the city. When he saw them, he got up to meet them and bowed down with his face to the ground. "My lords," he said, "please turn aside to your servant's house. You can wash your feet and spend the night and then go on your way early in the morning." "No," they answered, "we will spend the night in the square." But he insisted so strongly that they did go with him and entered his house. He prepared a meal for them, baking bread without yeast, and they ate. Before they had gone to bed, all the men from every part of the city of Sodom — both young and old —

surrounded the house. They called to Lot, "Where are the men who came to you tonight? Bring them out to us so that we can have sex with them." Lot went outside to meet them and shut the door behind him and said, "No, my friends. Don't do this wicked thing. Look, I have two daughters who have never slept with a man. Let me bring them out to you, and you can do what you like with them. But don't do anything to these men, for they have come under the protection of my roof." "Get out of our way," they replied. "This fellow came here as a foreigner, and now he wants to play the judge! We'll treat you worse than them." They kept bringing pressure on Lot and moved forward to break down the door. But the men inside reached out and pulled Lot back into the house and shut the door. Then they struck the men who were at the door of the house, young and old, with blindness so that they could not find the door. The two men said to Lot, "Do you have anyone else here — sons-in-law, sons or daughters, or anyone else in the city who belongs to you? Get them out of here, because we are going to destroy this place. The outcry to the LORD against its people is so great that he has sent us to destroy it." So Lot went out and spoke to his sons-in-law, who were pledged to marry his daughters. He said, "Hurry and get out of this place, because the LORD is about to destroy the city!" But his sons-in-law thought he was joking. With the coming of dawn, the angels urged Lot, saying, "Hurry! Take your wife and your two daughters who are here, or you will be swept away when the city is punished."
Gen 19:1-15

Lot, being oppressed in his soul by the evil around him, and fearful of all the men of Sodom actually being able to rape these angels, Lot was tempted and willing to do something terrible, which was to let these men rape his daughters instead, even with them being pledged to fiancés. However, had the men said yes to this offer, it is clear the angels would not have allowed the men to rape the daughters of Lot, but still would have stricken them with blindness. Lot's actions were very wrong, and were the actions of one oppressed and tempted, and fearful of what could happen if these angels were raped by these men, as to what God would do in reaction, most likely.

And this fear of God, however misplaced, seems to be what motivated him to be willing to allow this to happen to his daughters. However, the angels took care of the situation, and blinded the men.

But it cannot be denied that beyond this, even the "good" men of that time saw women as less than men, expendable, usable, property, and their hearts were hardened to their pain, feelings, and they did not see them as having rights. Even a "good" man at the time saw women as less than nothing. Much better for a woman to be gang-raped and helpless to a crowd of men, then for a man, especially an angel-man from God, to be raped. And the cowardice here also must be noted. But God delivered them all out of this situation.

And so that was Lot, a just man but who fell to temptation because he was oppressed by the evil around him, oppressed in his soul. And God was there to deliver him, as he was falling into temptation, but was delivered. The angels had their own way to deal with the men of Sodom, which it seems they intended from the beginning, as they had intended to stay the night in the square, and only went to Lot's home because of his insistence. Though Lot is still an example of how men saw women at that time, as less than men and expendable. It should also be noted that the Bible also states "So when God destroyed the cities of the plain, he remembered Abraham, and he brought Lot out of the catastrophe that overthrew the cities where Lot had lived." Which implies Lot was rescued for Abraham's sake. (Gen 19:29)

As for the men in Sodom, they were evil enough to be destroyed by God. They were not content to gang-rape 2 virgin girls, but were determined to gang-rape 2 men who had come to visit their city. And so it can be gathered by the way that women were treated at the time, that being able to rape a woman, either a slave, or take her to be your wife, had become so passé and common that it was just a normal thing, and did not give men a apparently desired feeling of ruling over another. Or perhaps by custom, if they did, they would have to provide for a child, and marry them.

But they were not seeking just sex, nor just to rule over a woman's body by rape. And what is rape but ruling over another's body as well as will? And to rule over a woman, was not as desirable for the men of Sodom. To rule over a free man was more desirable, and seemingly even to bond with other men in your city by doing this together seems to have had some aspect of feeling their superiority over foreigners. And for this, being so evil and vile, they were judged and destroyed. Keep in mind, they very likely had done this before, and did this when visiting men came to their city. The angels originally wanted to stay the night in the square, to see for themselves if the reports were true.

Gen 18:20-21 "And the LORD said, "Because the outcry against Sodom and Gomorrah is great, and because their sin is very grave, I will go down now and see whether they have done altogether according to the outcry against it that has come to Me; and if not, I will know."
And why was this sin against other men so great as for them to be destroyed, but slavery of men and women was not in itself enough for God to destroy men? This is an important question that deserves an answer, even begs for understanding, lest someone think sodomy is a worse sin than slavery and rape of a woman, both which Abraham committed, and Sarah participated in or did also.

And there is a satisfactory answer. It seems in many ways, that a man (or woman) was judged by God by his conscience, not by his actions. Truly the Bible says Abraham was declared righteous because of his faith, not because of his works. "for we say that faith was reckoned to Abraham for righteousness" (Rom 4:9). And his faith in God was likely very dependent upon his conscience.
 "Holding faith, and a good conscience; which some having put away concerning faith have made shipwreck" (1 Tim 1:19) A person who violates their conscience shipwrecks their faith, faith which was reckoned as righteousness in Abraham, and the same principle is true for Christians today.

It seems true that women and slaves were not considered as real people by most free men at that time.

In truth, they were not considered a man's "neighbors" to that man, but just his property, or less-than-neighbor, or less-than-man, less human than himself. And even a slave woman was considered less than human to a free woman. Violating slaves and women, as they were less-than-human, did not violate a man's conscience. Nor a woman's conscience. So sins against a woman or slave were not going to dirty a man's conscience and come between him and his faith in God. This seems to be precisely the case with men God chose, such as Abraham, not that they were sinless, but they were innocent in their sins because they truly did not understand they were wrong. Abraham was a slave owner, as was Sarah, and both were fine with raping a slave. But they did not understand this was wrong, and it did not violate their consciences. They were blind. And in this blindness, of a clean conscience, they still could have great faith in God. And it was because of Abraham's faith that God counted it to him as righteousness.

Which differed greatly from the men of Sodom. To violate another free man by rape did violate the conscience of a free man, because the free men recognized other free men as equally men, and as their neighbors. The men of Sodom did filthy their consciences before God, and ignored their guilt, and ignored that they knew what they did was wrong. They worked intentional evil, knowing it was vile and sin, but they did not care, and wanted to do evil and violation anyway, to those they actually did see as their neighbors.

Truly, the only way to make sense of many, many things in the Old Testament is to understand that these imperfect people, Abraham and Sarah, that God chose to work through, had faith in Him because of a much cleaner conscience, as they did not understand the wrongs they did. But from what they did understand of right and wrong, they truly did try to do right and to please God. Whereas the wicked people in Sodom knew a thing was wrong, and as a known wrong, they did it anyway, not caring to please or fear God. But Abraham repeatedly showed he had faith in God, leaving his home country when God told him to, moving to a distant land, being willing to sacrifice his son Isaac for God… his faith was such that he believed God was good, and just, and he held nothing back from God. At the same time, it seems his conscience was not shipwrecked, but rather was blind and unaware, in the things he did which were not loving his neighbor as himself, as in his mind few men really were his neighbors.

God is the same today, yesterday, and always. God loves everyone, all people, and He always has. It is not because of what we do or don't do, but because of who He is. And like we are given grace by our faith in Jesus Christ, and are thus counted righteous before God, Abraham was also given grace because of his faith in God, and counted righteous before God. But none of us are righteous on our own account, not today, and not then. That Abraham was a slave owner, even raping and impregnating a female slave of his, not seeing it was wrong, does not show us that God thinks slavery is ok, or that rape is ok. No, of course God's law of love is do unto others as you would have them do unto you. Why do we know slavery is wrong? Because we would not want to be a slave, or born into slavery. Why do we know rape is wrong? We would not want to be raped. Rather than showing God approves of either of these things, which He does NOT, Abraham's imperfections show us that God has THAT MUCH LOVE for each of us. That God loved people back then, even if they were immoral and vile and did not know it. The exact same God, who is the exact same way through all time, sent His Son to die for us, while we were still sinners. We were in sin, and did not know Him, and sometimes did not know what was right and what was wrong, and even when knowing did wrong anyway. Abraham also was in sin, but God loved him anyway, and had a relationship with him because he had faith in God.

This also shows us that God is the same now as He always was, and people back then were not counted righteous by works, but by faith in God. Abraham was ignorant of his sins, and so his conscience was pretty clean, and so he had faith in God, so God counted it as righteousness to Abraham. And today we have a relationship with God also, because we have faith in Jesus Christ, God's Son. Abraham's deficits throw no shadow of darkness upon our perfect loving God, but rather just highlight all the more what an amazing amount of true perfect Love God has for each and every person who ever was. And it shows us that our perfect Loving God is the same today, and yesterday, and always, and truly no man receives God's love or acceptance because of his or her works, but rather because of faith and God's totally Amazing Love for each of us.

Now, is it any coincidence that Abraham, a slave-owner, was shown by God that his descendents who would inherit the land God had promised, would live as mistreated slaves for 400 years in a foreign land? (Gen 15) And this was even before he impregnated Hagar. Truly, it seems he really did not understand that it was wrong to treat her this way, and it seems there was some barrier in his mind between him and a person who was a slave. He did not see a slave woman as his neighbor.

And there seems to be no lack of balance or lesson that Hagar was an Egyptian slave, and that his and Sarah's descendents would be slaves of Egypt for 400 years, and be mistreated. It seems clear that while God would make them the parents of a great nation, that first God had an intent to teach any view of slaves as not-being-people out of their descendents. And it does seem true, that sometimes for an apathetic person to have understanding and compassion for someone who is mistreated and helpless, that apathetic person has to experience being mistreated and helpless. And so whatever iniquities Abraham and Sarah possessed towards the mistreatment of slaves, or having slaves, was worked out through the firsthand experiences of their descendents. And so by the time they left Egypt under Moses, the house of Israel had much compassion for slaves, being freed slaves themselves, who were mistreated while they were in Egypt.

Now obviously, Egypt was no different in many ways than the land and culture that Abraham had come from. And his descendents were slaves in Egypt, where there still was polygamy, and women were still ruled over by their husbands. And as time passed in cultures all over the world, this only became more and more cemented as normal. This was all that people knew. It was normal for men to rule over other men, and for men to rule over women. And in Egypt, the Hebrew men came to learn what a terrible thing it was for another man to rule over their wife and self harshly, even to killing all of their sons. As the Hebrew women were slaves, they also likely were taken as concubines and at times for sexual use at times by Egyptian men. And so the Hebrew men also came to learn about this, that their daughters or even wives could be taken by men, against the will of the husband or father.

And so Moses was chosen by God to lead the Hebrews out of slavery, into the land that God had promised to give them as Abraham's descendents. The people that Moses led out of Egypt, that God led out of Egypt, saw certain institutions as normal, and had no concept of functioning without them. These were institutions such as a husband ruling over his wife, or "wives", concubines, and children, and also slavery. They already had a society and culture in place which had these institutions as fundamental building blocks and the normative way things functioned.

Please keep in mind that all of these concepts of a man ruling over a woman, or women, or over other men, were not institutions that God had created. God never had said that men should be slaves, and God did not invent slavery but rather men did. In the same way, while God warned Eve that Adam would in fact rule over her, this was in no way a sanction for such, and was not what God's intention was for marriage. God did not ever sanction a male-man ruling over a female-man, nor any man ruling over any other man. God did not put these institutions in place with the Hebrews, or with any people. Men made these things up, and by their sinful nature practiced them.

After God led the people out of Egypt, before God gave the Ten Commandments, Moses was spending all day judging the people. They would come to him and want him to settle their disputes. Moses was the only one that God had explained His Law and ways to, and so Moses was the only one who could settle their disputes and try to explain to them what was God's will.

Ex 18:13-27,
"The next day Moses took his seat to serve as judge for the people, and they stood around him from morning till evening. When his father-in-law saw all that Moses was doing for the people, he said, "What is this you are doing for the people? Why do you alone sit as judge, while all these people stand around you from morning till evening?" Moses answered him, "Because the people come to me to seek God's will. Whenever they have a dispute, it is brought to me, and I decide between the parties and inform them of God's decrees and instructions." Moses' father-in-law replied, "What you are doing is not good. You and these people who come to you will only wear yourselves out. The work is too heavy for you; you cannot handle it alone. Listen now to me and I will give you some advice, and may God be with you. You must be the people's representative before God and bring their disputes to him. Teach them his decrees and instructions, and show them the way they are to live and how they are to behave. But select capable men from all the people—men who fear God, trustworthy men who hate dishonest gain—and appoint them as officials over thousands, hundreds, fifties and tens. Have them serve as judges for the people at all times, but have them bring every difficult case to you; the simple cases they can decide themselves. That will make your load lighter, because they will share it with you. If you do this and God so commands, you will be able to stand the strain, and all these people will go home satisfied." Moses listened to his father-in-law and did everything he said. He chose capable men from all Israel and made them leaders of the people, officials over thousands, hundreds, fifties and tens. They served as judges for the people at all times. The difficult cases they brought to Moses, but the simple ones they decided themselves. Then Moses sent his father-in-law on his way, and Jethro returned to his own country."

And so Moses started to teach the people God's decrees and instructions in the way of a judge, to decide between parties in conflict. All of these parties were people who completely believed in the normalcy of slavery, and of men dominating women and ruling their families. For them, there was no concept that the righteous thing to do would be to not have slaves at all, because to them the idea was as outlandish and unmanageable as the idea of marriage itself not existing. And the idea that a woman should have equal rights as a man, was as unmanageably outlandish so as to be unthinkable. To them it defied all "common sense".

These cases probably included things like,
"This man had sex with my virgin daughter, and now refuses to pay me to take her as his wife"
and opposing this,
"I slept with his virgin daughter and would take her as a wife but the bride price he asks is so outrageously high, so I will not take her as a wife for I will not spend the money".

Now, if two men came to you and asked you, how would you decide a case like that? What would be best for the girl in her situation, possibly pregnant? What would be fair to the father and the man?
Would you endeavor even an hour to explain how the man should love the girl he had sex with enough to pay the price, or that the father should care enough about her well-being to not force her to be pregnant and unmarried? Would you try to explain to the girl that she was more than chattel to be bought and sold? Would an hour get you anywhere, with men that saw women as less-then-human property, and a girl that had known nothing but rule over her of her father her entire life, and who very likely saw herself as being less-than-a-man?
Would you spend two hours, or even a whole day, only to find vacant stares looking back at you?
And then they say respectfully, "Oh, well, that's very well and all, Moses, God's prophet, but now that you have shown us that God has no common sense, would you mind settling this dispute? Either he must pay, or I must lower the price, either he will take her as his wife or not, what says God?"
Did Moses himself understand these larger concepts to change, to teach them to the people?

This was their society, and ways that they insisted things be, and nothing could have persuaded them otherwise. They were sinful people and could not have understood, no matter had you spent a day trying to explain to them the truths that <u>we only understand</u>

by God's Holy Spirit living in our hearts!
Yet within these systems of slavery and men ruling over females, and families, which they would not have abandoned, God did set down judgments for them, that modified them doing things however they might have wished. Though at the time, probably no man had more than one wife, as they were all slaves, nor did a man have slaves, as he had just been one. But the way things were was all they knew, such as things had been with Abraham. But God intended to teach them and improve upon them just doing whatever they felt like, within these institutions of man ruling over other man.

And so after Moses teaching people how to judge, then God gave His Commandments directly, and explained how they were to live, through Moses, who wrote it down for the people to have, and taught it to them. And when you read through the Law, it is full of all sorts of fantastical notions that these men were ready to accept, having just been slaves and their families having been slaves, ideas which had appeal to them and they could understand from experience, despite their sinful natures to try to rule over each other.

Included in these ideas was the revolutionary notion that if a Hebrew man became a slave of another Hebrew, that he was to be set free after 7 years. Also, that if a master so much as knocked a tooth out from his slave, any slave, Hebrew or not, that the man could go free immediately on account of that tooth. Even that if a Hebrew man sold his land, as each were given a portion, that it would return to him or his family in 50 years. The laws God gave the Israelites greatly advocated for the rights of slaves, and insisted on the men of Israel viewing each other as brothers, regardless of social status or class. And on top of this, many restrictions were placed on slaves from other nations, that they also had to be treated just as well. And the rules in place by God did everything possible to restrict Hebrew men from ruling over each other long enough for a slave system or class system to form in which one man viewed another as some sort of sub-human inferior, as was the case in Abraham's time.
On top of this, God advocated for the rights of women, and many

of his laws regarding them were for their protection. For instance, a child was told to honor his mother and obey her, not just his father. Also, they could no longer be "taken" as wives without their father's agreement, and a man absolutely had to pay a bride price for them. If a man seduced a woman, he had to marry her, as long as her father would allow it, and if not he still had to pay a God-determined bride price for her. God placed a value on daughters that their fathers could understand was both high and set. She could no longer be given away, or taken away for nothing, but was given a very high value, fixed and set by God. And this was placed on her being a Hebrew woman who was a virgin, not on her being of a poor or rich family. Hard to conceive, but a rich daughter had been worth more than a poor one, but God set all of their prices to be equal, and high. Which meant a daughter's value was inherent on what she was, not on if her family was well-to-do or not. And in the case of the poor, if a man sold his daughter as a slave, she had to be treated as a daughter or a wife of someone in the house, whether her master, his son, or one of their slaves. She had to be treated as family, and provided for. If she was not treated right, then she was given her freedom. This is FAR more rights than a female slave had previously. And FAR more rights and value placed on women than they had previously.

And so the law is full of instances in which a slave is given more rights, and a woman is given more rights. God obviously sought to protect women and slaves in the laws He gave, far more than the ZERO amount of rights or protections they had previously, when men could do whatever they felt like doing. If you read the books of the law, the first 5 books of the Bible, you can see this. If you start out with a chaos and no law in which men would do whatever they could do to other men and to women, with nothing to stop them but the will of other men, then it becomes clear that God's laws to the Israelites served to help to protect and free the oppressed. But the institutions inherit in the law which were already present, invented, and held by men, such as men dominating women and enslaving other men and women, were not commanded by God to be put into place, nor affirmed by their mere existence and acknowledgement in the law.
God considered slavery wrong, and oppression of women as

wrong. Besides their complete inability to accept more radical changes, is there another reason why God did not abolish these things altogether in the law Moses gave to them?

Just looking at this from a historical perspective, we know that the Israelites could not manage to even obey what laws God gave them. They were corrupt and disobedient, bound by the sinful nature of the flesh, and failed to obey even what laws God did give them. And these were laws that God must have considered them potentially able to follow. Instead, ultimately, they ignored what laws they did not like, did whatever they wanted, and even added their own rules and tried to pass them off as God's laws. Jesus repeatedly rebuked the Pharisees for this, that they made their own traditions and rules, and by them made the laws God had given them, even the Commandment to honor your mother and father to no effect (Matt 15:6). The fact is that no matter what perfection of law God had tried to give then, they would have failed. The law that was given to Israel was not ever intended to be a black and white portrayal of absolute perfection for humanity, but rather was correct to improve them closer to perfection. That was its purpose. It helped them to see their own sin, and how evil they were, and to admit how impossible it was for them to not sin. Which helped prepare them for the coming Messiah.

And it was meant for all of us to learn and understand, that not a single one of us could be sinless on our own. No one can be sinless on their own, and no one could be good enough. The entire law of Israel was intended from the beginning not to bring anyone to perfection, even if they followed the law. It was intended to teach them, and improve them, as they learned that they needed something else, something more, that they simply could not be good enough on their own. And that was even within a system which did not see women as equals, and a system which allowed slavery of other men. And even if men were still allowed to treat others in ways they would not want to be treated, like women, like foreigners, like the poor, they STILL couldn't be righteous.

By men's own will men started ruling over women and other men, and made these flawed institutions. And even though God still allowed these flawed institutions, but perfected them as far as God could, men still could not stop from sinning, even within the institutions that they had thought up. Men created rule over women and other men, in place of God's direct rule over men and women. Israel and the law God gave them showed that men's creations of institutions of rule over each other were inherently flawed, and even if God perfected them to the utmost as they could be as broken sinful creations, that men could not bear up under them, to be without sin before God.

God put men as priests, to teach and manage God's laws over the people, but these priest became corrupted, abused their power, added their words and presented them as God's Words (like Adam), and also set themselves to rule over others as much as they could, until in the time of Jesus we see the Pharisees and Sadducees that He repeatedly rebuked. It was man's idea to have men that ruled over other man. Those men that God placed to let rule over other men, between God and other men, the priests, were not able to correctly handle their role any better than Adam did his. They did not, for the most part, live up to what God wanted them to do any better. Where they could get away with it, they added to God's Words, and presented their will as God's will. The priests' failure just shows again that man's idea of ruling over other men was inherently flawed, and would not work.

It is true also that God never originally wanted to give Israel a king, but upon the people's insistence, God eventually allowed them to have a king. And this also failed, as God never intended for a man to rule over others, not women or men, but for God to rule over all. And so it failed miserably. And most of the Old Testament is full of descriptions of one failure and violation of the law after another, both violations of women by sinful men who still would not keep the law, as well as many other sins. Including the many failures of the kings of Israel, even the better kings. And when all this failure had proven true, and the priesthood charged to keep the law had been so corrupted, and the rules of men had superseded the rules of God, and the kingdom itself lived under foreign rule, and it all had been shown as an utter failure, then God sent Jesus Christ.

Just as Abraham, in Israel the people were counted as righteous because of their faith, not because of their perfection. But it was through Israel that the Messiah would be born, the same who God prophesied about to Adam and Eve, who Israel also hoped for. And this Messiah was what Israel was all about, and the laws God gave Israel, was all to prepare the people for the Messiah.

And whereas all of history had been filled with men ruling over women, and the free ruling over slaves, and then also the Israelite ruling over the Gentile or visa versa, when Jesus Christ came it was intended to change all of this, so God alone Himself would rule over His people.

Jesus Christ is THE LORD of us all. Jesus Christ is our only King. Jesus Christ is our High Priest. Jesus Christ makes the rules, and gives them to each Christian personally, and gives us each His Holy Spirit to write His laws on our mind and in our hearts personally and directly. And He is God!

And so Jesus Christ, a man, and God Himself, was anointed by God to be the only man fit to rule over any other man, which restored things to God's original intent and design, which was for God to have a direct and personal relationship with each of us, for God to rule over each of us individually and directly, with no other man in between us and Him, because Jesus Christ is also God. And by God ruling directly over each man, this could change the world, in a way that a law given through other men never could, and bring a perfection with the indwelling of the Holy Spirit, which was never possible before. This was a change not from the outside-in, but from the inside-out. For:
There is neither Jew nor Greek,
there is neither slave nor free,
there is neither male nor female:
for you are all one in Christ Jesus.
Gal 3:28

God made it clear to us as Christians that ALL people are our neighbors, and we are to love them as we love ourselves, and to treat them as we would want to be treated, regardless of gender, class, or race, or nationality. Jesus Christ showed us that we all are each other's neighbors, and we all should see each other as equal. And He alone is the Lord of each of us Christians, personally and directly.

And this HAS changed the world in many ways and in many places! And while in this time, and for a time, while the Gospel is preached to all the world (and it has not been yet), we are in this world but not of it. We suffer by being in the systems of men who are rulers, but we also know that this is only for a time. And someday, soon, Jesus Christ is returning to establish His kingdom on Earth, and He will be the government and King of all people, and reign Himself for 1000 years on Earth. Even now, He is above all things, though Satan still is prince of this world, but Jesus Christ is far above Satan, as God has given Jesus Christ all power and authority. For now, a war rages, which we fight in, as we wait for all of those who would be saved to come into salvation in the Lord Jesus Christ. Jesus Christ has already won the war and has the Victory. We each know we are to obey God, and that Jesus is our Lord, and for this the rulers and people of the world persecute us, even until we become martyrs. But despite this, we still proclaim Jesus Christ as our Lord and King.

"Therefore I make known to you that no one speaking by the Spirit of God calls Jesus accursed, and no one can say that Jesus is Lord except by the Holy Spirit." 1 Cor 12:3

And who can say that their president, that their owner, that their king, their boss, or whatever manner of man rules over you, whether in a democracy or not, who can say that not any of them is your lord, but your Lord is Jesus Christ, except by the Holy Spirit? And in a time of Caesar as Emperor, and Herod as a King, and Pilate as a King, even some of them slaves with masters, in a world with men as rulers most obviously, who were these Christians that said that their personal Lord and King was Jesus Christ?

While they were told to submit to these rulers where they did not conflict with obedience to God, they said that Jesus Christ was their actual Lord and King, and not earthly rulers.

And so with God's people, He alone rules over them personally and directly in Jesus Christ.

Chapter Sixteen
Jesus, Women, and the Law

What did Jesus teach about the law? In the last chapter I covered that the law was not ever intended to be a perfect black and white portrayal of absolute perfection for humanity. The truth is that it inherited within itself, from man, corrupted institutions like slavery, and men ruling over women, things which God never intended to be, but men themselves created.

What does Jesus have to say about the law as it pertains to women?

"Some Pharisees came to him to test him. They asked, "Is it lawful for a man to divorce his wife for any and every reason?" "Haven't you read," he replied, "that at the beginning the Creator 'made them male and female,' and said, 'For this reason a man will leave his father and mother and be united to his wife, and the **two** will become one flesh'? So they are no longer two, but one flesh. Therefore what God has joined together, let no one separate. "Why then," they asked, "did Moses command that a man give his wife a certificate of divorce and send her away?" Jesus replied, "**Moses permitted you to divorce your wives because your hearts were hard**. But it was not this way from the beginning. I tell you that anyone who divorces his wife, except for sexual immorality, and marries another woman commits adultery." Matt 19:7-9

And the Pharisees came to him, and asked him, Is it lawful for a man to put away his wife? tempting him. And he answered and said unto them, What did Moses command you? And they said, Moses suffered to write a bill of divorcement, and to put her away. And Jesus answered and said unto them, For the hardness of your heart he wrote you this precept. But from the beginning of the creation God made them male and female. 'For this reason a man will leave his father and mother and be united to his wife, and the **two** will become one flesh.' So they are no longer two, but one flesh. Therefore what God has joined together, let no one separate." When they were in the house again, the disciples asked Jesus about this. He answered, "Anyone who divorces his wife and marries another woman commits adultery against her. <u>And if she divorces her husband and marries another man, she commits adultery.</u>" Mark 10:2-12

First off, Jesus confirms here that marriage in God's eyes is between 1 man and 1 woman, whom God joins together. Men have no rule or authority over this. Men cannot make God join them to more than 1 wife, even if they say they have 2 or 3 or 300 wives. And men cannot get a divorce before God unless she has committed sexual immorality. God won't do it, no matter what they pretend, or what rules they make up, God still rules sovereign. This also shows that when you add it all up, that God acknowledges that women can get a divorce by human law, but it can be taken that the same rules apply to her, that she cannot get a divorce before God except for sexual immorality committed by her husband. Which in truth, adultery is what men have done repeatedly to wives throughout history, but being ruled over by men, they had no recourse. Men with many wives, even David and Solomon, while they were under God's Grace, they were still all adulterers. Their first wife God joined them to was the only wife they ever had in God's eyes.

But more to the point: here Jesus says that Moses, not God, permitted divorce. Jesus Christ says that Moses permitted divorce and wrote this precept in the law, in the Bible. But Jesus makes clear that what was written in the law was not God's ideal of what He wants of us. That would be what is written in Deut 24, and it is also referenced in Deut 22:19, 22:29, and even in the prior book of Lev 21:7.

And so we can see here that what Moses wrote in the law for Israel was NOT meant to be moral perfection. And it is true that the men refused to accept the truth, because their hearts were hard, so what Moses wrote and has been handed down to us as the law was not meant to be perfect. The law was therefore not ever a complete expression of God's will.

And it really is true that the law was filtered to some extent through Moses, a man who was a product of the time he was living in, speaking to other people who were also in that culture. This is what Jesus makes clear! And these men Moses dealt with were men who already practiced divorce, as history shows the Egyptians did, and they were not willing to give it up.

That may mess up some people's view of the Bible, but <u>this is what the Bible itself teaches</u>:
Either God allowed Moses to allow or not allow things into the Bible at his discretion, which cannot be true as all scripture is God-breathed,
or God compromised with man in what was to be written in the law, in that the law was what THEY could strive for and even attain, though it was still not perfect.

The latter is the truth, which Jesus Himself teaches, with 2 witnesses of this truth. And more witnesses actually, as where the law said not to murder, Jesus said not to be angry, where the law said not to commit adultery, Jesus said not to have adultery in your heart. (Matt 5) And so it is clear that <u>the truth is God compromised with man in what was to be written in the law</u>, even allowed Moses to compromise with men as well, and this means very clearly that the law was <u>never</u> meant to teach us God's perfection and truth of morality.

Repeatedly Jesus and the writers of the New Testament choose to not call the law "the law of God" like it is some perfect portrayal of what God wants, but rather they call it "the law of Moses", etc.

Jesus said: "And he charged him to tell no man: but go, and shew thyself to the priest, and offer for thy cleansing, according <u>as Moses commanded</u>, for a testimony unto them." Luke 5:14

"<u>Did not Moses give you the law,</u> and [yet] none of you keepeth the law? Why go ye about to kill me? Moses therefore gave unto you circumcision; (not because it is of Moses, but of the fathers;) and ye on the sabbath day circumcise a man. If a man on the sabbath day receive circumcision, that the law of Moses should not be broken; are ye angry at me, because I have made a man every whit whole on the sabbath day?" John 7:19,22-23

"And he said unto them, These [are] the words which I spake unto you, while I was yet with you, that all things must be fulfilled, which were written in the <u>law of Moses</u>, and [in] the prophets, and [in] the psalms, concerning me. Then opened he their understanding, that they might understand the scriptures, And said unto them, Thus it is written, and thus it behoved Christ to suffer, and to rise from the dead the third day: And that repentance and remission of sins should be preached in his name among all nations, beginning at Jerusalem. And ye are witnesses of these things." Luke 24:44-48

And here is a picture which well shows the law is a mixture of man's will and God's will,
"And when the days of her purification <u>according to the law of Moses</u> were accomplished, they brought him to Jerusalem, to present [him] to the Lord; (As it is written <u>in the law of the Lord</u>, Every male that openeth the womb shall be called holy to the Lord)" Luke 2:22-23
It is the Lord's law, and it is Moses' law, both. Which shows yet again, that a man between other people and God does not teach us God's perfect will, but we each needed Jesus Christ directly.

Which is not to say the law is wrong, but merely to acknowledge it for what it is, and for what God intended it to be, which as Jesus makes clear, was not for it to be taken as a perfect expression of God's truth. It was from the Lord, but it also was filtered through Moses. "For the law was given by Moses, [but] grace and truth came by Jesus Christ." John 1:17
In fact, here we can see the law is contrasted with the truth that came by Jesus Christ.

The law was not ever to make anyone sinless,
"Be it known unto you therefore, men [and] brethren, that through this man is preached unto you the forgiveness of sins: And by him all that believe are justified from all things, from which <u>ye could not be justified</u> by the law of Moses." Acts 13:38-39

In truth, the Bible teaches that no one could be justified by following the law of Moses, even if any of them could have followed it. It was their <u>faith</u> that they tried to follow it which made them counted as righteous, and faith in God shown in following the law of Moses, that justified them to God as Jews. It was not the Law itself, which would make nothing perfect, but their faith.

The Law was good, and beneficial, but <u>the Law made nothing perfect</u>.

How can I claim "the Law made nothing perfect"? I only am saying what the Bible says:
"If therefore perfection were by the Levitical priesthood, (for under it the people received the law,) what further need was there that another priest should rise after the order of Melchisedec, and not be called after the order of Aaron?
For the priesthood being changed, there is made of necessity a change also of the law. For He of whom these things are spoken pertaineth to another tribe, of which no man gave attendance at the altar. For it is evident that our Lord sprang out of Juda; of which tribe Moses spake nothing concerning priesthood. And it is yet far more evident: for that after the similitude of Melchisedec there ariseth another priest, Who is made, <u>not after the law of a carnal commandment,</u> but after the power of an endless life. For he testifieth, Thou art a priest for ever after the order of Melchisedec. For there is <u>verily a disannulling of the commandment going before for the weakness and unprofitableness thereof. For **the law made nothing perfect**</u>, but the bringing in of a better hope did; by the which we draw nigh unto God." Heb 7:11-19
Truly, the law made nothing perfect, but was a step in a process, of bringing in a better hope, who is Jesus Christ. Who is THE answer and was always intended to be, from the beginning and the fall.

The Bible also says:
"For the Law, since it has <u>only a shadow</u> of the good things to come and not the very form of things, can never, by the same sacrifices which they offer continually year by year, make perfect those who draw near." Heb 10:1

And so this is a second witness and confirmation that the law makes nothing perfect, and cannot make perfect those who try to follow the law. Whereas Jesus Christ is the very form of the good things to come, the Law was only a shadow. How different can a shadow be from the thing it is the shadow of? Looking at a shadow by itself can greatly distort your understanding of what the actual object looks like, leaving out much information. A shadow of a tree, for example, cannot tell you about its leaves and trunk and fruit. And the shadow of a man, will tell you nothing of his eyes, or his hair, or many many things about him. And so also the Law was like the shadow of Jesus Christ, and in Him, the indwelling of His Holy Spirit, and the gifts and fruits of His Holy Spirit, and becoming adopted by God, which were all good things to come.

What else does the Bible says about the Law?
"Brethren, my heart's desire and prayer to God for Israel is, that they might be saved. For I bear them record that they have a zeal of God, but not according to knowledge. For they being ignorant of God's righteousness, and going about to establish their own righteousness, have not submitted themselves unto the righteousness of God. For <u>Christ is the end of the law for righteousness</u> to every one that believeth. <u>For Moses describeth the righteousness which is of the law, "That the man which doeth those things shall live by them"</u>. But the righteousness which is of faith speaketh on this wise, Say not in thine heart, Who shall ascend into heaven? (that is, to bring Christ down from above:) Or, Who shall descend into the deep? (that is, to bring up Christ again from the dead.) But what saith it? The word is nigh thee, even in thy mouth, and in thy heart: that is, the word of faith, which we preach; That if thou shalt confess with thy mouth the Lord Jesus, and shalt believe in thine heart that God hath raised him from the dead, thou shalt be saved. For with the heart man believeth unto righteousness; and with the mouth confession is made unto salvation. For the scripture saith, Whosoever believeth on him shall not be ashamed. For there is no difference between the Jew and the Greek: for the same Lord over all is rich unto all that call upon him. For whosoever shall call upon the name of the Lord shall be saved." Rom 10:1-13

"Ye shall therefore keep my statutes, and my judgments: which if a man do, he shall live in them: I [am] the LORD." Lev 18:5

The law was meant to lead people to Christ, as He is the end of the Law for all who believe, He is what was intending to be waiting at the end of the road, the goal to be reached, which the Law was to lead to. And truly, the Law of the Old Covenant was that if a person did these things, that person would live in them. This was Israel's agreement and covenant with God, that they would do these things, and they would live, and God would bless them. If they did not do these things in the law, then God would punish them and they would die. But in all cases, following the law could not by works justify anyone, it could make no-one perfect, it was not enough. But those who had faith, who believed God, would try to follow the law, and in this, because of faith they would have salvation.

What, do you think that a man who missed his last guilt offering on his deathbed, but who had true faith and obedience for God, would not be saved? Do you think a man who found every loophole in the Law, without fear of God, but not technically breaking it for appearance's sake, while keeping up perfectly with his offerings, that he would be righteous? It was not following of the Law which saved anyone, but rather their faith in God, by which God counted them as righteous, that they may live. And by live, I mean live eternally. For the just shall live by faith. Looking above, the righteousness of God, which is faith in God, is directly contrasted by men trying make their own righteousness, by the law and works.

The Bible teaches about this:
"Even as Abraham believed God, and it was accounted to him for righteousness. Know ye therefore that they which are of faith, the same are the children of Abraham. And the scripture, foreseeing that God would justify the heathen through faith, preached before the gospel unto Abraham, saying, In thee shall all nations be blessed. So then they which be of faith are blessed with faithful Abraham. For as many as are of the works of the law are under the curse: for it is written, Cursed is every one that continueth not in

all things which are written in the book of the law to do them. But that no man is justified by the law in the sight of God, it is evident: for, The just shall live by faith. And the law is not of faith: but, The man that doeth them shall live in them." Gal 3:6-12

Doing the law showed one had faith, and believed God, which is accounted as righteousness, and this is how those in Israel were given life eternal who had faith and believed God, as Abraham was also, as we have covered in the last chapter. But in itself doing the law justified no man in God's sight. The law made nothing and no one perfect.

The Apostle Paul understood this fact, and taught it.

"Christ hath redeemed us from the curse of the law, being made a curse for us: for it is written, Cursed is every one that hangeth on a tree: That the blessing of Abraham might come on the Gentiles through Jesus Christ; that we might receive the promise of the Spirit through faith. Brethren, I speak after the manner of men; Though it be but a man's covenant, yet if it be confirmed, no man disannulleth, or addeth thereto. Now to Abraham and his seed were the promises made. <u>He saith not, And to seeds, as of many; but as of one, And to thy seed, which is Christ. And this I say, that the covenant, that was confirmed before of God in Christ, the law, which was four hundred and thirty years after, cannot disannul, that it should make the promise of none effect.</u> For if the inheritance be of the law, it is no more of promise: but God gave it to Abraham by promise." Gal 3:13-18

Truly, Christ was Abraham's seed through whom all nations would be blessed, and this was God's original intent, and He freed people from the law, including all of its many spiritual curses for disobedience to any part of it. We can see Jesus Christ was God's original intent because it was what God promised Abraham 430 years before the law was given. Jesus Christ was never an afterthought of the law, or an "oops, that law thing didn't work, let's think of something else..." No!

The truth is Jesus Christ was intended to come since the fall, the seed of the woman who would crush the head of the serpent. And Jesus Christ was intended to come since Abraham, the seed of Abraham.

Keeping that in mind, what was the ultimate purpose of the law? "Wherefore then serveth the law? <u>It was added because of transgressions, till the seed should come to whom the promise was made;</u> and it was ordained by angels in the hand of a mediator. Now a mediator is not a mediator of one, but God is one. Is the law then against the promises of God? God forbid: for <u>if there had been a law given which could have given life, verily righteousness should have been by the law. But the scripture hath concluded all under sin, that the promise by faith of Jesus Christ might be given to them that believe</u>. But before faith came, we were kept under the law, shut up unto the faith which should afterwards be revealed. **Wherefore the law was our schoolmaster to bring us unto Christ, that we might be justified by faith. But after that faith is come, we are no longer under a schoolmaster.** For ye are all the children of God by faith in Christ Jesus. For as many of you as have been baptized into Christ have put on Christ. There is neither Jew nor Greek, there is neither bond nor free, there is neither male nor female: for ye are all one in Christ Jesus. And if ye be Christ's, then are ye Abraham's seed, and heirs according to the promise." Gal 3:19-29

The law was given to curtail sin, which is a good reason. It was also intended to be like a schoolmaster, teaching people about sin and showing people that they were sinners and could not attain righteousness by their own actions, so that they would realize their need for Jesus Christ to save them. And also to lessen the amount of sin taking place.

This is very important to understand:
Many people today act like the reason God had to send Jesus was because when God gave this perfect law of sinlessness, that no one could keep it perfectly without one mistake, and that the point of the law was to prove no one could keep God's perfect law that would make a person righteous.
This is not true!

The law, even if followed perfectly, would still not make a person perfect. The law was a shadow, and did not justify anyone, because only faith in God can justify anyone! And this only by God's Grace!

The law was only ever intended to teach people and to curtail sin, and to be a measuring line by which for people to see who was of faith in God, and tried to follow the law, and who was not of faith and God, and ignored the law, and to teach everyone that they could not reach any standard of perfection set in front of them on their own; but it also was closer to the truth, a shadow of the truth.

What commandments did Jesus teach over and over again?
"And Jesus answered him,
The first of all the commandments is, Hear, O Israel; The Lord our God is one Lord: And thou shalt love the Lord thy God with all thy heart, and with all thy soul, and with all thy mind, and with all thy strength: this is the first commandment. And the second is like, namely this, Thou shalt love thy neighbour as thyself. There is none other commandment greater than these." Mark 12:29-31

And so the law did contain the first of all commandments and the second, of which there were none greater, and these commandments were the truth that God really wanted us and Israel to follow!

And so much of the rest of the law was just describing these commandments, as best as they could be understood at the time. And that included being understood in a culture that viewed women, and slaves, and foreigners as inferiors to men, and not truly a man's neighbor. For if you truly loved your neighbor who was a slave, you would not rule over him but free him and pay him, and if you truly loved a woman, you would not rule over her but love her and free her to be able to submit herself to you, which she cannot do if you rule over her. (Which is what the rest of the New Testament relating to marriage teaches.)

But the people then were not yet able to understand the truth, that there was no male nor female, nor Jew nor Gentile, nor free nor slave barrier that separated them from who was their neighbor. Everyone was their neighbor, but they could not see it. And so the law contains many descriptions of loving your neighbor as yourself, that were filtered through ignorance, and were incomplete, imperfect shadows, making the law not able to justify anyone, nor perfect, but a schoolteacher, a lesson, towards a better understanding, to lead to a better way, who was Jesus Christ who is the Truth.

He did not come to abolish the law, but to fulfill it!
"Do not think that I have come to abolish the Law or the Prophets; I have not come to abolish them but to fulfill them." Matt 5:17
And the law could not be fulfilled until everyone understood that everyone was their neighbor, that they should love as themself, whether slave or free, Jew or Gentile, male or female. The first and second greatest commandments in the law could not be fulfilled in truth, until we all could see we were each equal and equally loved by God. And this is the understanding that Jesus taught, and made personally possible for each of us, in that we are all God's children, receiving the same gift of forgiveness and life, and with the same Holy Spirit indwelling each of us, so we could see and learn we were all equal and equally loved by God.

It seems many Christians today, for some reason, look at the law in the same way that the Jews looked at it, misunderstanding it. And it seems many Christians today look at the Old Testament in the same way that the Jews looked at it, misunderstanding it. In fact, there seems to be a heavy emphasis in some Christian circles to look at the Old Testament by leaning on the understanding of either ancient Jews, or modern ones… who do not have the Spirit of Truth in their hearts unless they are in fact Christians. Paul repeatedly taught early Christians against trying to follow the law to be justified and made righteous, which is where many of the above verses come from. Reading with an eye for this truth, there is plenty in the Epistles about this problem, which you can read on your own.

Included in this, and a great summary of the problem in viewing the Old Testament in the way that the Jews did, is the underlined portions below from 2 Corinthians:
"Not that we are adequate in ourselves to consider anything as coming from ourselves, but our adequacy is from God, who also made us adequate as servants of a new covenant, not of the letter

but of the Spirit; for the letter kills, but the Spirit gives life. But if the ministry of death, in letters engraved on stones, came with glory, so that the sons of Israel could not look intently at the face of Moses because of the glory of his face, fading as it was, how will the ministry of the Spirit fail to be even more with glory? For if the ministry of condemnation has glory, much more does the ministry of righteousness abound in glory. For indeed what had glory, in this case has no glory because of the glory that surpasses it. For if that which fades away was with glory, much more that which remains is in glory. Therefore having such a hope, we use great boldness in our speech, and are not like Moses, who used to put a veil over his face so that the sons of Israel would not look intently at the end of what was fading away. **But their minds were hardened; for until this very day at the reading of the old covenant the same veil remains unlifted, because it is removed in Christ. But to this day whenever Moses is read, a veil lies over their heart; but whenever a person turns to the Lord, the veil is taken away.** Now the Lord is the Spirit, and where the Spirit of the Lord is, there is liberty. But we all, with unveiled face, beholding as in a mirror the glory of the Lord, are being transformed into the same image from glory to glory, just as from the Lord, the Spirit." 2 Cor 3:5-18

And so the Bible teaches us that as Christians, we are better equipped, by the Holy Spirit and Him alone, to understand the first 5 books of Moses, than the Jews were, or are. And so whatever Christians have accepted about the books of Moses that the Jews have handed to us ready-made, should be assumed to have been interpreted with a veil over the person's heart. And the same is true of any non-Christian reading God's Words, whether Jews or anyone else. The Bible can only be understood with the Holy Spirit, who lives in the unveiled heart of a Christian. So then, if the verses above are understood, is it any surprise that a Christian view might contain an interpretation of the books of Moses which is very different from the standard interpretation of the ancient Jews? For it is true that the Bible teaches that Christians were going to see things in the Bible, the Word of God, even that they should see things, which had not been realized by the ancient Jews…

Because in fact they are still in school, under a schoolmaster, the law, which was and still is meant to lead them to Jesus Christ. And in many cases, it still does, Praise God! But we are no longer under the law, the schoolmaster, the tutor.

"Now I say, That the heir, as long as he is a child, differeth nothing from a servant, though he be lord of all; But is under tutors and governors until the time appointed of the father. Even so we, when we were children, were in bondage under the elements of the world: But when the fulness of the time was come, God sent forth his Son, made of a woman, made under the law, To redeem them that were under the law, that we might receive the adoption of sons. And because ye are sons, God hath sent forth the Spirit of his Son into your hearts, crying, Abba, Father. Wherefore thou art no more a servant, but a son; and if a son, then an heir of God through Christ." Gal 4:1-7

And so as adopted children of God, we are only to view the law as like our tutor, our schoolmaster, from a time when like a young child we were like a servant, but in Christ, we are no longer like a servant, like a child, under our schoolmaster, the law, but more like grown children of God and heirs. We have graduated, not to forget what we learned in primary school, but to move on to college, beyond the law, to its fulfillment who is Jesus Christ, who came not to abolish the law but to fulfill it.

As Christians we are not to see the law as Jews do, nor to try to be under it, as Paul said,
"I desire to be present with you now, and to change my voice; for I stand in doubt of you. Tell me, you that desire to be under the law, do you not hear the law?
For it is written, that Abraham had two sons, the one by a bondmaid, the other by a freewoman. But he who was of the bondwoman was born after the flesh; but he of the freewoman was by promise. Which things are an allegory: for these are the two covenants; the one from the mount Sinai, which gendereth to bondage, which is Hagar. For this Hagar is mount Sinai in Arabia, and answereth to Jerusalem which now is, and is in bondage with her children. [the law]

But Jerusalem which is above is free, which is the mother of us all. For it is written, Rejoice, thou barren that bearest not; break forth and cry, thou that travailest not: for the desolate hath many more children than she which hath an husband. Now we, brethren, as Isaac was, are the children of promise. [Jesus Christ the seed of Abraham]
But as then he that was born after the flesh persecuted him that was born after the Spirit, even so it is now. Nevertheless what saith the scripture?
Cast out the bondwoman and her son: for the son of the bondwoman shall not be heir with the son of the freewoman. So then, brethren, we are not children of the bondwoman, but of the free." Gal 4:20-31

In summary, the law could make no one perfect, as it was not meant to, even if a person followed it to the letter, and it could not work to fulfill the greatest commandments it contained, to love God with all of your being, and to love your neighbor as yourself. Only Jesus Christ was meant to and could serve to fulfill the law, and it was always God's plan for Him to. The law is good, but it is just a school lesson compared to the greater understanding of truth that we have in The Truth and the Holy Spirit of Truth who is in each of us. And it was always God's original plan to send Jesus Christ, and never for the law to justify anyone, as all are counted as righteous by their faith in God and because of His Grace and Mercy and Love and Goodness. Alleluia!

And so all that the law speaks about women, and slaves, and foreigners, which was not reflective of loving your neighbor as yourself, was made void as God gave His Holy Spirit to anyone who would believe on Jesus as Lord and Savior, so we could see the truth. And in the truth we can all see God loves us all equally, no matter of gender, race, class, or nationality. And so in every way the truth we learn in Christ Jesus to love our neighbor as ourself, and the truth we understand that our neighbor is every human there is, the law is shown and proven to be more and more just a shadow of the good things to come. And so everything in the New Testament about women supersedes the oppression of women found in the law, and the same for slaves, and the same for foreigners. The law was a step in the right direction, as it was able to be handled at the time, and was a lesson unto the people of the time, but we as Christians are to come to a much greater understanding of the truth, and love, and this was always God's will and intention. And in this, Jesus and His Holy Spirit work to perfect us.

"But you are to be perfect, even as your Father in heaven is perfect." Matt 5:48

To be perfect, we must do much better than the law describes.

Chapter Seventeen
1 Peter 3 – Actions Louder Than Words

Now we are going to look at 1 Peter, from about 2:18 through 3:18.

"Servants, be submissive to your masters with all respect, not only to the good and gentle, but also to the harsh. For this is commendable, if because of conscience toward God one endures grief, suffering wrongfully. For what credit is it if, when you are beaten for your faults, you take it patiently? But when you do good and suffer, if you take it patiently, this is commendable before God."

Here Peter explains to servants, which could also mean slaves, that they may end up suffering under the hands of their masters, and should take this suffering patiently, as this is commendable before God.

Peter then goes on to explain that as Jesus suffered, we also are called to suffer,
"For to this you were called, because Christ also suffered for us, leaving us an example, that you should follow His steps: " Who committed no sin, Nor was deceit found in His mouth"; who, when He was reviled, did not revile in return; when He suffered, He did not threaten, but committed Himself to Him who judges righteously; who Himself bore our sins in His own body on the tree, that we, having died to sins, might live for righteousness – by whose stripes you were healed. For you were like sheep going astray, but have now returned to the Shepherd and Overseer of your souls."
This echoes the words of Paul in Rom 8,
"And if children, then heirs; heirs of God, and joint-heirs with Christ; if so be that we suffer with Him, that we may be also glorified together."
So as Jesus suffered for us, we also suffer.

Why do we suffer? So as not to impede the spread of the Gospel as 1 Cor 9:12 alludes to, of this righteous attitude:
"If others share the right over you, do we not more? Nevertheless,

we did not use this right, but we suffer all things so that we will cause no hindrance to the gospel of Christ."
In this case Paul is referring to the apostles not taking money from the Corinthians, but supporting themselves, although they do have the right to receive support for teaching them. But Paul says he does not use this right, as he would rather suffer than to hinder the Gospel. Which speaks to the fact that as Christians, we may see we have rights, because of what we know is right, but are not to demand our rights for the Gospel's sake.

How does this work? Let's look at slavery as an example:
While as Christians we may see that slavery itself is wrong, and other such things, that we are trying to preach the Gospel to those who may think such institutions are fine.

Will a master think well of Christianity if his Christian slave tried to explain to him he is asserting his right to be free, because slavery is evil? If all the other slaves are submissive and accept their lot as slaves, then it is the Christian slave who seems evil and rebellious to their master, who sees his own good as a ruler as "good". And this will not make a sinful blind master who is lost receptive to the teachings of the Christians. As far as a slave-owner is concerned, slavery is right and accepted and "good". In truth it is not, because it violates the 2nd most important commandment, to love your neighbor as yourself. But the master's view, as he owns slaves, is that this wrong is right, and this evil is good, at least for him. And so the only way to impress him that Christianity is good, is for a Christian slave to be good in his eyes, as good as or more impressive and superior to the non-Christian slaves. Then the master may think well of Christianity and be interested in learning more about Jesus Christ.

The first sin came about from the evil desire of one man to rule over another man, not treating his neighbor as he would want to be treated. This was the driving force through history of the development of many evil institutions, both against men and women, as was covered in the last 2 articles. And this was never God's will, but rather God wanted rule over each human individually Himself, and this is seen in that He will in Heaven.

But in giving people free will to choose good from evil, the most fundamental and first evil desire that man chose was to rule over other man, not treating her as he would have wanted to be treated. This basic assumption that it is ok for a man to rule over another man against his will, and dominate another man against the law of love, is the most primary sin, in which a man in pride thinks it is ok to do this.

For any man to let go of this pride, a man must humble his or her self before God, and admit their own sinful depravity, and accept God is the ruler of all. Which is what happens when a sinner is convicted of sin, acknowledges God's sovereignty and judgment, and their need for a Savior. As such, it is completely putting the cart before the horse, and nigh near impossible, to have a lost person in a sin of ruling over his neighbor understand that God's intent is rule over each person personally and directly, each obeying His law of love. Nor can he understand that in the coming world God Himself will be the only king, and have the only power, over any man, instead of men taking their own power by their own wills, and using it in the ultimate hypocrisy by treating any other man as they would not want to be treated.

And so, for the sake of the Gospel, the servant or slave is told it is commendable before God to suffer not only for their mistakes, but also even when they have done nothing wrong. Why? For the sake of the Gospel, and to impress their master. The only good a master understands is his own rule and authority and what is to his benefit, as he plays god ruling over other men. To him this is good, and to most of the world this was seen as good, and governments acknowledged the rule of man over man, not because of God, but because each and every man seeks to be like the Most High, and play god, having power over other man, not to have God's will be done of love, but their own will to be done. In this all mankind is evil, and history shows man has been from the beginning.

And so the institutions in which we live were created by sinful man, and we are still in this world, though not of it. And to reach this world with the Gospel, we suffer by the hands of this world and the lost. Similar to how Jesus was crucified by the very people he died to try to save, under the rulers of this world, so also we suffer (or die) at the hands of the people we are trying to save. And nothing in our interactions with the lost is more important than trying to lead the lost to salvation in Jesus Christ. And so, like Jesus suffered, we also suffer. And so a servant or slave is instructed to even suffer, and to submit to his master, so that the master and the sinful world will see him as a good slave, and be impressed, so that they might be led to Christ. But at the same time, 1 Corinthians 7:21 says that if a man is a slave and has a chance to be free, that he should take it.

Also later in this book, Peter emphasizes that suffering for being a Christian, purely for that reason, is good, and suffering for doing good is good, and it is good to lead the lost to Christ, but to suffer for doing anything that impedes the way to Christ for the lost, or for committing sin, is bad. Even if that bad thing is to meddle with the lost and their institutions of rule,

"Dear friends, do not be surprised at the fiery ordeal that has come on you to test you, as though something strange were happening to you. But rejoice inasmuch as you participate in the sufferings of Christ, so that you may be overjoyed when his glory is revealed. If you are insulted because of the name of Christ, you are blessed, for the Spirit of glory and of God rests on you. If you suffer, it should not be as a murderer or thief or any other kind of <u>criminal</u>, or even as a <u>meddler</u>. However, if you suffer as a Christian, do not be ashamed, but praise God that you bear that name. For it is time for judgment to begin with God's household; and if it begins with us, what will the outcome be for those who do not obey the gospel of God? And, "If it is hard for the righteous to be saved, what will become of the ungodly and the sinner?" So then, those who suffer according to God's will should commit themselves to their faithful Creator and continue to do good." 1 Pet 4:12-19

And in this, we are to rejoice insomuch as we participate in the sufferings of Christ. For we are His body and we do His work, continuing it, which includes His suffering at the hands of an unjust world in the efforts of trying to save it and help it and heal it. As the church is His body, we do the same.

And so slaves are to be submissive to their masters, even patiently enduring suffering. Under the same principle of suffering for the sake of the Gospel, so as to lead people to Christ, wives are also given instructions:

"In the same way, you wives, submit yourselves to your own husbands so that even if any of them are disobedient to the word, they may be won without a word by the behavior of their wives, as they observe your chaste behavior in fear."

What does this mean? Well, first off, this is "in the same manner" as slaves are to patiently endure suffering, and Christ also endured suffering, so that people might be saved. Wives here are instructed to submit themselves to their own husbands, including even those who are "disobedient to the word". What does this phrase mean?

The meaning is to be found in context, as earlier in this same letter in 1 Pet 2:8 this same term "disobedient to the word" is also used. Here is the section:

"And coming to Him as to a living stone which has been rejected by men, but is choice and precious in the sight of God, you also, as living stones, are being built up as a spiritual house for a holy priesthood, to offer up spiritual sacrifices acceptable to God through Jesus Christ. For this is contained in Scripture: "BEHOLD, I LAY IN ZION A CHOICE STONE, A PRECIOUS CORNER stone, AND HE WHO BELIEVES IN HIM WILL NOT BE DISAPPOINTED." This precious value, then, is for you who believe; but for those who disbelieve, "THE STONE WHICH THE BUILDERS REJECTED, THIS BECAME THE VERY CORNER stone," and, "A STONE OF STUMBLING AND A ROCK OF OFFENSE"; for they stumble because they are <u>disobedient to the word</u>, and to this doom they were also appointed." 1 Pet 2

And so those who are "disobedient to the word" are the lost, the unsaved, the non-Christian. Here the reference is more to Jewish men, but in general the term refers to all men who stumble at Jesus Christ, and are disobedient to the particular word that "he who believes in Him will not be disappointed", as the lost refuse to believe in Jesus Christ. The term refers to an unsaved husband. And so Christian women are instructed to submit themselves to their own husbands, whether they are Christian or not. The reason for this is so that even if they are unsaved, that they might be won to Christ by the behavior of their wives.

Referencing back to what submission is and is not, there is limitation on what a Christian wife has to submit to with an unsaved husband, same as with a Christian husband. First off, she should not sin, nor do anything that violates her conscience. She also has a right to and should serve God as He has gifted and called her. If she does not do this, then it is God she is disobeying. Included is that it is right for her to have equal authority over her husband's body, as he has over hers, and she should not have to be violated or do things she is against in the bedroom. In fact, she is under the same marching orders as all Christians, and if a lost husband would restrict her, then she to obey God and not man, if it comes down to one or the other. She also retains the right to divorce if her husband is sexually immoral.

While keeping in mind that as a person she has many rights, and even instructions from God to her that she should do certain things which express those rights, or can do certain things which express those rights, the ultimate goal here is that through her submissive behavior she may win him to Christ. Which is contrasted with her trying to win him through words.

"they may be won <u>without a word</u> by the behavior of their wives," Why does this read "without a word"? The point here is that behavior speaks louder than words, and her submissive behavior towards her husband is more likely to win him to Christ than anything she might say that has the aim of winning him to Christ. This phrase "without a word" seems to reflect the idea or assumption that women are likely to say words towards winning him to Christ, and that the husband will not find this as ideal, or at least some people take this verse that way.

Some people make the argument that this "without a word" references to 1 Cor 14:34-35 in which women are told to be silent in order to show submission in church, not so much to their husbands, but to all men. I have already covered that these verses are a gloss in great detail. As these verses are a gloss, and were not in the original manuscript, they cannot be something that Peter was referencing to here in saying "without a word" (nor that God references to).

However, there is something that Peter may have been referencing to by saying "without a word". This would be Genesis 3:16.

When it is read with the understanding that the correct word is "teshuba" and not "teshuqa" in the place of the word "desire", then it refers to a wife arguing and debating with her husband as one of the negative effects of the fall into sin. It reads, "your repetitive verbal answerings will be to your husband" in a figurative sense. Or it reads "your repetitive returnings will be to your husband" in a literal sense.

This is the same word "teshuba" which is used in Job, in his long heated debate with his friends,
"Oh, that Job might be tested to the utmost for answering like a wicked man!" Job 34:36 (NIV)
"So how can you console me with your nonsense? Nothing is left of your answers but falsehood!" Job 21:34 (NIV)
And this also ties into some Proverbs in which a man is pointed out to have a problem with being annoyed at a wife he finds contentious or argumentative, likely in a verbal way with words.

And so if Peter is referencing to anything by "without a word", then he was most likely referencing to the negative effects of the fall into sin as are listed in Gen 3:16, which includes that a wife has a tendency to be verbally argumentative with her husband. As such, Peter is here cautioning wives to not fail in a verbal attempt to win their husbands by setting themselves up for temptation to argue, but rather that a superior way altogether it to try to win their husbands by their behavior, not by their words.

"as they observe your chaste behavior in fear."
The behavior that Peter wants wives to practice, so their husbands can observe, so they might be won to Christ, is "chaste behavior with fear". The word here for "observe" implies "to view attentively", and almost implies the sort of observance of one's behavior that contains scrutiny. This is fitting to a situation of a Christian wife with a non-Christian husband, especially in that culture in which women were ruled over by their husbands, who had much legal authority over them.

The word for behavior is also translated as conversation, and means, "*1) manner of life, conduct, behaviour, deportment*" as in the Strong's and Thayer's.
The word for "chaste" here means, in the Strong's and Thayer's: "*1) exciting reverence, venerable, sacred 2) pure a) pure from carnality, chaste, modest b) pure from every fault, immaculate c) clean*". So another way to put this is a "reverent and pure manner of life".

The word above for "in" is "en" in Greek and it usually is translated as "in".
The word here for "fear" is "phobos" and it is a noun form of the verb "phobeo", both of which mean fear or reverence. It is used many times meaning fear of God, and in this is often translated as reverence or even respect. The noun and the verb are related in their meaning and usage.

Who is the wife meant to be in fear of? The same word for fear "phobos" as well as the same word for "behavior" are used earlier in this same letter in 1 Peter 1. Their usage here gives us the context that Peter used, and makes clear what he was referring to: "But like the Holy One who called you, be holy yourselves also in all your behavior; because it is written, "YOU SHALL BE HOLY, FOR I AM HOLY." If you address as Father the One who impartially judges according to each one's work, conduct yourselves in fear during the time of your stay on earth; knowing that you were not redeemed with perishable things like silver or gold from your futile way of life inherited from your forefathers, but with precious blood, as of a lamb unblemished and spotless, the blood of Christ." 1 Pet 1

Who is meant to be feared here? It is **God** who is meant to be feared, and in this fear of God, people are to be holy in their behavior. This is very synonymous with Peter's later instructions for wives to have "pure" or "chaste" behavior. And so when Peter later gives the instructions to wives, he is in fact referencing back to his earlier words in this same letter, which instruct all Christians to be holy in their behavior out of fear of God.

And so when Peter later says to wives, "as they observe your chaste behavior in fear" this has nothing to do with marriage or submission or being a woman or wife, but rather is a rephrasing of the same instructions that Peter earlier gave to all Christians. Christian men and husbands are also told to have 'holy behavior in fear', but this is not in fear of men, but fear of God, and the same goes for Christian wives and women. And so the "chaste behavior in fear" that a non-Christian husband observes has nothing to do with him, or his will, or his standards, but is entirely determined by a Christian woman's relationship with God and her fear of God. The fear referenced here is fear of God, not fear of her husband. <u>**She is not instructed here to fear her husband, nor to "reverence" or "respect" her husband, but rather this is the fear she has for God.**</u> And this is consistent with the rest of the Bible, as Jesus taught in Matt 5:28:
"And fear not them which kill the body, but are not able to kill the soul: but rather fear him which is able to destroy both soul and body in hell."
And the same concept is in Psalm 111:10, "The fear of the LORD is the beginning of wisdom…"
And so the fear here of the wife is the fear of God, our Father, who judges, her knowing she was redeemed with the precious blood of Jesus Christ. This is reverence and fear of God, not the husband.

In fact the only time in the New Testament in which "fear" of a husband is mentioned, is in Eph 5:33 in which husbands are told to love their wives as themselves <u>in order for</u> the wife to "phobeo" her husband, and in this usage refers to "respect". That he must love her as himself <u>in order for, so that,</u> the wife will have respect for him, is a description of a <u>cause and effect</u> relationship.

Never at any point are wives told that they <u>must</u> respect their husbands, as respect is an estimation and esteem which is either sincere and real, or simply does not exist, and in order for a husband to have his wife have respect for him, he must love her.

And so when this is all put together, it reads with this correct understanding:
"In the same way (suffering to spread the Gospel) you wives, submit yourselves to your own husbands so that even if any of them are disobedient to the word (non-Christian and lost), they may be won (to Christ) without a word (without any argument or opportunity for it) by the behavior (manner of life) of their wives, as they observe your chaste (holy) behavior (manner of life) in fear (of God)."

Peter then continues in this instruction for wives,
"Your adornment must not be merely external–plaiting the hair, and wearing gold jewelry, or putting on dresses; but let it be the **hidden** person of the heart, with the imperishable quality of a gentle and quiet spirit, which is precious in the sight of God. For in this way in former times the holy women also, who hoped in God, used to adorn themselves, submitting themselves to their own husbands; just as Sarah obeyed Abraham, calling him lord, and you have become her children if you do what is right without being frightened by any fear."

Here Peter says that women should adorn themselves not with physical adornments for beauty, but rather with a gentle and quiet spirit, in the hidden person of the heart, which is precious in the sight of God. He says this is also how holy women of old adorned themselves, submitting themselves to their own husbands. And this is just as the example of Sarah, who obeyed Abraham, calling him lord.

What does this mean? Should wives address their husbands as "lord" or as "sir" as this is most closely equivalent to? Peter here is referencing not a summary of Sarah's behavior, but rather is referencing a particular instance and story that is in the Bible.

Genesis 18:12 is the **only** time in which Sarah is recorded in the Bible to have called Abraham "lord". So let's read this particular specific story that Peter was referencing to, so we can understand what Peter meant in context:

"And the LORD appeared unto him in the plains of Mamre: and he sat in the tent door in the heat of the day; And he lift up his eyes and looked, and, lo, three men stood by him: and when he saw them, he ran to meet them from the tent door, and bowed himself toward the ground, And said, My LORD, if now I have found favour in thy sight, pass not away, I pray thee, from thy servant: Let a little water, I pray you, be fetched, and wash your feet, and rest yourselves under the tree: And I will fetch a morsel of bread, and comfort ye your hearts; after that ye shall pass on: for therefore are ye come to your servant. And they said, So do, as thou hast said. <u>And Abraham hastened into the tent unto Sarah, and said, Make ready quickly three measures of fine meal, knead it, and make cakes upon the hearth.</u> And Abraham ran unto the herd, and fetch a calf tender and good, and gave it unto a young man; and he hasted to dress it. And he took butter, and milk, and the calf which he had dressed, and set it before them; and he stood by them under the tree, and they did eat. And they said unto him, Where is Sarah thy wife? And he said, Behold, in the tent. And he said, I will certainly return unto thee according to the time of life; and, lo, Sarah thy wife shall have a son. And Sarah heard it in the tent door, which was behind him. Now Abraham and Sarah were old and well stricken in age; and it ceased to be with Sarah after the manner of women. <u>Therefore Sarah **laughed** *within herself,* **saying,** "After I am waxed old shall I have pleasure, **my lord** being old also?"</u> And the LORD said unto Abraham, Wherefore did Sarah laugh, saying, Shall I of a surety bear a child, which am old? Is any thing too hard for the LORD? At the time appointed I will return unto thee, according to the time of life, and Sarah shall have a son. <u>Then Sarah denied, saying, I laughed not; for **she was afraid**.</u> And he said, Nay; but thou didst laugh." Gen 18:1-15

Did Sarah address Abraham as "lord"? No, she did not. She did not address Abraham as "lord" when she spoke to him. She addressed him as "lord" within herself, laughing within herself, and talking to herself. This is clearly demonstrated by her fear and denial of laughing, which the Lord calls her on. If she had said this or laughed outloud, she would not have tried to deny it, as the Lord was right there. And she would not have been afraid to have been confronted by the Lord with what she said within herself, if she had said this outloud, because her fear was because He knew her private unspoken thoughts, and this made her feel afraid. As such, in her fear, she lies to God, and in this does the wrong thing. And so God corrects her and restates that she in fact did laugh. But this laughter, and calling Abraham "lord" was done within herself.

As such the only recorded time (and it is the only one) in which Sarah calls Abraham "lord" is within herself, in her private thoughts and in her heart. The term "lord" as it is used here most closely equates to our understanding of the word "sir". In her heart and thoughts, she called him "sir", and in this showed her gentle and quiet spirit, and her submission of herself to him.

Prior to this, Abraham had told Sarah, in a rush, to make bread quickly, and then rushed away to get meat for the guests to eat. The Bible does not specify that Sarah actually did make the cakes, as they are not included in the list of what is set before the angels and the Lord to eat. But here Peter lets us know that Sarah did in fact do as Abraham had told her to do, and did make the cakes, and we can gather this because she called him "my lord" within herself. And any woman who had that kind of submissive attitude towards her husband, so as to call him "my lord" within herself, surely did make the cakes when he told her to in a rush. The situation was not that he asked her to politely, nor did he explain why, but he just told her what to do, gave an order in a rush, and then rushed away.

People back then were not so different than now, and it was slightly rude for him to tell her and not ask her to make the cakes, and not even spend the time to tell her why. And so his behavior was a little rude, and therefore a little unloving. But in the situation, his behavior was not based on any lack of love for her, or resentment towards her, but rather was just the hurried situation of God Himself had come to dinner unexpectedly, and so he was in a sincere and understandable hurry!

And so Sarah obeyed Abraham in what he told her to do, ordered her to do, even though he did not politely ask her to, or explain why because of time. And we know she did "obey" his "order" to make the cakes because within herself she called him "my lord", so surely she did make the cakes, as Peter points out.

And at the end of the story, Sarah in fear tries to lie to the Lord, denying that she laughed at what He said He would do, giving her a son in her old age, because she is frightened, even terrified because He 'read her mind!' and knew her thoughts inside of herself, in her mind and heart. She was not afraid because He overheard what she said outloud, but because he knew her private inner monologue. Eventually, Sarah admits she laughed that day, after her son is born, and she says,
"God has made me laugh, and all who hear will laugh with me." and as God commanded they named their son Isaac, which means "he laughs". (Gen 21:6)

So let's look at this part again with the intended contextual meaning included of the story referenced:
For in this way in former times the holy women also, who hoped in God, used to adorn themselves, submitting themselves to their own husbands; just as Sarah obeyed Abraham (making him cakes when he was in a justified rush and slightly rude and unloving, not asking her but telling her, and not explaining a thing), (which we know she made the cakes because of her) calling him lord, (within herself to herself in her thoughts in her submissive gentle and quiet spirit) and you have become her children if you do what is right (being honest with God about what is on the inside) without being frightened (as Sarah was and lied) by any fear (terror or amazement that God knows what goes on in your thoughts and heart).

Wow! What an amazing way for God to make clear to Christian women that submission is about attitude and feelings and thoughts, and not just in doing what her husband wants her to do. Real submission of a wife to her husband is supposed to also include a loving and meek spirit about submission, with understanding, love, and affection for her husband, and ideally with acceptance inside that God wants her to submit to him. And so even if a wife submits herself on the outside, but not on the inside, this is a clear message that God knows your thoughts and feelings. And this also leads to the fact that if your thoughts and feelings are honest before God, and you know they are not right, a wife should know that God knows it too.

So Peter implies to wives, don't be like Sarah and in terror that God knows your heart and try to lie to God about it. Rather, accept that God does know your heart, and be honest with God. And even ask God to work a miracle for you, like He did for Sarah and Abraham. Ask for Him to help you to change to have a meek and quiet spirit on the inside, in the hidden person of your heart, so you submit yourself to your husband, yourself both inside and outside, which is what God wants women to do.

And this is what God designed women to do naturally, in a world without sin, a woman was designed to naturally follow and submit to her own husband. Because of the sinful nature, it can be hard, and also because when a woman is ruled over, it leaves little room for her to develop submitting herself, but nevertheless, in any situation, God can work in a wife's heart to help a wife submit to her own husband as God wants her to and originally designed for a woman to do in a marriage. And she should try to do her part that God has told her to do as best as she can, seeking God's help outside and inside, regardless of if her husband does as God has told him to do, and regardless of if he is Christian or not. And her submitting to him, with a quiet and gentle spirit, can be very important in winning him to Christ.

While this is not the same sort of suffering that a slave might go through in submitting himself to his master, it can be difficult for a woman to submit herself to her husband, in submission to God, and she might also suffer in this difficulty. Especially in this case, in which non-Christian husbands are the main subject. In that time and place, men had legal authority over their wives, and in some ways the husband could do what he wanted to his wife, much like a master could with his slave. If she offended him in her obeying God, such as refusing to participate in idol worship, he might beat her, and he might even kill her, and she might have no recourse or little for whatever he did to her. And so she had to balance obeying God, with also trying to submit to a non-Christian husband. And so in specific this verse refers to a Christian wife potentially having to suffer at the hands of her non-Christian husband, regardless of submission. Non-Christian husbands are the target of her potentially having to suffer, in the same way that Christ suffered at the hands of the world, and that slaves may suffer at the hands of their masters. While this verse does imply that a woman may have some level of suffering just in submitting herself to her Christian husband, the great aspect of suffering "in the same manner" even if she does well is specifically referring to her having a non-Christian husband. This verse does not refer to her suffering "in the same manner" as Christ did under rulers and slaves may under masters because of a Christian husband, but rather only under a non-Christian husband.

At the time, women were generally legally owned by their husbands, with few limitations. That is not the case today in the United States and many other countries. In so much as a free woman has recourse under the law for mistreatment, and has rights like freedom of religion, the legal situation of a Christian woman today is different than that of a woman 2000 years ago. But this is not true everywhere.

(The following few paragraphs are a bit USA or other developed-country centric pertaining to laws.)

Some people try to say that this verse teaches that if a Christian wife is abused by her Christian husband, that she should endure suffering it. This is not what the Bible teaches, and that entire concept is in direct contradiction of Jesus' direct instructions for any Christian on how to handle it if another Christian sins against you, as Jesus makes most clear in Matt 18:15-17:
"If another believer sins against you, go privately and point out the offense. If the other person listens and confesses it, you have won that person back. But if you are unsuccessful, take one or two others with you and go back again, so that everything you say may be confirmed by two or three witnesses. If the person still refuses

to listen, take your case to the church. Then if he or she won't accept the church's decision, treat that person as a pagan or a corrupt tax collector."

If a woman is abused by a Christian husband, she is not to suffer, but to address his sin. First she is to talk about it privately with him, then to bring 1-2 Christians with her and have them witness the case she makes to him. If he still will not repent, she is to take it to the church. If he won't listen to the church, then she is to treat him as someone who is lost. (But regardless of this, if he is breaking the law of the land, she has every right before God to take him to court and take legal action against him, including in the case of abuse or domestic violence which is a crime.)

One of the most sad things that takes place today that I have beheld with my own eyes, and heard with my own ears, multiple times, is Christians who will refuse to serve as witnesses for a Christian wife who is being abused. These are people who believe that this verse in 1 Peter 3 means she should suffer abuse from a Christian husband, and she should do nothing about it, and they refuse to serve as witnesses for her, and will not confirm her correct case to an abusive Christian husband, even if they will admit that yes, they agree with her, this Christian man is abusive. But they refuse to serve as witnesses on her behalf to correct him, and disobey the clear words of Jesus Christ in Matt 18, choosing instead to follow doctrines of men forged out of a more fuzzy view of 1 Pet 3.

And even worse, I have seen and heard where a woman has not only been turned away by other Christians who refuse to serve as her witnesses, even agreeing a Christian man's behavior is abusive, but also I have seen a church who refused to get involved to correct an abusive husband. Unknown, but it seemed likely this church also believed she should suffer her Christian husband's sins against her, and would not obey Jesus to offer her recourse through the church. It is appalling.

But for any woman in such a situation, if she cannot follow Matthew 18 steps 2 and 3 because of the disobedience to Christ of the Christians or the church around her, then God understands, and so if she must skip steps 2 and 3, then do, and proceed directly to step 4, to treat such a man as a pagan. But regardless of this she may take him to court, and get whatever help is legally available to her, for domestic abuse or domestic violence. (For more info on Domestic Abuse or Violence see the Resources section.)

If he has committed a crime or violent crime, the law of the land dictates the prescribed action, as the Bible teaches in this same book of 1 Pet 2:13, "Submit yourselves to every ordinance of man for the Lord's sake".
And so in a case of a clear crime, which there is an ordinance against, such as violence, threats of harm, theft, kidnapping or false imprisonment, rape, etc. etc. etc. a Christian wife does not need to go privately, nor go with witnesses, nor go to the church, but **should** go directly to the police and courts and herself seek help for abused women in her area

As for correcting him privately, it is ultimately her choice to try this or not, but if she does <u>she should have a plan in place for him to receive help in changing</u> for if he repents, and there are many domestic violence programs available to help abusive men change, likely one in her area. But if he does not repent, then she should go straight to the police and courts.

Looking over what God instructs us, what Jesus instructs us to do, looking through all the verses in the Bible, this is what the Lord generally instructs a wife to do if she and her husband are both Christians and he is practicing domestic abuse or domestic violence. And if the wife is a Christian and her husband is a non-Christian and he practices the crime of domestic abuse or domestic violence, then she should also go to the police and courts, and seek help for herself as an abused woman and help for him as an abusive husband.

In a Christian wife submitting herself to her husband, as God has told her to do, there may be no picking and choosing between God's instructions to her. She has also been told by God to follow Matt 18, and to submit to every ordinance of man for the Lord's sake, which includes all the laws of the land that domestic abuse and domestic violence are crimes. If a Christian woman chooses to obey God in submitting herself to her husband, but refuses to obey God in submitting herself to the ordinances or laws in her land, and refuses to obey Jesus Christ in following Matt 18 which the Lord told all Christians to follow, then she is like a hypocrite, though she may have been one in ignorance. And if other Christians do not recognize this is correct, then they are also like hypocrites, though perhaps in ignorance. But if the church leaders and teachers do not recognize this is correct, then they are also like hypocrites, but as they are teachers, they will be judged more strictly by God for their ignorance, and in calling themselves teachers but teaching ignorance, for their doubled hypocrisy.

Moving on, we have already covered a long and intensive study on the next verse, which is copied below to review, excerpted from Chapter 6, "Ephesians 5 Marriage Part 2 – Love Your Wife".

"Likewise, ye husbands, dwell with [them] according to knowledge, giving honour unto the wife, as unto the weaker vessel, and as being heirs together of the grace of life; that your prayers be not hindered." 1 Peter 3:7
Looking at the Greek, and the context in which the words in this passage are used, it becomes clear that this is a powerful verse.

The word "dwell with" here is "synoikeo" which is only used here in the Bible. It is a compound of 2 words, "syn" and "oikeo". If Peter had wanted to mean "live with" in a way that referred to just 2 people living together, he more likely would have used a term like "oikeo meta" which means "dwell with", and is the very phrase used in 1 Cor 7:12-13 for a husband or wife dwelling with each other in some residence. But Peter uses an uncommon composite word, that is used only here in the Bible.

"Syn" is used as a prefix to describe people equally doing something together. For instance, "syn-odia" is "a company of travelers", "synthapto" is "to bury together with" and "synistemi" is to "stand with". These compositions all imply participants that are each equally part of some activity. The Greek prefix "syn" has the same meaning as the Latin prefix "co". In English, we use terms like co-chair, co-pilot, co-author, or co-worker. In the verb form, we might say co-authoring, co-chairing, co-piloting, or co-working. In 1 Pet 3:7, "dwell with" would be more correctly translated "co-dwelling".

The word knowledge here is "gnosis", and in the New Testament its meaning in use is one of the knowledge of truth of God, Jesus Christ, salvation, and understanding of the Christian faith or religion. This is not just a general word for "knowledge", as in "I have knowledge about cars". If it were it would make sense that a more broad Greek word for knowledge would be used, "epignosis", which is used more this way. But "gnosis" is used speaking of the deeper understanding of what is true and good in the Christian faith. The Strong's reads:
1) *knowledge signifies in general intelligence, understanding*
a) the general knowledge of Christian religion
b) the deeper more perfect and enlarged knowledge of this religion, such as belongs to the more advanced
c) esp. of things lawful and unlawful for Christians
d) moral wisdom, such as is seen in right living
As such, husbands are instructed "co-dwelling with deep knowledge of the Christian religion and moral wisdom from such..."

The word here for "give" is only used here in the New Testament. Again, it is a unique composite word, "aponemo". The word "apo" used as a prefix indicates *"separation, liberation, cessation, departure... finishing and completion... refers to the pattern from which a copy is taken... or to him from whom the action proceeds"*. (Thayer's) The word "nomos" (-nemo) means "law" and is translated as such in every instance in the KJV (197x). It can refer to the Mosaic Law, or any rule or law. But in the context of the word "gnosis" above, referring to an understanding of the Christian faith and religion, the "law" referenced to here must be one of the Christian faith. In the Thayer's under "nomos" it says, " *3. Of the Christian religion... the law demanding faith, Rom 3:27... the moral instruction given by Christ, esp. the precept concerning love, Gal 6:2..."*
What does Gal 6:12 say?
"Bear ye one another's burdens, and so fulfil the law of Christ."

Gal 5:12 better defines this for us:
"For all the law is fulfilled in one word, [even] in this; Thou shalt love thy neighbour as thyself."
And note that in this letter something is pre-established in Gal 3 which says, "For you are all sons of God through faith in Christ Jesus. For as many of you as were baptized into Christ have put on Christ. There is neither Jew nor Greek, there is neither slave nor free, there is neither male nor female; for you are all one in Christ Jesus."
Yet the only specifically "new commandment" Jesus gave is in harmony with this one, and is found in John 13:34-35: "A new commandment I give unto you, That ye love one another; as I have loved you, that ye also love one another. By this shall all [men] know that ye are my disciples, if ye have love one to another."
The Thayer's defines the word "aponemos" based on extra-biblical usage in the works of Josephus and others, as meaning *"(nemo to dispense a portion, to distribute), to assign, portion out"* With a unique word that literally means "from-law", which means "to assign, portion out" (Strong's) the translation of "give" is not accurate. The word would better read "apportioning" or "apportion".

What is being apportioned? The word here for "honor" is "time" and the Strong's defines it as,
"1) a valuing by which the price is fixed a) of the price itself b) of the price paid or received for a person or thing bought or sold 2) honour which belongs or is shown to one a) of the honour which one has by reason of rank and state of office which he holds b) deference, reverence"
This is <u>not</u> the same word that Jesus uses for "honor thy father and they mother" (Matt 19:19) which is "timeo", and it is also not the same word for "honor widows" (1 Tim 5:3). Nor is it the same word as "honor all men" or "honor the king" as is used in 1 Pet 2:17 which is earlier in this same book. "Timeo" denotes a meaning of *"to estimate, fix the value a) for the value of something belonging to one's self"*. With "timeo" the value is estimated for something belonging to one's self.
This is not the case with "time". Rather, this word "time" is used again and again in a way that means a fixed value to God, a value fixed by God, as something which is valuable or worth something great, or honor to a rank or position (of value).

Peter uses this word earlier in the same letter in,
"That the trial of your faith, being much more precious than of gold that perisheth, though it be tried with fire, might be found unto praise and honour and glory at the appearing of Jesus Christ" 1 Pet 1:7
"Unto you therefore which believe [he is] precious: but unto them which be disobedient, the stone which the builders disallowed, the same is made the head of the corner" 1 Pet 2:7
And also in 2 Pet 1:17, "For he received from God the Father honour and glory, when there came such a voice to him from the excellent glory, This is my beloved Son, in whom I am well pleased."
This word "time" therefore refers to a value or price that God will set or has set on something.
It is the same word used twice in 1 Cor (6,7) repeated in "Ye are bought with a price".
This price is not left to be determined by men, but has been determined by God.
Therefore, in 1 Pet 3:7 the word "honor" means an honor which reflects value, and the value of a price that has been fixed by God, not by men. It implies a set value God has put on someone, not the value a man puts on something that is his.
So far, the verse reads, "Likewise, ye husbands, co-dwell with deep knowledge of the Christian religion and moral wisdom from such, apportioning honor from value set by God..."

The word here for "unto the wife" is "gynaikeios". Again, this word is only used here in the Bible.
It means, *"of or belonging to a woman, feminine, female"*. This word is an adjective, not a verb.
Again, the translation "unto the wife" is not accurate, as this word is referring to something which belongs to the woman or to the female. Nor does the word imply this belongs to the "wife" in particular, but rather implies this belongs to the "woman, feminine, female".
The verse so far should read, "Likewise, ye husbands, co-dwelling with deep knowledge of the Christian religion and moral wisdom from such, apportioning the honor (from her value or price as set by God) belonging to the woman/female..."

The next phrase here is "as unto the weaker vessel". The word here for "as" is "hos" which means "as, like, even as, etc". There are no words contained in the Greek here to be translated "unto the". The word for "weaker" is "asthenes" and it means weaker as it is spelled here for comparative use. The word here for "vessel" is "skeous". This word is used one time with the same spelling in Luke 8:16 which reads,
"Now no one after lighting a lamp covers it over with a container, or puts it under a bed; but he puts it on a lampstand, so that those who come in may see the light."
The same word "skeous" is used in 2 Cor 4:6
"For God, who commanded the light to shine out of darkness, hath shined in our hearts, to [give] the light of the knowledge of the glory of God in the face of Jesus Christ. But we have this treasure in earthen vessels, that the excellency of the power may be of God, and not of us."
And in 2 Tim 2:20-21,
"But in a great house there are not only vessels of gold and of silver, but also of wood and of earth; and some to *honour*, and some to dishonour. If a man therefore purge himself from these, he shall be a vessel unto *honour*, sanctified, and meet for the master's use, [and] prepared unto every good work." (Note: the word *honour* here is "time" in Greek, as above, both times.)

This meaning, this illustration, has the weight of how the Epistles use the word vessel when referring to Christians. Christians are vessels of God, as the Holy Spirit lives in us, and through God's power we are enabled to do good works.
The same meaning is inherent in 1 Thes 4:3-6,
"For this is the will of God, your sanctification; that is, that you abstain from sexual immorality; that each of you know how to aquire his own vessel in sanctification and honor, not in lustful passion, like the Gentiles who do not know God; and that no man transgress and defraud his brother in the matter because the Lord is the avenger in all these things, just as we also told you before and solemnly warned you."

In this verse on how men should go about acquiring a wife, she is called a "vessel". This can have 2 references and meanings. The first is that as a Christian, she is a vessel of the Holy Spirit, and God's power. The second is the usage of the word vessel in referring to a body, as the husband is the head of the wife, the wife who is like his body. So here the reference is how the husband is to go about getting "his own body" to be the head of; without fornication, in sanctification and honor.

Back to 1 Pet 3:7, the same 2 meanings are inherent. The wife is a vessel of the Holy Spirit, empowered by God. At the same time she is the "weaker vessel", which begs the question, weaker than what? A woman's body generally is weaker than that of a man's. And the repeated analogy in the Bible is that the wife is like the body, and the husband like the head of that body, in being one flesh. He is the head, and she is all of the other body parts, metaphorically. Nevertheless, in physical practicality, she has the weaker body. So this part should read "as a (weaker) vessel".

The word for "heirs together" is "sygkleronomos" (also from the prefix syn-) and would better be translated as co-heirs. The emphasis is on an equality of sharing. This word is also used of the Gentiles, in Eph 3:6
"That the Gentiles should be <u>fellowheirs</u>, and of the same body, and partakers of his promise in Christ by the gospel".

The word here for "life" is "zoe", which in context almost always refers to eternal life. The word for "that" is "eis" and would better read "so that" or "towards that".

When this is all put together, the meaning should read as thus: "Likewise, you husbands, co-dwell with deep knowledge (of the Christian religion and moral wisdom from such), apportioning the honor (from her value or price as set by God) belonging to the woman/female, as a (bodily weaker) vessel of the Holy Spirit and God's power, and as being co-heirs of the grace of eternal life; so that your prayers will not be hindered"

The first thing to note is that the word here "likewise" is the same word used above starting off the verses aimed at wives. Which means that Peter is still on the same thought here. Slaves have suffering, Jesus suffered, likewise wives may suffer submitting herself a husband, and likewise husbands may suffer… in obeying God.

Here husbands are told by God to apportion the honor of the female that is set by God, as a vessel of the Holy Spirit, and an equal co-heir as a man to the grace of eternal life. In other words, a man has to recognize and treat a woman as an equal before God, equally human, and especially equal in all ways pertaining to the Christian faith and the Holy Spirit. Which includes the gifts of the Holy Spirit and her calling from God. And this includes that she is completely of equal value before God as he is, and God in no way considers her of inferior worth than a man, but she is worth just as much to God and is just as important as he is as a Christian, in all ways, like gifts and callings.

And so while a man may feel suffering from it, he is told that in Christ, he must treat his wife as his peer before God, of equal worth, and containing and meant to equally be an instrument of God's power, being a vessel of the Holy Spirit and God's power. He is told by God that in all ways as a Christian, he must honor her as a Christian with the exact same value he places upon a Christian man, and himself.

And in doing this, who is the man submitting to? He is submitting to God. And he may experience suffering in doing this, nevertheless this is what he is told to do by God. And this is very clear that he is told to do this by God, because if he does this, it is (also) so that his prayers will not be hindered. Which implies very clearly that if he does not do this, that his prayers will be hindered. And we pray to God, so the meaning here is clear that he told by God to do this, and is submitting himself to God.

And whether or not his wife is already a Christian, he is still to do this. Because it is implied in the larger context of this section that in doing this, and showing her the honor of the equality of men and women before God, and the female's equal worth to God, and

God's equal love for them, and their potential equal indwelling of the Holy Spirit, and the potential gifts and calling that entails, even in the potential of treating a woman as an equal before God, and in her seeing the honor he apportions her <u>even potentially</u> for this if she is lost, all of this is implied to be a way for him to help lead her to Christ.

And in truth, as Chapter 6 covered, a Christian man cannot love his wife as God wants him to without doing this, and in doing this he is loving her, and if not then he is not loving his wife. This is regardless of whether she is a Christian, or is lost. This seems to be the only place where a husband is not told to love his wife, where marriage is addressed and her submitting herself is mentioned. But actually, that is not the case, because in doing all of the above, this is a description of what a husband must do to love his wife.

In order to love her, he must show he apportions complete honor to her as his equal, as completely equal to him in God's sight. He must also show he apportions honor to her as completely equal in her calling from God, and in the gifts the Holy Spirit has given her, as they are both vessels of the Holy Spirit and God's power, and they have the same general purpose and calling from God, and in this they are in all ways equal before God and have equal potential to have a calling, have gifts from God, and to equally use them for God in His service. Neither one is more important to God than the other. This is not a feeling he necessarily must have, that he feels honor towards her, or thinks this is correct. Whether he feels it or not, he is told to DO this as an action, he is told by God to do the verb of apportioning honor to her, something that is expressed in his actions, and not just in words. He must DO the apportioning of honor to her. He also must DO the co-dwelling with his wife, living with her, with this knowledge and in this way, in which he DOES and SHOWS he apportions the honor (from her value or price as set by God) which belongs (is owned by) the woman/female, as a (bodily weaker) vessel (of the Holy Spirit and God's power, gifts and callings), and as her being an (equal) co-heir of the grace of eternal life.

And it would make some sense that a husband might feel some suffering in having to apportion his wife this kind of honor, and co-dwell with her as his peer and equal before God. It would make some sense that a husband might feel suffering in doing God's will in this, to treat her as he wants to be treated in the Lord and as a Christian, as an equal, as not inferior to himself, but having all the same worth and importance in God's sight, and gifts and callings from God, as a vessel of the Holy Spirit.

And the reason this makes sense that he would feel suffering to do this is because this is exactly the same sort of problem that Adam had with Eve in Eden. Likely in envy and pride, and a desire to control her, he did not treat her as he would want to be treated, nor apportion her equal honor before God as himself, but lied to her about God's words, to keep her from doing what God told her she could do, just because God told him he could not do this, trying to violate and interfere with her independent relationship with God and direct instructions from God to her.
As Hosea 6:7 says,

"But like Adam they have transgressed the covenant; there have they dealt treacherously against Me."

And every man since has had this as the most fundamental core of his sin nature. Every man since has had the iniquity of Adam visited upon him, the temptation to not see his wife as his equal, equally loved by God, of equal worth to God, and to acknowledge that God has an independent relationship with her. As a Christian, a wife may receive gifts of the Holy Spirit and a calling that is different from her husband's, as she has her own personal relationship with God, and work to do for God, all independent of her husband's control. This is the very thing that Peter most acutely wants men to do, is to apportion to her the honor that is due her as the female, the same honor of an independent relationship and instructions that God gave the first woman, which is exactly equal to that God gives a man. God wanted the man to do one thing, and the woman to do another thing, and instructed them differently. God had an independent relationship with both of them. But Adam apparently could not handle this, and tried to control her and interfere with her direct relationship with God, and Adam sinned in result. And because of his abuse of her trust by lying to her, in trying to interfere with her direct relationship with God, he set her up to be deceived by Satan, set her up to be tempted and to then tempt him, and she became in his transgression as a result. And ever since, a man has been visited with Adam's iniquity, passed down to him, to interfere with his wife's relationship with God, and to try to control her.

This is a temptation and spiritual bondage that Christian men must reject and not succumb to, even fighting this curse with spiritual warfare if they need to, in order to overcome this curse. And that is because God has told husbands to co-dwell with her as an equal, and to apportion the honor to the wife that God has set upon her, as she is completely his equal before God, and as a Christian and as a vessel of the Holy Spirit, and all that entails.

And if husbands do not do this, their prayers will be hindered, meaning by God, as they would still be repeating instead of repenting of the original sin of Adam. And make no mistake that the original sin of Adam was not only a result from the evil desire to interfere with her relationship with God, lie to her about God's words, to envy what God gave her, but most fundamentally was his attempt to try to control her and rule over her, treating her as if she was inferior and he was superior in God's sight. And this was instead of telling her the truth of what God had told him, and not trying to control her with lies about what God had said, but rather to love her and in her free will respect her choice to follow him or not. Truly, God who loves the world perfectly and is Love, gives us all free will to choose.

"Likewise (even suffering), you husbands, co-dwell with deep knowledge (of the Christian religion and moral wisdom from such), apportioning the honor (from her value or price as set by God) belonging to the woman/female, as a (bodily weaker) vessel (of the Holy Spirit and God's power), and as being (equal) co-heirs of the grace of eternal life; so that your prayers will not be hindered"

And if a man will not apportion his wife this honor that God gives her, his prayers will be hindered as the face of the Lord is turned away from those who do evil, as this chapter continues to explain:

"Finally, all of you, be like-minded, be sympathetic, love one another, be compassionate and humble. Do not repay evil with evil or insult with insult. On the contrary, repay evil with blessing, because to this you were called so that you may inherit a blessing. For, "Whoever would love life and see good days must keep their tongue from evil and their lips from deceitful speech. They must turn from evil and do good; they must seek peace and pursue it. <u>For the eyes of the Lord are on the righteous and his ears are attentive to their prayer,</u>
<u>but the face of the Lord is against those who do evil."</u>
Who is going to harm you if you are eager to do good?
<u>But even if you should suffer for what is right, you are blessed.</u>
"Do not fear their threats; do not be frightened." But in your hearts revere Christ as Lord. Always be prepared to give an answer to everyone who asks you to give the reason for the hope that you have. But do this with gentleness and respect, keeping a clear conscience, so that those who speak maliciously against your good behavior in Christ may be ashamed of their slander.
<u>For it is better, if it is God's will, to suffer for doing good than for doing evil.</u>
For Christ also suffered once for sins, the righteous for the unrighteous, to bring you to God.
He was put to death in the body but made alive in the Spirit."

Truly, it is better to suffer for doing good than doing evil. For all humanity has suffered from doing evil, which started with one sin, and it would have been better for Adam to suffer with Eve being able to do something he could not do, and God having an independent relationship with her, independent gifts for her, and independent instructions given directly to her, than for the evil he did in sinning and then all he suffered as a result of his sin.

And so as a slave his master, and as Jesus suffered under the rulers of the world, a Christian husband may suffer under the hands of

God in obeying God to treat his wife as a free equal in Christ with an independent relationship with God. And if he does not obey his Lord and King and Master, then whether it seems fair to him or not, his prayers to God will be hindered as his Lord turns His face away from him, His eyes not looking at him and His ears not listening to him.

If anyone finds the implications of this daunting, perhaps the people then did too, and this is why Peter said "Do not fear their threats; do not be frightened" above, as its actually a quote from Isaiah 8:
"For thus the LORD spoke to me with mighty power
and instructed me not to walk in the way of this people, saying,
"You are not to say, 'It is a conspiracy!'
In regard to all that this people call a conspiracy,
And you are not to fear what they fear or be in dread of it.
"It is the LORD of hosts whom you should regard as holy.
And He shall be your fear, And He shall be your dread.
He will be a holy place; for both Israel and Judah he will be a stone that causes people to stumble and a rock that makes them fall. And for the people of Jerusalem he will be a trap and a snare.
Many of them will stumble; they will fall and be broken, they will be snared and captured."
Bind up this testimony of warning and seal up God's instruction among my disciples.
I will wait for the LORD, who is hiding his face from the descendants of Jacob.
I will put my trust in Him."

The truth is that the Bible always says a Christian wife is instructed to "submit herself", and this instruction is given to her by God. A husband has no right to force a wife to obey God any more than she has a right to force him to obey God in any given way, as before God they are peers and equals as Christians. If a husband is trying to force her to submit, he is abusive. The Bible nowhere gives him any right to try to force her to submit to him, or rule over her, in fact this is specified as a negative consequence of the fall into sin. In him trying to force her to obey God, in this she only can submit herself to domination which IS abuse. God leaves her free to submit herself in obedience to Him, or to not, exactly as God does with a Christian man.

Christians or churches which refuse to serve as witnesses for an abused wife, take part in the husband's abuse. Churches who refuse to get involved are in direct disobedience to God by ignoring Matt 18. Witnesses may not be under the same compulsion to get involved, as the Bible does not seem to tell people that they must act as witnesses.

But as for Christians who refuse to serve as witnesses: if they acknowledge his behavior is wrong or abusive, but decide to do nothing, then they help him force her to submit to him by refusing to help, so then they take part in his abuse of her. And they are also in direct disobedience to God, not loving her as themselves, and not treating her as they would want to be treated, as she asks for help, and if they were asking for help, they would want to receive it. So they break the law of love, to love your neighbor as yourself, the second commandment of Jesus Christ.

But beyond this, they condone an idolater in their midst. Truly, a husband who tries to play god by dominating his wife **is an idolater**, caught in the sin of **self-idolatry**. This is the same as the covetousness of Adam, as her relationship with God was her own, and he tried to own it, and is why Col 3:5 states, "covetousness which is idolatry". A man who believes he has a right to rule over his wife, which God never gave him, is a self-idolater. Though it may be in ignorance.

And those who condone this with him could also be male-idolaters, that in opposition to God's will and God's Word, are setting men as a creation above God the Creator: Who alone is Lord, Who alone gives a wife her orders, and freedom to obey Him or not, and Who never gave her husband any authority to force her to obey God, or try to stand between her and God Himself. But God did order him to co-dwell with her as an equal Christian. Though his self-idolatrous actions may be in ignorance.

So a Christian or a church who will not help her by following Matt 18 also disobeys what God says in 1 Cor 5:9-13,
"I wrote to you in my letter not to associate with sexually immoral people — not at all meaning the people of this world who are immoral, or the greedy and swindlers, or idolaters. In that case you would have to leave this world. But now I am writing to you that you must not associate with anyone who claims to be a brother or sister but is sexually immoral or greedy, **an idolater** or slanderer, a drunkard or swindler. Do not even eat with such people. What business is it of mine to judge those outside the church? Are you not to judge those inside? God will judge those outside.
"Expel the wicked person from among you."

Why is it important for the church to practice Matthew 18 in these cases? If an abused Christian woman whose Christian husband is sinning against her follows the steps in Matthew 18, and if the church agrees with her and rebukes him and he will not heed the church, then he is to be treated as an unbeliever, a pagan. He is to be regarded as an unbeliever and treated as one by the abused wife and the church. The Bible specifies that a Christian husband may not leave his wife, and that a Christian wife should not leave her husband. But if she does leave him she should remain single or go back to him. (1 Cor 7:10-11). In cases of domestic abuse or domestic violence, it is perfectly acceptable to God for a Christian woman to separate from her husband if such is needed for her well-being or safety (or that of the children). In fact, God Himself kicked Adam out of Eden after he had been mistreating his wife Eve, and allowed for her to stay in the Garden as long as she chose to, even for the rest of her life if she wanted, separated from Adam. And Adam was barred from going to Eve by a cherub with a flaming sword. In more modern terms, if a husband is being abusive, God is fine with a wife separating herself from him, even if she stays in the house and he is restrained from coming near the home, such as if she would get a restraining order. Understanding the context better from what happened in Eden in the first marriage, 1 Cor 7:11 is not God frowning upon a woman leaving her husband if there is real need, nor does her leaving mean she is a "bad Christian", but rather God left Christian women this option knowing that in some cases there might be a real need for a Christian wife to separate from her husband. However, separation is not the same as divorce, and she must remain married-but-separated.

Today if Matthew 18 is followed by an abused Christian wife, and she gets the church involved, addressing the sin of a Christian husband who is abusing her, they should help, and there are many other options out there available to help. There are shelters to keep her (and children) safe, legal aid to get a restraining order, and programs for men to help them change their abusive behavior, there is counseling, anger management classes, and also once the woman is safe from being abused, there is marriage counseling. (Which for safety reasons must happen after she is safe from any potential retaliation, and his abusive behavior has been modified - in some states in the US marriage counseling is illegal in domestic abuse situations until requirements about her safety and changes in his abusive behavior have been met. It is also advisable that she be safe from retaliation before going to the step 2 in the Matthew 18 process.) With all of these options for help, it is possible for the abuse to stop and for a marriage to improve, heal, and continue.

But in cases in which an abusive Christian husband will not repent of sinning against his wife, the Bible-following church may declare him to be treated as an unbeliever, as per Matthew 18. In these cases, a Christian wife, whether separated from him or not, she may not divorce him (1 Cor 7:13). But whether she is living with him, or if she refuses to live with him and remains separated, if he will not repent, and the church has declared him to be treated as an unbeliever through the Matthew 18 process, then if this unbeliever husband divorces her, she is not bound in such a case (1 Cor 7:15). Again, if a Christian husband has been declared to be treated as an unbeliever by the church per the Matthew 18 process, and he divorces his wife, she is not bound in such a case. She is rightfully divorced in such a case, and so is free to remarry, as per God's Word (1 Cor 7:27-28). So if she does remarry, she does not commit adultery, nor does her second husband commit adultery. By God's Word in 1 Cor 7:15, in such a case it is not just a man putting asunder what God has joined together, but rather by God's Word, it is God who validates this as a divorce. God, our loving Father, has made provision in His Word for Christian women who are abused by their husbands to receive help, and have hope.

Chapter Eighteen
1 Timothy 3 – Female Deacons, etc.

According to the Bible, can women be deacons in the church? Can women be elders in the church?
First off, what are elders and what are deacons? I will attempt to answer all this based off of what the Bible actually says, not so much by the current use of the terms in modern interpretations or tradition.

An elder means an "overseer" or "superintendent", and according to the New Testament they can make decisions pertaining to the local church. Following the New Testament model, there are supposed to be multiple elders in each local church which make decisions together, as this is not left up to any one single person. It seems their ideal number may be twelve, as the first church was the one in Jerusalem which consisted of the 12 apostles.

It is known that elders could make decisions for the church based on the account of Acts 15:6-29
"<u>The apostles and elders met to consider this question</u>. After much discussion, Peter got up and addressed them: "Brothers, you know that some time ago God made a choice among you that the Gentiles might hear from my lips the message of the gospel and believe. God, who knows the heart, showed that he accepted them by giving the Holy Spirit to them, just as he did to us. He did not discriminate between us and them, for he purified their hearts by faith. Now then, why do you try to test God by putting on the necks of Gentiles a yoke that neither we nor our ancestors have been able to bear? No! We believe it is through the grace of our Lord Jesus that we are saved, just as they are." The whole assembly became silent as they listened to Barnabas and Paul telling about the signs and wonders God had done among the Gentiles through them.
When they finished, James spoke up. "Brothers," he said, "listen to me. Simon has described to us how God first intervened to choose a people for his name from the Gentiles. The words of the prophets are in agreement with this, as it is written: "'After this I will return and rebuild David's fallen tent. Its ruins I will rebuild, and I will

restore it, that the rest of mankind may seek the Lord, even all the Gentiles who bear my name, says the Lord, who does these things' — things known from long ago.

"It is my judgment, therefore, that we should not make it difficult for the Gentiles who are turning to God. Instead we should write to them, telling them to abstain from food polluted by idols, from sexual immorality, from the meat of strangled animals and from blood. For the law of Moses has been preached in every city from the earliest times and is read in the synagogues on every Sabbath." <u>Then the apostles and elders, with the whole church,</u> decided to choose some of their own men and send them to Antioch with Paul and Barnabas. They chose Judas (called Barsabbas) and Silas, men who were leaders among the believers. With them they sent the following letter:

<u>The apostles and elders, your brothers, To the Gentile believers</u> in Antioch, Syria and Cilicia: Greetings. We have heard that some went out from us without our authorization and disturbed you, troubling your minds by what they said. So we all agreed to choose some men and send them to you with our dear friends Barnabas and Paul — men who have risked their lives for the name of our Lord Jesus Christ. Therefore we are sending Judas and Silas to confirm by word of mouth what we are writing. <u>It seemed good to the Holy Spirit and to us not to burden you with anything beyond the following requirements</u>: You are to abstain from food sacrificed to idols, from blood, from the meat of strangled animals and from sexual immorality. You will do well to avoid these things. Farewell.

By this passage, we know that elders have the ability to make decisions for the church. By this same passage, we also know that apostles also have the ability to make decisions for the church. In this passage above the elders and apostles made decisions together. And truly, the writings of Paul and Peter that compose so many books of the New Testament, which we still follow today, were in fact written by apostles.

As we covered, women can be apostles, such as Junia the apostle that is mentioned in Rom 16:7. And we also covered that <u>the Holy Spirit gives His gifts as He chooses</u>. Which means that regardless of if women can be elders, they can be apostles, and as such women can still have the ability to make decisions for the church in being apostles. And it is both elders and apostles who together made decisions for the church in Acts 15. This passage confirms both the decision making ability of apostles and elders at the same time.

As such, there is no reason to object that women could not be elders based purely on the idea that women are not able to hold a position of decision-making for the church. As many women as are apostles, a gift given by the choice of the Holy Spirit, they are all in the position to have the same ability as elders in making decisions for a church, inherently by being apostles. People seem to sometimes forget that being an apostle is a gift of the Holy Spirit, and does not just refer to the 12 apostles and Paul from 2000 years ago, but rather that it is a gift of the Holy Spirit that He has given to many Christians ever since, both to men and women, as He sees fit.

A deacon is a "servant" or "minister" which works in a church, for an elder or an apostle. They are not recorded to have been able to make decisions for the entire church, but their role is more to serve in the context of different ministries and needs. But within serving those needs, such as a food distribution to widows, they are potentially managing people themselves. In Acts 6:1-6 the twelve apostles had the people choose seven men to serve as deacons.

"In those days when the number of disciples was increasing, the Hellenistic Jews among them complained against the Hebraic Jews because their widows were being overlooked in the daily distribution of food. So the Twelve gathered all the disciples together and said, "It would not be right for us to neglect the ministry of the word of God in order to wait on tables. Brothers and sisters, choose seven men from among you who are known to be full of the Spirit and wisdom. We will turn this responsibility over to them and will give our attention to prayer and the ministry of the word."

This proposal pleased the whole group. They chose Stephen, a man full of faith and of the Holy Spirit; also Philip, Procorus, Nicanor, Timon, Parmenas, and Nicolas from Antioch, a convert to Judaism. They presented these men to the apostles, who prayed and laid their hands on them."

Here we can see that the deacons were chosen, and then the apostles prayed and laid hands on them as part of the process of them becoming deacons. Timothy was likely a deacon, serving in the church of Ephesus when Paul wrote him. As 1 Tim 4:6 says, "If you point these things out to the brothers, you will be a good minister(deacon) of Christ Jesus, brought up in the truths of the faith and of the good teaching that you have followed."

This word "minister" is actually the same word for as for deacon, as it is used in the qualifications for a deacon. This can also be gathered by the same laying on of hands process that was followed in Acts being recounted also in Timothy's case in this same letter, showed in: "This charge I commit to you, son Timothy, according to the prophecies previously made concerning you, that by them you may wage the good warfare" 1 Tim 1:18
"Do not neglect the gift that is in you, which was given to you by prophecy with the laying on of the hands of the eldership." 1 Tim 4:14, and also mentioned in Paul's second letter, 2 Tim 1:6 "Therefore I remind you to stir up the gift of God which is in you through the laying on of my hands."

And so Timothy was actually a deacon, not an elder, and his role included setting an example and teaching sound doctrine to the church at Ephesus. He was charged with this by Paul: the instructions of the letter to him, and all of this teaching in the letter of 1 Timothy. And this was as a deacon.
There may be some confusion about this as the editors of the Textus Receptus and the KJV added into the Greek, as an editor's note, that Timothy was the first ordained bishop (elder) of Ephesus, however this is not in the oldest manuscripts nor any until then in the early 1500s, in short just being their personal opinion. But the scriptures say Timothy was a deacon.

The apostles seem to have ordained the first deacons by the laying on of hands. These deacons were selected by the people of the church, and then ordained by the apostles through the laying on of hands. In the case of Timothy and Paul, Timothy as a deacon had the task of teaching sound doctrine committed to him by Paul, who seems to have been one of the first to preach the Gospel at Ephesus, and spark the growing Christian church there. While Paul is not in Ephesus, he has Timothy stay there, and as a deacon he commits to him to teach sound doctrine. And so it seems that deacons could serve as teachers, as well as serving in capacities such as food distribution.

Before the first apostles ordained any elders, they first ordained the 7 deacons. As Paul and apostles traveled around to new churches in various cities, they left deacons there to teach. Some time later, they ordained actual elders in the churches, as Acts 14:23 states:
"So when they had <u>appointed</u> elders in every church, and prayed with fasting, they commended them to the Lord in whom they had believed."
The word here for "appointed" means *"1) to vote by stretching out the hand 2) to create or appoint by vote: one to have charge of some office or duty 3) to elect, create, appoint"* and it inherently describes the same process of laying on hands that was practiced with deacons.

It seems that generally, a new church was to be begun by an older church. It was first led by apostles. Then, in this case, the apostle put a deacon there to serve the baby church and help to grow it up, like a child of the parent church. Then once there were Christians who had grown up in the church enough to be more mature, the apostles would either directly, or have the deacon under the apostle, go through a process of the people of the church choosing elders from among them. And both the deacons and the elders of the new church were ordained by the laying on of hands of either the apostles, elders, or the deacons of an older church.
In this it seems that the elders were grown up to replace the apostles, and once ordained, they served the new church in the fashion that the apostles which founded the church once had served. And in this then they also ordained their own deacons, or

the apostles ordained deacons from among them as well. There seems to have been some flexibility in how this worked, but most definitely those more experienced in Christ acted parentally over a baby church until those in it has grown up to a more adult maturity, and then the younger church came to manage itself. In the elders being, in fact, a replacement for the apostles in a grown-up church, it is no wonder that apostles and elders seemed to both make decisions together for the church. In fact the apostles (or those ordained by them) had been like parents to the new church elders, who were later ordained.

In general, there seems to be much in all of this that was based off of necessity in a world of forming new churches in new places, and an ever-expanding growing of the Christian church. And it seems that once apostles or those ordained under them had established a new church, they often travelled on, starting more new churches. Elders and deacons were ordained from the people of that area, by choice of the people, and later with guidelines or qualifications being met, to keep fulfilling the roles of the apostles etc. who had started the church and then left.

Timothy was a deacon serving an apostle, and was to instruct the church on choosing its own elders and its deacons. Eventually Timothy seems to have left Ephesus, as Paul indicates in 2 Tim 4:13, "When you come, bring the cloak that I left with Carpus at Troas, also the books, and above all the parchments."

And so all of this indicates that a deacon had a varied role, of being under either an apostle or an elder, who served in some way, which could vary from food ministry to teaching ministry, even in enforcing the instructions of an apostle who was not present, like a deacon might teach or enforce the instructions of an elder in a church once it was grown and independent. And it seems that the elders replaced the role of the apostles who originally founded a church, which means an apostle already had all the authority and responsibility of an elder when the church started.

And so again, as Junia was mentioned as an apostle, it would seem she had this role as well, and just like Paul, for a time in some new church, she had all the authority of an elder, prior to ordaining elders in that new church once it reached independent maturity. And like Paul, she may have had deacons ordained which she charged to serve in some capacity in the church. Taking all this into account, again there seems little reason to object to a woman having the authority and responsibility of an elder in a church.

There are no women clearly mentioned as elders of the Christian church in the Bible. There is one woman mentioned specifically to be a deacon, and the word used of her "diakonos" is the same word that is used as in the requirements of deacons found in 1 Timothy 3.

"I commend to you Phoebe our sister, who is a <u>deacon</u> of the church in Cenchrea, that you may receive her in the Lord in a manner worthy of the saints, and assist her in whatever business she has need of you; for indeed she has been a <u>patroness</u> of many and of myself also." Rom 16:1-2
The word here for "patroness" is "prostatis", a feminine noun. It means, *"a woman set over others, a female guardian, protectress, patroness."* It is a noun form of the verb "proistemi" which means, *"to set or place before a) to set over b) to be over, to superintend, preside over c) to be a protector or guardian 1) to give aid d) to care for, give attention to 1) profess honest occupations"*. This verb is used specifically both in reference to the deacons and elders of a church:

"But we request of you, brethren, that you appreciate those who diligently labor among you, and <u>have charge over you</u> in the Lord and give you instruction." 1 Thes 5:12
"The one who exhorts, in his exhortation; the one who contributes, in generosity; the <u>one who leads</u>, with diligence; the one who does acts of mercy, with cheerfulness." Rom 12:8
"He must be one who <u>manages</u> his own household well, keeping his children under control with all dignity (but if a man does not know how to <u>manage</u> his own household, how will he take care of the church of God?)" 1 Tim 3:4-5

"Deacons must be husbands of only one wife, and good <u>managers</u> of their children and their own households." 1 Tim 3:12
"The elders who <u>rule</u> well are to be considered worthy of double honor, especially those who work hard at preaching and teaching." 1 Tim 5:17

And so if this verb means "to lead, to manage, to rule, to have charge over" then the feminine noun form of this verb means a female "leader, manager, ruler, lady in charge", in the same way that the verb "to run" equivalents in a noun form to "a runner". The reference here to elders, and in general to church leaders and those with charge over others, shows that in fact Phoebe's description of being a "patroness" could be better translated as "leader, manager" and directly ties to her being a deacon.
And so as a leader/manager in being a deacon, it seems that Phoebe, like Timothy, had responsibility and authority over others in the church through serving as a deacon.

And this means that at some point someone ordained Phoebe in the same way that Timothy was ordained as a deacon, by the apostles' laying on of hands, praying and prophesying over her.

Also mentioned regarding laying on of hands is receiving the Holy Spirit, as in Acts 8:14-17:
"Now when the apostles which were at Jerusalem heard that Samaria had received the word of God, they sent unto them Peter and John: Who, when they were come down, <u>prayed for them, that they might receive the Holy Ghost</u>: (For as yet he was fallen upon none of them: only they were baptized in the name of the Lord Jesus.) <u>Then laid they their hands on them, and they received the Holy Ghost</u>."

And also in Acts 19:2-6, "He said unto them, Have ye received the Holy Ghost since ye believed? And they said unto him, We have not so much as heard whether there be any Holy Ghost. And he said unto them, Unto what then were ye baptized? And they said, Unto John's baptism. Then said Paul, John verily baptized with the baptism of repentance, saying unto the people, that they should believe on him which should come after him, that is, on Christ

Jesus. When they heard [this], they were baptized in the name of the Lord Jesus. And when Paul <u>had laid [his] hands upon them</u>, <u>the Holy Ghost came on them; and they spake with tongues, and prophesied."</u>
Although on the day of Pentecost, and also the first time that any Gentiles received Him, the Holy Spirit simply was given to the believers, it is true that the apostles also laid hands on people and prayed over them for them to receive the Holy Spirit, after their baptism.

While deacons and elders were chosen by the congregation, following certain qualifications, and were ordained by the laying on of hands with prayer and prophecy, it may be that being an elder or deacon involved a gift of the Holy Spirit.
"We have different <u>gifts</u>, according to the <u>grace given to each of us</u>. If your gift is prophesying, then prophesy in accordance with your faith; if it is serving, then serve; if it is teaching, then teach; if it is to encourage, then give encouragement; if it is giving, then give generously; <u>if it is to lead, do it diligently</u>; if it is to show mercy, do it cheerfully." Rom 12:6-8
Here the gift of leadership is mentioned, and compared to gifts of the Holy Spirit such as prophesy and teaching. As such, it seems that leadership in the church is considered a gift of the Holy Spirit.

1 Cor 12:28 "And God hath set some in the church, first apostles, secondarily prophets, thirdly teachers, after that miracles, then gifts of healings, helps, <u>governments</u>, diversities of tongues."
Here a gift of the Holy Spirit of "governments" is mentioned, and this is sometimes called the "gift of administration". This is probably the same as the gift of the Holy Spirit of leadership.
It could be that this sort of ordination by the apostles carried with it a prayer for the Holy Spirit to give the gift of governments or leadership to the deacon or elder. This would be very much like the cases in which prayer and laying on of hands resulted in new believers receiving the gift of tongues for the first time. Only in this case, it was a gift of administration or leading.

And so in a very real way, it seems the Bible teaches that those who were deacons or elders were seen very much as servants of Jesus, doing administration, as a gift of the Holy Spirit. And that is while others had received the gift of apostle, or prophet, teaching, etc. and served in those ways.
It is interesting this gift of "governments" (in order) was the last of all gifts listed besides tongues. It could be that the church who selected its own elders and deacons from among themselves were led by the Holy Spirit to pick those who seemed to have already been given a gift of administration or leadership. And so when these people were ordained, the prayer and laying on of hands was for them to develop this gift in full which they already seemed to have been given by the Holy Spirit.

Perhaps much in the same way that the disciples served under Jesus, then served Him as apostles, the emphasis on the role of later elders were that they were supposed to be like the first disciples, serving under Jesus as their Lord. Truly, the leader of the church is Jesus, and so elders should be viewed not as the leaders of the church, but as the servants of Jesus Christ who is the leader of the church. As the first disciples were all apostles, starting new churches and travelling, this is the first gift listed, and the one that pertains the most to the great commission of spreading the Gospel to new people. Whereas elders and deacons of an established local church did more in the way of maintenance and administration of the foundation that the apostles had laid. While elders had decision making ability for the church once it was matured, their decisions were to largely be based on the foundation and rules and teachings and doctrines that the apostles had already established. The elders were not in a position to develop a new way, just like the disciples who followed Jesus, but rather to maintain the way which had been taught to them, as the disciples stuck to what Jesus had taught them, and the elders were only to make decisions in how what they had been handed applied in new minor variations of circumstances, for the established body of believers there.

It should also be noted that elders and deacons were not necessarily defined as teachers, prophets, evangelists or apostles in their role in serving the church. Apostles would be sent out, and teaching was a different gift also. Church gatherings at this time are also described to have been far more interactive with those of many different gifts participating in a more open fellowship. In many ways, the original Christian Church of the New Testament was very different than how the church looks today. And in some ways it was the same. But there is little to nothing described here in the Bible which resembles many churches today in which there is one pastor, who teaches, helps, administrates, and often leads in decision making, with a board of elders that usually follow the pastor. It has been said that 10% of the church does 90% of the work, but this was not so much the case back then, in which everyone used their gifts in a more shared way, and the emphasis was more on the Spirit of Jesus leading the church, speaking up through the many people of the congregation, rather than only more through any 1 man, or even a group of elders. There has been much either corrupted or changed through the last 2000 years, which may still need to be restored.

As for women as deacons, yes women could be deacons. Phoebe is mentioned as one in the Bible. So let's look at the qualifications which she must have met to have been ordained as a deacon:

Deacons — in like manner grave, not double-tongued, not given to much wine, not given to filthy lucre, having the secret of the faith in a pure conscience, and let these also first be proved, then let them minister, being unblameable. Women in like manner grave, not false accusers, vigilant, faithful in all things. Deacons let them be of one wife husbands; the children managing well, and their own houses, for those who did minister well a good step to themselves do acquire, and much boldness in faith that [is] in Christ Jesus. 1 Tim 3:8-13

Paul makes it clear here to specify that women can be deacons. It can be assumed that all of the same qualifications, of being grave, not given to much wine or filthy lucre, having the secret of faith in a pure conscience, being unblameable, being proved first, all apply to not only the male but the female deacons also. But in specific Paul wants them to make sure that women deacons are also grave, not false accusers, vigilant, and faithful in all things. Women are mentioned primarily for this, as he apparently thinks these are more likely problems a woman might have. But of course, not being a false accuser is a qualification for a male deacon also, and the qualifications more targeted to female deacons also apply to the male.

And he wants to make sure that if the deacon is a husband that he only has one wife. In a culture of polygamy this is very understandable to mention as a requirement. As we have covered, a man with more than one wife, in truth is an adulterer. This requirement did not apply to a woman, as she only was able to have one husband. This did not need to be specified as it was unheard of, and any woman trying this would simply be understood as an adulteress. In truth, a man may only have 1 wife, but men have long thought they could make this decision up for themselves, though in truth Jesus revealed that it is God alone who joins 2 people in marriage, and marriage has always functioned by God's rules, no matter what rules men made up about it. So a deacon must not be an adulterer, claiming 2 or more "wives" (or "concubines").

As for the children, both a woman or a man may lead their children or house well, so there is nothing gender-specific here. As 1 Pet 3 specifies, a husband and wife "co-dwell" together. And a woman is said to manage her children and house in 1 Tim 5:14 (this same letter)
"So I would have younger widows marry, bear children, <u>manage their households</u>, and give the adversary no occasion for slander."

Apparently in this list, because we know Phoebe was a deacon, we can also know that the phrase "one wife husbands" does not mean that a deacon must be married, nor a man. We can also gather this from the case of Timothy, who is not mentioned to have been married, but also was a deacon. So a better translation for understanding would be "a deacon if a husband must have only one wife". It can also be assumed that Timothy did not have children, so that portion should be understood as "if a deacon has children they must be well managed".

The language in this passage is obtusely gender-neutral in the Greek. It would have been possible to write this in a way which was very specific that deacons had to be men, like by saying "deacons must be men" however that is not said. Not only that, but the pronouns used are gender neutral, and open. In what ways the words do seem masculine, it is not specific, but in keeping with the all-inclusive use of the masculine tense in Greek. In other words, if Paul wanted to indicate only men could be deacons, his writing style seems to go out of the way to confuse the reader as to let the reader think that gender is not a qualification.

And this is the exact same style as is used in the passages regarding elders, which also seem to have been intentionally written to be open and gender neutral, and could have easily been written to be very masculine specific, but were not. And again, they could have specified "an elder must be a man" or even "if any man wants to be an elder" but they do not, instead saying "If any one wants to be an elder", and nothing in here says definitively that an elder must be a man. Below is a translation from the Greek reflecting the earliest manuscript of these passages, the Codex Sinaiticus. I have highlighted in gray anything that seems to indicate only a man can be an elder.

"Stedfast the word: If any one the oversight doth long for, a right work one desireth; it behoveth, therefore, the overseer to be blameless, of one wife a husband, vigilant, sober, decent, a friend of strangers, apt to teach, not given to wine, not a striker, not given to filthy lucre, but gentle, not contentious, not a lover of money, own house managing well, having children in subjection with all gravity, (and if any one own house [how] to manage hath not known, how an assembly of God shall take care of?) not a new convert, lest having been puffed up may fall to a judgment of the devil; and it behoveth also to have a good testimony from those without, that may not fall into reproach and a snare of the devil."
1 Tim 3:1-7

1 πιςτος ο λογος ει τις επιςκοπης ορεγε ται καλου εργου επι 2 θυμει δι ουν τον επιςκοπον ανε πλημπτον ει ναι μιας γυναικος ανδρα νηφαλιο ςωφρονα · κοςμι ον · φιλοξενον 3 διδακτικον · μη

παροινον · μη πληκτην · αλλα επιεικη αμαχο 4 αφιλαργυρον του ϊδιου οικου κα λως προϊςτανο μενον · τεκνα ε χοντα εν υποτα γη μετα παςης ςε μνοτητος 5 ει δε τις του ϊδιου οικου προςτηναι ουκ οιδεν πως εκ κληςιας θυ επι μεληςεται 6 μη νεοφυτον ϊ να μη τυφωθεις εις κριμα εμπεςη του διαβολου 7 δει δε και μαρτυρι αν καλην εχιν α πο των εξωθεν ςεμνους ϊνα μη εις ονιδι ςμον εμπεςη και παγιδα του διαβο λου ·

"If any one is blameless, of one wife a husband, having children stedfast, not under accusation of riotous living or insubordinate, for it behoveth the overseer to be blameless, as God's steward, not self-pleased, nor irascible, not given to wine, not a striker, not given to filthy lucre; but a lover of strangers, a lover of good, sober-minded, righteous, kind, self-controlled, holding according to the teaching to the stedfast word, that may be able also to exhort in the sound teaching, and the gainsayers to convict." Titus 1:6-9

6 ξαμην ει τις εςτι ανηεγκλητος μιας γυναικος ανηρ τεκνα εχων πιςτα μη εν κατηγορια αςωτιας η ανυπο
7 τακτα · δει γαρ τον επιςκοπον ανεγ κλητον ειναι ως θυ οικονομον μη αυθαδη μη οργιλον μη παροινον μη πληκτην μη αιςχροκερδη
8 αλλα φιλοξενον φιλαγαθον ςωφρονα δικαιον οςιον εγκρατη
9 αντεχομενον του κατα την διδαχην πιςτου λογου ϊνα δυνατος η και πα ρακαλειν εν τη δι δαςκαλια τη ϋγιαι νουςη και τους αν τιλεγοντας ελεγχι

As seen above, the only thing in these verses that indicates that an elder must be a man is the qualification that he must be the husband of one wife. The exact same phrase is found in the qualifications for a deacon. As is clear in the case of deacons this only means, "(to be a deacon) if a husband must have only one wife". We can tell this by the context that Timothy was a deacon, and seems to have been single, and because Phoebe, a woman, was a deacon.
As such, there is every reason to think that the phrase has the exact same meaning in the list of qualifications for elders, namely that "(to be an elder) if a husband must have only one wife".

In the qualifications for deacons, it can be assumed that all the qualifications that seem to be more specific towards women are also applicable to men, such as "not false accusers". And vice versa, women deacons should not be "given to filthy lucre" same as the men. As such, it seems that if the qualifications for elders are written in the same way, that all the qualifications for a woman to be an elder would be the same as for a man, excepting that it is assumed she only will have one husband if she is married.

It could be argued that Paul specifically mentions women as deacons, but does not specifically mention women as elders. This would not be surprising, as at that time it may be that women were not anticipated to be elders. There are in fact no female elders mentioned in the New Testament. However, this in itself in no way precludes women from being elders today, as the Words of the Bible in no way seem to restrict a woman from being an elder. While Paul seems to have written expecting that elders would be men, it also is clear that <u>his God-breathed words left it completely open for women to be elders as well</u>. Because, truly, Jesus is the Word, and God wrote the Bible.

The argument could be made that all of the 12 apostles were male, and as they were the original church leadership, that women should not be elders based on this precedent. But this argument fails in that Junia is mentioned as a female apostle, and as such it is clear that the first 12 apostles being male really doesn't matter, as later apostles were female. In the same way, even though the first deacons were male, it is clear that later deacons were also female, because of Phoebe the deacon.

If anything, the pattern is that while men were first to be apostles and deacons, later women were also. And so if this pattern were to be continued, it would show that while men were the first to be elders, then later women were to be also.

And so it is clear women can be deacons, and there are also many reasons to think women can also be elders. To sum up the reasons:

1. Because the qualifications for elders contain no qualifications to preclude women, excepting "husband of one wife" which obviously only applied to men

2. Because "husband of one wife" means in context "if a husband, he must have only one wife" as shown by the cases of both Timothy (single) and Phoebe (female)

3. Because the qualifications for deacon are obviously for both men and women regardless of who it is more targeted at, they applied to both genders

4. Because the language is intentionally broad and gender-neutral in the qualifications

5. Because if elders were to only be men the text could have clearly stated "elders can only be men".

Therefore, it seems that the most Biblical view to take of these passages, looking at the contextual meanings, is that women can be elders the same as men can.

6. This is further supported by women being able to be apostles, who have the role of ordaining elders and deacons, and have charge over them at least temporarily. Also that in being apostles, women can make decisions for a church, and teach them as Paul did in his letters to Timothy, a deacon under him who was raising up a newer church. This is also supported by women being able to be deacons, who also seem to be able to teach and guide a newer church, and under an apostle, even facilitate the ordaining of elders and deacons. Without even looking at the qualifications for elders, it is clear that between women being apostles and deacons that they may teach, make decisions for the church, start new churches and guide them, and also ordain elders and deacons. This is weighty in and of itself.

7. Added to this, is that the lists of qualifications for elders do not clearly specify men, nor preclude women, but rather are written to be unnecessarily gender-neutral (if specifying men-only).

8. Even if in fact women were not yet elders at that time, which is in truth an unknown either way, this is not an argument that they can't be, but only that they weren't yet. However, the pattern of apostles and deacons was that men were the first, and then women followed and were as well. This is 2 witnesses to a pattern that men doing something first was irrelevant in whether or not a woman could do the same thing later. And it adds weight to a precedent that female elders were to follow male elders.

Adding it all together the argument becomes very strong that women can be elders. As such, the stance of a Bible-believing Christian who believes women today can be elders is completely justifiable and supportable by the Word of God. The Words of God seem to completely allow for women to be elders, ever since then, and this includes that they definitely can be now.

The fact is that most arguments that some people make that women cannot be elders are based not on the language of the qualifications listed here in 1 Timothy or Titus, but self-admittedly their arguments are based on passages like 1 Cor 11, 1 Cor 14, and 1 Pet 3, none of which in truth teach anything that shows that women cannot be elders.

The objection that a wife cannot be an elder or deacon because she would be in a position of authority over her husband if he is not one, ignores that God is fine with a wife being able to do or have something that her husband can not do or does not have. God did not have a problem with Eve being able to eat from a tree that her husband Adam could not eat from, but rather Adam was the one that seemed to have a problem with this. God is fine with a wife being able to have something more than her husband, which he does not have, or her being able to do something that he cannot do.

The same goes for any gifts of the Holy Spirit, which actually arguably include gifts of administration to be an elder or deacon. As in a marriage love means the husband seeks the way of his wife, to do as she wants, and she seeks to do what he wants in submitting herself to him, neither one has more authority than the other in decision-making, but rather the Bible teaches they should <u>meet in the middle, if each is loving and submitting equally</u>. As such, it affects a marriage no more for a husband to be an elder, or have a "greater gift" than his wife, than for a wife to be an elder or have a "greater gift" than her husband (though again, in 1 Corinthians 12 the gift of administration is the last gift listed besides tongues). The Bible does not teach a double-standard, but rather the Bible teaches equality and acceptance of God's will for each person's calling and giftings from God, without any discrimination from gender or marital status (except for the adultery of polygamy).

Women in fact can be deacons, and can be elders, and this is a completely Biblical position to take, which can be supported by scripture accurately and taking the Bible most literally as the Word of God.

Chapter Nineteen
The Truth of the Church's History

If all this prior is true about women, and the understanding so far presented is or is closer to what the apostles Peter and Paul understood, and what Jesus knew, then a question arises. How did we get from the situation of women then, to the situation of women later in the church?

"In those days when the number of disciples was increasing, the Hellenistic Jews among them complained against the Hebraic Jews because their widows were being overlooked in the daily distribution of food. So the Twelve gathered all the disciples together and said, "It would not be right for us to neglect the ministry of the word of God in order to wait on tables. <u>Brothers and sisters, choose seven men from among you</u> who are known to be full of the Spirit and wisdom. We will turn this responsibility over to them and will give our attention to prayer and the ministry of the word."
This proposal pleased the whole group. They chose Stephen, a man full of faith and of the Holy Spirit; also Philip, Procorus, Nicanor, Timon, Parmenas, and Nicolas from Antioch, a convert to Judaism. They presented these men to the apostles, who prayed and laid their hands on them." Acts 6:1-6

In review, the first deacons were first chosen by the people, and then went through an ordination by the apostles. As such it makes sense that later, elders and deacons were also chosen by the people, and then ordained by a pre-existing apostle, elder, or deacon.
Under this system in which new elders and deacons were chosen by the people, it make sense that the women, composing half the church, would have been commonly ordained as deacons, and even eventually come to be ordained as elders. The fact is that the pre-existing apostles, elders, and deacons who did the ordination of new elders and deacons were only serving the local congregation. In fact, the element here of a democratic method of choosing church leadership is very clear. Those who were to serve as leaders were to be elected by all the people in the church, and

the pre-existing leaders simply did the process of ordaining them. Of course there were certain qualifications that had to be met, but in the case of deacons most clearly, and also in the case of elders, the qualifications left the positions open to women.

So what happened?

The church seemed to have followed the original model at least through around 95 AD, in which Clement of Rome mentions in 1 Clement that elders which had been chosen by the approval of the people and ordained by the prior leaders, *"with the consent of the whole Church"*, could not be fired when they had served well and done nothing wrong, Clement says they had *"blamelessly served the flock of Christ in a humble, peaceable, and disinterested spirit"* (chap 44). Apparently a couple of men started trouble and tried to convince the church to basically impeach the elders for no reason. Clement seems to think the reason was simple envy (chap 3), and perhaps the desire of these trouble-making men was to try to replace the elders and to rise to what they saw as power in being *"leaders"* (chap 14). But in truth the elders were servant leaders, likely in the capacity of a gift of the Holy Spirit, just as anyone else functioning in the church in a gift of the Holy Spirit (Chap 37, 38).
It should also be noted that Clement sent this letter on behalf of a group of elders of which he was only one.

The view of women and marriage seems to have been in consistently high esteem as in the New Testament through around 120-140 AD as is seen in the writings of Polycarp to the Philippians. First of all, his writings hint that women were deacons. Of deacons he says, *"They must not be slanderers"* which matches "Women in like manner grave, not false accusers", and there is nothing in the qualifications for deacons of "not slanderers" that is targeted at male deacons, or more closely matches, than this qualification more targeted at female deacons. So there is some reason to think they did have female deacons at that time, and nothing specifies that they did not.

On women and marriage he says:

"And when absent from you, he wrote you a letter, which, if you carefully study, you will find to be the means of building you up in that faith which has been given you, and which, being followed by hope, and preceded by love towards God, and Christ, and our neighbour, "is the mother of us all." For if any one be inwardly possessed of these graces, he hath fulfilled the command of righteousness, since he that hath love is far from all sin. But the love of money is the root of all evils." Knowing, therefore, that "as we brought nothing into the world, so we can carry nothing out," let us arm ourselves with the armour of righteousness; and let us teach first of all ourselves to walk in the commandments of the Lord, then [teach] the women [to walk] in the faith given to them, and in love and purity tenderly loving their own husbands in all truth, and loving all [others] equally in all chastity; and to train up their children in the knowledge and fear of God. Teach the widows to be discreet as respects the faith of the Lord, praying continually for all, being far from all slandering, evil-speaking, false-witnessing, love of money, and every kind of evil; knowing that they are the altars of God, that He clearly perceives all things, and that nothing is hid from Him, neither reasonings, nor reflections, nor any one of the secret things of the heart. Knowing, then, that "God is not mocked," we ought to walk worthy of His commandment and glory."

Here Polycarp seems to say that first everyone needs to teach themself to walk in the commandments of the Lord. The commandments referenced are the ones to love God, Christ, and our neighbor. He also seems to reference to faith or love as "the mother of us all". I do not know what he is quoting, but it seems to hold motherhood and women in a good light with respect for women. He then says the love of money is the root of all evils, and that we can take no possession with us. He then advises everyone to teach themself to follow these commandments of love to God, Christ, and neighbor. This is immediately followed by advice to then teach the women how to walk in the faith given to them. He earlier references to the letter of Paul, which he says if studied will teach them how to build themselves up in the faith which has been given to all of them, advising them to study the scriptures. And so it seems that his teaching is that once they all have taught themselves to follow the commandments of loving God and neighbor, that then the they also need to make sure to teach the women to build them up in the faith, likely by teaching the women the scriptures. In context this is the most clear meaning. Also for the church to teach the women to love their husbands, be chaste, and to train up their children in the knowledge and fear of God, which of course would go far better if they were taught the scriptures. This is in keeping with the understanding of 1 Timothy 2 found in this book. It is also in keeping with the understanding of 1 Peter 3 found in this book, to husbands. Polycarp goes on to give instructions to widow women, and references to nothing being hidden from God, but Him knowing all the secret reasonings and reflections and secret things of the heart. This is also in keeping with the understanding found in this book of 1 Peter 3 to wives; and here by Polycarp is directed to widow women.

As such it seems as late as 120-140 AD that women were still serving as deacons, and were held in high esteem, encouraged to be taught the scriptures, and this was seen as the responsibility of the church, and also likely as assumed appropriate as part of husbands loving their wives as their neighbors. It should also be noted that Polycarp sent this on behalf of several other elders along with himself, of which he was only one.

However, looking at the writings of Ignatius, (98-117AD) which are questionable in their preservation as to whether they have been added to by later writers, it seems that this was not the case in all of the churches. In some churches, an odd new structure had developed in which 1 elder was considered THE "bishop", and all of the other elders seemed to be under him in authority. These churches seemed to have made the mistake of thinking that who an elder was ordained by made a particular elder more important. It could also be that an elder claimed himself to have more authority than the other elders because he was ordained by one of the original 12 apostles or the apostle Paul, and the other elders were not. This should have been recognized as heresy, in contradiction to the scriptures written at the hand of the Apostles, but it apparently was not recognized as heresy.

Soon enough, the churches with a "bishop" as a more "in charge" elder spread, and overtook the number of churches with multiple equal elders in leadership.

Why? Because men were used to a man ruling over others. And because men themselves had the desire to rule over other men. As we have covered looking at the Old Testament, the same kind of man who seeks to rule over other men is also the kind of man who seeks to rule over women. The same desire for power that led a single elder to have more power than the other elders, is the same desire that brought about polygamy, and slavery, and the first sin. Certain men in the church must have sought this, and other men must have accepted it, all ignoring Jesus' words in Luke 22:25-27

"And He said to them, "The kings of the Gentiles lord it over them; and those who have authority over them are called 'Benefactors.' "But it is not this way with you, but the one who is the greatest among you must become like the youngest, and the leader like the servant. "For who is greater, the one who reclines at the table or the one who serves? Is it not the one who reclines at the table? But I am among you as the one who serves."
and in Matt 20:25-28
"But Jesus called them to Himself and said, "You know that the rulers of the Gentiles lord it over them, and their great men exercise authority over them. "It is not this way among you, but whoever wishes to become great among you shall be your servant, and whoever wishes to be first among you shall be your slave; just as the Son of Man did not come to be served, but to serve, and to give His life a ransom for many."
The twelve apostles understood this, as did Paul. But in a couple of generations, the elders of the church, whose positions were to replace that of the original apostles, seem to have forgotten this.

As such, in the early 200s it is recorded that more and more importance was placed on a single "bishop" and whether or not he was ordained by an original apostle. Tertullian was of this time, and writing in his Prescription Against Heretics, said,
"Let them produce the original records of their churches; let them unfold the roll of their bishops, running down in due succession from the beginning in such a manner that [that first bishop of theirs] bishop shall

be able to show for his ordainer and predecessor some one of the apostles or of apostolic men, – a man, moreover, who continued steadfast with the apostles. For this is the manner in which the apostolic churches transmit their registers: as the church of Smyrna, which records that Polycarp was placed therein by John; as also the church of Rome, which makes Clement to have been ordained in like manner by Peter. In exactly the same way the other churches likewise exhibit (their several worthies), whom, as having been appointed to their episcopal places by apostles, they regard as transmitters of the apostolic seed."(Chap 32)

And so more and more emphasis was placed on the "bishop", and who they had been ordained by, completely disregarding (in this case) that both Polycarp and Clement seemed to have considered themselves just one of many elders. They also encouraged others to follow the elders of their church, without reference to a "bishop" or more important elder. Surely they practiced this that they taught, and themselves did not consider themselves to be a more important elder or bishop, but rather others at the time or later in churches with a "bishop" insisted on viewing them this way. Which was probably for no better reason then they happened to be the one, of many equal elders, which wrote the letter which was preserved. Those who placed more emphasis on 1 man ruling a church over all others were of such an inclination to make who ordained Polycarp and Clement of Rome to be of more importance than the democratic eldership clearly taught and practiced by those who ordained them. But there is no indication that Polycarp and Clement placed this sort of importance on themselves, but rather were just 1 of many equal elders. But soon people began to ignore this fact.

And so the desire of man to rule over other man, as old as humanity, slowly crept into the church, transforming it from a democracy of servants of a single Lord, led by Him through His Holy Spirit, into something resembling more of the monarchy of man ruling over other man. And the type of men who would do this and accept this, are also the type who would seek to rule over women.

Such as Tertullian, same writer as above, who said,
De Cultu Feminarum, book 1, chap 1. ("Every woman should be ....)
walking about as Eve mourning and repentant, in order that by every garb of penitence she might the more fully expiate that which she derives from Eve,-the ignominy, I mean, of the first sin, and the odium (attaching to her as the cause) of human perdition. "In pains and in anxieties dost thou bear (children), woman; and toward thine husband (is) thy inclination, and he lords it over thee."
And do you not know that you are (each) an Eve? The sentence of God on this sex of yours lives in this age: the guilt must of necessity live too."
"You are the devil's gateway: you are the unsealer of that (forbidden) tree: you are the first deserter of the divine law: you are she who persuaded him (Adam) whom the devil was not valiant enough to attack. You destroyed so easily God's image, man. On account of your desert-that is, death-even the Son of God had to die."
On the Veiling of Virgins, chap. 9. "It is not permitted to a woman to speak in the church; but neither (is it permitted her) to teach, nor to baptize, nor to offer, nor to claim to herself a lot in any manly function, not to say (in any) sacerdotal office."

And Tertullian also taught that women should wear a veil and a head covering, twisting Paul's meaning in 1 Cor 11, as many still do today, and his arguments also twisted the scriptures as much as the above. It is entirely possible that Tertullian or a follower of his teachings may have had a hand in the gloss of 1 Cor 14:34-35. In any case, he seemed to have a hatred of women, and twisted the scriptures in a misogynistic effort to support his hatred, and also made his own rules up that a woman must not speak in church, could not be a deacon, nor could teach, all in a fashion of either outright total ignoring of the Scriptures, or in twisting of them.

And so it can easily be seen in this example that the same sort of man who would falsely teach that men have a right to rule over other men, would also find reasons to attack women and try to establish that they could be ruled over by men as well. But with the high level of esteem for women in equality that was taught by Jesus, Paul, and the apostles, this sort of false teacher had to ignore much and twist much on a very high level of hatred in order to give a rise to hatred of women which would take away their newfound equal and esteemed position as Christians in the church.

And this is seen above, for instance in the complete ignoring on Paul's teachings in Romans 5 that Adam committed the first sin, and also that woman is clearly stated to have also been made in the image of God in Genesis. Let it also be noted that Tertullian taught questionable ideas that were anti-Trinitarian for some time, and then eventually went and joined what was regarded at the time as an openly anti-Trinitarian cult.

The bottom line is that at some point, someone had to have made a choice to seek personal power over teaching the truth of the Word of God. And in this, someone chose to seek power over men, and also over women, and twisted the scriptures and ignored the Word of God in their teachings in order to do so. There is a simple term for this which is a "false teacher". And as Paul warned about repeatedly, at some point false teachers did creep into the church, seeking the rule of men, not God. It is the same story as all of the rest of history, and as such the church began to be filled with false teaching which was not ever meant to be the true way, teaching, model or practice of Christianity.

What happened next, over the 200s in a nutshell:
At some point the next "bishop" seems to have been chosen not by the people, but rather at the discretion of the presiding bishop and elders under him. Which is also very much like a monarchy, not a democracy. And the same also happened for elders and deacons, in which the practice changed from the people of the church choosing their leaders, to the leaders choosing the leaders who would follow them. These practices of course all reek of men who seek power. Then they apparently took the liberty upon themselves to choose among themselves "bishops" who would be over several "bishops" in a certain region; a "bishop" of the "bishops". And also the "bishops" in Rome tried to assert that they had more authority than the other bishops of other churches, and in fact that the bishop of Rome had the right to have authority over the bishops in all other regions.

Eventually, this all led to the development of the early Catholic church. Later, as Christianity was legalized by Constantine emperor of Rome in the early 300s, and the state set to enforce the decisions of the bishops as "true" and "false" doctrine, all of this false teaching cemented. In 380 AD Christianity under the "bishops", and the "bishops of bishops", was made the official religion of the Roman Empire. And from this came the Catholic church that we still know today, which grew to have great political power.

And so the early false teachers that changed the structure of the church so that men could rule over other men, and have power over the people, also were the type that sought men to have power over women. They taught all of these things hand in hand, as almost all of the big names of the 200s both contributed towards the development of the bishops-led church, and also to a view of women which set to reverse all that Jesus, the apostles, and Paul had done and taught to change men's view and treatment of women to one of equality to men, and equal participation in the Christian church.

Just to sample their views from then, and after:
[Churchfather, venerated as a Saint up to the 17th century] Clement of Alexandria (150?-215?): *"Every woman should be filled with shame by the thought that she is a woman."*

[Churchfather] Tertullian (160?-220?): *"Woman is a temple built over a sewer, the gateway to the devil. Woman, you are the devil's doorway. You led astray one whom the devil would not dare attack directly. It was your fault that the Son of God had to die; you should always go in mourning and rags."*

[Saint] Ambrose (339-97): *"Adam was deceived by Eve, not Eve by Adam... it is right that he whom that woman induced to sin should assume the role of guide lest he fall again through feminine instability."*

Saint John Chrysostom [349-407] commanded every Christian father to instill into his son *"a resolute spirit against womankind ... Let him have no converse with any woman save only his mother. Let him see no woman."* — Christianity and Pagan Culture In the Later Roman Empire, by M.L.W. Laistner

[Saint] Augustine (354-430): *"Woman was merely man's helpmate, a function which pertains to her alone. She is not the image of God but as far as man is concerned, he is by himself the image of God."*

Pope Gregory I (540-604): *"Woman is slow in understanding and her unstable and naive mind renders her by way of natural weakness to the necessity of a strong hand in her husband. Her 'use' is two fold; [carnal] sex and motherhood."*

"In 584 CE, the Council Of Macon was held at Lyons.
43 Catholic bishops attended as well as 23 male representatives of other bishops.
On the question of "Are women human?", 32 voted Yes, and 31 No (that would make the remaining 5 still undecided)."

[Saint] Thomas Aquinas (1225-74): *"[Woman] was made only to assist with procreation."*

Martin Luther (1483-1546), leading Reformer, founder of Lutheran Protestantism:
"If [women] become tired or even die, that does not matter. Let them die in childbirth–that is why they are there." — Martin Luther
— The Dark Side of Christianity by Helen Ellerbe

[Reformer, founder of Scottish Presbyterianism]
John Knox (1513-72): *"Woman was made for only one reason, to serve and obey man."*

Lutherans at Wittenberg [1595] debated whether women were really human beings at all.
— The Dark Side of Christianity, by Helen Ellerbe

[Reformer, founder of the Methodist movement]
John Wesley (1703-91): *"Wife: Be content to be insignificant. What loss would it be to God or man had you never been born."*
(All from http://freetruth.50webs.org/A3.htm)

Perhaps the Gentile converts had a poor view of women to start with. It is important to keep in mind that generally the Gentile world was no different than that of the time of Abraham. They had slaves, they owned women as wives who had very little to no rights, and they also in many places practiced polygamy, or had concubines. And all of this was mostly without any influence of the Law of Moses, let alone an acceptance of that law in society as the law of the land.

The Jews had been living with more of strict moral code than the Gentile nations around them, even with all their failures and breaking of the Law. When the Jews became Christian they had more of a foundation and understanding of the changes which took place, a better understanding of the scriptures than they had carried as Jews before their conversion. But when Gentiles became Christian, they were starting as people who had little no knowledge or practice of the Jewish Law and Old Testament. For them the Law of the Old Testament was probably in many ways a step up from the morals in their own culture which they had been brought up in and practiced. Just to comprehend the Law and Old Testament was probably a challenge for Gentile converts who were prior unlearned and unfamiliar with it.

And so as more and more Gentiles became converts, even became bishops and rose to power and established teachings, it is no wonder that the new insights of Christianity that the Jewish 12 apostles and Paul, etc. had obtained, were lost, and replaced. And they were replaced with the most banal and basic misinterpretation of the New Testament, regarding slaves and women, as filtered by the Old Testament, with the Law no longer viewed as merely a step in the right direction, but again as something more justified to perfection and ideal. But this was only a view and understanding which confirmed their own biases as those with power over slaves and women. This did not reflect the newer insights and direction that the first apostles and Christians understood, during their personal transitions from Judaism to Christianity. It may have been the prejudices of the converts, which caused them to misunderstand so much about everything which the New Testament writers and early Jewish Christians had understood had changed and must change in their perceptions. As those who personally knew Jesus and wrote the New Testament fell asleep, understanding was lost, and important information about women was misread and misinterpreted.

But nevertheless, it cannot be ignored that a better understanding once had been attained, and was being taught, and at some point someone entrusted with the truth made a choice to seek power, over seeking the truth. The prejudices of the people, both Gentile and Jew, were conducive and stacked to accept this sort of false teaching… but these prejudices were not the sole cause of this false teaching emerging and gaining hold in the church. Someone knew the truth, as the apostles knew it and taught it and established it, but over time someone decided to ignore the truth in favor of personal power, and in total compromise with a sinful world. False teachers and hirelings somehow slipped into the flock, and led the Christians astray. This is what Paul warned would happen, and as the early church is recorded to have fought repeatedly, but eventually the battle was lost with consequences that would last for millennia.

And so for a brief time, women were treated well in the church and seen as equals, neighbors to love as oneself, equal before God in the gifts and Grace they had received, just as the men were.

And then the Church plunged back into the darkness of the world, worldly understanding, worldly systems of ruler-ship, worldly systems of slavery and rule over other men and women. Soon enough misunderstood twisting and perversion of scripture became not only publicly taught false teaching, but not long after became cemented in political systems of worldly governments. Elders became bishops, and bishops became priests, and like the Jewish priests of the Old Testament, Christian priests became Pharisees, and developed traditions of men, from false teaching of the scriptures.

In short the history of the church is that was invaded by antichrists and false teachers, which led it all astray. And this same error continued for almost 2000 years, and in some places still continues today. And piece by piece the errors established then have fallen away, in minor leaps and spurts in places, and then more widespread. Over a long time, the Gentiles came to reach the morality of the Law, and even to surpass it in places. Until we reach today, in which at least some of the world has democracy, and slavery is almost universally outlawed, at least on paper. But the same struggles continue for men to find new and inventive ways to rule over other men. Even within democracies, money has become a means of power, and the system is full of personal agendas of self-service.

The birth of democracy centered greatly around men getting tired of being ruled over by other men, and wanting to rule themselves. Men were tired of being born into a world in which they had no voice in the laws, were victims of the power of monarchies and elite men, from birth subject to unfair laws. Democracy also sprang forth from the desire of men to live without religious persecution, which was tied to the government and national churches. Men wanted to be able to practice their religion before God without being told how they must believe, but to be free to believe as they did without oppression.

This was why many left Europe, and came to America, to flee religious persecution. And eventually men decided they should make the laws for themselves that they had to live under, and rule themselves. This is where the United States came from. The same sort of ideals have founded many other democracies and republics the world over. The bottom line is that a man did not want to be treated with no voice in his own government, and so they endeavored to change the system of men ruling over other men, so that men would have a voice, and choice, on how the government would treat them. In the US, the first words of the Declaration of Independence, to found a republic, showed the heart of what these men wanted. They believed that men who were ruling should treat those they ruled over as equals in the sight of God. And the best way they found to ensure this was for the rulers to be temporary representatives of the ruled, serving as rulers in commonly agreed upon laws. They wanted those in government to treat them as those in government would want to be treated.

"We hold these truths to be self-evident, that all men are created equal, that they are endowed by their Creator with certain unalienable Rights, that among these are Life, Liberty and the pursuit of Happiness. That to secure these rights, Governments are instituted among Men, deriving their just powers from the consent of the governed, That whenever any Form of Government becomes destructive of these ends, it is the Right of the People to alter or to abolish it, and to institute new Government, laying its foundation on such principles and organizing its powers in such form, as to them shall seem most likely to effect their Safety and Happiness." -The Declaration of Independence

It was the desire for equality, and liberty, that started the US. Of course, in the beginning, the men who were created equal were only land-owners, typically white, and this statement in no way prevented slavery, nor stated that men and women were created equal. It was a long time coming before these words would be fully realized to how we see them today, which is that "all people are created equal".

Slavery in the US of men was only made illegal about 150 years ago. But slavery is still practiced in the world, and it is estimated that some <u>27 million people today</u> are living in slavery as slaves. And still entirely too much of the world still practices the enslavement of women, and in multiple forms. The first is still that of a sex-slave or concubine, and many children are violated this way also. Many of those 27 million are women and children who are sex-slaves. For those who are aware of this problem in the world today, do remember all of this is nothing new!

Women only were recognized as full citizens and able to vote in the US a little over 90 years ago. Other countries gave women the right to vote only slightly more or less recently. And the right of women to vote, in the UK was preceded by the sacrifices of thousands of women who protested for suffrage. They were roughed, even beat up, by mobs of men and sexually molested by men at their protests, to the point of taking to carrying dog-whips in order to deter sexual molestation in self-defense, esp. as decent Christian women.

'Not the police, but the stewards at political meetings, and the men who volunteer to "keep the women in order," they'...'as they're turning us out they punish us in ways the public don't know... They punish us by underhand maltreatment – of the kind most intolerable to a decent woman'...'they were not only facing imprisonment, but unholy handling." - The Convert, Elizabeth Robins, pgs.158,163

They were imprisoned for political protest, in the US the charge was "obstructing traffic" as women stood on the sidewalk in front of the White House. They were sometimes beat in prison.
"Whittaker and his workhouse guards greeted 33 returning protestors on what has become known as the infamous "Night of Terror," November 14, 1917. Forty-four club-wielding men beat, kicked, dragged and choked their charges, which included at least one 73-year-old woman. Women were lifted into the air and flung to the ground. One was stabbed between the eyes with the broken staff of her banner. Lucy Burns was handcuffed to the bars of her cell in a torturous position. Women were dragged by guards twisting their arms and hurled into concrete "punishment cells."
womensenews.org/story/our-story/041029/night-terror-leads-womens-vote-1917

Both in the UK and in the US women who went on hunger strikes were tortured by force feedings of tubes down their throat or nose, or also in the UK in their rectum.
For many of these women, the worst feature of prison life was the 'public' violation of their bodies when being forcibly fed. Helen Gordon Liddle hated the lack of privacy when enduring the pain of forced feeding. Nell Hall spoke of the "frightful indignity" of it all. For Sylvia Pankhurst, the sense of degradation endured was worse than the pain of sore and bleeding gums, with bits of loose jagged flesh, the agony of coughing up the tube three or four times before it was successfully inserted, the bruising of her shoulders and the aching of her back. Sometimes, when the struggle was over, or even in the heat of it, she felt as though she was broken up into many different selves, of which one, aloof and calm, surveyed all the misery, and one, ruthless and unswerving, forced the weak, shrinking body to its ordeal. Although the word 'rape' is not used in the personal accounts of force fed victims, the instrumental invasion of the body, accompanied by overpowering physical force, great suffering and humiliation was akin to it, especially so for women fed through the

rectum or vagina. 'Janet Arthur', later identified as Fanny Parker, in Perth prison in 1914, was one such victim:

Thursday morning, 16th July ... the three wardresses appeared again. One of them said that if I did not resist, she would send the others away and do what she had come to do as gently and as decently as possible. I consented. This was another attempt to feed me by the rectum, and was done in a cruel way, causing me great pain. She returned some time later and said she had 'something else' to do. I took it to be another attempt to feed me in the same way, but it proved to be a grosser and more indecent outrage, which could have been done for no other purpose than torture. It was followed by soreness, which lasted for several days. When released, a medical examination revealed swelling and rawness in the genital region. -The Prison Experiences of the Suffragettes in Edwardian Britain, June Purvis, pgs. 122,123

They repeatedly were tortured by force-feeding up to 3 times a day for months on end, and several women died as a result, not of starvation, but of the injuries accrued by the violent force-feedings. They were no less than martyrs to death. And there is no doubt that the Suffragists in the UK inspired those Suffragettes in the US, all who through their sacrifices, willing to die for this cause, brought in a new era of freedom for women. Many, many, of these suffragist women were Christians. Also Christian were Elizabeth Cady Stanton and Lucretia Mott who wrote in the 1848 Declaration of Sentiments:

"We hold these truths to be self-evident: that all men and women are created equal; that they are endowed by their Creator with certain inalienable rights; that among these are life, liberty, and the pursuit of happiness; that to secure these rights governments are instituted, deriving their just powers from the consent of the governed. Whenever any form of government becomes destructive of these ends, it is the right of those who suffer from it to refuse allegiance to it, and to insist upon the institution of a new government, laying its foundation on such principles, and organizing its powers in such form, as to them shall seem most likely to effect their safety and happiness."

So suffragists were Christian women who by legal protests went to serve the Law of Love, to treat one's neighbor as one would want to be treated, even willing to be martyrs in this service.

In 6000 years of human history, it has only been in about the last 120 years or less that women have had equal legal rights whatsoever. In all of human history, that is only at most 2% of the time in which humanity has existed, in which women have had anywhere near equal rights as men. Which means that for at least 98% of human history, women have not had equal legal rights as men. That is not much of a precedent for freedom, and surely women should always keep in mind that it would be much easier by the nature of men for their equal legal rights to be lost to them again, as having them is no guarantee of continuing to have them. All it would take is a war and bad men to win, and the laws could change overnight, and that is either a tyranny possible from without, or even from within your own country. And even this is only speaking of <u>some</u> governments that exist today. Others still do not recognize women to have equal rights, even to today. What if those countries took yours over?

The truth is, that Christianity was the birth of the democratic systems we have today, as they are birthed from a belief in rights given by God, and treating others as we want to be treated as Jesus taught. This is their foundation, it was all about what they believed about how governments should be, as Christians following a higher moral code of love for other men. Christianity birthed democracy. Christianity birthed women voting.

And when it comes to women, men are the same today in their nature as they always have been, since the garden of Eden. The only reason why any men treat any women any differently now is because of Jesus Christ, and because of the influence that Christianity and its higher morals have had upon the world, especially through democracy. Within a system of laws chosen by the people, a system birthed of Christian ideals of morality and loving your neighbor as yourself, men are raised better now than in the past in how they view women, in some places. And they are limited to some extent by the laws of the land, in which now in many countries women have rights, and can prosecute for crimes committed against them. Many men are raised to treat women better than generations past. But the sinful nature of man is no different than since the beginning.

There are still governments which exist today which do not recognize women as having equal rights as men, and even see them as being the property of men. For them nothing has changed. But worse than this, there are some countries in which crimes like violence and rape, imprisonment, and violent abuse of women are not even crimes. <u>They are like property with which men can do whatever they want without repercussion.</u> (The worst of the crimes against women in these places, include such as violent facial mutilation with acid, and forced genital mutilation making sex very painful for them, forced marriage and raping of virgins before hanging them to death, the list goes on and on…) In this, the world is no better today than the time of Abraham, before the law was given, before Jesus came. But in some places it is in fact even worse. Truly a Satanic hatred of women fighting against all Christian progress of the Law of Love has led to an even more evil and crueler darkness. In some places, the life of women is worse with misogyny, worse than it has probably ever been in all of human history, either before the Law of Moses or after it being given. In some places the Law of Love from Christianity has not yet spread enough for these governments to have changed, to enact democracies in which women can have some hope of being treated by their male neighbors, as their male neighbors would want to be treated, nor treated by the government as those in the government would want to be treated.

And so it is of utmost importance to note that many false Christian teachings of the Christian church, which have allowed for either slavery of men or still allow for abuse/domination of women, make Christianity indistinguishable from worldly religions which allow for the same things. But this false teaching, and all remnants of it, is not, nor has it ever been, the true teaching of Christianity. The true teaching is that we are to love our neighbor as ourself, treat others as we would have them treat us, and there is no Jew nor Greek, slave nor free, male nor female barrier which separates any of us from our neighbor. And that a husband has no right to try to force his wife to submit to him, nor to dominate or rule over her. And that a wife's instructions are from God to her to submit herself, as a husband's are to love, and as love does not seek it's own way, that in truth submitting herself and him loving her balance out to show equality in decisions to be made in a marriage, teaching compromise between a husband and wife, not him ruling or dominating over her to his will. This is all the truth which was lost in the church's youth by the infiltration of the early Christian church with false teachers and false teachings justifying man to rule over man and woman. And as a result the church plunged into darkness in many ways (though not all), and cemented to not change to back to true restoration through political power and enforcement of false teachings as law, and thus truly has spent 2000 years trying to slowly recover!

And as a result, in the present day, Christianity overall is seen as indistinguishable from many other worldly religions, especially when it comes to women, the same double-standards seem to apply. But this was never God's original intent that women in Christianity would be treated with double-standards that are no better than those in the elementary schoolteacher of the Law of Moses, or worse by double-standards in worldly secular religions which were not in any way founded by God.

Until Christianity is restored, it is no wonder that so many lost people cannot see any major difference between Christianity and many other religions, and discard them all as irrelevant, especially non-Christian women. The ramifications of this on evangelism of the lost cannot be over-emphasized.

And even worse are those Christians who really see no difference either, and still as blind guides, approve and make excuses for the evils of the slavery or domination of women in the present world, under the auspices of religion, excusing the outright birth into slavery of women (married or not) in some countries, under the hypocritical vision of themselves still excusing their own domination of women.

And who among the non-religious can tell the difference between Christianity or another religion in how they view or treat women? And even if Christians disagree, saying another religion is worse, whereas Christians are justified, to the non-religious so many Christians look like total blind hypocrites! If you are in for a penny, you are in for a pound. And if you are not with the Lord, you are against Him. Truly, the detrimental ramifications of this on evangelism of the lost cannot be over-emphasized.

Now, is that to say that all Christians who have followed false teachings, or been false teachers, for the last 2000 years were in fact not Christians? No! How many Christians do you know that teach many things you believe are true, but a few things you think are incorrect? And so it has been the same. Surely some of those in power were not Christians and were antichrists over the ages… but being taught wrong and then teaching wrong does not mean someone is not truly a Christian. And so the same should be understood throughout history as well as today. But for those who have known better, and have chosen power over God's Truth, surely God will judge them for this. But many true Christians have lived over the last 2000 years, in all the many incarnations of the form of the church, and still do today, in all its varied denominations, whether they believe and teach false teaching or not. But as the Bible teaches in Rev 19, the Bride has not yet made herself ready for the Groom,
"Let us rejoice and be glad and give Him glory! For the wedding of the Lamb has come, and His Bride has <u>made herself ready</u>. And to her it was granted to be arrayed in fine linen, clean and white, for the fine linen is the righteous acts of the saints."
That is us, the church, His Bride. And the Bride to date has not made herself ready.

It is both sad and appalling how many Christian men today look down upon Christian women, and insist they have no right to have a voice in church governance, and how they may be ruled by their husbands will even by force and even with evil behaviors… But they cannot see that as there is no male nor female, they, these Christian men, in their own relationship with Jesus are considered His Bride and His Wife, and He never treats them this way, nor views them with contempt. Male and female, there is no difference to Him.

So, may the Bride make herself ready for the Groom to come get her, to be wed for all eternity.

Chapter Twenty
Many Who Are Last Will Be First

"For as the heavens are higher than the earth,
so are my ways higher than your ways,
and my thoughts than your thoughts." -Isa 55:9

May this last study serve as a comfort, and as a wake up call.

"Then one of the scribes came, and having heard them reasoning together, perceiving that He had answered them well, asked Him, "Which is the first commandment of all?"
Jesus answered him, "The first of all the commandments is: 'Hear, O Israel, the LORD our God, the LORD is one. And you shall love the LORD your God with all your heart, with all your soul, with all your mind, and with all your strength.' This is the first commandment. And the second, like it, is this: 'You shall love your neighbor as yourself.' There is no other commandment greater than these." -Mark 12:28-31

"Let no debt remain outstanding, except the continuing debt to love one another, for whoever loves others has fulfilled the law. The commandments, "You shall not commit adultery," "You shall not murder," "You shall not steal," "You shall not covet, and whatever other command there may be, are summed up in this one command: "Love your neighbor as yourself."
Love does no harm to a neighbor. Therefore love is the fulfillment of the law." -Rom 13:8-10

"Think not that I am come to destroy the law, or the prophets: I am not come to destroy, but to fulfil. For verily I say unto you, Till heaven and earth pass, one jot or one tittle shall in no wise pass from the law, till all be fulfilled. Whosoever therefore shall break one of these least commandments, and shall teach men so, he shall be called the least in the kingdom of heaven: but whosoever shall do and teach, the same shall be called great in the kingdom of heaven." -Matt 5:17-19

The greatest command is to love God with all your heart, mind, soul, and strength. The second greatest commandment is to love your neighbor as yourself. And it is by loving your neighbor as yourself that the law is fulfilled. Jesus came to fulfill the law, and how He fulfilled it was to make it so everyone is your equal neighbor, without regard to being male or female, Jew or Gentile, free or slave. For the only way for people to truly follow the first and second greatest commandments was for them to understand that all people are their equal neighbors, and that they should treat them equally as they want to be treated, doing to them as they would have done unto them.

In every case in which a man has not loved a woman, or a person has not loved a foreigner to them, or a master has not loved their slave, as they love themself, and as their equal neighbor, this has broken the 2nd commandment and violated the Law of Love. So if someone who breaks the least of the commandments and teaches others to do so will be called least in the kingdom of heaven, what will someone be called who has broken the second greatest commandment?

But even if there are only 2 listed here which encompass all others… if the 2nd commandment is the least of the 2 commandments, then those who have broken it and taught others to break it will be called the least in the kingdom of heaven.

And so all Christian men who have not loved their wives as themselves and as their equal neighbor, and have taught others to do the same, all masters who have not loved their slaves as themselves and who have taught others to do the same, and all those who have not loved foreigners as themselves and have taught others to do the same, these all will be called least in the kingdom of heaven.

If there are those who are called least in the kingdom of heaven, then there must also be those who are called great in the kingdom of heaven. What else does Jesus say about the kingdom of heaven?

"And He was passing through from one city and village to another, teaching, and proceeding on His way to Jerusalem. And someone said to Him, "Lord, are there just a few who are being saved?"
And He said to them, "Strive to enter through the narrow door; for many, I tell you, will seek to enter and will not be able. "Once the head of the house gets up and shuts the door, and you begin to stand outside and knock on the door, saying, 'Lord, open up to us!' then He will answer and say to you,
'I do not know where you are from. Then you will begin to say, 'We ate and drank in Your presence, and You taught in our streets'; and He will say,
'I tell you, I do not know where you are from; DEPART FROM ME, ALL YOU EVILDOERS.' In that place there will be weeping and gnashing of teeth when you see Abraham and Isaac and Jacob and all the prophets in the kingdom of God, but yourselves being thrown out. "And they will come from east and west and from north and south, and will recline at the table in the kingdom of God.
"<u>And behold, some are last who will be first and some are first who will be last.</u>"
-Luke 13:22-30

Here the meaning seems to be that some of the first Jews who first heard the Gospel will not be saved, who were of first importance, who knew of Jesus first. While many of those who come from all over and every direction (the Gentiles) will be saved, even though they were considered last, and heard of Jesus last. And so some of the Gentiles are last to hear the Gospel, but they will be first in that they are saved, and some of the Jews were first to hear the Gospel, but they will be last in that they will not be saved. And so those who were honored the most here on earth, will not receive it in heaven and will not be saved, but those who were honored the least here, will be far more honored in heaven, in being saved. This shows that the way things are here may be reversed in heaven, despite people's expectations and beliefs.

"Then Peter said to Him, "Behold, we have left everything and followed You; what then will there be for us?" And Jesus said to them, "Truly I say to you, that you who have followed Me, in the regeneration when the Son of Man will sit on His glorious throne, you also shall sit upon twelve thrones, judging the twelve tribes of Israel. "And everyone who has left houses or brothers or sisters or father or mother or children or farms for My name's sake, will receive many times as much, and will inherit eternal life. But many who are first will be last; and the last, first." -Matt 19:27-30

"Peter began to say to Him, "Behold, we have left everything and followed You." Jesus said, "Truly I say to you, there is no one who has left house or brothers or sisters or mother or father or children or farms, for My sake and for the gospel's sake, but that he will receive a hundred times as much now in the present age, houses and brothers and sisters and mothers and children and farms, along with persecutions; and in the age to come, eternal life. "But many who are first will be last, and the last, first."
-Mark 10:28-31

Jesus says that Christians in this age will receive a hundred times as much, in the way of family. Who might those be? Either in the millennial kingdom of Christ or Heaven, Christians will receive houses and/or land, and will all receive eternal life. Also, in heaven, Christians will receive many times more in the way of family than what they have left. <u>Jesus makes clear</u> that in heaven no one will be married to each other. Listed as family we will receive are brothers, sisters, mothers, and children. God of course is our only Father.

There is no special category here for a "wife" or a "husband". This is because in truth, a husband and wife now, are a brother and sister in Christ. Also note that people who have left everything to follow Jesus, receive many times as much in the categories of family, and land. But nowhere mentioned are slaves, or wives. This is because God does not recognize slaves as the property of other people, nor does God recognize wives as the property of their husbands. Land is property, but people are not. Christians are all considered as family by Christ. In this present age, we were intended to find new family in the church. In heaven, these same Christians who in truth are our family here, will also be our family in heaven, along with many more Christians.

There is nothing fake or sentimental or officious or metaphorical about the New Testament's repeated use of the terms "brethren" "brothers" "sisters" and "mothers".

"Then Jesus' mother and brothers arrived. Standing outside, they sent someone in to call him.
A crowd was sitting around him, and they told him, "Your mother and brothers are outside looking for you." "Who are my mother and my brothers?" he asked. Then he looked at those seated in a circle around him and said, "Here are my mother and my brothers! Whoever does God's will is my brother and sister and mother."
-Mark 3:31-35

"While Jesus was still talking to the crowd, his mother and brothers stood outside, wanting to speak to him. Someone told him, "Your mother and brothers are standing outside, wanting to speak to you." He replied to him, "Who is my mother, and who are my brothers?" Pointing to his disciples, he said, "Here are my mother and my brothers. For whoever does the will of my Father in heaven is my brother and sister and mother." -Matt 12:46-50

In Christ, we really are all family. If you do the will of God, then you believe in Jesus Christ, as did the disciples. And if you are disciple of Jesus Christ, then Jesus says you are His brother or sister or mother. And so if Jesus says you are His brother, and says your wife is His sister, and as Jesus Christ is the Truth and spoke the truth, then it is true that you are siblings. It is not really debatable if you take the words of Jesus as literal and true. In context, Jesus made it clear that His disciples were as truly and literally family to Him as his actual mother Mary, and His actual blood brothers by birth.

If you are His brother or sister or mother, then all other believers are your FAMILY. This is best understood as brothers and sisters, but sometimes it is easier for an older woman that she is like a mother to the younger believers, but in any case the point is that Jesus says we are His family, and what Jesus says IS the TRUTH.

Jesus did not say "they are like my brothers and sisters, metaphorically speaking".
Jesus said, "whoever does the will of my Father in heaven IS my brother and sister and mother."
So among Christians, if you ARE Jesus' brother, and a woman IS Jesus' sister, then you are siblings.
And so we ARE all family, in truth, and Jesus says this is just as much as family by birth and blood.
And so a Christian slave-owner makes his brother, as bonded as blood in Jesus' view, his slave.
And a Christian man who mistreats a Christian woman, mistreats his sister, or his mother,
as bonded as blood in Jesus' view, whether his sister as his wife, or in any other capacity.

Back to the ambiguous phrase above, "But many who are first will be last, and the last, first."
What does this mean? It says that many of those who are, currently, first will be last, and the last, first.
Who is first now? In the context above, "first" means those who are more important or honored in the current time. But in heaven, many of those who are first now will be last. And many of those who are last now will be first. Other verses give more clarification:

"For the kingdom of heaven is like a landowner who went out early in the morning to hire laborers for his vineyard. "When he had agreed with the laborers for a denarius for the day, he sent them into his vineyard. "And he went out about the third hour and saw others standing idle in the market place; and to those he said, 'You also go into the vineyard, and whatever is right I will give you.' And so they went. "Again he went out about the sixth and the ninth hour, and did the same thing. "And about the eleventh hour he went out and found others standing around; and he said to them, 'Why have you been standing here idle all day long?' "They said to him, 'Because no one hired us.' He said to them, 'You go into the vineyard too.'

"When evening came, the owner of the vineyard said to his foreman, 'Call the laborers and pay them their wages, beginning with the last group to the first.' "When those hired about the eleventh hour came, each one received a denarius. "When those hired first came, they thought that they would receive more; but each of them also received a denarius. "When they received it, they grumbled at the landowner, saying, 'These last men have worked only one hour, and you have made them equal to us who have borne the burden and the scorching heat of the day.'
"But he answered and said to one of them, 'Friend, I am doing you no wrong; did you not agree with me for a denarius? Take what is yours and go, but I wish to give to this last man the same as to you. 'Is it not lawful for me to do what I wish with what is my own? Or is your eye envious because I am generous?' "So the last shall be first, and the first last." -Matt 20:1-16

Here the meaning seems to be that God will give everyone who serves Him the same thing in heaven. This likely refers to eternal life, the family, and houses mentioned previously. In reference to the earlier verses with this phrase, it seems to indicate that all believers will receive the same thing. So it's likely we each shall receive the same in the way of life, family, and a home, as every one else.

For being God's servants, it is like He will 'pay' us all the same amount, no matter how much work we did in comparison to others. And for those that think they should have deserved more, this could be disappointing. On one hand, this may seem disappointing, but to others, it is uplifting. For instance, at a baseline level, a slave will receive the same as his master, and a wife will receive the same as her husband. In heaven, at a baseline level, everyone is given the same, and importance here on earth does not matter. This indicates that in heaven we will all be equal in what God gives each of us.

And for a heavy fixation on this verse, some people seem to think if they want riches, or honor, or power, or whatever, then they best get it here in this life, because in heaven we will all be repaid equally. They see that their time is now, to get what they can, in this life. However, in context, this verse only refers to the fact that all Christians will receive salvation, and family, and a home. As Jesus said in John 14:2, "In My Father's house are many mansions; if it were not so, I would have told you. I go to prepare a place for you." So this refers to family, to a home with God, and to eternal life, which will all be equal. This does not refer to rewards based on individual actions. This is clear, because no matter how much each worker did, they all received the same. As such, this does not explain anything about those who will be called least or great, nor many other verses that mention "rewards" in heaven that are based on individual actions of merit.

The verses on "rewards", the "least" and "great" we will cover next; verses that refer to individual rewards based on individual merits as a Christian, and not just on the basis that one is a Christian:

"By the grace God has given me, I laid a foundation as a wise builder, and someone else is building on it. But each one should build with care. For no one can lay any foundation other than the one already laid, which is Jesus Christ.
If anyone builds on this foundation using gold, silver, costly stones, wood, hay or straw, their work will be shown for what it is, because the Day will bring it to light.
<u>It will be revealed with fire, and the fire will test the quality of each person's work.</u>
If what has been built survives, the builder will receive a reward.
If it is burned up, the builder will suffer loss but yet will be saved
— even though only as one escaping through the flames.
Don't you know that you yourselves are God's temple and that God's Spirit dwells in your midst?
<u>If anyone destroys God's temple, God will destroy that person; for God's temple is sacred, and you together are that temple.</u> Do not deceive yourselves. If any of you think you are wise by the standards of this age, you should become "fools" so that you may become wise. For the wisdom of this world is foolishness in God's sight." -1 Cor 3:10-19

These verses say that each one will receive rewards for whatever they have built which survives the test. The Christian will be saved, but will suffer loss and only be as one escaping through the flames. The Christian therefore will only receive rewards if what they have built survives the test of fire.

But they still will receive the same gifts of eternal life, a house, and family, even if everything burns up and they receive no "rewards". Whatever they are rewarded with is to keep for all eternity, the same as eternal life, the family of believers, and their home. But their "rewards" will be based on their individual works, deeds, and what they have built, so these will vary person-to-person.

"Look to yourselves, that we lose not those things which we have wrought, but that we receive a full reward." -2 John 1:8

Again, it is confirmed that there is a full reward, and a lesser reward in which one has lost what they had built. While everyone receives the same baseline of eternal life, family, and home… some will receive a more full reward than others as some will lose part of what they built in a test of fire.

"For the Son of Man is going to come in his Father's glory with his angels, and then <u>he will reward each person according to what he has done</u>." -Matt 16:27

Jesus says he will reward each person according to what they have done. As a Christian if you have done more deserving of reward, then you will have more for all eternity.

"And behold, I am coming quickly, <u>and My reward is with Me, to give to every one according to his work</u>. I am the Alpha and the Omega, the Beginning and the End, the First and the Last."
Blessed are those who do His commandments, that they may have the right to the tree of life, and may enter through the gates into the city. But outside are dogs and sorcerers and sexually immoral and murderers and idolaters, and whoever loves and practices a lie.
I, Jesus, have sent My angel to testify to you these things in the churches. I am the Root and the Offspring of David, the Bright and

Morning Star."
And the Spirit and the bride say, "Come!" And let him who hears say, "Come!"
And let him who thirsts come. Whoever desires, let him take the water of life freely." -Rev 22:12-17

In heaven, all Christians will be there, and will receive rewards according to their works. So just to make it clear, all Christians will receive the same in the way of eternal life, the family of believers, and a home. As His bride, Jesus said He was going to prepare a place for each of us, and in His Father's house there are many mansions. This applies to all believers equally. We all receive the same of these gifts from the Lord by His Mercy and Grace, because we are saved by Jesus Christ. We are God's children, so He gives us eternal life, in a home with Him, and each other as family.

But on top of this, there are also "rewards" that Christians can receive based on what they have done, according to their works, and what they have built. And this will vary by individual person. These "rewards" are not the same for all believers. These "rewards" are given based on merit of a person's actions, not on the basis of simply being a Christian. When you add it all up, this means that some Christians will have more "rewards" for all eternity, than will other Christians. And this will be entirely fair, as the "rewards" are based on a person's own works, as judged fairly by the same standard for every one. They are not based on God loving one person more than another, or any sort of favoritism, especially among His children, but only on a Christian's works.

To make an analogy:
It is like a child who is adopted into a family, they receive a home and a family, and a life there.
But each child may bring their personal belongings with them from the orphanage, which are theirs. What we build in this life that passes the test of fire and receives an eternal "reward", is our Father letting us keep what is ours, which is allowed in our new home, which He has adopted us into.
Our Heavenly Father adopts many children into His family, giving them all a life with Him, a home, and each other as family. But Our

Heavenly Father also lets His adopted children carry what good things they had from the orphanage to their new home, which does vary.

And so some will have more "rewards" than others, in the kingdom of heaven, for all eternity. And as it seems that Jesus implies there are those who will be called least in the kingdom of heaven, then there also must be those who are called great. As such, who is least and who is great very well may relate to these "rewards".

What are the sorts of things that God gives out "rewards" for? He does tell us. In fact, Jesus had much to say about the way things are going to work out once we get to heaven, and much to say comparing it to the way things are here. Some of what is said below applies to believers in comparison to non-believers, but <u>some also applies to believers in comparison to other believers.</u>

"Looking at His disciples, He said:
"Blessed are you who are poor, for yours is the kingdom of God.
Blessed are you who hunger <u>now</u>, for you <u>will be</u> satisfied.
Blessed are you who weep <u>now</u>, for you <u>will</u> laugh.
Blessed are you when people hate you,
when they exclude you and insult you and reject your name as evil, because of the Son of Man.
"Rejoice in that day and leap for joy, because <u>great is your reward in heaven.</u>
For that is how their ancestors treated the prophets.
"But woe to you who are rich, for you have already received your comfort.
Woe to you who are well fed now, for you will go hungry.
Woe to you who laugh now, for you will mourn and weep.
Woe to you when everyone speaks well of you,
for that is how their ancestors treated the false prophets.
"But to you who are listening I say: Love your enemies, do good to those who hate you, bless those who curse you, pray for those who mistreat you. If someone slaps you on one cheek, turn to them the other also. If someone takes your coat, do not withhold your shirt from them. Give to everyone who asks you, and if anyone takes

what belongs to you, do not demand it back. Do to others as you would have them do to you. "If you love those who love you, what credit is that to you? Even sinners love those who love them. And if you do good to those who are good to you, what credit is that to you? Even sinners do that. And if you lend to those from whom you expect repayment, what credit is that to you? Even sinners lend to sinners, expecting to be repaid in full.
But love your enemies, do good to them, and lend to them without expecting to get anything back.
<u>Then your reward will be great</u>, and you will be children of the Most High, because he is kind to the ungrateful and wicked. Be merciful, just as your Father is merciful." -Luke 6:20-36

Rewards seem to be given for loving your enemies, for loving those who mistreat you, loving those who insult you, loving those who steal from you, and dominate you, and doing good to those who practice hate towards you. Jesus also makes it clear that the have and have-nots will be reversed. Rewards are also given for those who are hated, excluded, and insulted "because of Jesus". These verses do not just apply to non-believers, but also apply to Christians, as it relates to heaven.

Every Christian woman or slave who has ever been hated, and excluded, and insulted, by those in the church who say they do all this "for Christ", or by her husband who says he does this "for Christ", here Jesus says that her reward in heaven will be great. So much so, she should rejoice and leap for joy!
And for every slave or woman who has ever loved in futility a master or husband who behaved as their enemy, and insulted them, excluded them, forced them, and took from them, esp. "for Christ", that slave or woman will be rewarded greatly in heaven. And this is among the body of Christian believers.

However...
No rewards are mentioned for those who exclude others for the reason of Christ. No rewards are mentioned for those who force others to do what they want, or act hatefully, or insult others, even if they say the reason is Jesus, is God, or is the Word of God, the Bible, who is Jesus.

And so those Christians who have been masters, or husbands who have been hateful, or men who have been hateful towards women and excluded them all saying it is justified by the Bible and Jesus and God…. they aren't going to get any reward for this. But the Christian people, the slaves, the women, that have been mistreated "because of Jesus, God, and the Bible" are going to get a reward, according to their works. And these "rewards" will be theirs for all eternity.

The concept is in more specific in Luke, but understanding that things in heaven will be reversed, and those who love their enemies will be rewarded, let's look at the same paralleled in Matthew.
"Blessed are the poor in spirit, for theirs is the kingdom of heaven.
Blessed are those who mourn, for they will be comforted.
Blessed are the meek, for they will inherit the earth.
Blessed are those who hunger and thirst for righteousness, for they will be filled.
Blessed are the merciful, for they will be shown mercy.
Blessed are the pure in heart, for they will see God.
Blessed are the peacemakers, for they will be called children of God.
Blessed are those who are persecuted because of righteousness, for theirs is the kingdom of heaven.
<u>Blessed are you when people insult you, persecute you and falsely say all kinds of evil against you because of me. Rejoice, and be exceeding glad: for great is your reward in heaven:</u> for so persecuted they the prophets which were before you. -Matt 5:3-12

But I tell you, do not resist an evil person. If anyone slaps you on the right cheek, turn to them the other cheek also. And if anyone wants to sue you and take your shirt, hand over your coat as well. If anyone forces you to go one mile, go with them two miles. Give to the one who asks you, and do not turn away from the one who wants to borrow from you.
You have heard that it was said, 'Love your neighbor and hate your enemy.' But <u>I tell you, love your enemies and pray for those who persecute you</u>, that you may be children of your Father in heaven. He causes his sun to rise on the evil and the good, and

sends rain on the righteous and the unrighteous. <u>If you love those who love you, what reward will you get</u>? Are not even the tax collectors doing that? And if you greet only your own people, what are you doing more than others? Do not even pagans do that? Be perfect, therefore, as your heavenly Father is perfect."
-Matt 5:39-48

Who is more poor in spirit and meek, a woman who submits to being dominated, doing good to her husband, or a husband that dominates her? A slave or her master? Who mourns more? If the poor in spirit and meek will inherit the earth and the kingdom of heaven is theirs, then is it not the woman and the slave who will inherit more or more fully? (This among Christians.) Comparing between believers, this seems assured.

Women have had all sorts of evil said against them, as have slaves, and Christians have claimed it was because of Jesus, who is the Word of God. So every time a woman has been insulted and attacked using the Bible, or a slave has been, and the accuser was a Christian claiming justification by the Word of God... that Christian woman or slave is going to get a reward! And so again, when women or slaves or foreigners are insulted, persecuted, and people say all sorts of evil against them, saying it is for Christ, the Word of God, the Bible, for God, the reward of the abused Christian will be great, and will be for all eternity.

No such great reward is mentioned for the abusive Christian master, or husband, or persecutors. The meek and abused will inherit a reward that the more powerful persecutors and abusers seem to not inherit. <u>And this reward is in the kingdom of heaven which will last eternally!</u>

"Lay not up for yourselves treasures upon earth, where moth and rust doth corrupt, and where thieves break through and steal: But lay up for yourselves treasures in heaven, where neither moth nor rust doth corrupt, and where thieves do not break through nor steal: For where your treasure is, there will your heart be also."
-Matt 6:19-21

A slave, or wife that is treated as if she is property, and wealth... no man will keep in heaven. No man will possess other people as property in heaven. And in mistreatment, and not loving your neighbor as yourself, there is no reward. But those loving Christians who are mistreated here in Jesus' name, they will receive a reward. They will receive rewards in heaven that will last for all eternity, treasures for the slaves and treasures for the mistreated women like slaves, who this is said to be done because of Christ, and who knows what these "treasures" or "rewards" will be. But one thing we do know about them is that they will last for all eternity.

Surely Christian slave-owners, and wife abusers, who mistreat their neighbor saying the reason is Christ, and God, and the Bible, and religion... and the slave or wife took it lovingly, returning good for evil for the sake of Christ.... the abusers have not realized the truth! Which is that their slaves and their wives will likely have more treasures in heaven than they do, for all eternity. With every act of mistreatment stated for the reason of Christ, or God, which the meek accepted and returned with love, they assure and have assured more and more that the person they are mistreating will have more rewards than them in heaven, that last for all eternity.

And if it is the humble, the servant, the slave, the meek, those who try to love, and women who seek to submit under conditions of being dominated, and insulted for being a woman, who is treated as insignificant and unimportant, and a slave who is treated as subhuman, and a woman who is treated as subhuman, who will receive rewards for not resisting, and for submitting to abusive rule, who love their enemies who treat them like possessions, and serve their enemies who are like their owners... if it is these humble that will receive more rewards than those who mistreated them, then doesn't it make sense that among Christians, that the abused will be greater in heaven, and the abusers will be lesser? In the kingdom of heaven, which lasts for all eternity... could it be that those with more rewards (the abused here) will be the greater in the kingdom of heaven, forever, than those with less rewards (the abusers here) will be the lesser in the kingdom of heaven, forever?

"And they were bringing children to Him so that He might touch them; but the disciples rebuked them. But when Jesus saw this, He was indignant and said to them, "Permit the children to come to Me; do not hinder them; for the kingdom of God belongs to such as these. "Truly I say to you, whoever does not receive the kingdom of God like a child will not enter it at all." And He took them in His arms and began blessing them, laying His hands on them." -Mark 10:13-16

The disciples, as it is commonly taught, did not see children as important enough to take up Jesus' time. Men were important, women far less so, and little children not really at all. But Jesus said that whoever does not receive the kingdom of God like a child will not enter it at all, and that the kingdom of God belongs to such as these. There are a couple of meanings to look at here. The first is that there will be many children in heaven, many many children, who for whatever reason died early in innocence. They will be in heaven, and perhaps there will be many more children there than adults!

But there is another reference here, which is seen by comparing other similar verses:
"At that time the disciples came to Jesus, saying, "Who then is greatest in the kingdom of heaven?" Then Jesus called a little child to Him, set him in the midst of them, and said,
"Assuredly, I say to you, unless you are converted and become as little children, you will by no means enter the kingdom of heaven. Therefore <u>whoever humbles himself as this little child is the greatest in the kingdom of heaven.</u> Whoever receives one little child like this in My name receives Me.
"Whoever causes one of these little ones who believe in Me to sin, it would be better for him if a millstone were hung around his neck, and he were drowned in the depth of the sea. Woe to the world because of offenses! For offenses must come, but woe to that man by whom the offense comes! "Take heed that you do not despise one of these little ones, for I say to you that in heaven their angels always see the face of My Father who is in heaven.
"If your hand or foot causes you to sin, cut it off and cast it from you. It is better for you to enter into life lame or maimed, rather

than having two hands or two feet, to be cast into the everlasting fire. And if your eye causes you to sin, pluck it out and cast it from you. It is better for you to enter into life with one eye, rather than having two eyes, to be cast into hell fire.
For the Son of Man has come to save that which was lost. "What do you think? If a man has a hundred sheep, and one of them goes astray, does he not leave the ninety-nine and go to the mountains to seek the one that is straying? And if he should find it, assuredly, I say to you, he rejoices more over that sheep than over the ninety-nine that did not go astray. Even so it is not the will of your Father who is in heaven that one of these little ones should perish."
-Matt 18:1-14

Unless they become like little children, they will not enter the kingdom of heaven. And whoever is humble as a little child will be the greatest in the kingdom of heaven. Surely, men have often been less humble than women, and masters less humble than slaves. So who is more like a humble child? <u>The more humble like a child you are, the greater you will be in heaven, for all eternity.</u>

It is also interesting here that Jesus seems to advocate harming yourself rather than sinning against a child who is a believer, and makes it clear that they must not despise or hate children, which seems most likely to refer to despising a child by their actions. Jesus also references to causing or tempting a Christian child to sin. Rather than in any way act hatefully, they should cut off their hand or foot… and this implies rather than harm a child with any sort of hateful violence, they should instead injure themselves.

"An argument started among them as to which of them might be the greatest.
But Jesus, knowing what they were thinking in their heart, took a child and stood him by His side, and said to them, "Whoever receives this child in My name receives Me, and whoever receives Me receives Him who sent Me; <u>for the one who is least among all of you, this is the one who is great.</u>"
-Luke 9:46-48

"They came to Capernaum; and when He was in the house, He began to question them,
"What were you discussing on the way?" But they kept silent, for on the way they had discussed with one another which of them was the greatest. Sitting down, He called the twelve and said to them,
"<u>If anyone wants to be first, he shall be last of all and servant of all</u>."
Taking a child, He set him before them, and taking him in His arms, He said to them,
Whoever receives one child like this in My name receives Me; and whoever receives Me does not receive Me, but Him who sent Me."
-Mark 9:33-37

Here Jesus makes it clear that to be the greatest and first among them, then one must be last and servant of all. In context of the other verses on the greatest and the least, this is a truth that applies both to being the greatest Christian on earth, and also the greatest Christian in heaven. And in context, this means being a servant even to a child, by receiving a child. Jesus says that whoever "receives" a child, actually receives Jesus and God. A child was one who was thought to be of the lowest importance, lower than men or even women.

What does "receive" mean?

1) to take with the hand a) to take hold of, take up 2) to take up, receive a) used of a place receiving one b) to receive or grant access to, a visitor, not to refuse intercourse or friendship 1) to receive hospitality 2) to receive into one's family to bring up or educate c) of the thing offered in speaking, teaching, instructing 1) to receive favourably, give ear to, embrace, make one's own, approve, not to reject d) to receive. i.e. to take upon one's self, sustain, bear, endure 3) to receive, get a) to learn (Strong's)

It means to welcome and accept in friendship, help, hold up, accept as family, and not to reject. And so by doing this to a child, they were doing this to Jesus and to God.

This is very similar to:

"When the Son of Man comes in his glory, and all the angels with him, he will sit on his glorious throne. All the nations will be gathered before him, and he will separate the people one from another as a shepherd separates the sheep from the goats. He will put the sheep on his right and the goats on his left.
"Then the King will say to those on his right, 'Come, you who are blessed by my Father; take your inheritance, the kingdom prepared for you since the creation of the world. For I was hungry and you gave me something to eat, I was thirsty and you gave me something to drink, I was a stranger and you invited me in, I needed clothes and you clothed me, I was sick and you looked after me, I was in prison and you came to visit me.' "Then the righteous will answer him, 'Lord, when did we see you hungry and feed you, or thirsty and give you something to drink? When did we see you a stranger and invite you in, or needing clothes and clothe you? When did we see you sick or in prison and go to visit you?' <u>"The King will reply, 'Truly I tell you, whatever you did for one of the least of these brothers and sisters of mine, you did for me.'</u>
"Then he will say to those on his left, 'Depart from me, you who are cursed, into the eternal fire prepared for the devil and his angels. For I was hungry and you gave me nothing to eat, I was thirsty and you gave me nothing to drink, I was a stranger and you did not invite me in, I needed clothes and you did not clothe me, I was sick and in prison and you did not look after me.' "They also will answer, 'Lord, when did we see you hungry or thirsty or a stranger or needing clothes or sick or in prison, and did not help you?' "He will reply, 'Truly I tell you, whatever you did not do <u>for one of the least of these</u>, you did not do for me.' "Then they will go away to eternal punishment, but the righteous to eternal life."
- Matt 25:31-46

Again here Jesus mentions those who are His brothers and sisters. And he mentions even the "least of these", His brothers and sisters. And so if a child is the least important in the eyes of men, but the greatest will be a servant to even a lowly child, then this same understanding can apply to both a slave, or a woman, if men also regard them as not important. And so as for welcoming, befriending, accepting as family, and helping the lowly and unimportant, if you accept them, then you accept Jesus and God with them, but if you reject them, then you reject Jesus and God along with them.

"And there arose also a dispute among them as to which one of them was regarded to be greatest. And He said to them, "The kings of the Gentiles lord it over them; and those who have authority over them are called 'Benefactors.' "But it is not this way with you, but the one who is the greatest among you must become like the youngest, and the leader like the servant.
"For who is greater, the one who reclines at the table or the one who serves?
Is it not the one who reclines at the table? But I am among you as the one who serves.
"You are those who have stood by Me in My trials; and just as My Father has granted Me a kingdom,
I grant you that you may eat and drink at My table in My kingdom, and you will sit on thrones judging the twelve tribes of Israel." -Luke 22:24-30

As Jesus was here as one who serves, the greatest and leader must be like the youngest and a servant. Which means that those who have been like servants, such as Christian slaves and women, are in fact greater, and more leaders for God, then those Christians who have been served and who have lorded authority over others as their leaders. In the case of a Christian husband who tries to claim and lord authority over his wife, he is like the worldly Gentiles, and there is nothing Christlike to be found there to reward. In contrast, a wife who is treated like a servant, she is in fact the leader in what is real Christian leadership. She is more like Jesus, and the husband is more like a pagan. Between Christians, the abusive-ruling husband, and the serving wife, she is the greatest. And the same is true of a slave being greater than a master.
And also note that in this verse Jesus again references to the kingdom of Heaven, and reassures the disciples that they will all eat and drink at His table and also that they will sit on thrones judging the twelve tribes of Israel. This is to reassure them, in

context, about their greatness in the kingdom of heaven. And so it is clear that again all this references not to just on earth, but also to the kingdom of heaven and to eternity.

"But Jesus called them to Himself and said, "You know that the rulers of the Gentiles lord it over them, and their great men exercise authority over them. "It is **not** this way among you, but <u>whoever wishes to become great among you shall be your servant, and whoever wishes to be first among you shall be your slave</u>; just as the Son of Man did not come to be served, but to serve, and to give His life a ransom for many." -Matt 20:25-28

"Calling them to Himself, Jesus said to them, "You know that those who are recognized as rulers of the Gentiles lord it over them; and their great men exercise authority over them. "But it is **not** this way among you, but <u>whoever wishes to become great among you shall be your servant; and whoever wishes to be first among you shall be slave of all</u>. "For even the Son of Man did not come to be served, but to serve, and to give His life a ransom for many." -Mark 10:42-45

Here twice more, 3 times total, Jesus makes it very clear that Christians are not to be like the Gentiles, exercising authority over each other, but rather that they should serve each other. To be great, one must be a servant of the others, but to be first (the greatest) one must be a slave of the others. And so the more one is like a slave, the more one is honored, but those who try to rule over others with authority, they have no honor to them. And so among Christians, the slave is greater than the master, and the wife forced by rule to be like a servant, is greater than her husband that rules over her.

"Then Jesus spoke to the crowds and to His disciples, saying: "The scribes and the Pharisees have seated themselves in the chair of Moses; therefore all that they tell you, do and observe, but do not do according to their deeds; for they say things and do not do them. "They tie up heavy burdens and lay them on men's shoulders, but they themselves are unwilling to move them with so much as a finger. "But they do all their deeds to be noticed by men; for they broaden their phylacteries and lengthen the tassels of their garments.

"They love the place of honor at banquets and the chief seats in the synagogues, and respectful greetings in the market places, and being called Rabbi by men.

"But do not be called Rabbi; for One is your Teacher, and you are all brothers.

"Do not call anyone on earth your father; for One is your Father, He who is in heaven.

Do not be called leaders; for One is your Leader, that is, Christ.

<u>But the greatest among you shall be your servant.</u>

<u>Whoever exalts himself shall be humbled; and whoever humbles himself shall be exalted."</u>

- Matt 23:1-12

For anyone that has questioned what I have said in this book, that the rule of man over other man is from sin, and not from God, please examine the words of Jesus on this matter, in all the passages above. Christians are not to be called leaders, as in worldly systems of authority, nor to be called father, as in the church gone astray in the last 2000 years, nor for men to exalt themselves as teachers coveting the position as an honor, reserved for men, while they use rule and authority to deprive women of being able to teach. Men in fact turn teaching from being a service of a servant into a worldly honor as did the Rabbis, any time a man teaches that women may not teach, but only men.

"So when He had washed their feet, and taken His garments and reclined at the table again, He said to them, "Do you know what I have done to you? You call Me Teacher and Lord; and you are right, for so I am. If I then, the Lord and the Teacher, washed your feet, you also ought to wash one another's feet. For I gave you an example that you also should do as I did to you. Truly, truly, I say to you, a slave (any Christian) is not greater than his master (Jesus), nor is one who is sent (any Christian) greater than the one who sent him. (Jesus) "If you know these things, you are blessed if you do them." -John 13:12-17

Truly, Jesus sought for his people to follow His example, and to ALL serve, and only through service and loving others, to gain their respect and esteem and the desire for them to follow a servant by choice as a loving servant of others. This is who Jesus was to us, and we followed Him by His love for us. There is no place here in Jesus' teachings for Christians to imitate worldly models, which have all come from sin, of "authority" and man ruling over another man. Over and over Jesus tried to teach this, that humble service is the ONLY right way to lead others, but so many have and do mangle His message by polluting it with worldly understanding. Many teachers have reduced the wisdom of God to only the foolishness of men, and teach the lowly thoughts of men, only seasoned at best with a dash of the high thoughts of God. God loves us, and gives us all free will. No one has been forced to follow Jesus, but we do because of His love for us, and because He served us by giving up His life for us in Love so that we could be saved. He helped us and served us and loved us, and still does help us and serve us and love us. This is why we follow Jesus, and by free will we choose to obey Him. He never has forced us, He never lorded His authority over us as God, or violated our free will. He is our only example of how to get others to follow us the right way, and it is through service and love. But the ways of mankind, of domination and rule and authority, have no right place amongst believers who are trying to have others follow them.

What shows more faith and trust in God? Service to others, or forcing rule over others? Which is more an act of faith and shows trust in God? When you force rule over others, the tool to bend their free will to yours is fear of something negative. When you serve and love others, it is left up to God, in the nature He made people to have, to follow their heart and by free will choose to follow, out of love.

Jesus showed His faith and trust in God even to death. He was a servant of all of us, helping us, serving us, loving us more than His life, even to death, all showing His faith in God. Service and love, not forcing rule, is what He has told us to do. When we serve and love, to help someone follow out of a free choice, instead of forcing rule, we show our faith in Jesus Christ, by doing what He said to do.

There is only one right way to do it, and it has nothing to do with positions of power as in worldly systems. These were invented by man in sin, and while sometimes good can work in the world through them, they are inherently based on a lie, as God was always meant to rule directly over each person individually, and He will restore the world to this in the kingdom of heaven.

And when we get there, many Christian slaves and women will be rewarded for their works, in loving those and submitting to the forceful rule of those who abused them, even their own brothers and sisters. The abusers will not receive a reward for this, and so many of these women and slaves will find themselves to be greater in rewards in the kingdom of heaven than Christians who abused them.

And in this, the abused will also be greater in the kingdom of heaven than the abusers.

"Then a voice came from the throne, saying: "Praise our God, all you his servants, you who fear him, both great and small!" Then I heard what sounded like a great multitude, like the roar of rushing waters and like loud peals of thunder, shouting: "Hallelujah! For our Lord God Almighty reigns. Let us rejoice and be glad and give him glory! For the wedding of the Lamb has come, and his bride has made herself ready. Fine linen, bright and clean, was given her to wear." (Fine linen stands for the righteous acts of God's holy people.) Then the angel said to me, "Write this: Blessed are those who are invited to the wedding supper of the Lamb!" And he added, "These are the true words of God." -Rev 19:5-9

Someday, we Christians are going to be invited to the Wedding supper of the Lamb, our wedding to Him, in which we will all take our places at the table.

"And He began speaking a parable to the invited guests when He noticed how they had been picking out the places of honor at the table, saying to them, "When you are invited by someone to a wedding feast, do not take the place of honor, for someone more distinguished than you may have been invited by him, and he who invited you both will come and say to you, 'Give your place to this man,' and then in disgrace you proceed to occupy the last place.
"But when you are invited, go and recline at the last place, so that when the one who has invited you comes, he may say to you, 'Friend, move up higher'; then you will have honor in the sight of all who are at the table with you.
"For everyone who exalts himself will be humbled, and he who humbles himself will be exalted."
And He also went on to say to the one who had invited Him, "When you give a luncheon or a dinner, do not invite your friends or your brothers or your relatives or rich neighbors, otherwise they may also invite you in return and that will be your repayment.
"But when you give a reception, invite the poor, the crippled, the lame, the blind, and you will be blessed, since they do not have the means to repay you; for you will be repaid at the resurrection of the righteous."
When one of those who were reclining at the table with Him heard this, he said to Him, "Blessed is everyone who will eat bread in the kingdom of God!" -Luke 14:7-15

Let every one be careful of where they sit at a wedding supper. For those who have been humble will be exalted, and those who have been exalted, even exalting themselves, will be humbled. This is what Jesus said concerning wedding suppers. At the wedding supper of Jesus and the church, is there any reason to think that the caution Jesus gave would not also apply? It seems that the situation may likely be the same in heaven, that some will be assigned to the more honorable seats, and some to the less honorable seats. It would also make sense that those who are greatest in the kingdom of heaven would have the more honorable seats, and those who are least in the kingdom of heaven would have the less honorable seats.

"Then the mother of the sons of Zebedee came to Jesus with her sons, bowing down and making a request of Him. And He said to her, "What do you wish?" She said to Him, "<u>Command that in Your kingdom these two sons of mine may sit one on Your right and one on Your left.</u>" But Jesus answered, "You do not know what you are asking. Are you able to drink the cup that I am about to drink?" They said to Him, "We are able." He said to them, "My cup you shall drink; <u>but to sit on My right and on My left, this is not Mine to give, but it is for those for whom it has been prepared by My Father.</u>" -Matt 20:20-23

From this passage, we can understand that there will be assigned seats in heaven. Where does the Bible say we will sit with Jesus? At the wedding feast of the Lamb. So there is every indication that the wedding supper will have assigned seats. God, who judges righteously, who repays each according to their works, will choose where each one will sit and what is their proper place. Jesus said the seats of honor are to be decided by God, who will judge justly and reward righteously. These seats are assigned by God. And as here on earth, those in heaven with greater rewards and therefore more distinguished, they are honored by sitting at the head of the table. Which is why Jesus warns us Christians to all go to the foot of the table at the wedding feast, so we will not risk being publicly humbled by being asked to move down to a less honored seat at the foot of the table.

Just as an illustration, to make a point, this is what I picture, after all have been shown to their reserved seats, assigned by God :

There is a table that stretches far and wide, at the wedding supper of the Lamb. All Christians are invited. Everyone there is celebrating and happy, and every single person is rejoicing.

And what you see there is Jesus sitting at the head of the table. Sitting by Jesus are many loving and humble Christian women and some men who were slaves, who have been greatly rewarded, and many loving and humble women who as wives were treated like slaves and mistreated "because of Jesus, God and the Word of God" and took it lovingly. The Christian women and slaves are great in the kingdom of heaven, and are given seats of more honor.

Zooming back a ways to look at this long table, it becomes clear that many of those who are sitting near Jesus are women, with some men also, but many are women, likely even more women than men.

And as you look farther and farther away, towards the foot of the table, there are an increasing number of men, masters of slaves, and those who ruled over their wives. Sitting nearer to the foot of the table are those who are lesser in the kingdom of heaven, who have received less rewards, and are less honored.

And among these are many Christian men (and women) who practiced the abusive forcing of rule of man over other man, with fear and threats and even lies about the Word of God, those who did not love women or slaves as themselves, and would not acknowledge them as their equal neighbors. These are those who succumbed to teachings to not love your neighbor as yourself, and abused and mistreated their Christian sisters and brothers.

At the very foot of the table are those who are least in the kingdom of heaven. These are those teachers who both practiced, and taught others to not love your neighbors as yourself, and to not treat others as you would want to be treated. These are those who taught others to be hateful and prejudiced against women, or slaves, or foreigners, teaching men's superiority, the exclusion of women from equal participation in the church, and who said this was all the will of God as per the Word of God, the Bible, who is Jesus. These are those Christians who both taught this, and practiced their own teachings. These Christians who were false teachers are at the very foot of the table, the least in the kingdom.

If they look around, they would likely not see the familiar faces of their slaves, or their wives, their brothers and sisters who they abused and mistreated. This is because their sisters and brothers who were their slaves or wives are far away towards the head of the table sitting nearer to Jesus.

And these seats represent the honor God gives that person, their assigned seat, for all eternity.

And so for those who need comfort, and for those who do not understand how God could have made this world in which there are slaves, and in which women have been treated as subhuman servants for almost all of human history, for those who find the history of humanity and the church to be so unfair towards women that they wonder how a just God could have made woman at all, knowing she would go through this, and for her to have gone through all of this…

Please, take comfort, for the sorrows of this life and the unfairness, cannot compare with the joys and justice of the eternal never-ending life we will have in the kingdom of God with Jesus. Those who have lovingly accepted abuse and mistreatment here, will be greater in the kingdom of heaven, more honored for all eternity, while those who abused and mistreated and taught such will be lesser in the kingdom of heaven, and less honored for all eternity, if they are there at all.

God is Just, and will reward every one with justice. This is portrayed in the illustration or analogy seen above at the table, which is a picture of the accumulation of the many things Jesus had to say about the greatest and least in the kingdom of heaven. The Lord has told us of His justice and His thoughts and His ways. The humble will be exalted, and the exalted will be humbled, for all eternity.

Romans 8:15-18
"For you did not receive the spirit of bondage again to fear, but you received the Spirit of adoption by whom we cry out, "Abba, Father." The Spirit Himself bears witness with our spirit that we are children of God, and if children, then heirs—heirs of God and joint heirs with Christ, <u>if indeed we suffer with Him, that we may also be glorified together. For I consider that the sufferings of this present time are not worthy to be compared with the glory which shall be revealed in us!</u>"

So, love your enemies, even other Christians who act like your enemies, and do not resist them when they force you, repay evil with good, bless those who curse and persecute you, pray for them, and rejoice when you are mistreated "because of Jesus". Your reward in heaven is great, and is everlasting. And so in this, I hope those who needed comfort are comforted.

And for those who needed a wake up call, I hope you have it.

Chapter Twenty One
In Conclusion – Full Equality

In the broadest scope:
God created all men and women as equals, each meant to have a direct relationship with Him.
Men and women were both equally created in the image of God, and are equally human.
God made the male-man and the female-man, and both are equally man.
God gave equal dominion over the earth, animals, etc. to both women and men.
God equally told men and women to be fruitful and multiply and have dominion over the earth.
Men and women were each meant to take their instructions directly from God, not each other.
Men and women were meant to be equally ruled by God, and not each other.
Men and women have in all ways the exact same living spirit and soul inside of them.

In the church:
God designed the church to have servant-administrators who were meant to be servants, who were chosen by both the men and women of the church. These servant-administrators chosen by the men or women could be either men or women, chosen to fill the roles of deacons (servants) or elders (overseers) for the church.
God gives gifts and callings of any of the gifts of the Holy Spirit to whomever He chooses, both to men and women, without gender discrimination.
As such, in the model of the church, women are meant to do anything and everything that men do, and there is meant to be no discrimination based on gender. Women may vote to choose elders and deacons, and also may serve as elders and deacons, same as men. Women may be called to be pastors, apostles, teachers, and have any calling that a man might have, and any gift that a man might have. The church also has a responsibility to make sure not only men, but also women, are taught before they teach. In all ways in the church men and women are equal, and are not to be

discriminated against. Women are able to equally participate in church services and fellowships as the men are. Women are able to choose what they want to wear, as men are, and how to have their hair, as men are. There is nothing required by God that women have to wear to distinguish them from the men, nor does God require men to cut their hair to distinguish them from the women. Women and men are equally able to speak in church.

In worldly systems of government:
Men ruling over other men in domination was invented by men, not God. Men arrange themselves in these governments, and in instituting governments. God permits these governments of whatever type to exist for the reason that they work towards punishing those who commit evil. Democracy is founded on New Testament principles of treating others as you want to be treated, and on the true church structure of the people choosing their own leaders, as God leads them. Democracy therefore is modeled after God's model for the church government. To be true to the model of God it resembles, any democracy should therefore also allow for women to vote equally as men, and allow for women to occupy any positions of public-service equally as men can. Systems of government which are not essentially democratic are also not based on God's model of government for the church. While all human governments are flawed, a democracy which treats all people as equal neighbors, regardless of gender or race or monetary social class, is superior to all other forms of government. And governments which allow for slavery of men, or do not treat women with equal rights as men, are not governments which follow God's model for Christian governance, and are therefore inferior to those which accurately do. In God's model of church governance, without regard to gender, race, or social class, all people may follow whatever calling God gives them in personal religious freedom. As such, any governments which prevent all people from equally choosing their religion, or from among legal professions, are not based on God's model for Christian governments, and are inferior. Therefore, Christians who live under such systems of government rule are living in oppressive systems, and Christians can know these governments are below the standards of God's model for governance.

As Christians, our only King is Jesus Christ, and His kingdom is not of this world, same as we are in this world but not of it. Our most important focus should be on the spread of the Gospel of Jesus Christ, regardless of and working around whatever worldly governmental systems are in place. Only secondary to this and where this priority intersects with politics, the most important political focus for Christians, nationally or internationally, should be to use whatever political voice they have towards having democratic systems of government that do not discriminate based on gender, class, or race in any way, specifically so that they will allow freedom of religious choice to all people without discrimination. Tertiary to this would be so that they allow freedom of professional expression, and equal say in the government both as voters and as elected officials, being available to all people and fellow Christians everywhere.

In marriage:
Marriage was meant to be an equally voluntary symbiotic relationship between 2 equal humans.
Men and women have equal value before God, and are to be completely equal in the church, as well as in any democratic political system of governance based on God's model for the church.
When it comes to authority in a marriage, God's instructions to a wife and to a husband balance out so that neither person has more authority than the other, but rather are equals in authority.
Neither one was ever meant to dominate the other, and this always has been sin.
God makes it very plain that in the bedroom, a husband and wife have completely equal authority.

To review,
"1 Cor 7:2-4 spells out, "Nevertheless, to avoid fornication, let every man have his own wife, and let every woman have her own husband. Let the husband render unto the wife due benevolence: and likewise also the wife unto the husband. The wife hath not power of her own body, but the husband: and likewise also the husband hath not power of his own body, but the wife."

If there is not mutual agreement in the bedroom, then logically spouse A can tell the other with authority "Don't do that with your body" while spouse B says "Yes do this with your body" and in effect, if the two spouses are not in agreement, then they cancel each other out. So unless there is mutual agreement in the bedroom, nothing should happen."

God's instructions are meant to lead to compromise in marriage. This is seen best is comparing the husband's instructions to love his wife to the wife's instructions to submit herself to her husband. In all His instructions on marriage God has made it very clear that men are not to use sinful tactics to try to dominate or rule over their wives, but rather than her submission is to be completely voluntary.

To review, on Submission,
"It means to choose to do what someone else wants to do, to go with another's judgment, and in this case for the wife to decide to do, to go with, what the husband wants to do. Hupotasso never means a man forces his wife to submit, rather the wife must submit herself, as the word is reflexive.
Truly, these verses nowhere give a husband any right or authority to try to force his wife to submit to him. The husband is given no authority by God to force her to submit. God instructs the wife to submit herself to the husband. The wife is submitting because of the authority of God. In every case of a wife submitting herself, she is actually submitting to the authority of Jesus Christ when she does so."

As such the wife does not submit herself to her husband because of any authority the husband has over her, but in her submitting to Jesus' authority. The husband has been given no authority over her. She is his equal and peer. God has given a husband no authority over his wife. God never gave any husband authority over a wife, not with Adam and Eve, and not since. The wife submits to God's authority by doing what God tells her to do, which is to submit herself to her husband. This is the same as the husband submits to God's authority by doing what God tells him to do, which is to love his wife. Like submission, love includes for the husband to do what the wife wants to do. The wife has no authority given by God over her husband in this either. The wife has no authority to try to force her husband to love her, which includes her husband doing what she wants. When a husband does what his wife wants he is submitting to God's authority, not the wife's authority, as she has no authority over him either, just as he has no authority over her. Both the husband and wife have equal authority in a marriage, and neither has authority over the other. Their marriage is meant to function as a symbiosis, like the head of a body, and the rest of the body beside the head, function together in a symbiosis.

To review, on the head and the body, as in 1 Cor 11 with correct understanding,
"Christ is the head of every Christian, who are His body, and the husband is the head of a wife, who is like his body, and God is the head of Christ, who is the fullness of the Godhead bodily."
This is an analogy by which to understand the reason, by nature, that the wife should submit herself, as body parts submit to the head, and why the husband should love his wife as himself, as the head loves all the other parts of the body. Nothing in this concept gives a husband authority over his wife, or vice versa, but rather just illustrates the natural symbiosis that God designed marriage to have.

"Wives, submit yourselves unto your own husbands, as unto the Lord. Because the husband is the head of the wife, even as Christ is the head of the church: and He is the saviour of the body… Husbands, love your wives, even as Christ also loved the church…. So ought men to love their wives as their own bodies. He that loveth his wife loveth himself. For no man ever yet hated his own flesh; but nourisheth and cherisheth it, even as the Lord the church: For we are members of His body, of His flesh, and of his bones. For this cause shall a man leave his father and mother, and shall be joined unto his wife, and they two shall be one flesh. This is a great mystery: but I speak concerning Christ and the church…" Eph 5

A husband and wife are 1 person, 2 people in one body. The husband is the head, and the wife is all of the body parts besides the head. It is simply natural that the body submits to the head, and that the head shows love to the body. But the head does not have more authority because it is the head, nor does the body have more authority because it is the body. They are 2 parts of one person. Submission and Love balance out when it comes to decision making. The head is supposed to do what the body wants (in love), and the body is supposed to do what the head wants (in submitting itself). Neither one was given more authority over the other by God, just natural symbiotic roles to play out in mutuality and equality.

To review on Love,
"love does not seek its own"
The word here for "seek its own" means "*to seek i.e. require, demand a) to crave, demand something from someone*". This phrase is also translated as "self-seeking" or "seeking its own way" or "demand its own way". The emphasis is on self-centeredness, and being self-satisfying.
So if a husband is seeking or demanding his own way, with his wife, he is not being loving to her.

This concept deserves further exposition, as it is important. While a wife is told to submit to her husband, at the same time the husband is told to love his wife. To love his wife a husband has to not seek or demand his own way. Which means he should be seeking another's way, his wife's way.
On the one hand, the wife is told to submit to her husband, which means she should try to do what he wants, let him have his way. On the other hand, the husband is told to love his wife, which means he is to not seek or demand what he wants, not to seek or demand his own way. He should be seeking his wife's way, he should try to do what she wants, let her have her way.
This truth about love is echoed in 1 Cor 10:24,
"Let no one seek his own good, but that of his neighbor."

So when it comes to decision making in a marriage, in loving the wife, the husband is told to seek what the wife wants, but not demand what he wants. And the wife is told, in submitting to her husband, to try to do what he wants. What does this mean?
The wife is supposed to do what the husband wants to do, but the husband is supposed to do what the wife wants to do. As such, there is meant to be equality in decision making in a Christian marriage, which means there should be compromise. Another way to put this is,
"If he's loving her as much as she's submitting to him,
then they should meet somewhere in the middle."
And of course, both should be seeking what it is that God wants of each of them.

The husband in loving his wife is to do what she wants to do.
The wife in submitting herself to her husband is to do what he wants to do.

Therefore, any decisions should be by 50/50 compromise if they are both equally obeying God.
They are one person, with two equally important parts, and so decisions should always be mutually agreed upon and compromised with a 50/50 ideal goal when there is disagreement.

When it comes to decision-making authority, the equality of the principle of compromise is shown in the following table, along with God's instructions for men to not try to dominate their wives. (This is mutually save barring anything on which one cannot do something based on moral grounds, whether of God's commandments on what to do or not do, or on matters of conscience. But all things being equal and allowable, is attempted to be reflected in the table.)

Domination is inherently sinful because it does not treat someone as you want to be treated.
Domination, controlling another, is the ever-present core of domestic abuse and domestic violence.
This list draws from the Chapter on Ephesians 5, Love Your Wife, specifically the portions on what love is not.

If she ideally submits	+ If he ideally loves	= then there is compromise
she does what he wants	he does what she wants	50/50 fair goal of compromise
If she doesn't submit	**+ he reacts being unloving**	**= he's a hypocrite**
she won't do what he wants so	he won't do what she wants	he's not loving her, he's a hypocrite
she won't do what he wants so	he demands his own way	he's not loving her, he's a hypocrite
she won't do what he wants so	he won't be self-sacrificial	he's not loving her, he's a hypocrite
she won't do what he wants so	he acts selfishly	he's not loving her, he's a hypocrite
she won't do what he wants so	he acts self-centeredly	he's not loving her, he's a hypocrite
she won't do what he wants so	he won't compromise	he's not loving her, he's a hypocrite

she won't do what he wants so	he starts to get angry	he's not loving her, he's a hypocrite
she won't do what he wants so	he gets angry	he's not loving her, he's a hypocrite
she won't do what he wants so	he gets bitter	he's not loving her, he's a hypocrite
she won't do what he wants so	he gets harsh	he's not loving her, he's a hypocrite
she won't do what he wants so	he tries to lie to her	he's not loving her, he's a hypocrite
she won't do what he wants so	he tries to deceive her	he's not loving her, he's a hypocrite
she won't do what he wants so	he gets envious of her	he's not loving her, he's a hypocrite
she won't do what he wants so	he gets jealous about her	he's not loving her, he's a hypocrite
she won't do what he wants so	he gets impatient	he's not loving her, he's a hypocrite

she won't do what he wants so	he is unkind	he's not loving her, he's a hypocrite
she won't do what he wants so	he is inconsiderate	he's not loving her, he's a hypocrite
she won't do what he wants so	he brags about himself	he's not loving her, he's a hypocrite
she won't do what he wants so	he extols himself	he's not loving her, he's a hypocrite
she won't do what he wants so	he extols his greatness	he's not loving her, he's a hypocrite
she won't do what he wants so	he extols his rightness	he's not loving her, he's a hypocrite
she won't do what he wants so	he extols his experience	he's not loving her, he's a hypocrite
she won't do what he wants so	he extols his intelligence	he's not loving her, he's a hypocrite
she won't do what he wants so	he extols his superiority	he's not loving her, he's a hypocrite

she won't do what he wants so	he gets proud	he's not loving her, he's a hypocrite
she won't do what he wants so	he gets prideful	he's not loving her, he's a hypocrite
she won't do what he wants so	he gets arrogant	he's not loving her, he's a hypocrite
she won't do what he wants so	he gets rude to her	he's not loving her, he's a hypocrite
she won't do what he wants so	he gets rude to others	he's not loving her, he's a hypocrite
she won't do what he wants so	he gets rude in private	he's not loving her, he's a hypocrite
she won't do what he wants so	he gets rude in public	he's not loving her, he's a hypocrite
she won't do what he wants so	he disregards her life-goals	he's not loving her, he's a hypocrite
she won't do what he wants so	or her long-term wellbeing	he's not loving her, he's a hypocrite

she won't do what he wants so	he counts up her faults	he's not loving her, he's a hypocrite
she won't do what he wants so	he lists her past wrongs	he's not loving her, he's a hypocrite
she won't do what he wants so	he infers she is up to evil	he's not loving her, he's a hypocrite
she won't do what he wants so	he thinks she is evil	he's not loving her, he's a hypocrite
she won't do what he wants so	he thinks to do evil to her	he's not loving her, he's a hypocrite
she won't do what he wants so	he weighs to do evil or not	he's not loving her, he's a hypocrite
she won't do what he wants so	he thinks on evil he could do	he's not loving her, he's a hypocrite
she won't do what he wants so	he plots against her	he's not loving her, he's a hypocrite
she won't do what he wants so	he does evil against her	he's not loving her, he's a hypocrite

she won't do what he wants so	he plots to tempt her to sin	he's not loving her, he's a hypocrite
she won't do what he wants so	he sins against her	he's not loving her, he's a hypocrite
she won't do what he wants so	he is glad to see her fail	he's not loving her, he's a hypocrite
she won't do what he wants so	he is glad to see her sin	he's not loving her, he's a hypocrite
she won't do what he wants so	he won't act to protect her	he's not loving her, he's a hypocrite
she won't do what he wants so	he won't believe her	he's not loving her, he's a hypocrite
she won't do what he wants so	he won't stay with her	he's not loving her, he's a hypocrite
she won't do what he wants so	he seeks revenge	he's not loving her, he's a hypocrite
she won't do what he wants so	he bears a grudge	he's not loving her, he's a hypocrite

she won't do what he wants so	he **won't co-dwell** with her	
	acknowledging as follows	(spiritual abuse)
	she is his equal before God	
	has equal worth before God	
	equal function in the church	
	equal potential for God	
	equally important to pursue	
	her spiritual gifts & callings	
	equal in marital co-dwelling	
	equal co-heirs of eternal life	
	equally vessels of God	
	apportion honor due her of	

	honor of equal worth to God	
	honor of equal worth as him	
	honor of being his neighbor	he's not loving her, he's a hypocrite
she won't do what he wants so	he lies about the Bible	he's not loving her, he's a hypocrite
she won't do what he wants so	he lies about its teachings	he's not loving her, he's a hypocrite
she won't do what he wants so	he lies about God's Words	he's not loving her, he's a hypocrite
she won't do what he wants so	he treats her in a way he	
	wouldn't want to be treated	he's not loving her, he's a hypocrite
she won't do what he wants so	he threatens anything above	he's not loving her, he's a hypocrite

If she submits	+ If he does not love	= then he dominates
she does what he wants	he does any of the above	he is abusive, he is disobeying God, she gets rewards in heaven
she does what he wants	he won't compromise	he is abusive he is disobeying God, she gets rewards in heaven
If she does not submit	**+ If he ideally loves**	**= then there is no domination**
she won't do what he wants so	he does what she wants	she is disobeying God, he loves self-sacrificially like Jesus, giving himself up for her per Eph 5, and he gets rewards in heaven
she won't compromise so	he does what she wants	she is disobeying God, he loves self-sacrificially like Jesus, giving himself up for her per Eph 5, and he gets rewards in heaven

As is shown clearly in this table, God's plan for marriage is 50/50 compromise.

A husband who uses the tactics in the table above to try to control his wife is unloving and abusive and is disobeying God.
A husband who responds to a wife's lack of submission with anything on the above list is a hypocrite, and also is disobeying God as much as she is. In order for a husband to dominate his wife, he has to be disobeying God. If a husband is obeying God, then he is loving his wife, which can only result in a lack of domination, either by compromise in decision-making, or self-sacrificially loving her and so choosing to do what she wants to do. In fact any time a husband uses the Bible to tell a wife she must do what he wants because the Bible says to submit to him, or promotes anything besides a 50/50 compromise ideal goal on decision-making, that husband is in fact in disobedience to God.

Love and submission both are shown by letting the other person have their way, and doing what the other person wants, and so the Bible teaches a 50/50 compromise as God's ideal will for marriage when it comes to decision making. Neither the husband nor the wife have more authority than the other in a marriage. The husband being the head of a body gives him no more authority than the wife being the rest of the body parts. God never gave the husband dominion over the wife, nor men over women. In general in a Christian marriage a husband, to love his wife, must recognize her equality with him as a Christian, in all things pertaining to gifts, callings, and participation in the church.

In Parenting:
While the life-giving spirit or "breath of life" comes only from the father of a child, the building and forming of the child's body is done only through a mother's body during pregnancy, and the mother carries and births the child. Both the mother and father contribute something that is equally essential to having a child, that only they can do, and so their contribution is equal, as neither one can do this without the other. The body, mind, and heart of a child, which compose what is often termed the "soul", are a composition from both the mother and the father. As such, the contribution of both mother and father are equally essential in the multiplying process of a child. The child is equally from both of them, though made by God.

When it comes to children, both the mother and father have equal authority over their child. The child is told to obey both their mother and father. The child is told to honor both their mother and father. The family equally belongs to the mother and to the father in a marriage. Both the mother and father have equal responsibility to teach the child God's Word. This shows the same need for compromise between parents when it comes to decisions in parenting, and that they both have equal authority.

In the Future:
This particular combination of Biblical arguments and concepts which together join to form these conclusions are unique in how they have been pieced together (as far as I know), and perhaps would do better to not be confused with other views or combinations of arguments out there. As to a name for this particular combination of Biblical arguments, and the conclusions that follow from them, of which many are listed above, the most accurate description may be "Christian Suffragism Theology". Those who ascribe to these beliefs could accurately be called "Christian Suffragists". This is an accurate term, as the word suffrage means "the right to vote". And the word suffragism means "The belief that the right to vote should be extended (as to women)". As the above conclusions make clear, the main stance of these teachings are that the Bible teaches:
1. Wives have an equal voice and participation in decision-making in marriage, as does a husband.
2. Mothers have an equal voice and participation in decision-making in parenting, as does a father.
3. Women have an equal vote and right to participation in the church in all ways, as do men.
4. Women are in all ways equal in everything concerning their relationship with God, as are men.
5. It is right that women should have an equal vote and participation in governments, as do men.
So this particular combination of Biblical arguments and conclusions could accurately be described as "Christian Suffragism Theology", because the emphasis of its conclusions is on how God wants a woman to have equal decision-making voice as a man, and His Word teaches a woman should have an equal decision-making

voice as a man. All of these arguments and teachings are from the Bible, which is the Word of God, who is Jesus Christ. The Bible teaches women are to be treated as equals to men in all ways, in every sphere, whether the church, in marriage, in family, or in worldly models of governance. The Bible may have been taught incorrectly for almost 2000 years, but this is no excuse for Christians to continue to teach the Bible incorrectly.

Jesus was not sexist towards women in his life, He spoke up for women's rights in His Word, and He gave women the right to equally vote and participate in His church. Jesus gave instructions for husbands to love their wives, and to treat them as equals, and for children to obey both their parents. His instructions for a Christian marriage balance out to teach the ideal goal in marriage is for a 50/50 compromise between husband and wife in decision-making, and show the husband and wife to have equal authority in the marriage, and over the family. As such, Jesus Christ was both a suffragist who believed women should have an equal voice as men, and as the Lord, He gave women an equal voice as men in His instructions to Christians in His Word the Bible. Jesus still is trying to teach the truth through His Word today.

I would like to end this with some songs and some words from women who were suffragists, and who were Christians, who fought for women today to be able to vote in this country and have legal equality with men, 100-150 years ago. They were workers in a field that was ripe for harvest, and still is being harvested by some workers today. But though the harvest is plenty, the workers are few. There is no telling how many more women out there would come to Christ, and how many more Christian women would do more to serve God, fulfilling His will for their lives, if women were to be able to work in the field to the fullest extent which God intended for them to, without being deterred or hindered by false teachings or unbiblical unrighteous traditions of men that are held in many churches.

The women of 100-150 years ago who demanded women's right to equal decision-making and participation in the country as men, also (I believe by God's leading) sought for equal fair rights in the church, in marriage, and in parenting, as well. Their goal remains unreached, as their goal was towards God's truth, and God's truth remains unknown and unpracticed by so many Christians today.

And this is seen in their songs and writings from 100-150 years ago. While some paint them that way, I do not believe the Christian women of the Suffragist movement were rebellious, but rather that they were led by the Holy Spirit of Truth, and were seeking what is right and just, even though they could not explain many things from the Bible at that time, which can be explained today.

The ability to vote in their own government was only one issue for which these Christian suffragists were protesting for change, as Elizabeth Cady Stanton wrote in the 1848 Declaration of Sentiments:

"In the covenant of marriage, she is compelled to promise obedience to her husband, he becoming, to all intents and purposes, her master–the law giving him power to deprive her of her liberty, and to administer chastisement. He has so framed the laws of divorce, as to what shall be the proper causes, and in case of separation, to whom the guardianship of the children shall be given, as to be wholly regardless of the happiness of women–the law, in all cases, going upon a false supposition of the supremacy of man, and giving all power into his hands.

He closes against her all the avenues to wealth and distinction which he considers most honorable to himself. As a teacher of theology, medicine, or law, she is not known.

He allows her in church, as well as state, but a subordinate position, claiming apostolic authority for her exclusion from the ministry, and, with some exceptions, from any public participation in the affairs of the church. He has created a false public sentiment by giving to the world a different code of morals for men and women, by which moral delinquencies which exclude women from society, are not only tolerated, but deemed of little account in man. He has usurped the prerogative of Jehovah himself, claiming it as his right to assign for her a sphere of action, when that belongs to her conscience and to her God.

He has endeavored, in every way that he could, to destroy her confidence in her own powers, to lessen her self-respect, and to make her willing to lead a dependent and abject life. Now, in view of this entire disfranchisement of one-half the people of this country, their social and religious degradation–in view of the unjust laws above mentioned, and because women do feel themselves aggrieved, oppressed, and fraudulently deprived of their most sacred rights, we insist that they have immediate admission to all the rights and privileges which belong to them..." .

They were seeking to end spiritual abuse in Christian marriages, and moving towards God's truth.

"Let Us All Speak Our Minds"
As sung by Elizabeth Knight, Songs of the Suffragettes

Men tell us tis fit that wives should submit to their husbands submissively weakly, that whatever they say their wives should obey, unquestioning, stupidly, meekly.
Our husbands would make us their own dictum take without ever a wherefore or why for it.
But I don't and I can't, and I won't and I shan't,
No, I will speak my mind if I die for it
For we know its all fudge to say man's the best judge of what should be and shouldn't and so on. That woman should bow, nor attempt to say how she considers that matter should go on.
I never yet gave up myself as a slave,
however my husband might try for it
For I can't and I won't and I shan't and I don't,
but I will speak my mind if I die for it.
And oh ladies I hope who with husbands do cope,
with the rights of the sex will not trifle.
We all if we choose, our tongues but do use, can all opposition soon stifle.
Let man if he will then bid us be still and silent,
a price he'll pay high for it.
For we won't and we can't and we don't and we shan't,
let us all speak our minds if we die for it!

They were seeking to end spiritual abuse in the church as well, as is shown in the context in this song, that they wanted to be able to vote in the church (as the Bible teaches that only elders can do), as well as voting in the government of the country:

"Oh Dear, What Can the Matter Be?"
As sung by Elizabeth Knight, Songs of the Suffragettes

(Oh Dear what can the matter be? Dear, dear, what can the matter be? Oh Dear what can the matter be? Women are wanting to vote.)
Women have husbands, they are protected. Women have sons, by whom they're directed. Women have fathers, they're not neglected.
Why are they wanting to vote?
Women have homes, there they should labor. Women have children, whom they should favor. Women have time to learn of each neighbor.
Why are they wanting to vote? (chorus)
Women can dress, they love society, women have cash with its variety, women can pray with sweetest piety.
Why are they wanting to vote?
<u>*Women are preaching to sinners today, women are healing the sick by the way, women are dealing out law, as they may.*</u>
<u>*Why are they wanting to vote?*</u> *(chorus)*
Women are traveling about here and there, women are working like men everywhere, women are crowding then claiming tis fair.
Why are they wanting to vote?
Women have reared all the sons of the brave. Women have shared in the burdens they gave. Women have labored your country to save. That's why they're wanting to vote. So its, Oh Dear what can the matter be? Dear, dear, what can the matter be? Oh dear what can the matter be? When men want every vote.

And little seems to have changed in the attitudes found in some circles of the church on the matter of women's rights in marriage, and in the church, over the course of the past 100-150 years. Women suffragists who fought for women's rights to vote in the country's government, faced opposition from what seems to be pretty much identical attitudes from men, as many women still face today:

"Keep Woman in Her Sphere"
As sung by Elizabeth Knight, Songs of the Suffragettes

I have a neighbor, one of those not very hard to find, who'd know it all,
without debate, and never change their mind.
I asked him "What of women's rights?" He said in tone severe,
"My mind on that is all made up: keep woman in her sphere."
I saw a man in tattered garb forth from the grog shop come.
He squandered all his cash for drink, and starved his wife at home.
I asked him, "Should not woman vote?" He answered with a sneer,
"I've taught my wife to know her place.
Keep woman in her sphere."
I met an earnest thoughtful man, not many days ago.
Who pondered deep all human law, the honest truth to know.
I asked him, "What of woman's cause?" The answer came sincere,
"Her rights are just the same as mine.
Let woman choose her sphere."

After 150 years, the goals of the Christian suffragists have still not been attained for many Christian women in the contexts of Christian marriage, family, and the Christian church. And in 2000 years the Christian church has not managed to attain what Jesus Christ intended for it. He is returning soon for a spotless Bride without wrinkle or blemish. It's about time we get this right.

In closing,
"Men have got their rights, and women have not got their rights. That is the trouble. When woman gets her rights man will be right. How beautiful that will be. Then it will be peace on earth and good will to men. But it cannot be until it be right…. It will come…. Yes, it will come quickly. It must come."- Sojourner Truth 1867

The solution? Learn the truth, spread the truth, and walk in the truth.
"Dear friend, I pray that in all respects you may prosper and be in good health, even as your soul prospers. For I was very glad when brethren came and testified to your truth, that is, how you are walking in truth. I have no greater joy than to hear that my children are walking in the truth." - 3 John 1:4

Resources:

More resources linked from my website www.WalkInTruth.net

Domestic Violence or Domestic Abuse, and Help
Search www.helpguide.org
www.theduluthmodel.org/documents/PhyVio.pdf
www.letswrap.com/usadv/

Also search online for Domestic Violence Counseling or Shelters in your state.

Help for him as an abusive husband
www.heart-2-heart.ca/women/page15.htm

See What Works Best According to Statistics
www.libraryindex.com/pages/2063/Treatment-Male-Batterers-NATIONAL-STUDY-BATTERER-INTERVENTION.html

Laws that domestic abuse and domestic violence are crimes
www.baddteddy.com/abuse/abuse_laws_index.htm

Christian Coalition Against Domestic Violence – www.ccada.org

Christians for Biblical Equality – www.cbeinternational.org

Clearinghouse of Information Against the Teachings of NGJ Michael and Debi Pearl – www.whynottrainachild.com

No Longer Quivering – www.nolongerquivering.com

Resources on Spiritual Abuse
www.pureprovender.blogspot.com/2011/03/helpful-sites-on-spiritual-abuse.html

Recommended Book: Why Does He Do That? Inside the Minds of Angry and Controlling Men – by Lundy Bancroft

Jesus Christ Was A Radical Feminist
www.jesuscentral.com/ji/life-of-jesus-modern/jesus-feminist.php

The Jesus Style Online Audiobook - www.servant.org
(Best study on getting to know Jesus personally, ever!)

Also see my other Bible study books on the topics of Spiritual Warfare, Angelology and Demonology, at ParadoxBrown.com

www.ingramcontent.com/pod-product-compliance
Lightning Source LLC
Chambersburg PA
CBHW020345170426
43200CB00005B/56